THE !KUNG OF NYAE NYAE

≠Toma

The !Kung
of Nyae Nyae

Lorna Marshall

Harvard University Press
Cambridge, Massachusetts
and London, England 1976

Copyright © 1976 by Lorna J. Marshall
All rights reserved

Library of Congress Catalog Card Number 76–19152
ISBN 0–674–50569–7
Printed in the United States of America

To Stephanie

Contents

Acknowledgments

The foremost expression of my gratitude and that of my family is to the !Kung whom we know in the Nyae Nyae region. They accepted our presence among them in friendliness, and they willingly helped us in our endeavor to understand their ways.

My husband, Laurence Kennedy Marshall, and I had the great pleasure of having our daughter and son working and sharing experiences with us in the field for large portions of the time. Laurence and I speak of them with open pride. Both are exceptionally gifted in minimizing cultural differences and in creating warm, friendly relations. They have no trace of condescension in them for anybody or anything. Our daughter, Elizabeth Marshall (now Mrs. Stephen Thomas), gathered ethnographic material, as I did, and has put her notes at my disposal. In some cases I am able to give her due credit for them, but in other cases our work is so merged that hers is inextricable from mine, and I can only express my gratitude for it. From her work has come her book on the /Gwi and !Kung Bushmen, *The Harmless People,* now so widely known and enjoyed that it can be called a classic in Bushman studies.

The special field work of our son, John Marshall, was to make a film record. The experiences of his first field trip led him to feel that the way to let ethnographic film best speak for the people it photographs, minimizing the intrusion of the observer who holds the camera, is to film events as completely as possible as they happen to occur. The bodies of film of both ordinary and extraordinary events filmed just as they occurred he calls "sequences." In producing the films, he has preferred to work with sequences rather than to construct thematic films that use material from different bodies of footage to illustrate a theme. In my opinion, both sequences and thematic films are valuable. The film record in unedited state has been a valuable documentary resource to me in my work.

In organizing and typing field notes, cataloguing and filing photographs, and typing manuscripts, I first had the invaluable assistance of Evelyn Brew, later at different times that of Ilona Daly, Marilyn Wood, and Constance Coulopoulos. Philip Yampolsky was an invaluable assistant in preparing manuscripts and charts and in editing. My esteemed friend, Frances Panton, helped me in immeasurable ways. Each gave me the advantage of special skills, the enjoyment of sharing an interest, and the pleasure of a warm relationship. I am grateful to them all.

When our project to make a study of Bushmen was first thought of, our family had the benefit, which we acknowledge with gratitude, of much advice and encouragement from members of the anthropology department of Harvard University. J. O. Brew, then director of the Peabody Museum, appointed a committee to discuss aims and procedures with us. The committee was composed of Brew, the late Lauriston Ward, Douglas Oliver, and Hallam Movius. Several others, including the late Clyde Kluckholn, also discussed our project with us at length. Gradually our plans for field work took form. Brew, whose interest in our work has been unceasing, visited us in the field for six weeks in 1952.

In Africa, as well, we were fortunate in our early advisors. Raymond Dart, Vivian F. M. FitzSimons, and the late Charles Koch (who joined our field trips in 1951 and 1958), all gave us their lively interest and sound suggestions. We also profited greatly by conversations with Phillip V. Tobias, Monica Wilson, and F. L. Maingard.

Professors Oswin Köhler and Ernst Westphal have very kindly responded to my questions on Bushman language. Theodore August Wagner awakened my interest in studying the star lore of the Bushmen and thoughtfully provided me with a copy of Norton's *Star Atlas.*

While first preparing my material for publication, I had the pleasure of discussing it with the following scholars, each of whom read one or more of the manuscripts: Mary Douglas, the late Daryll Forde, Donald Menzel, George Peter Murdock, Douglas Oliver, David M. Schneider, and N. J. van Warmelo. I am grateful to them for their perceptive comments and their encouragement.

More recently, I have had the pleasure and benefit of discussing several particular aspects of my work with Nancie Gonzalez, who has been most generous with time and counsel. Kristi Cannon has kindly provided some current information which is incorporated in Chapter 1. I am deeply grateful to James Fox, who has read the manuscript, for his encouragement as well as his interest and his comments. My thanks are due to Megan Biesele quite especially. She has not only read manuscripts with the utmost attention and critical acumen but has assisted me in the final stages of preparation of this book. Her knowledge of the !Kung with whom she worked in the Dobe area, her mastery of their language, her deep interest in all aspects of their lives, her understanding, and her attitudes make her assistance very special indeed.

Since Richard Borshay Lee (he formerly used the middle name Barry) conducted his intensive studies with !Kung in the Dobe area in Botswana, beginning in 1963, I have had discussions and exchange of ideas with him that were of great value and great pleasure to me. He has been generous in his correspondence on Bushman questions as well as in discussion. Irven DeVore and Richard Lee together organized the Harvard Bushman (San) Research Project in 1963, which has brought scientists of several disciplines to study the !Kung in the Dobe area. The members of this project are sometimes called the Harvard Group. Lee's work, which I cite often, and that of the others of this group have added new dimensions to Bushman studies. I have immensely enjoyed talking with several members of the group about our mutual interests in their special fields of interest, especially Irven and Nancy DeVore, Melvin Konner and Marjorie Shostak Konner, Pat Draper, Nancy Howell, Richard Katz, and John and Alison Yellen.

Nicholas England, who was with us in the field in 1958, 1959, and 1961, made a collection of Bushman music and is the author of a superb study of the music of Nyae Nyae which I have cited several times. He was an unusually companionable member of our group in the field, with his flair for bringing people of all kinds, colors, and persuasions into friendly relationships. Over the years, discussion with him on any aspect of our work in Bushman studies has been a benefit and a pleasure.

Robert Story made his collection of Bushman food plants in the Kalahari while on expedition with us in 1955 and 1958. His published material has been of great use to me (see Chapter 2), and he has been kind, meticulous, and entertaining in responding to my questions on the botanical identification of the food plants. His replies have come to me from South Africa, Patagonia, and Australia.

Brian Maguire, now of the Bernard Price Institute for Paleontological Research, was a welcome member of our group in 1953. He collected the food plants in the Tsho/ana area.

Charles O. Handley, Jr., of the Smithsonian Institution, was collecting small mammals while with us in 1952. He has made his report to the Smithsonian available to us. I have several times had occasion to refer to it and want to express my thanks.

We owe a special debt to Robert H. Dyson. In 1951, when he was a graduate student in archaeology at Harvard University, he came with us on our first field trip into the Nyae Nyae area and was a particularly effective and helpful member of our group. Fritz Metzger, author of *Narro and His Clan*, Eric Williams, Senior Laboratory Assistant in the Department of Anatomy at the University of the Witwatersrand, and Claude V. McIntyre, whom I mention later, were also with us on that trip. It was with this group that we first made contact with the !Kung of Nyae Nyae. We stayed six weeks with them at that time. Dyson with Fritz Metzger and his two !Kung interpreters made the first ethnographic observations of those !Kung. Dyson took meticulous notes and made the notes available to us. He and Eric Williams also made face masks of the !Kung. These masks hang on the walls of the Department of Anatomy at the Witwatersrand.

In the articles I have published up to now, I have been dealing with my own observations and have had occasion to cite only a few of Dyson's. I make several more citations from his notes in this volume and hereby express my thanks. The largest section of Dyson's notes records his detailed, precise observation of artifacts and the techniques of making them. I hope that those notes will be published as a chapter in some other volume of Bushman studies.

During our stay in the Nyae Nyae area, Dyson made a collection of stone artifacts of Late Stone Age industries from several sites on the surface of the ground at Gautscha and elsewhere. Pressure of work has prevented him from analyzing his collection himself, and he has given the collection to us. It has been analyzed by Larry Lepionka, who kindly provided me with a summary (see Chapter 1). I want to express my gratitude to both.

Several other members of the field trips were, in the years indicated, companionable and welcome participants. Three were scientists from the Transvaal Museum in Pretoria who made collections and observations in their own special fields, namely: the late Charles Koch, entomologist (1951, 1958), Wolf Haacke, zoologist (1961), and O. P. M. Prozesky, ornithologist (1961). Robert G. Gardner, Director of the Film Study Center at the Peabody Museum (Harvard), was a member of the 1958 trip; he participated in the filming during his stay.

Carey McIntosh (1951), William Donnellan, M.D. (1955), and C. J. Mathias (1961) assisted us in a variety of ways. Theunis Burger of D'Kar in Botswana holds a special place in our memories of the 1955 trip, and we give him special thanks. He guided our trucks across the central part of Botswana over trackless country from Molepolole to Ghanzi. He was helped by a Bushman guide. They took direction from the sun, and after eighteen days of travel, we came out at exactly the spot he was aiming for, a certain spot marked by a broken spring. Burger interpreted for us during the month we stayed with the /Gwi on that trip and was in every way most helpful.

The thanks of our group as a whole are due to the administrative officers of South West Africa who gave us their courteous assistance and arranged our permits to enter the native territories. We are particularly grateful to those officers who helped us to arrange our first expeditions. They were: Colonel P. I. Hoogenhout, Administrator; John Neser, Secretary; and H. J. Allen, Senior Native Commissioner, and Claude McIntyre, Senior Welfare Officer. The last two men were then in the Department of Native Affairs in the South West Africa Administration. In 1955, the Administration of Native Affairs in South West Africa was taken over by the Department of Bantu Administration and Development of South Africa, and Mr. Allen and Mr. McIntyre held office under that department. We owe Mr. McIntyre a special debt of gratitude. He accompanied and guided us on our first expedition to Gautscha in 1951. He was the first administrative officer ever to enter the Nyae Nyae area as far as we know. He is a master of desert travel, and he was of the utmost help in all aspects of expedition life. In 1959, he was appointed to be the first Bushman Affairs Commissioner, and in 1960, he established a government post at Tsumkwe.

We are grateful to George B. Silberbaurer for his help with permits to enter Botswana (then the Bechuanaland Protectorate), and we have enjoyed following his Bushman studies and publications and discussing all manner of Bushman matters with him.

A. J. Duarte, of the Instituto do Investigação Cientifica de Angola, was our kind host in Angola in 1951. His knowledge of the country and his many languages opened the world of Angola to us.

Our transportation was made a matter of adventure and not misad-

venture owing to the effort and skills of several people. I want especially
to thank Heiner Kretzchmar, Casper Kruger, Foppe Hoogheimstra, and
Kurt Ahrens, who were with us at different times. We enjoyed their
company and relied on their skills. I also want to mention John Marshall's
able contributions to the struggles with the trucks. The struggles are a
vivid memory.

It is impossible for me to name individually all the members of our
staff over the years whose abilities and efforts helped us to travel and
live in the desert; I can only assure them all of our sincere thanks for
their cheerful and effective cooperation and express special thanks to
their senior member who was with us the longest, Philip Hameva.

I wish to name with pleasure and gratitude the interpreters, photographers, and sound recorders whose work was so essential to our
record of the Bushmen. The interpreters are listed below. Those marked
with an asterisk are Bushmen:

>   Kernel Ledimo, 1953, 1955, 1957–58, 1959
>   *Ngani, 1952–53, 1957–58, 1961
>   *Katukwa, 1951
>   *Katembehe, 1951
>   Frederick Gaeb, 1952 (July–December)
>   */Gao, 1952 (July–December)
>   Ebsom Kopunko, 1952 (October–December)
>   Joseph Tsanigob, 1952 (December)
>   Wilhelm Camm, 1955, 1957–58
>   *Dabe, 1955
>   */Gishay, 1955

With the aid of these interpreters, in varying combinations, we were
able to communicate in fifteen languages: English, Afrikaans, German,
Portuguese, Ovambo, Herero, Tswana, several dialects from the Okavango area, !Kung, Heikum, Nharo, !Kõ, //Gana, /Gwi, and Nama.

Katembehe and Katukwa were our first interpreters. Fritz Metzger
had brought them with him in 1951, and it was through them that we first
introduced ourselves to the !Kung. We think these two little old men, like
two cheerful gnomes, put in a good word for us, Bushman to Bushman,
and that they helped us very much to win trust and good will.

I am especially grateful to Kernel Ledimo and Ngani. Ledimo, a member of the Tawana tribe of the Tswana Nation, was my interpreter on every expedition, except that of 1961, since early January 1953. He had spoken !Kung from his childhood, having lived with !Kung on his father's cattle post in western Botswana. His father came to the Gautscha area to hunt on many occasions and was remembered by several of !Kung of the older generation. Ledimo learned English at an Anglican school in Botswana. Ngani, a Heikum, had lived in the household of Courtney Clark in South Africa for several years. He had a gift for languages and spoke nine. Both these young men understood our purposes and our methods and strove faithfully to translate as accurately as they could, not to embellish or distort information the !Kung gave us, not to offer their own interpretation or explanation of what the !Kung meant. They tried painstakingly to unravel the misunderstandings and nonunderstandings in which we were so often entangled.

The major photographic contributions to the field work were made by Laurence Marshall and John Marshall. Laurence Marshall worked in still photography, taking mainly color photographs but also many black-and-whites. John Marshall's primary activity in the field (1950, 1951, 1952–53, 1955, 1957–58) was filming the Bushmen. From this film record he has since produced the documentaries *The Hunters* (which won the Flaherty Award in 1958), *Bitter Melons, !Kung Bushman Hunting Equipment,* and *N/um Tchai,* as well as numerous *Sequences* on Bushman life.

Three other members of the expeditions were primarily engaged in photography, in this instance still photography, and credit is due them for many fine pictures: Anneliese Scherz (June 6–July 3, 1953), a professional photographer at Windhoek, worked mainly in black-and-white while she was at Gautscha; Daniel Blitz (1955), an engineer at Sanders Associates, Nashua, New Hampshire; Robert Gesteland (1957–58), then a graduate student at the Massachusetts Institute of Technology.

Many expedition members worked on sound recording—of music especially, and also of speech. Chief among them were Elizabeth Marshall Thomas, John Marshall, myself, Daniel Blitz, Nicholas England, and two specialists from South West Africa who did intensive and excellent work in 1953: Frank Hesse (May 5–May 30) and Hans Ernst (June 6–July 3).

Four of the chapters in this book, Chapters 5, 6, 8, and 9, originally appeared as papers in *Africa,* the journal of the International African Institute, and it is with the kind permission of the Institute that they are republished here. The original titles were "!Kung Bushman Bands," "The Kin Terminology System of the !Kung Bushmen," "Marriage among !Kung Bushmen," "Sharing, Talking and Giving: Relief of Social Tensions among !Kung Bushmen." The dates of original publication are given in footnotes to the chapters.

I have made some revisions in these papers—principally changes in the order in which material is presented. Corrections, additions, and revisions of significance are signaled in footnotes.

Notes on the Text

ORTHOGRAPHY

My orthography is codified in the following key, which shows the values I attribute to various letters and combinations. Some letters represent more than one sound. This orthography does not transcribe the !Kung sounds with high phonetic accuracy; in many instances it allows only an approximation of the !Kung sounds.

a	*father*
e	*end*
i	*feet*
o	*note*
u	*moon*
ai, ae	*lie*
ao, au	*thou*
aú	Raúl (Spanish)
ei, ay	*say*
dj	ju*dge*
g	*g*ap
j	*je* (French)
kh	*k* with strong aspiration
k"	ejective *k* or "glottal croak" as Dorothea Bleek calls it (*A Bushman Dictionary*, p. 117)
n	sometimes *not*, sometimes *sing*; n before a click is always nasalized
ng	*sing*

tsh	*chance.* To avoid the ambiguity of the hard *ch* as in *character* and the soft *ch* as in *chance*, I changed to tsh.
x	no*ch* (German).

I attribute the common English values to the letters *b, d, h, k, m, s, t, w,* and *z,* and the combinations *qu* and *sh.*

In addition to the above letters, I use the symbols for clicks (see below); I use the tilde to indicate nasalization of a vowel, an apostrophe ['] to indicate the glottal stop. !Kung has three tones, high, middle, and low. High tone is indicated by a line above the word as in ⁻*di,* "female"; low tone by a line on the lower level of the word as in ₋!*ga,* "rain." Middle tone is conventionally not marked. I fear I have failed to note high and low tones in every instance in which they should be noted.

I am not a competent linguist and feel very humble about my rendering of the !Kung words. I do not want my spellings to be taken as authoritative. In view of the recent works of Nicholas England and members of the Harvard Bushman (San) Research Project, I revised some spellings to conform with theirs, but for the sake of consistency with my own earlier work, I limited those changes to a few. There has been no general conformity in orthography in the past, and there still is not. Time will tell if a standard is ever developed and agreed upon. My principal changes are as follows:

tai	"mother," formerly spelled *dai*
k''xau	"owner," formerly spelled *kxau*
n	to conform with !Kung pronunciation, the *n* that indicates nasalization of a click is now placed before the click instead of following the click. Thus the name formerly written *!Nai* becomes *N!ai.*

Some place names that appear in this volume have established spellings that are found in maps and official publications. I have not altered these, although in some cases they conflict with the key given above. The most important of these are:

Barachu	*ch* = my *tsh*
Chadum	*ch* = my *k*

Châsis   This name is pronounced like—in fact, it *is*—the
            French and English word for the underpart of an
            automobile.

Gautscha   *tsch* = my *tsh*. The !Kung pronounce this name
            with an initial dental click that is ignored in the
            established spelling; a more nearly correct render-
            ing would be /*Gausha.*

Ghanzi   *gh* = my x; *z* = my *ts*

Nyae Nyae   *ae* = my *ai*.

A few minor improvements have been made in the spelling of several place names. The changes, I believe, are not confusing, except perhaps the change from Cho/ana to Tsho/ana. Incidentally, at one time
in the past another name was bestowed upon Tsho/ana and that name
appears on various maps: it is Sigaret, the Afrikaans spelling of cigarette.

CLICKS

Clicks are called velaric suction stops (Heffner) or velar injectives
(Greenberg). There are five click sounds in the Khoisan languages. !Kung
employs four, all of them lingual. (The fifth click of the southern Bushman languages is labial.) To make the four lingual clicks, one forms a
cavity at the top of the mouth by pressing the back of the tongue against
the velum, the sides of the tongue against the inside of the upper teeth,
and the tip against the back of the front teeth or the alveolar ridge. The
center of the blade of the tongue is then drawn downward (Doke and
Heffner). This enlarges the cavity a little, and the air in it becomes
slightly rarefied. To produce the click sounds, the closure at the velum
is maintained while the tongue is released at some other point. The rush
of air into the cavity makes the different click sounds according to the
place of the release. To produce the fifth, the labial click, closures are
made at the velum and the lips; the closure at the lips is then released
with a gentle smack. In all clicks, the velar closure is released almost
immediately after the frontal release; the manner of velar release is indicated in writing by the letter that follows (or in the case of n, precedes)
the click. The release may be unvoiced (with a *k* sound), voiced (with a g
sound); these sounds may be aspirated or not. The click may be followed
directly by a vowel or by a glottal stop. The whole click may be nasalized.
The standard symbols for the clicks are:

/   Dental click. The tip of the tongue is placed against the back of the upper front teeth; in the release, it is pulled away with a fricative sound. English-speakers use a similar sound in gentle reproof; it is sometimes written "tsk tsk."

≠   Alveolar click. The front part of the tongue, more than the tip, is pressed against the alveolar ridge and drawn sharply downward when released. The sound produced, a snap, is often (not always) accompanied by a slight sucking sound.

!   Alveolar-palatal click. The tip of the tongue is pressed firmly against the back of the alveolar ridge where it meets the hard palate and is very sharply snapped down on release. A loud pop results.

//   Lateral click. The tongue is placed as for the alveolar click. It is released at the sides by being drawn in from the teeth while the front part of the tongue remains pressed against the alveolar ridge. The click has a fricative sound. Drivers of horses, at least American and Canadian drivers, traditionally use lateral clicks as sounds to signal their horses to start or go faster. My interpreter, Kernel Ledimo, said that in making this click the !Kung release both sides of the tongue. Doke, however, says that in all instances that he observed carefully among the !Kung, only one side, the right side, was released.[1]

⊙   Labial click. This click is found only in the southern Bushman languages. The velar closure is the same as for the lingual clicks, but the frontal closure is made with pursed lips rather than the tongue. When the lips are released, the sound is like a kiss (hence the name "kiss click").

VOCABULARY

I am dropping three Afrikaans words that I had formerly adopted because they seemed convenient or colorful at the time and am replacing them with English words. They proved not to be convenient; it became a nuisance continually to define them: *veldkos* is replaced with "wild plant

---

1. Clement M. Doke, "An Outline of the Phonetics of the Language of the (hũ: Bushmen of North-West Kalahari," *Bantu Studies* (December 1925), p. 148. Elsewhere Doke uses the spelling *Qhung* for the people we call !Kung.

foods" or "plant foods"; *werf* is replaced with "encampment"; and *scherm* is replaced with "shelter."

Band: I am using the term "band" for the group of people who live together in !Kung society. The !Kung word is *n//abesi.* The bands are traditionally structured on ties of kinship and affinity. See Chapter 5.

Groups: Ordinarily the word is used loosely through the book and refers to an aggregation of people. The kind of aggregation becomes apparent in the context. However, in one context, the word has special meaning. I use it to refer to !Kung who are living with Bantu. I say these people live in groups, distinguishing them from those who live in the traditionally structured bands.

N/um k"xau: I am using the !Kung term *n/um k"xau* ("medicine owner") in place of the term "medicine man."

K"xau n!a: I use this term, which literally means "big owner," in place of the earlier word, "headman." See Chapter 5 for explanation.

San: The members of the Harvard Bushman (San) Research Project (called also the Harvard Group) take the position that the name Bushman is derogatory. They are encouraging the adoption of the name *San* in place of Bushman. I quote Richard Lee in the introduction to the forthcoming book, edited by Irven DeVore and Richard Lee, to which members of the Harvard Group and others have contributed chapters on their special fields. The book is entitled *Kalahari Hunter-Gatherers* (Cambridge, Mass., Harvard University Press, 1976). Lee says:

> Recently, African scholars have complained that "Bushman" is a term of derogation with racist overtones and have suggested that "San" be adopted as a more dignified and respectful term of reference (Wilson and Thompson 1969). San means "aborigines, or settlers proper" in the Cape Hottentot dialect (Hahn 1881). They called the "Bushman" the "Sanqua (Sonqua)" and the term San was used by Isaac Schapera in the title of his classic, "The Khoisan Peoples of South Africa" (1930).

While I believe that the name Bushman was definitely derogatory when it was first applied by European voyagers and settlers in South Africa, I have felt that it need not continue to be considered derogatory unless the speaker is imputing derogation in using it. In my feelings, I accord "Bushman" the dignity of any dignified race name. However, I can see the other point of view and may follow the young scholars in adopting *San* in future articles, but it is too late for me to do so in my books.

IDENTIFICATION OF INDIVIDUALS

Charts have been made of ten bands in the Nyae Nyae region, namely, Bands 1–7, 9, 10, 12. See Table 3 for a list of the bands. The charts are in Appendix 1. Their principal purpose is to show the consanguineous and affinal relationships on which bands are formed. In the charts, each person has been assigned a number composed of the number of the band of which he is a member and a number within the band according to the place in which his name falls in the chart. Thus, Zuma [2.2] means that Zuma is a member of Band 2 and has been given the number 2 within that band. An "X" before a number indicates that the person was dead. Through the text these chart numbers are used to identify individuals.

I refer to several individuals much more frequently than others. Instead of endlessly repeating their band chart numbers and explaining who they are, I shall identify them herewith. If a name appears in the text without a chart number, the person is the person of that name in the following list. The list does not give every member of each family. For the complete family, see the band charts.

≠Toma [1.16], called ≠Toma Word
!U [1.15], his wife
Tsamgao [1.17], son of ≠Toma and !U
/Gaishay [1.18], son of ≠Toma and !U
!Ungka Norna [1.19], daughter of ≠Toma and !U,
   named for ≠Toma's sister and for me.
   Norna is the !Kung rendering of Lorna. The
   !Kung cannot or do not pronounce "l."
Lame ≠Gao [1.14], brother of !U
Old N/aoka [1.13], mother of !U, Lame ≠Gao, aud Di!ai [1.9]

/Qui [1.24], called /Qui Navel by the !Kung
      (We called him Neanderthal; Claude McIntyre
      called him Lazy /Qui.)
//Kushay [1.23], his wife
Little ≠Gao [1.26], son of /Qui and //Kushay
Old Gaú [1.20], father of //Kushay
!Ungka [1.21], his daughter
/Gishay [1.22], his son

Gao [1.8], called Gao Feet. (We called him
      Gao Medicine.)
N/aoka [1.7], his first wife

//Khuga [1.4], daughter of Gao and N/aoka
Crooked /Qui [1.5], her husband
Di!ai [1.9], Gao's second wife, sister of !U [1.15]
N!ai [1.12], Di!ai's daughter by a former husband, Gumtsa
/Gunda [2.23], N!ai's husband
/Gao Music [1.1], husband of Gao's daughter, N≠isa [1.2]

Old /Gaishay [4.1], father of Gao
Old Di//khao-!Gun≠a [4.2], his wife

Old ≠Toma [2.16]
Old /Gam [2.17], his wife
//Ao [2.20], son of Old ≠Toma and /Gam,
    called //Ao Wildebeest

Old /Gasa [2.35], the mother of five sons and daughters
    (Gaú [2.25], ≠Gao [3.4], Gao [7.12], ≠Gisa [2.31],
    N/aoka [2.36])
Gaú [2.25], son of Old /Gasa
Be [2.26], his first wife
Khuan//a [2.24], his second wife, mother of / Gunda [2.23]
Short /Qui [2.37], husband of N/aoka [2.36]. (We called
    him /Qui Hunter. This is the man who lost his foot as
    a result of a puff adder bite. He is described by Elizabeth
    Marshall Thomas in *The Harmless People*, Chapter 13.)
Gao Beard [2.9]. (At first we called him Gao Helmet.)
//Kushay I [2.10], his first wife
Xama [2.14], daughter of //Kushay I and Gao Beard
//Kushay II [2.8], second wife of Gao Beard
Old Xama [2.7], mother of Gao Beard

/Ti!kay [9.8]
N/aoka [9.7], his first wife. She will be so identified each
    time to distinguish her from Gao's first wife
Baú [9.6], daughter of /Ti!kay and N/aoka
N!ai [9.9], /Ti!kay's second wife. N/aoka and N!ai are sisters.
    This N!ai will be distinguished from N!ai [1.12] by being
    called /Ti!kay's wife.

Old Demi [6.4]

Old /Gaishay, the bachelor [3.8].

THE !KUNG OF NYAE NYAE

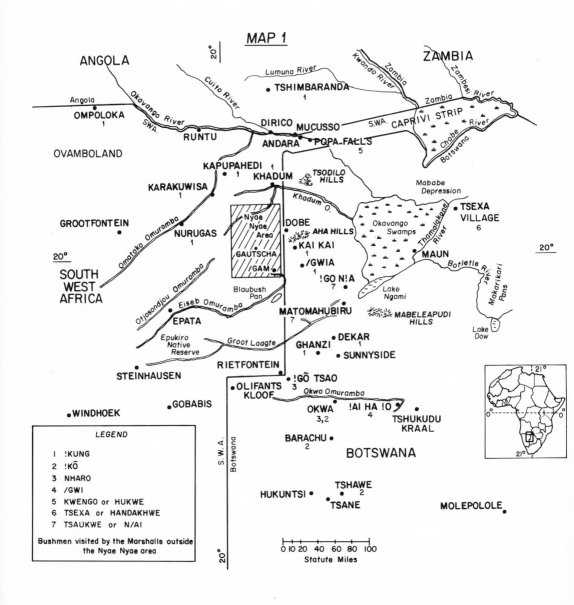

MAP 1

ANGOLA

ZAMBIA

Lumuna River

Cuito River

Kwando River

Zambia

Zambesi River

• TSHIMBARANDA
1

Zambia

Angola

Okavango River

OMPOLOKA
1

S.W.A.

DIRICO   MUCUSSO

Zambia

S.W.A.   CAPRIVI STRIP

Chobe River

OVAMBOLAND

RUNTU

ANDARA • POPA-FALLS
5

Botswana

KAPUPAHEDI   • 1
        • 1   KHADUM

✳ TSODILO
HILLS

*Mababe
Depression*

KARAKUWISA
1

Khadum O.

*Okavango
Swamps*

• TSEXA
VILLAGE
6

GROOTFONTEIN •

Omatako Omuramba

NURUGAS
1

Nyae
Nyae
Area

• DOBE
  • AHA HILLS
✳ KAI KAI
1

Thamalakane River

20°

20°

SOUTH
WEST
AFRICA

GAUTSCHA
/GAM

/GWIA
1

• MAUN

Botletle River

*Makarikari
Pans*

Otjosondjou Omuramba

Eiseb Omuramba

*Blaubush
Pan*

!GO N!A
7

*Lake
Ngami*

EPATA •

Epukiro
Native
Reserve

Groot Laagte

MATOMAHUBIRU
7

✳ MABELEAPUDI
HILLS

*Lake
Dow*

• DEKAR
1

GHANZI
1

RIETFONTEIN •

• SUNNYSIDE

STEINHAUSEN •

• !GŎ TSAO
3

S. W. A.

Botswana

• OLIFANTS
KLOOF

Okwa Omuramba

• WINDHOEK

• GOBABIS

OKWA
3,2

!AI HA !O
4

• TSHUKUDU
KRAAL

LEGEND

1   !KUNG
2   !KŌ
3   NHARO
4   /GWI
5   KWENGO or HUKWE
6   TSEXA or HANDAKHWE
7   TSAUKWE or N/AI

Bushmen visited by the Marshalls outside
the Nyae Nyae area

BARACHU
2

BOTSWANA

TSHAWE
2

HUKUNTSI •

• TSANE

MOLEPOLOLE
•

20°

0 10 20 40 60 80 100
Statute Miles

21°

0°

0°

21°

Introduction: The Expeditions and Conditions of Study

The expeditions my family and I made into the Kalahari Desert to conduct our Bushman studies were instigated and led by my husband, Laurence Kennedy Marshall. The first three (1950, 1951, 1952–53) were sponsored by the Peabody Museum of Harvard University; the following five expeditions (1955, 1956, 1957–58, 1959, 1961) were sponsored by the Smithsonian Institution and by the Transvaal Museum of Pretoria, as well as by the Peabody Museum. The first three expeditions were formerly called "Peabody Museum Kalahari Expeditions," and the latter five were called the "Peabody-Harvard Smithsonian Kalahari Expeditions." They have also been referred to as the "Marshall Expeditions." I shall use the latter designation as it is the least cumbersome, or call them simply our expeditions.

Laurence Marshall was present on all these expeditions; John Marshall, our son, was present on all except 1956, 1959, and 1961; Elizabeth Marshall, now Elizabeth Thomas, our daughter, was present in 1951, 1952–53, and 1955; and I was present on all except 1950, 1956, and 1957–58. During each expedition we[1] were joined for varying periods of time by scientists in several disciplines and other participants who for one reason or another were interested in accompanying us.

On the expedition in the summer of 1951, we had the welcome assistance of Robert Dyson, then a graduate student in archaeology at Harvard University. His main interest was in archaeology rather than ethnography, and he did not join our later Bushman expeditions. Looking

---

1. Most often it is my family I have in mind when I say "we" in describing experiences we shared. Sometimes—and I think it can be easily deduced from the context—my "we" refers to members of the expedition as a whole. I avoid the editorial "we."

back, it is interesting to remember that in 1952 when we planned to stay the year through in the field, we could not find an ethnographer to go with us, to help with the enormous amount of work that lay before us. Anthropologists were intrigued by the mystery of Bushmen's origin and race affiliation, by their unique click languages and certain unique physical characteristics, and by their small stature and the various hypotheses offered to explain it. But Bushmen were so far from the mainstream of the American anthropologists' studies in those days that no one known to the Harvard anthropology department, either at Harvard or elsewhere, wanted to take time out to spend a year with them.

I have often been asked by friends and acquaintances to tell how it came about that our family undertook a study of Bushmen when none of us were anthropologists and we had had no training in preparation. Laurence (born 1889 in Massachusetts) had studied civil engineering at Tufts. I (born 1898 in Arizona) had studied English literature at Berkeley and Radcliffe and taught English at Mount Holyoke. Elizabeth (born 1931) had only begun college and John (born 1932) was just finishing high school. Laurence, who had founded the Raytheon Company in 1922 and had been its president thereafter, had retired in the spring of 1950. The hard war years had deprived him of spending time with his family; he had had no vacations with us, not even whole weekends. He wanted to be with us and, now that he was free to do so, he wanted us to undertake some interesting project together. First of all, however, he wanted to take a trip to Africa with his son. As he and John began to plan the trip, they became intrigued with the Kaoko Veld and the Kalahari Desert. Although none of us was an anthropologist, anthropology was a common interest of the whole family, and it was a natural step for Laurence and John to consult their anthropologist friends, asking what would be interesting to see in those two areas, and if anything they could do would be useful. They were told that anthropologists would like to know if any remnant groups of Bergdama could still be found in remote parts of the Kaoko Veld, living in their ancient ways, apart from Hottentots or Herero. The anthropologist friends also pointed out that in the portion of the Kalahari that lies in northeastern South West Africa and northwestern Botswana (then Bechuanaland), in another veld called the Kaukau Veld, were !Kung Bushman hunter-gatherers, and that not a great deal was known about those particular Bushmen.

Laurence and John spent most of the summer in 1950 traveling in the Kaoko Veld. They found fascinating people, especially the Shimba, but they found no trace of remnant Bergdama. They then went to northwestern Botswana to look for unacculturated Bushmen. At Kai Kai they learned that there were !Kung over the border in South West Africa who were living in complete independence from Bantu or white people. Laurence and John then knew what they wanted our family project to be. Although the miles of travel to those !Kung from Kai Kai were relatively few, Laurence and John were not well enough equipped that year to venture into an untraveled part of the desert. They did not have sufficient gasoline or means of carrying enough water, but they began forming their plan.

In 1951, we fulfilled that plan and as a family we made our first expedition into the area, which I later called the Nyae Nyae area. I call the !Kung who live there the Nyae Nyae !Kung. (Nyae Nyae is pronounced *ny ny*, rhyming with *high*.)

Good fortune attended us then and after. ≠Toma's reception of us was one of the greatest portions of our good fortune. He is the leader of Band 1, an uncommonly intelligent, able man, much esteemed by his people. After observing us and talking with us for three days, he seemed to approve of us and to understand our purpose. We had said simply that we believed it good for people with different ways of life to learn to understand each other as best they could, and that we wanted to learn and understand the customs of the !Kung. ≠Toma agreed. As time went on, more than once in different contexts, the idea was suggested or expressed that no white people had ever before wanted to understand the customs of the Nyae Nyae !Kung and that the Nyae Nyae !Kung were not averse to having a little attention paid them. Such an idea may have crossed ≠Toma's mind during his three days' observation of us, but he did not express it explicitly at the time. He just gave us his approval and agreed to let us live with him. He bestowed Bushman names on us, the names of his own family. In this way, we were favorably presented to the whole of the Nyae Nyae area and no time was lost in overcoming shyness and suspicion on the part of the !Kung in other bands.

The 1951 stay at Gautscha was short, only six weeks, but we were assured that a longer stay was feasible. We were captivated and left determined to return to stay the year through.

In 1952–53, the most productive period of our study, we were based in three places: /Gam in the south of the area, Gautscha Pan in the central part, and Tsho/ana in the north. In July 1952, when we arrived at /Gam, we found a severe drought in progress, a circumstance exceed-

Laurence Marshall and Gao of Band 1

ingly unfavorable to the !Kung, but favorable to us. All the small temporary waterholes and most of the semipermanent ones had dried. The
!Kung of the area had no choice but to stay within range of the waterhole
at /Gam. The wonderful /Gam waterhole, always a permanent one, had
been blasted and deepened by a Bantu family from Tsau, Botswana, the
family of Musindjan, a Tawana, and Kavasitue, his Herero wife. They
had come to /Gam with their cattle a few years before. The waterhole supplied the cattle, the Bantu family, the !Kung, and our expedition.
Every day the water was taken down to the mud, every night the waterhole filled again.

No fewer than five !Kung bands, about 158 persons, had congregated
around /Gam. The waterhole belonged (in the Bushman sense) to Bands

12 and 13. Those bands and Bands 14, 15, and 16 were interlaced by many kinship and friendship ties. Traditionally, the latter bands shared the /Gam water with Bands 12 and 13 during drought. Our good fortune was to find so many !Kung there instead of dispersed in the vast countryside where we might never have made contact with them. Every few days some departed to gather food, going varying distances to places they knew. They took ostrich eggshells filled with water and stayed gathering for two or three days, and returned to /Gam when their shells were empty, bringing with them what food they had obtained. But always some people remained in the encampments. We would visit them, count them, and ask for their genealogies. (Genealogies were a good beginning with those people; they seemed to enjoy telling us who they were.) We had the opportunity of seeing the bands as clearly visible units. They were encamped a mile or more apart, each about a mile from the water-hole. Within itself each band was a huddle of people, fires, and shelters drawn close together. The bands maintained their separateness of residence consistently, but the people mingled amicably at the waterhole,

Elizabeth Marshall Thomas, on return to /Gam, greeting !Kung women

Lorna Marshall greeting !Kung women at /Gam

and when they visited our camp, and, most importantly, when they held several great ritual curing dances and sang and danced together the night through. They appeared to enjoy being together, and I considered that the social contact compensated to some extent for the hardships the drought imposed on them in procuring food.

At Gautscha Pan, where we moved next, at the end of August 1952, we settled ourselves with ≠Toma, who had sponsored us the year before, and his band, Band 1. The other band based on the Gautscha water, Band 2, soon joined us, building their shelters close to those of Band 1. It was not long before members of all the bands in the central part of the area began to visit—a family or two at a time, or the whole band. Bands 1 to 10 are the central bands—about 210 persons. Soon we knew them all. The drought had not been as severe in the central part of the area as it had in the southern part. It was not need for water that brought the !Kung together at Gautscha in abnormal aggregation, but curiosity about us. They came and went. The distances between the waterholes of these bands is not great. For example, the distance from Gautscha to Tsumkwe is about eighteen miles, from Gautscha to Deboragu about twenty-five. Visitors also came from Kai Kai, Kubi, and other communities in Botswana. Sometimes up to 75 !Kung would be encamped around us at a time. The Gautscha waterhole, another wonderful permanent one, miraculously supplied us all, like the widow's cruse, without ever being completely emptied down to the mud.

Late in December 1952, when the big rains were about to begin, we had to leave Gautscha and move to Tsho/ana on the northern periphery of the area, for we could not have got out of the Gautscha area with our trucks in the rains, however dire our need. At Tsho/ana, we had access to a track kept passable and used twice a month by the convoys of trucks of the Witwatersrand Native Labor Association (W.N.L.A.) that take Ovambo back and forth to work in the mines in the Transvaal.

≠Toma, /Qui, and their families from Band 1 agreed to come with us and stay with us till we could return to Gautscha (at the end of April), so that we could continue our work with them.

At Tsho/ana and at Samangaigai the Department of Native Affairs of South West Africa (this was before the South African Department of Bantu Administration and Development took over native administration in South West Africa) had established posts on the track followed by the W.N.L.A. truck convoys. The convoys stopped at one or the other of these posts for the night. Both posts were in the charge of Tawana men who were married to Kwangare wives: Moremi at Tsho/ana and Matambo at Samangaigai.

Moremi's post was the point of entry into South West Africa from Botswana, and his responsibility was to make customs inspections of luggage, and, in an attempt to control hoof-and-mouth disease, disinfect tires and boots. A group of !Kung worked for him, tending his cornfields and his cattle. Tsho/ana was also the waterhole of Band 24; the band lived independently of Moremi's post.

We had opportunity to observe the !Kung contacts with the Bantu there. When the convoys—especially those returning from the mines—arrived, all the almost naked, slender, little brown !Kung men would stand in groups staring with awe at the big, black Ovambo with their mine uniforms, boots, helmets, headlights, and sunglasses, and their sewing machines and whatever other worldly goods they were bringing home to their wives. This was indeed the outside world to those !Kung. They told us explicitly that they feel shy, naked, and inferior in the presence of these big black men with their goods.

Officially Moremi and Matambo were called "Bushman Guards." I was at a loss to know whether they were to guard the Bushmen from the outside world or the outside world from the Bushmen. Robert Morris, the Native Commissioner at Runtu, considered that the former was their function, but in the opinion of some white people in South West Africa, the guards were there to protect the outside world from the Bushmen. The !Kung, so friendly and courteous to us, may feel shy, even timid, themselves, but to many white people they were "wild" Bushmen.

"Tame" Bushmen live as laborers on farms and may have done so for two or three generations; "wild" Bushmen live in the brush, and wild Bushmen have a bad reputation. Knowing our interests, virtually every white person we met talked to us about Bushmen. Rarely had anyone a personal experience to tell us, but there was much recounting of the well-known stories in the literature of the deeds of the "vermin," and people were given to remembering everything they had ever heard about murders and cattle killing. They told over and over again certain episodes— of the murder of a judge by a poisoned arrow, for example—and we were warned in all seriousness to take guns for our protection and to beware of the little poisoned arrows that fly no one knows whence. I mention these opinions and warnings in order to suggest the degree to which the Bushmen and the whites were isolated from each other. Actual experience with the !Kung contradicts these fearsome stereotypes.

Our contact and that of the !Kung with the Bantu who passed through Tsho/ana consisted only of staring at each other for an hour or so, once in two weeks, and had no significant influence upon our life there. Our relations with Moremi and his family were very friendly and satisfactory. They did not impinge at all upon our relations with the !Kung. Once the rains began, the !Kung were free to move around the country, and many came to Tsho/ana to visit. However, at Tsho/ana our daily life took place mainly with only the two !Kung families who had come with us, and we were not in such constant and close contact with large numbers of people as we had been at Gautscha.

The aggregations at Gautscha, though abnormal in !Kung life, were favorable to our work. In our close association with the many !Kung there, we had the opportunity to observe more social interaction, such as sharing meat with a large number of people present, to see more activities that take place in an encampment, such as the making or mending of artifacts, to see more dances and games, to hear more music, more talk, more telling of tales than if we were with only a small group of two or three families at a time. Also, we never lacked informants. People went out to hunt and gather for days at a time but, with the large number of people assembled, there were always some spending the day in the encampment.

Much of our information was gathered through interrogation. Our method was, in addition to observing what we could see being done, to ask questions about many subjects: kin terms, for example, marriage regulations, the names of the gods, beliefs about the stars, food avoidances, and so forth. We worked on the same subject over and over with different informants, hoping to allow misunderstanding and confusions resulting from inept questioning on our part and confusion and error in translation to fall away. These interrogations entertained the !Kung, who found them much more interesting than some of their usual leisure occupations, so each session of talk would be attended by a sizable group. Instead of one person answering questions, many would put a word in, to add to the information given, to confirm, contradict, or correct it, to give another opinion, or to describe a variant custom.

Except on a few occasions, we did not provide food for the !Kung with whom we lived or those who visited, nor did we deplete their limited food supplies by living off the land ourselves; we brought our food in tins. The Gautscha bands continued in their hunting-gathering patterns. !Kung visitors to Gautscha usually brought some food with them and received gifts of food from the Gautscha relatives whom they visited. At Tsho/ana, however, where we had taken Band 1 away from their own food resources, we provided them with food from our supplies.

We regularly gave tobacco to the members of Bands 1 and 2 with whom we lived. We gave visitors a present of tobacco when they arrived and when they gave us interviews or worked with us in some special way. The !Kung are ardent smokers. In those days, we were ardent smokers, too. Not a shadow of guilt crossed our minds when we shared cigarettes and gave handfuls of pipe tobacco in appreciation of the !Kung's cooperation. We regularly gave presents, also, of cocoa, coffee, tea, sugar, salt, matches, and empty cans, which were very much appreciated.

The !Kung did not make importunate demands upon us. They had their own artifacts, which fully satisfied their needs in their traditional way of life, and were not in want of ours. In the very beginning of our making arrangements with ≠Toma, we had explained what we could and could not do. We explained that we had only the food we brought with us and that we could not give it to all and sundry in any substantial amounts, but that we could give tobacco and salt, and so forth. ≠Toma and others appeared to understand, and they agreed to our arrangements, saying they would be glad to have what we could give. When they made requests of us it was never in the mode of persistent begging, only gentle and polite hints that they would like some little thing such as an empty tin or a box of matches. They asked mostly for our medicines. (The ailments we treated most often were inflammations of the eyes, abrasions, burns, and intestinal upsets.)

When we were leaving in 1953, we rewarded the people who had given us much time and information with gifts. (They were the members of Bands 1 and 2, /Ti!kay's family in Band 9, Old /Gaishay and his wife in Band 4, and several others.) It was with soul searching as to what was fair and helpful to them, and after we learned to some extent what they wanted, that we made the decisions and sent out for the objects. We gave shorts and shirts to the men, bright scarves and cloth to the women, blankets, beads, heavy wire for arrow points, chisels, knives, pipes, and a few pots. The people were enchanted with their gifts, and we departed still searching our souls and wondering if we had done the right thing.

In addition to conducting our field work with the Nyae Nyae !Kung, we traveled elsewhere in the Kalahari Desert and in adjacent areas to visit Bushmen of other language groups, in the northern part of South West Africa, in southern Angola, and in Botswana. Our visits were rela-

TABLE 1. Places and Periods of Work with !Kung in the Nyae Nyae Area

Time		Location
1951	Mid-June through July	Gautscha
1952	July, August	/Gam
1952	September through December	Gautscha
1953	January through April	Tsho/ana
1953	May through July	Gautscha
1955	August	Nama
1957–58[a]	November through June	Tsumkwe
1959	July	Nama
1961	September	Tsumkwe

[a]The emphasis of the 1957–58 expedition was upon film by John Marshall and the collection of music by Nicholas England. I was not present that year.

tively short, but they gave us opportunity to make some comparative observations.

Table 1 gives the times and places of our work in the Nyae Nyae area. (The places are shown on Map 2 in Chapter 5.) Table 2 shows the places and times of our travels and the Bushmen with whom we stayed. (See Map 1.)

TABLE 2. Bushman Groups Visited outside of the Nyae Nyae Region

Year	Group	Location
1952–53	!Kung	Central dialect speakers, Nurugas, Karakuwisa, Khadum
1955	!Kung	Central dialect speakers, Mr. Lewis' farm near Ghanzi, Botswana
1955	!Kõ, also known as !Xõ, ≠Hũa, Magon	Near Okwa and at Barachu, Botswana
1955	Nharo, also known as Naro and Naron	Near Okwa
1955	/Gwi, also known as /Gwikhwe or /Gikwe	!Ai Ha !O Pan and vicinity Botswana c. 23°1′ E, 22°25′ S
1956	!Kung	Central dialect speakers near Omboloka, South West Africa
1959	Kxoé, also known as Kwengo, Mbarakwengo, Hukwe, and !Xũ	At Popa Falls on the Okavango River, South West Africa
1959	Ts'ixakhoe, also known as Tsexa and Handákhwe	Near the M'Babe Depression, Botswana
1959	!Kung	Northern dialect speakers at Tshimbaranda, 50 miles north of Dirico, Angola
1961	!Kung	Central dialect speakers at Dekar, east of Ghanzi, Botswana
1961	Nharo	!Gõ Tsao, c. 50 miles southwest of Ghanzi
1961	Tsaukhwe, Tsaukwe, also known as N/hãi	Xaxa, c. 22°15′ E, 21°5′ S Matomahubiru, c. 22°10′ E, 20°50′S !Go N!a, c. 22°12′ E, 20°35′ S
1961	Kõ, ≠Hũa, !Xõ, Magon	Tshawe, near Tsane, Botswana

1 Orientation and Perspectives

The Bushmen described in this volume are !Kung Bushmen, whose name for themselves is *jū /wāsi*. They live in a portion of the Kalahari Desert that lies in South West Africa, in an area centered approximately at 20° south latitude and 20° east longitude, near the border that divides South West Africa from Botswana. I call the area the Nyae Nyae area (to be defined presently), and I call the people the Nyae Nyae !Kung.

The material I present was gathered mainly in 1951, in 1952–53, and in 1955. On subsequent visits in 1959 and 1961, I added to and updated some of the material, but my most productive periods of study were in the first-mentioned years. Unless other indications are given, those years (1951, 1952–53, 1955) are to be taken as the *ethnographic present* of the descriptions. (Table 1 in the Introduction shows the places and the times of our work with the Nyae Nyae !Kung. Also see Map 2.)

At that time, the Nyae Nyae !Kung were living in complete independence, wholly by hunting and gathering, with no agriculture, no herds, no dogs, no beasts of burden. With the exception of the three Bantu families previously mentioned, none but !Kung inhabited the area.

Since that time, changes have been taking place. The descriptions in this book should be construed as applying to the Nyae Nyae !Kung in the above-mentioned years, not to later times and not to Bushmen in general, or even to !Kung in general—unless a wider application is specifically mentioned. Only a minority of Bushmen lived as independent hunter-gatherers, even in the years of my ethnographic present. Others lived in a variety of economic conditions. Although some customs and beliefs may have been widely shared, many varied, as did the conditions under which Bushmen lived. Without comparative study, there is no knowing how general a given custom or belief was.

Circumstances and the aridity of the desert had favored the independence of the Nyae Nyae !Kung. With few permanent waterholes and absence of other permanent surface water, the Nyae Nyae area had apparently not attracted the early white colonials of South Africa and South West Africa; the colonials had found better lands. Hence, these Bushmen escaped extermination at the hands of settlers, the fate that extinguished the Bushman race in South Africa.

At the time we arrived, the !Kung in the Nyae Nyae area were protected by government regulation. Although the area was not formally defined by the government of South West Africa as a native reserve for Bushmen, nonetheless it was "crown land" and was closed to white settlers and to Bantu, either from South West Africa or the Botswana side of the border. There had been occasional temporary defiances of those regulations. Herero or Tawana had on occasion brought cattle from Botswana into the area and had settled temporarily, but no permanent settlements had been established except the kraals of the three Bantu families: one in Samangaigai, one in Tsho/ana, and one in /Gam. The Nyae Nyae !Kung visit the !Kung who live on the Botswana side of the border. There they have had contact for decades with Herero and Tawana, who have cattle posts in the border country. The !Kung engage in trade with them, mostly for metal for arrow points, knives, tobacco, and pots, but they are not dominated by Bantu, not even much influenced by them.

White influence on the Nyae Nyae !Kung was at a minimum at the time we were in the area. No administrative post, no mission, school, or labor-recruiting office had been established. In fact, no government official had ever penetrated the area, as far as is known, beyond the Bantu staffed posts on the northern periphery till 1951, when Claude McIntyre entered it as a member of our first expedition. A few travelers, hunters, and prospectors had crossed the area in ox wagons, some had carved their names on the baobab trees (see the section below, The !Kung Historical Perspective), twice a police patrol on camels went through; but no whites had settled. Later, the difficulty of travel into the area by motor vehicle had served as a deterrent to casual incursion upon the !Kung by white people from the South West Africa side seeking labor for their farms. A stretch of 100 to 150 miles of uninhabited country, waterless most of the year, at the time trackless, lay between the easternmost of these farms and the Nyae Nyae area. When we started out in 1951 equipped to make the journey, we were eight days traveling the 150 miles, crossing from Epata to /Gam, following the Eiseb Omuramba (see Map 1). Our four trucks, laden with gasoline drums, water drums, food, and gear, stuck in the sand, first one, then another. They were plagued with hourly punctures and daily broken springs; they crashed into huge aardvark burrows; and one time the main frame of one of our Dodge power wagons was broken in two. Furthermore, the seeds of tall dry grasses clogged the radiators and they boiled. That was a crucial difficulty. Many times the radiators had to be taken off and cleaned. We could not afford their boiling, for the water we carried in our water drums had to take our whole expedition not only in but out. We were going into an unmapped, undescribed area looking for Bushmen who might accept us or might refuse to do so and disappear, and we did not know whether or not we would find water adequate to our expedition needs. I mention the difficulties of the journey because I believe the conditions of travel were so important a protective factor for the !Kung in maintaining their own way of life.

Looking at the situation from another point of view, we can say that while white people and Bantu had not taken the area from the !Kung, the !Kung had not left it. It seems probable that they had inhabited it for a very long time and were not recent refugees driven into it, and that we observed a way of life that had not changed radically in ages.

Change did begin for the !Kung, however, in the late 1950's, and in 1960 extensive and profound changes began. The Department of Bantu Administration and Development established the office of Bushman Affairs Commissioner. Claude McIntyre was the first to be appointed to the office in late 1960, and with his wife, Beryl, he established a post, a dwelling, and a bore hole at Tsumkwe. For the eight years before McIntyre's retirement, the McIntyres devoted themselves to the !Kung. With a group who were eager to make the attempt, McIntyre experimented with growing corn and millet and later with raising goats. Kalahari aridity and the cycle of drought turned much of this experiment into disappointment, but developments continued. An airstrip and a road were built. A Dutch Reformed Church mission was established. The !Kung were no longer remote. Today, the effort is under way to find ways to bring them into the modern world, and the problems that attend that process are upon them in all their complexity and gravity.

This book is about the !Kung as they were before profound change began.

NAMES AND DIALECTS

A multitude of names surround Bushmen in their many language groups —names they give themselves, names their Bushman neighbors give them (often descriptive of the place or terrain they inhabit or the food that is the staple), names Bantu and white people give them (often corruptions of the Bushman words).

The name *!Kung* has been traditionally used in the literature on Bushmen for the group of Bushmen to which the Nyae Nyae !Kung belong—both for the people and their language.

The name here spelled *!Kung* is the word in the !Kung language that means "person" or "people." The word has been rendered in different orthographies, in a profusion of spellings, by those engaged in Bushman studies: Isaak Schapera in his classic work, *The Khoisan Peoples of South Africa: Bushmen and Hottentots,* gives the spellings *!Khŭ* or *!Kuŋ* and says the people are commonly called *Kung.*[1] I was influenced by Schapera's statement but I was not omitting clicks, so the spelling *!Kung* became my choice. *!Kung* was also the choice of spelling of Estermann, De Almeida, Metzger, and members of the Harvard Bushman (San) Research Program.[2] Theophilus Hahn has *!Kuong;* Passarge has *²Kung* (he uses the numeral 2 to represent the alveolar click symbol, ≠). Fourie

1. Isaak Schapera, *The Khoisan Peoples of South Africa: Bushmen and Hottentots* (New York, Humanities Press, 1951), pp. 5 and 33. The term *Khoisan* was coined by Leonhard Schultze-Jena in *Zur Kenntnis des Körpers der Hottentotten und Buschmänner* (Jena, Gustav Fischer, 1928), p. 211. Schultze says *kxoï-kxoïn*, meaning "true (echte) people," is the name the Hottentots use for themselves; *Sān* is the word they use for Bushmen. Schapera adopted *Khoisan* as a convenient generic term for the two peoples and has made the term well known.

2. Padre Carlos Estermann, *Etnografia Do Sudoeste De Angola*, Memórias, Série Antropológica E Etnológica, IV (Porto, 1956), passim; António De Almeida, *Bushmen and Other Non-Bantu Peoples of Angola: Three Lectures* (Johannesburg, Witwatersrand University Press for the Institute for the Study of Man in Africa, 1965), p. 1; Fritz Metzger, *Narro and His Clan* (Windhoek, South West Africa, John Meinert Ltd., 1950), p. 8. The Harvard Bushman (San) Research Program was begun in Botswana in 1963 and has been continuing. Its leaders are Irven DeVore and Richard Borshay Lee. Scientists in social anthropology, physical anthropology, and archaeology have participated. Lee points out that the adoption of a standard form for the word *!Kung* is desirable and recommends *!Kung* because it has been the most widely used in the literature. See his *Subsistence Ecology of !Kung Bushmen* (Ann Arbor, Mich., University Microfilms, 1968), p. 27.

has !Kūng; Lebzelter has !Kun and //Khun; Vedder has !Kũ; Doke has Qhung; Maingard, !Khũ; Köhler and Westphal, !Xũ; England, !Kxõ. Dorothea F. Bleek in her monumental work, A Bushman Dictionary, has !Kũ, Kun, and Kung.³

In this same work, Bleek's overall classification of Bushman languages into three divisions—northern (N), southern (S), and central (C)—makes !Kung a northern language. Bleek divides the northern group into three languages as follows: Auen or //K"au -//en (NI), spoken in the vicinities of Ghanzi (Botswana) and Gobabis (South West Africa); !Kũ, !Kuŋ or Kung (in my spelling !Kung) (NII), spoken north of NI in Botswana and South West Africa; !O!kuŋ (NIII), spoken in Angola. These are now classified by linguists as one language with three dialects that are mutually intelligible.

Richard Lee prefers to call the three dialects by the same name, !Kung, and to differentiate them as northern, central, and southern.⁴ Thus, his northern !Kung is Bleek's NIII, his central !Kung is Bleek's NII, and his southern !Kung is Bleek's NI. I follow Lee's lead in this classification. The !Kung described in this volume, whom I call the Nyae Nyae !Kung, are among the speakers of the central !Kung dialect.

The northern !Kung, whom we studied briefly at Tshimbaranda in Angola, call themselves !Kung, and, as far as they know, all the !Kung in Angola do also. The Bantu, however, call those !Kung who live east of the Okavango River Sekele; those west of the Okavango they call Kwankhala. De Almeida tells us these words mean "porcupine people" and "crabfish people" respectively.⁵

The southern !Kung, who have traditionally been called Auen or //K"au-//en in the literature, are called Makaukau by the Herero and Tswana as well as by the white farmers of Ghanzi area. Lee tells us that

3. Theophilus Hahn, Original Map of Great Namaqualand and Damaraland, 1879; Siegfried Passarge, Die Buschmänner der Kalahari (Berlin, Dietrich Reimer [Ernest Vohsen], 1907), p. 19; for the works of Fourie, Lebzelter, Vedder, and Doke see Schapera's bibliography in The Khoisan Peoples of South Africa; L. F. Maingard, "The Three Bushman Languages," African Studies, 16 (1957), 39; Oswin Köhler by personal communication (the spelling appears in "Noun Classes and Grammatical Agreement in !Xũ (Zû-/hoà dialect)," Annals University Abidjan, Série H [Linguistique], Fascicule hors serie, 1971; E. O. J. Westphal, "A Re-classification of Southern African Non-Bantu Languages," Journal of African Languages, 1 (1962), 7; Nicholas M. England, "Music among the Zũ'/'wã-si of South West Africa and Botswana," Ph.D. diss., Harvard University, 1968; Dorothea F. Bleek, A Bushman Dictionary (New Haven, American Oriental Society, 1956).
4. Lee, Subsistence Ecology, pp. 27, 28.
5. De Almeida, Bushmen of Angola, p. 1.

all these terms appear to be corruptions of the Nharo word ≠d"au//ae, which means "north side," reflecting the fact that the southern !Kung have traditionally lived north of the Nharo. Lee finds that this is the name the Nharo use for the southern !Kung and the southern !Kung use for themselves.[6] They feel that *Makaukau* is a derogatory term.

The speakers of the central !Kung dialect do not call themselves *!Kung*; their name for themselves is *jũ /wãsi*.[7] If explicitly asked, our informants accepted the name *!Kung* but made it clear that they were not pleased with it. They say the black people call them that.

Tswana call Bushmen in general *Sarwa*; Herero call them *Ovaku-ruha*. Both names refer to living in the bush, as our general name "Bushman" does, and living in the bush is considered a lowly state. Bantu in general look down on Bushmen in general, and they look down especially on those who live wholly by hunting and gathering. Hunters and gatherers they consider to be backward, ignorant, poverty-stricken bush-dwellers, without livestock or crops, without proper garments, without dwellings, without status or amenities or possessions of any kind to which they could point with pride. I think for that reason the names that Bantu use for Bushmen come to have a ring of derogation in Bushman ears—the general names Sarwa, Ovakuruha, and also the names that distinguish the different language or dialect groups, !Kung and Makaukau, and so forth.

In the name *jũ /wãsi*, *jũ* means "person" and *si* is the plural suffix. */Wã* has been translated several ways. Westphal translates it "true" or "real" and says "any translation which reflects the fact that the people are identifiable and worth knowing (i.e., good, loyal, honest, correct, right) would be acceptable." Lee translates */wã* as "proper" and "true." England thinks that "common," "usual" are concepts the word holds.[8] Kernel Ledimo, our interpreter, thought that the word also held the idea of perfection, cleanliness, purity. He said pure water could be called *!gu /wã*, and a perfectly clean pot could be called *kxo /wã*. He said also that if one man were suspicious of another and of what he might be carrying and asked, "What have you got in your hand?," the other might open his hands and reply, if he had nothing harmful, "*Mi* [I am] */wã*." In the

6. Lee, *Subsistence Ecology*, p. 28.

7. Jũ/wãsi has been spelled in many ways. The one I most enjoy is Passarge's ssu²-gnássi (*Die Buschmänner*, p. 23). The Harvard Group currently uses the spelling zhũ/twãsi.

8. Westphal, personal communication; Lee, *Subsistence Ecology*, p. 27; England, "Music," p. 59.

title of her book about the !Kung, Elizabeth Marshall Thomas para-
phrases jũ/wãsi, which she writes Zhu twa si, as The Harmless People.
She says, "Twa means 'just' or 'only' in the sense that you say: 'It was
just the wind' or 'It is only me.' "[9]

For the jũ /wãsi, the name holds dignity and honor, but not for Bantu
and not for all Bushmen or even all !Kung. The northern !Kung at Tshimbaranda in Angola do not use this appellation. They consider it derogatory and think it impolite. Perhaps this is because Bushmen in other
economic conditions tend to look down on Bushmen who have remained
hunter-gatherers as backward, ignorant, and poor, and most of the !Kung
who have continued to live as hunter-gatherers are in the central dialect
group, that is, they are jũ/wãsi. Isaak Utuhile, the Tawana administrative
chief at !Xabe in Botswana, said that in the name jũ/wãsi the Bushmen
were declaring, in effect, "We are not animals, we are humans." But the
idea that they needed to assert that they were humans, not animals, was
not one that we detected in the thinking of the jũ/wãsi.

THE NYAE NYAE AREA, THE DOBE AREA,
THE NYAE NYAE REGION

The Nyae Nyae *area* lies in the western portion of the Kalahari Desert in
South West Africa between approximately 19°5′ and 20°20′ south lati-
tude and 20°10′ and 21° east longitude. The border between South West
Africa and Botswana is at 21° E at this latitude. The extent of the area in
the north-south dimension is about ninety miles, and, in the east-west
dimension, from the meridian of 21° E to the farthest point west that the
!Kung go, the distance is about sixty miles. Near the center of the Nyae
Nyae area is a circle of thirteen pans, some of them exceptionally large.[10]
Gautscha Pan, at which our expedition of 1952–53 was based much of
the time, is at about 19°48′30″ S, 20°34′36″ E. I take the coordinates and
the names Nyae Nyae and Gautscha from a map issued by the Surveyor
General of South West Africa at Windhoek, dated July 11, 1935.[11]

---

9. Elizabeth Marshall Thomas, The Harmless People (New York, Alfred A. Knopf,
1959), p. 24.
10. The pans are natural depressions with surfaces that are more impervious than
loose sand. Water collects in them during the rains; they dry up in the dry season.
11. Comparison was made with the map of Bartholomew and Sons, South Africa
and Madagascar, Edinburgh, 1959; also with World Aeronautical Charts, numbers
1178 and 1274 (revised 1952). No accurate survey of that part of the world has been
made except for the border on 21° E. Specific places are indicated on the several
maps only approximately, and the maps differ slightly, or more than slightly, one
from the other. I depend principally on the Surveyor General's map.

The coordinates serve to locate the area approximately but should not be thought of as boundaries. Except for the meridian of 21° E, the area has no boundaries, and to delimit it at all is a matter of definition.

Theophilus Hahn on his map of 1879 calls the general region in which the Nyae Nyae area lies "Dorst Veld" (Thirst Veld). He writes "!Koung Bushmen" on the map in the space of the Dorst Veld, which is otherwise empty (that is, without place names or symbols of topographical features, indicating that the area was unexplored). The general area is called Kaukau Veld on South African maps.

The name Nyae Nyae comes from the map of the Surveyor General. So spelled, it appears in the center of the circle of pans, which is approximately the center of the area. Needing a convenient appellation for the whole area as I define it, I adopted Nyae Nyae.

The name is a corruption of the !Kung name N//hwã!ai. The corruption has been used before. It is spelled Neinei on German maps and Nyae-Nyae or Nyainyai on Afrikaans and English maps, and England tells us it is rendered O-njeinje by Herero.[12] The !Kung apply the name N//hwã!ai to a portion of the Nyae Nyae area that includes the circle of pans and the land around them. The pans, outcroppings of rock, and several waterholes are the special features of N//hwã!ai; the ground in N//hwã!ai is somewhat firmer than the loose sands found elsewhere. !Kung who live in this locality call themselves "owners of N//hwã!ai."

We estimated a population of 567 !Kung in the whole of the Nyae Nyae area. There were three families of Bantu in the area, the family at /Gam and the "Bushman Guards" at Tsho/ana and Samangaigai; they were the only non-Bushman inhabitants. Three groups of !Kung worked for and lived with the Bantu families. The majority of !Kung lived in their traditionally organized bands. The bands, nineteen in number, are described in Chapter 5 and listed there in Table 3. The locations of their waterholes are shown on Map 2.

Our most rewarding study was with Bands 1–7, 9, 10, and 12 in the years 1951, 1952–53, 1955. Bands 1–7, 9, and 10 are in the central portion of the Nyae Nyae area, and they are the "owners of N//hwã!ai"; Band 12 is one of the bands based at the /Gam waterhole.

In 1963, the Harvard Bushman (San) Research Project began intensive study of the !Kung in western Botswana, in the area that roughly parallels the Nyae Nyae area in latitude. They based themselves at Dobe,

12. England, "Music," p. 44.

and since then the area in which they worked has become well known as
the Dobe area. It became necessary to make a distinction between the
two areas. Since the name Nyae Nyae is associated with our work on the
South West Africa side, I am retaining the name to distinguish that area
from the Dobe area.

Richard Lee records a !Kung population of 433 in the Dobe area.
Of those, 311 were living independently by hunting and gathering, 122 of
them were living with Bantu. They were based at eight waterholes. In his
Subsistence Ecology of !Kung Bushmen, Lee defines and describes the
area and discusses the subsistence of the !Kung within it in full detail.[13]

Our travels and observations in the Dobe area had been only cur-
sory. We saw nine bands of !Kung living independently and six groups
living with Bantu (see Table 3). We learned something of the area from
visiting Isaak Utuhile, the administrative chief at !Xabe, and from !Kung
from the Dobe area who came to visit relatives in the Nyae Nyae area. In
1961, we spent two weeks with a band of !Kung at /Gwia, south of Kai
Kai, a band we had not met before. We did not happen to go to Dobe itself in our Botswana travels, which seems ironic to me now, since Dobe
has become so well known to all who are interested in Bushman studies.

The !Kung of the Nyae Nyae area in South West Africa and those of
the Dobe area in Botswana form a loosely united population. They have
no structured political unity, but the population is a pool of people who
intermarry. I include in this statement both the !Kung who live in traditionally organized bands and those who live in groups working for Bantu.
Kinship bonds link the working groups with the !Kung population as a
whole, and they are part of the pool of !Kung who intermarry.

In the distant past there was no political border between the coun-
tries, and the now-established border for a time had no effect on the
movements of the !Kung. The government authorities did not restrain
them from crossing back and forth as they wished, to visit or to live on
either side. I therefore wanted a convenient means of referring to the
land which this population inhabits as a whole. In previous publication,
I used the appellation "region of Nyae Nyae" for that purpose, and I have
decided to retain it. It is awkward to use the name Nyae Nyae within
two frames of reference in this way, but it is more awkward to change
the appellation. Once something is in the literature, it is impossible to get
it out and very difficult to modify it.

13. Lee, *Subsistence Ecology,* pp. 38–68.

Intermarriage of the !Kung within the Nyae Nyae region took place over a long period of time, and the people are woven by blood and marriage ties into a web of relationships. They are not constrained by formal social rules from marrying outside this population, nor are outsiders constrained from entering it by marriage, but such outside marriages have been rare. The !Kung within this population all apply kinship terms to each other. They do so on the basis of their names, in what I call the name-relationship (see Chapter 6), whether or not they have close consanguineous or affinal ties. This contributes greatly to their sense of being one people. Much visiting has given many of them face-to-face acquaintance. If they do not have that, they at least know each other's family connections. They are not strangers to one another.

I identified the perimeters of the region on the basis of statements made by the !Kung in the central part of the Nyae Nyae area, that is, the owners of N//hwã!ai. I must emphasize the fact that I am taking their point of view before great changes came upon them. Also I must emphasize the fact that the !Kung on the peripheries of the area had somewhat wider contacts. For example, the !Kung at /Gwia knew central !Kung further south, and there were three marriages between the /Gwia !Kung and Bushmen of other language groups, two with Nharo women and one with a N/hãi man. The !Kung in Tsho/ana and Samangaigai knew central !Kung further north in the area of Khadum. However, for the owners of N//hwã!ai, the region was almost their whole world.

They include in the north !Kung who live at or near Tsho/ana and Samangaigai but not those who live at Khadum, Kapupahedi, Karaku-wisa, or Nurugas, although the Nyae Nyae !Kung know that the !Kung at those places are central-dialect speakers like themselves. They include !Kung who live to the south as far as N//o!gau but not those who live further south. To the east, they include !Kung in Botswana in the Dobe area, including those at Kai Kai and /Gwia. To the west, beyond the region, is the stretch of uninhabited country 100 to 150 miles wide which we were eight days in crossing. In the rainy season, the Nyae Nyae !Kung can cross that country and occasionally do so. I think of them passing through it as quietly as shadows in contrast to our traversing it in roaring, banging trucks. The Nyae Nyae !Kung have kept contact with a few central-dialect-speaking !Kung in the zone of the South West Africa farms. Three !Kung families from the west have married into Nyae Nyae !Kung families. For this reason, I say the Nyae Nyae region is almost their whole world but not entirely so.

Although the Nyae Nyae !Kung know that there are more !Kung than those in their region who speak the same dialect that they speak, if they have no relatives or acquaintances among them, they count them as strangers and call them *ju dole.*

Dole means "strange," "bad," "worthless," "harmful," or "potentially harmful" (the strange *is* potentially harmful in !Kung thinking), and, according to Bleek's translation, "different" or "other." *Dole* is widely used in all the above senses. A bad person may be called *ju dole;* a good and close friend may also be called *ju dole* if one is displeased with him. Land that produces no food is *dole.* Any strange people, be they white, black, or Bushmen of other language groups, and those of the same language and even the same dialect, if they are strangers, are *ju dole.* By contrast, the !Kung within the region are all *jū /wāsi* to themselves and to each other.

Because there are so many consanguineous and affinal ties among the !Kung within the region, I wondered for a time if we should find a kin group of the type Murdock proposes in hypothesis, and for which he proposes the term *deme.* If such a kin group were found, Murdock says it would be bilateral and endogamous and "comparable to the sib both in size and in the traditional rather than demonstrable bonds of kinship which unite members."[14] Though the social relationships of the Nyae Nyae region show elements suggesting a deme, I am convinced that the region does not constitute, strictly speaking, an organized kin group of which the people are conscious as a social form. The endogamy of the region is customary and preferred, but it is not required by social rule; and the population is not united in such a way that social regulation derives from the unity.

BUSHMAN POPULATION AND DISTRIBUTION OF !KUNG

Several decades ago, estimates of the number of surviving Bushmen were as low as 7,000 to 7,500, and Bushmen were thought to be dying out. However, as time went on and more data became available, estimates increased. In 1957, Phillip Tobias, who had taken an interest in collecting not only official data but local estimates made by district commissioners and others, published an estimate of 55,000. He surprised everyone. Richard Lee in 1964, when still more government reports and other data

14. George Peter Murdock, *Social Structure* (New York, Macmillan, 1949), pp. 62, 63.

had become available and his own observations in the field were considerable, lowered the estimated figure to 44,100.[15] The variations in the estimates are not to be taken as an indication that the Bushman population rose and fell that much, but only that direct counts of Bushmen were few and estimates of nomadic desert-dwellers difficult to make.

Lee places 24,600 Bushmen in Botswana; 15,000 in South West Africa; 4,000 in Angola; 100 in the Republic of South Africa; 200 in Zambia; 200 in Rhodesia.[16]

Of Bushmen in all the surviving language groups, the !Kung are the most numerous. Lee's estimate is 13,000. Of those he estimates that 4,000 are northern dialect speakers, 2,000 southern dialect speakers, and 7,000 central dialect speakers.[17]

The northern dialect speakers are mainly in southern Angola. They are to be found also in the northeastern part of Ovamboland, and in the vicinity of Runtu, in South West Africa. In Angola, according to the maps of Estermann and De Almeida, !Kung groups are found from the southern border as far north as about 13° south latitude and from about 14° east longitude to the Zambia border.[18] In their various localities they live as neighbors of the several Bantu tribes that have settled in southern Angola, among them Ambo, Kwangare, Mbwela, Humbe, Mbukushu, and Ganguela. We made a brief study of two !Kung groups who live among Ganguela at Tshimbaranda, east of the Cuito River, about fifty miles north of Dirico.

The southern dialect speakers are to be found in the vicinity of Ghanzi in Botswana and somewhat to the north, south, and west of that vicinity. They are also found around Gobabis in South West Africa. Practically all of them are on the farms of the white people in those areas. We made no study of southern !Kung and had only a minimum of contact with some who worked for a white farmer in the vicinity of Ghanzi.

The central dialect speakers live in South West Africa and Botswana in three geographic areas.

(1) Central !Kung groups are found working for or living in some degree of dependence on white farmers in South West Africa on the easternmost farms in the zone of the white inhabitants, those farms that

15. Phillip V. Tobias, "Bushmen of the Kalahari," Man, 57 (March 1957), 33; Lee, Subsistence Ecology, p. 13.
  16. Ibid.
  17. Ibid., pp. 19, 26.
  18. Estermann, Etnografia, vol. I; De Almeida, Bushmen of Angola, p. 43.

border upon the desert and upon the Eastern and the Epukiro native re-
serves of the Herero. The farms extend from the vicinity of Gobabis
northward to Grootfontein, Neitsas, and Nurugas. Central !Kung are
found also on the farms of the white inhabitants in the Ghanzi area of
Botswana working or living as squatters.

(2) Further to the northeast in the Okavango Native Territory in
South West Africa, other !Kung of the central dialect live in some degree
of relationship with the Okavango tribes on the south side of the river
where it turns from its north-south direction and flows east and southeast toward the Okavango swamps. Those Bantu tribes are Kwangare,
Sambio, Dirico, and Mbukushu. We saw a few !Kung children in one of
the schools of the Roman Catholic missions that serve the Okavango
tribes at Andara. Other !Kung of the central dialect live as hunter-gatherers independently of the Bantu, some south of the government post at
Runtu, and some in the vicinity of the government post at Nurugas and
Karakuwisa, and others live at or near Kapupahedi and Khadum.

(3) The remaining !Kung of the central dialect are those of the Nyae
Nyae region.

LINGUISTIC PERSPECTIVE

For many reasons, the languages that employ clicks have intrigued not
only linguists but also scholars interested in the origins and movements
of peoples in Africa.[19] Clicks are not known to occur anywhere in the
world outside of the southern part of the African continent except in
Tanzania, where two click languages, Sandawe and Hadza, are found.
The origin and early distribution of clicks, the relationships of the languages, especially the Bushman and Hottentot languages, and the possible borrowings of one language from another are matters of ongoing interest. Many of the languages have not yet been fully analyzed, but work
on them is proceeding.[20]

19. For her help in the preparation of this section, I am indebted to Megan Biesele.
20. Oswin Köhler's dictionary of Kxoé is forthcoming. He is also working on !Kung
as spoken in the area of Andara, in the Caprivi Strip. J. W. Snyman has published a
book on !Kung as spoken in the Nyae Nyae area, *An Introduction to the !Xũ (!Kung)
Language* (Cape Town, A. A. Balkema, 1970). His work on Žu/'hõasi phonemics and
his Žu/'hõasi dictionary are also to be published by Balkema. In the future he plans
to complete his comparison between Nama (Hottentot) and Žu/'hõasi vocabularies. E.
O. J. Westphal continues to make research trips to the Tshu-Khwe and !Xũ areas. He
has computerized his Bushman dictionaries: the coding was done by D. J. Cranmer
of the linguistics department of Cornell University. He is also corresponding publicly

There has been considerable recent discussion about the classification of the languages that employ clicks and the nomenclature used for them. Schapera called these languages "Khoisan," the convenient term with which he bracketed the Bushman and Hottentot peoples.[21] Oswin Köhler retains that appellation. In 1955, Joseph H. Greenberg called the Hottentot and Bushman languages "Khoisan," but used the designation "the Click Languages" when he included the two Tanzanian languages.[22] By 1966, he had expanded "Khoisan" to include the entire group of related languages. For clarity he distinguished between South African Khoisan (Hottentot and Bushman) and East African Khoisan (Sandawe and Hadza). E. O. J. Westphal opposes the use of "Khoisan" for linguistic purposes and has settled upon the term "non-Bantu click languages," which he proposes to subdivide into "Khwe-Kovab" or Hottentot, Bush, and East African click languages. Westphal feels that the Tanzanian languages cannot as yet be associated with the South African click languages by regularly accepted linguistic procedures.[23]

---

in South African journals with Anthony Traill about the classification of the Bushman languages. Traill himself has done a study of the !Xõ clicks using cineradiographic techniques. He has a continuing twofold project of (1) providing a complete account of one dialect of !Xõ (a Southern Bushman language), and (2) surveying the dialectal diversity found over the entire !Xõ area. He has also discovered a hitherto unknown Bushman language he calls Eastern ≠Hûã near the Khutswe Game Reserve in Botswana. This language, though centrally located and in contact with only the Tshu-Khwe language group, exhibits linguistic features that would make it seem a link between northern and southern Bush languages, Westphal's A and B. (Traill, "N4 or S7: Another Bushman Language," *African Studies Quarterly Journal*, vol. 32, Johannesburg, Witwatersrand University Press, 1973).

21. In Notes on the Text, I mentioned that there is a movement among anthropologists to abandon the name *Bushman* and to adopt *San* instead. That movement includes the abandoning of the name *Hottentot*, as well, and the adoption of *Khoikoi* instead (see n. 1 above). When the names *Bushman* and *Hottentot* were bestowed by the first Europeans to arrive in South Africa, the names ridiculed the way of life of the bush dwellers and the clicking speech of the pastoral Hottentots. I think the names have lost their original denotation and that in this day and age they are not used in derogation; but still they are unfortunate. They are deeply entrenched, however, and it remains to be seen whether or not the movement to abandon them will gain enough momentum to dislodge them.

22. Oswin Köhler, "Studien zum Genussystem und Verbalbau der zentralen Khoisan-Sprachen," *Anthropos*, 57 (1962), 529; J. H. Greenberg, *Studies in African Linguistic Classification* (Branford, Conn., Compass Publishing Co., 1955; repr. from *Southwestern Journal of Anthropology*, vols. 5 [1949], 6 [1950], 10 [1954]).

23. J. H. Greenberg, *Languages of Africa* (The Hague, Mouton, 1966); E. O. J. Westphal, "The Click Languages of South and East Africa" (1971), in J. Berry and J. H. Greenberg, eds., *Linguistics in Subsaharan Africa*, vol. 7 of Thomas A. Sebeok, ed., *Current Trends in Linguistics* (The Hague, Mouton, 1971), pp. 369–378; E. O. J. Westphal, "The Linguistic Prehistory of Southern Africa: Bush, Kwadi, Hottentot and Bantu Linguistic Relationships," *Africa*, 33 (July 1963), 242.

Clicks have been borrowed by several Bantu languages in southern Africa, but are not an inherent element of those languages. The Kwadi language (also called Curoca) in southwestern Angola employs clicks, but Kwadi does not have other features in common with the other click languages. Westphal says of it that "up to the present, all linguistic attempts at linking Kwadi with any other language in Africa have been entirely negative."[24]

The Bushman and Hottentot languages have generally been regarded as belonging to one language family, and a common language source in the distant past has been assumed for them. In the past decade, Köhler and Greenberg classified them as a language family. Westphal's research has led him to take issue with that classification. He claims that the fact that all these languages employ clicks does not necessarily indicate that they have a common language source. He has been concerned to show that they lack grammatical and lexical relationship and says it is possible that they have acquired the clicks by contact and borrowing. Throughout his writings, Westphal emphasizes the fact that none of the languages have been recorded at several different periods of their development, and as yet no rules for sound shifts can be set up between any of the click languages.[25] Anthony Traill makes the point that we really have no idea about the sorts of linguistic changes that characterize the click languages. He says these languages have great phonetic complexity and would be good testing ground for the theory of linguistic change.[26]

In Westphal's classification, Bush and Hottentot languages do not together constitute one language family, but the Hottentot languages within themselves do constitute a language family. They are genetically related.[27] Characteristics they have in common are a system of twenty-seven pronouns and the differentiation of masculine, feminine, and common gender in singular, dual, and plural.[28]

In his reclassification of the languages, Westphal makes another

24. Ibid., pp. 242, 247.
25. Oswin Köhler, "Studien zum Genussystem," p. 529, and Greenberg, *Studies in African Linguistic Classification*, p. 87; E. O. J. Westphal, "Linguistic Prehistory," pp. 242, 237.
26. Anthony Traill, "The Compleat Guide to the Koon," a research report on linguistic field work undertaken in Botswana and South West Africa, July 1972 and January 1973 (unpub. typescript, 1973), p. 2.
27. E. O. J. Westphal, "Linguistic Prehistory," pp. 249–251.
28. E. O. J. Westphal, "A Re-classification of Southern African Non-Bantu Languages," p. 3; Oswin Köhler, "Die Khoe-sprachigen Buschmänner der Kalahari," Sonderdruck aus Forschungen zur allgemeinen und regionalen Geographie, *Festschrift für Kurt Kayser* (Kölner Geographische Arbeiten, Sonderband, 1971), p. 375.

change from traditionally held views. He reclassifies the languages Bleek calls her central group of Bushman languages as Hottentot and calls the people who speak them Hottentots. According to modern research, there are five main groups of related languages and dialects within Bleek's central group. Westphal calls them the Tshu-Khwe Hottentot languages.[29]

Bleek recognized the similarity of her central group to the Hottentot languages and called Hottentots "the linguistic brothers of the Central Group." She called the central languages Bushman, nevertheless. Both Köhler and Greenberg classify the central group with Hottentot. Köhler proposes that the languages traditionally classified as Hottentot and Bleek's five central group languages (Westphal's Tshu-Khwe) be called Central Khoisan and that the speakers of the five central group languages be called Khoe-speakers. Köhler prefers that Bushman and Hottentot be used for the two peoples when they are being classified as races and cultures and that the names be disassociated from language.[30]

The problem that interests me is not so much what we call the Hottentot and Bushman languages (though that problem is very interesting), but what we call the peoples. Are the people of Bleek's central group Hottentots who live in the Bushman manner without herds, or Bushmen who speak Hottentot?

There are differences between the two branches of the Capoid race, as this race is called by Carleton S. Coon. Hottentots, in general, are taller and lighter-skinned than Bushmen. Other precise somatic differences have been recorded by Schultze and summarized by Schapera.[31] Investigations into differences in blood characteristics have been carried out by researchers from the University of the Witwatersrand and the University of Capetown, and from Harvard University. It will not be until further somatic and serological studies have been completed, however, that we can answer the question about the central group: are they Hottentots who have taken on Bushman culture or Bushmen speaking Hottentot languages? There is no doubt of their culture being like that of the pres-

29. Dorothea F. Bleek, *Comparative Vocabularies of Bushman Languages*, University of Cape Town, Publications of the School of African Life and Language (Cambridge, The University Press, 1929); E. O. J. Westphal, "A Re-classification of Southern African Non-Bantu Languages," pp. 1–8.

30. Bleek, *Comparative Vocabularies*, p. 11; Köhler, "Die Khoe-sprachigen Buschmänner," p. 375, and Greenberg, *Studies in African Linguistic Classification*, p. 87; Köhler, "Studien zum Genussystem," p. 529.

31. Carleton S. Coon, *The Origin of Races* (New York, Alfred A. Knopf, 1962); Coon, *The Living Races of Man* (New York, Alfred A. Knopf, 1965); Isaak Schapera, *Khoisan Peoples of South Africa*, p. 60.

ent Bushmen. They have the ritual curing dance, the Eland Music of the menarchal rite, the manner of living, similar artifacts, and many other cultural features in common. I have an open mind on the subject, but admit to being somewhat influenced by impression. To me these people look and act so like Bushmen that I lean to calling them Bushmen till they are proved to be Hottentot. Both peoples have had a long history in which to make their several divergences, with possible absorptions of language or of ritual or other aspects of culture from each other and from peoples they passed in their early migrations. Their historical relationships still remain shrouded in mystery.

As to the extant Bush languages, which he clearly distinguishes from Hottentot languages, Westphal finds, according to his recent research (1971), three language families, each including several languages and/or dialects. He finds these language families unrelated to each other. He calls the families the Ju, the Taa, and the !Wi according to the way each family renders the word "person."[32] (Formerly he considered the languages to fall into four families, which he called Bush A, B, C, and D.) The Taa and !Wi languages are spoken by relatively small groups. The Taa speakers are in the region of the Nossob and Auob rivers in South West Africa and Botswana. The !Wi are in South Africa; they include the ≠Khomani in Gemsbok Park and the remnant of Bushmen at Lake Chrissie, the //Xegwi. The !Kung language with its three dialects comprises the Ju family, a language unrelated to any other in this world. As a language it is spoken by the largest numbers of living Bushmen in any Bushman language group.[33]

BUSHMAN ORIGINS AND MIGRATIONS

There are two main theories concerning the origins of the Bushmen on the African continent.[34] One, the theory that they originated in North Africa and migrated south, has been propounded by Carleton Coon in *The Origin of Races*. The second, held by Phillip Tobias and other South African scholars, is that the ancestral Bushman population arose in southern Africa and spread northward.

Both of these theories utilize the same repertoire of fossil and sub-

---

32. Westphal, "The Click Languages of South and East Africa," pp. 380–381.
33. Ibid.
34. Megan Biesele wrote this section, "Bushman Origins and Migrations." I wish to express my gratitude.

fossil findings. Probable post-Pleistocene ancestors of the modern Bushmen have been found across South Africa and in a sweep along the high plateaus of East Africa. The direction of this sweep is the subject of the two differing interpretations.

Tobias' analysis of these remains in 1961, reinforced in the same year by his consideration of the genetic forces that have shaped living Bushmen, followed a twenty-year hiatus since the previous overall review of race formation in Africa.[35]

During this twenty-year period, there had been a change in emphasis in biological anthropology from racial typology and race formation to population thinking and emphasis on natural selection and human diversity. At the same time, the realization of the limits of the fossil and subfossil evidence had led to a much more balanced and scientific viewpoint about prehistoric human populations. The earlier, racial typology minimized the all-important genetic and phenotypic variation (an extremely vital aspect of a population, as it allows evolution to occur). In 1941, R. Broom could write, "It seems to me not improbable that the Bushmen will prove to have been descended from a North Asiatic brachycephalic race remotely allied to the ancestral North American Indian, and the Korana to have come from a dolichocephalic Central Asiatic race."[36] Tobias was concerned to show that racial typologies and speculations about the immigration of racial types from remote parts were no longer necessary to explain the emergence of the Bushmen. Instead, he concentrated upon the evidence for their evolution from existing populations within southern Africa, postulating the derivation of the Bushman groups from Rhodesian Man.

The Capoid subspecies of *Homo sapiens,* to which the Bushmen belong, is differentiated from the Congoid (Negro) and other subspecies by pedomorphy (infantile physical characteristics) and a certain amount of dwarfing. Tobias' argument for the southern origin of the Capoids is based on the way in which he interprets the fossil record. Not only do the earliest Bush remains in Africa date from the Middle Stone Age of southern Africa, he says, but all pre-Bush remains from southern Africa are of larger people than the Bushmen. These last can be divided into

35. Phillip V. Tobias, "New Evidence and New Views on the Evolution of Man in Africa," *South African Journal of Science,* vol. 57, 1961; Phillip V. Tobias, "The Physique of a Desert Folk: Genes, Not Habitat, Shaped the Bushman," *Natural History,* vol. 70, 1961.

36. Robert Broom, "Bushmen, Koranas, and Hottentots," *Annals of the Transvaal Museum,* 20 (1941), 251.

two groups, the earlier Rhodesioid groups—"Neanderthaloid" fossils of great size, with craggy browridges—and a later Boskopoid group which resemble, but are larger than, present-day Bushmen. Tobias suggests that these forms underwent two main changes during the Upper Pleistocene. The Rhodesioids experienced differentiative changes, rendering them more infantile. Later their descendants, serially represented in finds from Boskop, Matjes River, and Fish Hoek in South Africa, underwent progressive dwarfing changes that eventually produced the modern Bushmen.[37]

Coon challenged this theory by asking why Bushman-like remains found further north in Kenya, for instance, were unreduced in size. If Tobias' ideas about the origin of the Bushmen in southern Africa were right, he said, later Bushmen who migrated northward would have been dwarfed, as were their southern forebears.[38] Coon's own theory would account for the East African unreduced forms by locating the original ancestors of the Bushmen in Morocco.

Interesting new Middle Pleistocene finds at Ternefine, Littorina Cave, and Temara in Morocco had been made a few years before 1961; Tobias, however, did not accord them the weight Coon was to place on them, by the middle of the sixties, as the earliest ancestors of the Bushmen. Coon coalesced an ancestral "Ternefine-Tangier Line" from the new Moroccan finds of the 1950's and his own Tangier discovery of 1939. This line was neither Caucasoid nor Negroid and resembled, he felt, both the Australopithecines and Sinanthropus of Asia. Coon is criticized for these ideas because the Australopithecines of South and East Africa are separated in time from the Middle Pleistocene by at least several hundred thousand years. Furthermore, the number of different Australopithecine populations represented by the material we have remains unclear.

Coon found his Ternefine-Tangier line also morphologically similar to finds from Singa in the Sudan, Homa in Kenya, and the Boskop group in South Africa. Tools found with the Ternefine-Tangier forms, he felt, were "as good as the recent work of Bushmen."[39]

The Capoids thus evolved as a subspecies, in Coon's theory, in the apparently periodic isolation from Congoids provided by the waxing and waning Sahara Desert. Then when the present Palearctic fauna invaded

37. Tobias, "New Evidence," pp. 31–32.
38. Coon, *Origin of Races*, p. 641.
39. Coon, *Origin of Races*, discussion pp. 588–600.

North Africa at the end of the Pleistocene, the Caucasoids who accompanied it drove the Capoids southward. The refugees crossed the (then
well-watered) Sahara by way of the central Saharan Tibesti highlands, where the last remains of a more humid vegetation survive even
today.[40]

In East Africa, fossil finds as well as pockets of living Capoid populations (such as the Duwwud of Libya and the Sandawe of Tanzania) indicate the course of their subsequent spread down the East African highlands to their present home in southern Africa.[41] In southern Africa, they
entered an underpopulated area inhabited by relatives of the ancestral
Negroes and Pygmies (Congoids) living farther north and west. These
people, of a lower evolutionary grade, were absorbed by the Bushmen,
according to Coon. Later, West African Negroes with agriculture and
metallurgy moved into the area, arriving at the same time as the Dutch.
Bantu and Boer together drove the Bushmen out of the lusher parts of
southern Africa and into the Kalahari.[42]

Coon supports his thesis that the Ternefine-Tangier line was ancestral to the Bushmen with an image from the folklore of the Riffians of
northern Morocco, descendants of the Mouillians. These people preserve
a vivid memory of their predecessors, food-gatherers who took refuge
in the inaccessible Riffian mountains.[43] The thesis is further bolstered
by the discovery of Bushman-like rock paintings in the Sahara. Archaeo-
logical evidence may give the theory some support: the Wilton culture
which has survived among the Bushmen, Coon writes, is "a micro-blade
derivative of the Capsian which had entered Africa from western Asia
some eight to nine thousand years earlier." Coon later concluded that "if
the Ternefine-Tangier folk were not the ancestors of the Bushmen, they
were a sixth subspecies that uniquely died without modern descendants,
and the Bushmen would have had no discernible ancestors."[44]

But like the southern theory, this northern theory also holds that
the infantilization and shrinking of Bushmen from larger ancestors must
have taken place in southern Africa. The South African Boskop remains,
unreduced, are the same size as Bushman-like fossil finds from Kenya

40. Ibid., and E. W. van Zinderen Bakker, "Paleobotanical Studies," in the Symposium on Early Man and his Environments in Southern Africa, *South African
Journal of Science*, 59 (1963), 334.
41. Coon, *Origin of Races*, p. 590.
42. Ibid.
43. Coon, *Origin of Races*, p. 601.
44. Coon, *Living Races of Man*, p. 89; Coon, *Origin of Races*, p. 602.

and the Sudan. Dwarfing and pedomorphy begin to be evident in the later specimens from Zitzikama, Matjes River, and Fish Hoek.

These reduction processes can be dated as having begun only a few thousand years ago, and as yet there is no satisfactory explanation of them. Ancestors of Bushmen never lived in tropical forests where humidity selects for the short stature conducive to rapid heat loss. Nor can their size be due to a shortage of food, because they once had all the game they could eat, according to Coon. Coon points out further that the size reduction has not affected all Capoids to the same extent. Since Hottentots and Strandloopers (pastoralists and fishermen) are larger than the Bushmen, he tentatively postulates that the hunting life may select for smaller stature.[45]

Following Alice Brues' suggestions in "The Spearman and the Archer," Tobias has related the size of Bushmen to their use of small bows and poisoned arrows. Coon too accepts this idea, calling Brues' essay "brilliant." Her main point is that selection in body build can come about through the influence of cultural factors as well as physical environmental factors. "A dominant weapon or tool may alter the average physique of a race using it over the course of time by giving a selective advantage to individuals of a body build best adapted to its use," she writes.[46]

An evolutionary sequence that went hand in hand with the use of various weapons can be traced as follows. The heavy build of the Neanderthalers facilitated the use of the bludgeon for killing prey. Then the invention of the spear directed selection toward favoring a long, light build well adapted to swift running. Even the act of taking aim requires motion, for the spearman. The power of the entire body gathers behind the spear to deal the deathblow; small size is therefore not favored.

But when the bow was invented, some of these selective effects were reversed. The prey is approached by stalking. Aim is taken at a stationary moment. The power behind the arrow itself is the power that will reach and penetrate the hide sufficiently to wound the animal. Thus, the archer needs short, thick arm muscles, a characteristic contrary to the best structure for spearmen. The bow favored the development of a

---

45. Ibid, pp. 645–646.
46. Phillip V. Tobias, "Bushman Hunter-Gatherers: A Study in Human Ecology," in D. H. S. David, ed., *Ecology in Southern Africa* (The Hague, W. Junk, 1965), p. 77; Alice Brues, "The Spearman and the Archer," *American Anthropologist*, 61 (1959), 457–458.

short, mesomorphic type with a laterality of build particularly well expressed in the shoulder and arm.[47]

The addition of arrow poison has made further reductions in size and arm-musculature possible, says A. R. Willcox, since it reduced the

Small size is a distinctive Bushman physical characteristic. Kuara, a visitor from /Gam, who is greeting John Marshall so warmly, is 4 feet, 11 inches in height (149.86 cm). John is 5 feet, 9 inches. Of sixteen men measured at Gautscha, Kaura was the shortest. Gao at 5 feet, 7 inches (170.18 cm) was the tallest. The men of Gautscha averaged 5 feet, 2 inches (157.48 cm). Ledimo, our interpreter, is on the right. The boy in the middle is Tsamgao, ≠Toma's son. The photograph shows a gradation of skin color from Ledimo's dark brown (so-called black), through the Bushmen's lighter yellowish-brown, to John's so-called white. Bushman skin tans. The underarm skin near their armpits, especially when scrubbed, was several shades lighter than the exposed body skin; it was lighter in several instances but less reddish than the back of Lorna Marshall's fully tanned hand.

47. Brues, "Spearman," p. 307.

≠Gisa, wife of Dam, is 4 feet, 11 inches in height, the average height of thirty-one women measured at Gautscha. The minimum height was 4 feet, 8 inches (143.08 cm). One very tall woman was 5 feet, 5 inches (165.10 cm), another was 5 feet, 3 inches (160.02 cm). The rest were near the average. A common physical characteristic of !Kung women, though not invariably present, is an area of black pigmentation on the breast (shown here). The one newborn baby girl we saw (Norna) had jet black nipples at birth. That pigmentation faded away in a few weeks. Many !Kung children have the so-called Mongolian spot at birth, an area of black pigmentation on the buttocks which disappears after a few months. Notice ≠Gisa's fine necklace of ostrich-eggshell beads and the scarification on her cheeks. All !Kung women have scarified lines on their faces, upper legs, and buttocks. One woman scarifies another by pinching up

size of the bow needed. The bow must now merely cause the arrow to pierce the skin of the animal, rather than actually wound it. It is significant, he feels, that both Pygmies and Bushmen, as well as other small peoples of the world, use a poison technology in hunting. Tobias supplements this line of thinking by saying that a Bushman's "very hunting methods have placed a premium upon other qualities than broad shoulders—namely smallness of build, staying power, [and] . . . an acute reliance on veld-craft in the tracking of wounded animals."[48]

Tobias and Willcox agree that large size is not necessarily an advantage to man under all circumstances. "Unless larger size confers some specific advantage it is in itself a handicap in the evolutionary struggle . . . as the dinosaurs discovered," Willcox adds.[49] If the hunter does not depend on brawn behind bludgeon or spear to kill by the force of his blows, small size can be advantageous to him. Lightness and agility are assets to stalking. A small, slender man requires less food and water to sustain him than a large man.

Tobias thus concurs with Coon in dismissing the idea of the Bushman physical type as a direct result of desert conditions. As we have seen, a refinement in hunting technology can account for their stature, and cultural knowledge in the form of veld-craft further explains their successful exploitation of the harsh desert environment. Also, unlike Eskimos, Bushmen lack specialized basal metabolic adaptations to heat and cold. Instead they use cultural means—the fire, the karosses of antelope skin—to manipulate a microclimate about themselves against winter cold.[50] They use various combinations of shade, evaporation, and rest against the heat.

These facts support the belief held by some anthropologists that Bushmen may not have lived in the desert very long. It also underlines a primary point Tobias has made concerning their adaptation to it. In facet after facet of their lives, it is cultural rather than anatomical features that allow them to survive there. In defending the theory of their southern origin, he has relied heavily on this point to explain the apparent rapidity

a fold of skin and cutting a line of tiny vertical cuts along it with a knife. She rubs into the bleeding cuts a mixture of charcoal and fat. The skin forms around the fragments of charcoal and the lines remain dark for a lifetime.

48. A. R. Willcox, "Size and the Hunter," *South African Journal of Science,* May 1971, pp. 306–307. Tobias, "Bushman Hunter-Gatherers," p. 77.
49. Willcox, "Size and the Hunter," pp. 306–307.
50. Tobias, "Physique of a Desert Folk," p. 23.

of their emergence from Rhodesioid stock. Coon had said to him in 1956 that if a Bushman could develop from the large, gerontomorphic Rhodesian Man in a mere 50,000 years, anthropologists would have to revise considerably their ideas about the rate of human evolution.[51] Tobias' reply, worked out between 1956 and 1961, was that evolution occurs

The !Kung protect themselves from cold with fire and with karosses made of antelope hide. The people in the photograph (members of Band 5) have been gathering tsi seeds and are settling for the night near the place where the tsi grows. They have made a fire and are at home in the land, as intimately a part of it as any of its creatures. They cook their tsi seeds in the hot coals and ashes, scape them out with a fire paddle, and crack them between stones. Note the man's kaross. At night men, women, and children wrap themselves in karosses and sleep in them, beside their fires. By day, the men wear only breechclouts, the children perhaps only beads, but women wear their karosses constantly. The men's breechclouts have butterfly-shaped tabs on the back at exactly the right place to sit on.

51. Tobias, "New Evidence," p. 32.

Women wear karosses made of the whole hide of an antelope. Gemsbok hide is preferred. The hide is scraped, tanned, pulled, and rubbed by the men till it is like suede. The girl on the left is bundled against a winter wind. Some of the white hair of the animal's belly has been left on this kaross for decoration.

more rapidly when natural selection and cultural selection are pulling in the same direction.

In the case of the Bushmen he felt that cultural selection played a major role. Long ago and even into present times Bushmen have occupied extremely diverse environments, from the Kalahari Desert to the cold Basuto Highlands. In all these environments their anatomy was essentially the same. Tobias therefore has sought cultural explanations to add to natural ones in accounting for the physical peculiarities of the Bushmen.

Women in clement weather tie their karosses over one shoulder and have their arms free as seen in the photograph of !Ghia. The kaross is tied firmly around the waist with a strong thong and is pulled up so that it bulges over the thong and forms a pouch in which a woman carries all her belongings. The baby does not bounce among the belongings. The baby is tied to the mother's side in a special leather sling which is tied over the mother's shoulder. Under the kaross, the women wear a back apron of leather and a front apron of beads or leather ornamented with beads.

Their steatopygia, for instance, he sees as possibly the result of cultural and natural forces acting together. This question of the fat deposits on the buttocks of Bushmen and Hottentots has long been problematical and remains so. Tobias found after much initial skepticism that steatopygia does indeed diminish during famine and drought. He postulates that it may be, thus, an adaptive trait not associated with desert life as such but with the hunter-gatherer cultural economy. The periodic shortages of food in such an economy may be mitigated by drawing on this reserve. Beyond that there is the cultural explanation, that there has been sexual selection for this trait, as it is much admired in women. By making a cultural virtue of a biological necessity, Tobias feels, the Bushmen have accelerated their own evolution.[52]

Rose E. Frisch of the Harvard Center for Population Studies suggests another dimension to our understanding of steatopygia. She and her associates find that in general in women of child-bearing age, a minimum weight representative of a minimum store of fat is necessary for the onset and maintenance of menstrual cycles.[53] During the adolescent growth spurt the amount of fat stored is almost doubled within a short period of time. By menarche enough has been stored to provide the extra 50,000 to 80,000 calories necessary to carry a pregnancy to term, as well as several months' supply of the 1000 calories per day needed for lactation. In times of famine, energy stored as female fat would thus have selective advantage.[54] Frisch postulates, further, that where food supply is precarious and the weather is hot as well, it may be of advantage in cooling the body to localize the fat store in the buttocks and thighs rather than to distribute it over the body surface.[55] The problem with this idea, of course, is what to make of the apparent steatopygia (shown in rock paintings) of past Bushmen who inhabited nondesert environments. Perhaps, as Tobias suggested, steatopygia can best be seen as a special adaptation to the periodic shortages of the hunting-gathering way of life.

For the pedomorphic features of the Bushmen, however, no explanation has been advanced. These features include some of their most strik-

52. Tobias, "New Evidence," p. 33.

53. Rose E. Frisch, "Critical Weights, a Critical Body Composition, Menarche and the Maintenance of Menstrual Cycles," in E. Watts, F. Johnston, and S. Laskar, Biosocial Interrelations in Population Adaptation (The Hague, Mouton, in press).

54. Rose E. Frisch, Roger Revelle, and Sole Cook, "Components of Weight at Menarche and the Initiation of the Adolescent Growth Spurt in Girls: Estimated Total Water, Lean Body Weight and Fat," Human Biology, 45 (Sept. 1973), 469–483.

55. Rose E. Frisch, personal communication, Dec. 6, 1973.

Steatopygia is exemplified by this woman of /Gwia. We were unable to observe to what extent steatopygia existed among the women in the Nyae Nyae area because the women there flatly refused to take off their karosses from around their backs. We did not want to offend the women and did not press our request. In /Gwia, in 1961, nine women performed the Eland Dance of the

ing characteristics: low, flattened skull; poor development of sinuses; tiny mastoid processes; bulging or vertical forehead; small, flat face; wide distance between the eyes; flat nasal bridge; light skin pigment; hairlessness; and semierect penis. These traits cannot be attributed to desert conditions, because Bushman-like remains have been found in wet areas of Africa as well. There are also other hunter-gatherers, for instance the Australian aborigines, who show no infantilism. Negroes in the same setting as Bushmen do not show it either.[56] Nor can dwarfing be regarded as an adaptation to the desert, as it too was found among Bushmen when they were living elsewhere. Tobias provisionally suggests that short stature may be not only an advantage in hunting but a desired trait in the community as well.[57] Careful studies of the physical attributes the modern Bushmen find most desirable might help to support or negate theories like these. Of course genetic characteristics can only be selected for if the people·who possess them produce more offspring than others in the same population. It has yet to be demonstrated that steatopygia confers reproductive advantage by sexual selection.

Serological investigation has yielded no final answers as yet to the problem of Bushman relationships with other groups such as Hottentots and Bantu. One broad conclusion that has emerged, however, is that red-cell enzyme allele frequency constellations do not support in any

---

Menarchal Rite. For that occasion, women customarily take off their karosses, and we were able to observe that steatopygia does occur among !Kung women. Note the shape of the buttocks which protrude at a sharp angle from the back and are almost flat on top. Compared to two Hottentot women whom we saw, who had buttocks half again as large as those of the /Gwia woman, the /Gwia steatopygia can be considered moderate. Only one other of the nine /Gwia women had buttocks as large as these in the photograph. The others were decidedly plump but not so fully developed. This observation fits with the statement that occurs in the literature on Bushmen that northern Bushman women are not as steatopygous as Hottentot women. Note the scarification of the thighs and buttocks. All !Kung women are scarified in this way. The women of Nyae Nyae as well as those of /Gwia said the scarification is made for beauty alone, that it has no other significance. One wonders, however, if the significance has only been lost to memory. The fact that the girls are scarified at about the age of twelve suggests that the scarification may once have been part of a fertility rite practiced in the past.

56. Tobias, "Physique of a Desert Folk," pp. 19–20.
57. Tobias, "New Evidence," p. 34.

way the notion that Bushmen and Hottentots descended from Asian populations.[58] Another conclusion is that both the Hottentots, long erroneously regarded as a separate race of Hamitic origin or connections, and the Bushmen can with reason be regarded as Negroid peoples of the same stock as the Bantu.[59] Because they must have obtained cattle and metallurgy from the northeast, some anthropologists have postulated that they got these from the Caucasoid Hamites whom they absorbed racially.[60] But the blood-group studies of Ronald Singer and his associ-

The ubiquitous little ≠Gao (right), son of /Qui and //Kushay of Band 1, exhibits the lordosis characteristic of Bushmen, with the accentuated curve in the lower back and the resultant protruding abdomen. His semi-erect penis is a characteristic of the race. ≠Gao is wearing his father's cocoon dance rattles wound around his legs. These three children standing on an anthill are at a stage in which they are both eating solid food and still nursing.

58. M. C. Botha, et al., "The HL-A System in the Bushman (San) and Hottentot (Khoikoi) Population of South West Africa," release of the Provincial Blood Grouping Lab, Cape Town, South African Institute of Medical Research (Copenhagen, Munksgaard, forthcoming), p. 10.

59. Staff reporter, "Hottentots Are of Negro Stock," *The Cape Argus*, Thursday, Aug. 24, 1961 (based on the work of Ronald Singer).

60. Coon, *Living Races of Man*, p. 114.

/Qui, a young boy, son of /Gao Music, has typical Bushman characteristics: black hair, the curliest hair on earth, called "peppercorn" because it spirals into little black lumps; wide-apart, dark brown eyes; eyefolds; wide nose with flat nasal bridge; the nostril openings forward in the nose; short rounded ears with little or no lobe, the helix wide and well turned in; everted lips; high cheekbones in a heart-shaped nonprognathous face. /Qui, as the French would say, has "beaucoup de race."

!U, wife of ≠Toma, also has features typical of her race.

ates have established that the Hottentots had no Hamitic physical characteristics at all.[61] Rather, both Hottentots and Bushmen tend to be associated, on the basis of blood groups, with the Bantu peoples. Tobias suggests that long ago Bushmen and Negroes might have had a common

61. *The Cape Argus*, Aug. 24, 1961.

ancestor. It is difficult to go further with this suggestion, he explains: we have virtually no fossil remains of the precursors of the Negroes, though much fossil evidence is available for the ancestors of the Bushmen.[62]

Then, too, a recent blood-group study done by the South African Institute of Medical Research and H. C. Harpending of Harvard University presents evidence for considerable biological *distance* between Khoisan and Bantu. A cluster analysis of blood traits showed that Bushmen and Hottentots do constitute a group with some distinctness from other populations. Among the genetic markers used in this differentiation were the gammaglobulin allele $Gm^{1, 13}$, the sickle hemoglobin gene, and G6PD electrophoretic polymorphisms.[63] Other differences between Congoid and Capoid blood groups are found in the frequencies of O and of cDe, the "African" Rh gene, as well as of haptoglobin Hp^1.[64]

To complicate the picture further, in a recent study of the HL-A blood system in South West Africa, a Khoisan (common to Bushmen and Hottentots) feature has *not* emerged. M. C. Botha, who made this study, writes that "the Nama [Hottentots] are clearly distinguished from the !Kung and Heikum [Bushmen] as well as Negro samples, serologically if indeed not genetically. Hottentots, thus, as Coon writes, are like Bushmen in some ways and like Negroes in others, as well as having peculiarities of their own.[65] Few definite conclusions on the relationships of the three groups can be drawn from these diverse genetic clues as yet, but further studies are under way.

E. O. J. Westphal has approached the more recent relationships of the Bushmen with other peoples of southern Africa through linguistics and oral tradition. He has traced the migrations and the mixings of these groups in his informative article, "The Linguistic Prehistory of Southern Africa." The Capoid group has long been associated with certain non-Bantu or "Khoisan" languages. Westphal's intent has been to provide "a cartographical statement of the earliest distribution of the non-Bantu languages that technical linguistic information will permit."[66] Of course, the dates and nature of any Early Stone Age languages are certainly open to wide interpretation, so that their use is limited for establishing

62. Tobias, "Physique of a Desert Folk," p. 19.
63. T. Jenkins, H. C. Harpending, H. Gordon, M. M. Keraan, and S. Johnston, "Red-Cell-Enzyme Polymorphisms in the Khoisan Peoples of Southern Africa," *American Journal of Human Genetics*, vol. 23, 1971; ibid., pp. 523–524.
64. Coon, *Living Races of Man*, p. 287.
65. Botha et al., "The HL-A System"; Coon, *Living Races of Man*, p. 114.
66. P. 239.

Old N/aoka, the sister of Old /Goishay who was the mother of /Ti!kay's wives, has the deeply wrinkled skin characteristic of aged Bushmen. She was the only childless woman, and she was the one and only blind person that we met in the Nyae Nyae area. Her sister led her around with a stick (each holding one end). Note how her peppercorn hair twirls into separate spirals that show the scalp between. She, too, has the characteristic nonprognathous profile.

Gentle Old Demi is in his seventies, but he has energy and vigor and a lively interest in life. His hair and beard are gray. He is more heavily bearded than many !Kung men, who typically have scant face and body hair.

or confirming population relationships. Nevertheless, Westphal has found that the early (and perhaps the late) Stone Age in southern Africa was characterized by a great number of different so-called Bush languages. The heterogeneity of these languages, in contrast to the relative homogeneity of Bantu and Hottentot languages, suggests that the subcontinent was sparsely inhabited by hunter-gatherer groups who had little contact with each other across cultural borders.[67]

Westphal's article goes on to show that Bantu historical lore points to an area within which the Hottentot and Bush languages could have developed in isolation. He located this area unreservedly within southern Africa, however, saying that the click languages of Tanzania cannot as yet be associated with the southern African click languages by accepted linguistic techniques. His point of view, thus, extends no promise of support for Coon's theory of northern origins. On the other hand, he does not explicitly deny the possibility.

Westphal summarizes the findings of his study on early migrations this way:

> Folklore and language seem to indicate a relatively early presence of an organized Bantu people along the eastern escarpment [of *southern* Africa]. At a later stage, a more primitive and perhaps more agricultural people moved eastwards along the Zambezi and down the east coast. Associated with the latter or perhaps preceding them were the Northern Bushmen mentioned above. The earliest Bantu made contact with the Hottentots who were living either in the western half of Southern Rhodesia or in the eastern highveld areas of the Transvaal. It is suggested that Hottentot itself is the product of an unknown (and clickless) language and a Bush language of Southern Rhodesia.[68]

That Bushmen were once spread widely over this subcontinent is supported by fossil evidence and by Tobias' estimate that as many as 55,000 of them survive even today in widely scattered areas.[69] They appear to have been driven from the more fertile areas into marginal ones by Bantu invasions from the north along the east coast and by Europeans moving east and north from the Cape. Coon has written that the key to African cultural history is "resistance in depth to penetration or, more simply, lag. As L. Frobenius said long ago, in Africa peoples and cultures

67. Ibid., p. 256.
68. Ibid., p. 264.
69. Phillip V. Tobias, "On the Survival of the Bushmen," *Africa* 26 (1956), 174–186.

do not replace one another, they simply move aside."[70] But Coon can see, of course, only the surviving populations of today. Perhaps the best way to survive often *is* to move aside.

In any case, Bush peoples are to be found today in the southern Kalahari sandveld, the northeastern South West Africa sandveld, a variety of bush and forest areas in Angola, and in the Eastern Transvaal around the Lake Chrissie pans. Within recent history they lived in the Karroo and the Highveld (grasslands of the Orange Free State, southern Transvaal, and parts of Natal and the Cape), and in the mountains of Basutoland and Natal.[71]

Increasingly, even these marginal areas are subject to encroachment by pastoralism and other means of livelihood. There are few places left into which people can "move aside." Thus most of the Bushmen live today in one of several economic relationships with Bantu or Europeans. A few thousand continue to live by hunting and gathering, the mode of organization for which their physical type has been adapting itself for, at the very least, 50,000 years.

THE !KUNG HISTORICAL PERSPECTIVE

The region of Nyae Nyae was inhabited in the distant past by people who made stone artifacts. Robert Dyson, when he was with our expedition in 1951, collected many microlithic artifacts of the Late Stone Age from the surface of the ground in several locations in the vicinities of Gautscha Pan and Tsho/ana in the Nyae Nyae area.

In Botswana there is abundant evidence of such early habitation where !Kung live. John Yellen, a member of the Harvard Group, spent three years in the Dobe area collecting Middle and Late Stone Age artifacts from numerous surface and excavated sites. I quote, with his permission, from his paper, "Ethnoarchaeology: Bushman Settlement Patterns":

> Surface scatters of the Late Stone Age material abound in the Dobe region, and very often they mark the presence of stratified sites. I surveyed most of this area with Bushman assistance and was able to plot areal distributions. The places with the largest and most dense surface scatters are just those where today Bushmen establish

70. Coon, *Living Races of Man*, p. 91.
71. Westphal, "Linguistic Prehistory," pp. 238–239.

their winter dry season camps. At best, sparse scatters were present near the small pans which hold water only during the rains.

Analysis of faunal remains indicates that Late Stone Age peoples hunted basically the same range of game as their present-day counterparts, including such small and difficult-to-catch animals as springhare. These prehistoric peoples must have utilized what, on geological evidence, was a drier climate, in much the same way as their modern-day counterparts.

We can no longer support the traditionally held view that the northern fringe of the Kalahari is a refuge area into which Bushmen fled or were driven in relatively recent times. Of course, before the appearance of both the Bantu and the Europeans, the well-watered areas in South Africa and in southern Zambia most likely did support larger Bushman populations. However, the Dobe Late Stone Age sites, which in their lower levels contain neither pottery nor metal, refute this refuge idea. Although there is no direct proof that ancestors of the present-day Bushmen in this area left the abundant Late Stone Age remains, it seems most likely that this was the case. In comparing modern and prehistoric populations however, it is not necessary to assume a genetic link.[72]

Pressure of work has kept Dyson from analyzing the material of the surface site he found at Gautscha and Tsho/ana. Larry Lepionka kindly agreed to make the analysis, and he gave me the following information by personal communication:

The materials consist of eleven separate lithic collections. Excluding one set of Levalloisian-produced flakes of Middle Stone Age vintage (obtained near Encocua, southern Angola) for spatial reasons, the remainder probably all pertain to the Late Stone Age. There is interassemblage variation in that four of the collections contain a plurality of blade implements while three are virtually or entirely lacking in this form. Accompanying the blades are blade-like flakes and crescentoid flakes, the three forms providing a majority of the total implement number in each of the first four collections and in a fifth as well. These five can be considered as a microlithic class in opposition to the latter three, wherein the majority of tool forms are varieties of small side and end scrapers on discoid flakes or split pebbles. Such forms are not eschewed in the "microlithic" assemblages; rather, there is implement type overlap (though frequencies are far different) with the microlithic collections having the

72. John E. Yellen, "Ethnoarchaeology: Bushman Settlement Patterns," paper presented at the Bushman Symposium, American Anthropology Association Meeting, New York City, November 1971, p. 1.

wider range of variation. The remaining two groups are intermediate in their constituents but closer in affinity to the microlithic class.

Consideration of type distributions and nonlithic (ceramics, European artifacts) associations makes it possible to postulate a historical development with the addition of blade technique to the repertoire of an earlier tradition. However, this is suggested only as the most logical explanation of the observed differences; the evidence for it is obscured by problems of adequate sample preservation, the presence of "transitional" elements in several collections, and possible functional differentiation. Regardless of the determinants of intercollection variation there is no justification for exclusion of any of these assemblages from the Late Stone Age. Six (including one nonmicrolithic) contain crescentoid flakes, the type marker of the "Wilton Industry," and two other collections (the "intermediate" ones) contain sufficiently similar forms to make their association with the majority beyond doubt. Of the remaining two, one consists of only nine implements and so may be inadequately represented.

These collections are of value in that they indicate another Late Stone Age locale in the Kalahari; chronologically they are less clear. Three groups contain potsherds, limiting them to the Iron Age, a span of two thousand years at the most; one of these also includes European glass and is therefore much more delimited in time. Others (though none of the nonmicrolithic groups) were found in the general vicinity of ceramics or European artifacts but not in direct association. As most collections are not datable by such methods there is only negative evidence for the assumption of any great antiquity. While such age is unlikely, the presence of fairly varied stone assemblages could be considered as evidence of a minimal amount of Bantu or European influence, whence the use of iron might have been derived, in this region. There is also one tool form that can be interpreted functionally as a projectile point; these are relatively large pieces made on discoidal flakes and occur in five collections (excluding the three most representative microlithic groups, two of which are associated with ceramics). If the interpretation is valid these forms can be considered as evidence for a shift in hunting technology between the time of their production and the observed practices of the Bushmen in modern times. These two factors and the typological differences would suggest that some time depth is represented by these collections, though it is impossible to estimate how great it may be.

Our informants among the Nyae Nyae !Kung had apparently not noticed the little stone artifacts that Dyson found in their area, and when their attention was called to them, they said they had never known peo-

ple to make stone blades or arrow points and had never been told anything about them by the old people. Their grandfathers, they said, had
metal knives and arrow points, as they do now. Our informants showed
little or no interest in the stone artifacts and seemed not to wonder who
those people might have been who lived in the land before them, or
whether they were their own ancestors or others.

In a recent personal communication, Yellen corroborates that no
!Kung to whom he spoke in Botswana had any knowledge about Late
Stone Age tools of the kind collected in South West Africa by Dyson.
Yellen excavated over 5,000 of these microliths in the Dobe area and
showed them to the people. They were not recognized as tools made by
human beings until Yellen explained them as such. However, he feels
that direct ancestors of the present-day !Kung were, in fact, most probably the makers of these tools. This is the most reasonable and parsimoni-
ous explanation, he says, since Late Stone Age tools in southern Africa
are definitely associated with Khoisan groups and were still being made
in South Africa in historic times.

Ground stone tools, on the other hand, are known to living !Kung.
Yellen interviewed an old man at Dobe who had lived at /Gam, in South
West Africa, as a young man. The old people there, he said, hacked stone
out of rock faces and shaped it into axes by grinding. When the old
people died, and as iron became more readily available, the art died out.
Iron was known and available to a limited extent when the old man (now
perhaps seventy-four years old) was a young boy.

Lack of wonder, such as our informants showed when we spoke to
them about the stone artifacts, is characteristic of the !Kung. They know
extremely little about the world outside their own region and their
own time. Except for the past depicted in their ancient tales, other times
and other people are blanks to them. Instead of being stimulated by
curiosity, the !Kung imagination, faced with the unknown and having
nothing concrete to work on, becomes inactive and indifferent. It is the
here and now that engages the !Kung.

No proof came to light that the makers of the microlithic artifacts
at Gautscha and Tsho/ana were ancestors of the present !Kung inhabitants, but, on the other hand, no proof to the contrary appeared, and
nothing suggested that the !Kung had come recently into the area. The
oldest persons we met had never heard their forebears tell of living elsewhere, and they have no legend of migration, no stories of having been
driven by enemies—Bushmen, Hottentots, blacks, or whites—from lands

they previously inhabited. They think their people lived in the Nyae Nyae region since time began. That the !Kung do not remember a golden age in which they did not inhabit the desert is corroborated by the collections of their mythology made by members of the Harvard Group and other researchers. The most comprehensive collection of !Kung oral literature, made in 1970–1972 by Megan Biesele of the Harvard Group, contains no hint of such a time, though she searched for stories of a past in a different land.

Knowing these nonaggressive people now, one cannot imagine that when they did come into the area they took it by force from former inhabitants. Among the !Kung, no tales are told of battles; no praise of warrior heroes is sung. The !Kung are strongly set against fighting and accord it no honor. To have to fight is to have failed to find a solution by wiser means. As /Ti!kay of Band 9 remarked, "Fighting is dangerous—someone might get killed."

The !Kung look to a mythical past which they do not define in time except to say it was long ago. They consider that past to be actual, not mythical. The old old Bushmen who lived in those days were different from themselves. They could speak with the great God, the Creator of all things. The Creator instructed the old old people in the ways of life, gave them the knowledge of arrow poison, taught them their skills and crafts and the customs that they should follow. The old old people passed on this knowledge to the generation that came after them, and so it has been passed on from generation to generation till today. The !Kung do not worship their ancestors or perform any rites of reverence for them, but they respect them, Ju n!a, old person, is a term of respect. The old are the conveyors of knowledge and wisdom. The young know nothing, they have no sense, the !Kung say, till they are taught by the old. Very often adults, even elderly ones, when they do not know an answer to a question, will take refuge in a claim of youth. "We are but young," they say, "we do not know. The old old people knew these things."

Although they look respectfully to the past, they are not history-minded. They make no effort to hold actual past events systematically in mind or teach them to their children—neither events that concern the living people nor those concerning their forebears. They remember what they happen to remember their father and grandfathers telling them.

They have no calendar, and they do not count years. They can only vaguely place events in time by saying that they were children or young men or old men when the event occurred. Often they point to someone and say, "I was the age of that person." They reckon the recent past by the seasons; they may remember two or three dry or rainy seasons back and can place the birth of a child, for instance, within that range, but after that they lose track. Placing events in measured time is not significant to them.

We do not know how long the !Kung have lived in the Nyae Nyae region, but we can place the advent of Bantu in recent times. Murdock tells us: "The last wave of Bantu expansion, occurring within the historical period, carried the Tswana branch of the Sotho peoples westward into the country now known as Bechuanaland, where they engulfed the indigenous Bushmen. This began around 1720 and continued until after the beginning of European contact in 1801."[73]

The Tawana tribe of the Tswana people had moved west as far as Tsau at some date but, Lee tells us, it was not till the 1880's and 1890's that they began to bring their herds for summer grazing to the western border country which the !Kung inhabit, and not till 1925 that the Bantu began to live in that part of the country the year around.[74]

Contact and trade with the Tawana brought the use of metal to the !Kung. Our elderly informants told us their grandfathers obtained knives and scrap metal with which to make arrow points and assagai blades. Lee's informants, however, made the point that their grandfathers did not have metal till they were beyond their youth, and he provisionally dates the beginning of its use by the !Kung to the 1880–1890 period.[75]

No white people settled in the Nyae Nyae area, but over the years hunters, prospectors, soldiers, police, and possibly the men who surveyed the border between South West Africa and Botswana passed through. Old people among the !Kung told of having seen various parties of white people in ox wagons, on horses, or on camels. The memories go back to the last quarter of the nineteenth century. However, many of the !Kung we knew had not been present when any of the various parties passed through and had not seen any white people before us. The meetings of the !Kung and the white people had been haphazard and fleeting, in any case; none of the parties had remained any length of time in the region.

The !Kung call white people !hũ. They also use color adjectives as we do. They call us red people, ju-s-a-!gaa, and they call the Bantu black people, ju-s-a-djo.

73. George Peter Murdock, *Africa: Its Peoples and Their Culture History* (New York, McGraw-Hill, 1959), p. 386.
74. Lee, *Subsistence Ecology*, pp. 57, 64.
75. Ibid., p. 54.

Testifying to the presence of the white people are names and dates carved on three baobab trees—two trees at Gautscha and one at Gura. About forty names and initials are legible or fairly legible; a few more are illegible. The dates range from 1878 (or 1876) to 1945, and, in addition, there is the date we carved in 1951.

The legible names and initials are listed below. Our photographers took pictures of the inscriptions but did not always keep a clear record of which tree was being photographed. My memory and a few notes lead me to think that the names or initials marked with a single asterisk (*) are on the largest Gautscha tree, those marked ** are on the second largest Gautscha tree, those marked *** are on the Gura tree. I am uncertain of the location of the unmarked names. The two Gautscha trees are about a hundred yards apart. A third, smaller, baobab at Gautscha, standing between the two large trees, had no inscription, insofar as we know.

Name	Date
* N.L.	1878 [or 1876? The upper part of the last figure is not clear; our consensus is that it is 8.]
* REES [the S is reversed]	1887 [In same photo, apparently made at the same time and in the same style of lettering, are illegible inscriptions of initials including PEPT [?]; also the legible intials F.J.S. and L.S.]
[?] Rush	10.13.1903
* PÜSCHEL	1905
* W. KUSTER	11.V.05
F. Crim	11.[?].05
** G. Klein	[?] v.OV
** Kipping	11.V.OV
** Wolf	1905
** WARDEL	1905
** C. Thorp	1905
Ehrt[?]Rüipmer	1905
*** [F?] R. P. Frenzel	11.5.05
*** R. Goldmann	11.5.05
Shün	11.5.05
* KAHLE	1911
* W. MATTENKLODT [the D is reversed]	17
* [I?] Berger	8.4.33
* E. v.d. BERG	10.9.33
* WERNER	[?] V.35

Name	Date
* W. Zillmann	10.5.35
* G. BARRY	1937
* C. C. Bone	V.VIII.37
* J. Lewis	1945
[The s is reversed]	
* The inscription of our expedition is simply the date	1951

Names with No Clearly Associated Dates

P. BECK
[?] EYSER [Keyser?]
McDonald
Stöhr
Vogt
Jerry
Clersmann
L. Thomas

Initials without a Date

* D.P.B.
* [J?] W.
* F.K.
* P.B.
* M.P.

* G.W.
** h.g.t
** P.O.Z.
F [or T?] V.D.
W.P.

Old /Ti!kay of Band 14 gave us the earliest account of white people passing through the area. His father had told of first seeing white people at /Gam. Old /Ti!kay, an old man himself in 1952, was not yet born at the time. His father told him that the white people were traveling in ox wagons. There were men and women in the party. Some of the men walked ahead of the oxen. They came from the southwest and were on their way to the Okavango River. They were hunting elephants, collecting their "teeth," as /Ti!kay put it. They were also killing ostriches for their feathers and were collecting ostrich eggs.

My surmise is that this party went on from /Gam through Gautscha, that N.L. was one of its members, and that he carved his initials and the date 1878 (or 1876) on the biggest baobab tree.

It seems obvious that the party was engaged in the trade that J. H. Esterhuyse described in his history of South West Africa. Esterhuyse

The largest of the three Gautscha baobab trees has W. Mattenklodt's name, among others, carved in its bark. Pegs have been driven into the immense tree so that men can climb it to scan the countryside for game and boys can climb it for the fun of climbing.

tells us that by the decade of the 1870's, there were 137 Europeans in South West Africa, and "apart from the Rhenish Missionaries, they were all directly or indirectly connected with trade." In addition to guano from the islands and cattle obtained from Herero, Nama Hottentots, and Basters, the principal items of trade and export were ivory and ostrich feathers. Hunters traveled as far as Lake Ngami depleting the elephant and ostrich population. Twenty thousand pounds of ivory were exported annually. Esterhuyse says ostrich feathers were worth £45 per pound.[76]

Two other early encounters with white people were at /Gam and Kai Kai. Hendrik Van Zyl, whom Silberbauer in his survey aptly calls "the redoubtable Van Zyl," well-known in Botswana annals as the first white settler of Ghanzi (in 1874), was in /Gam on a hunting trip in 1879.[77] His party may well have been one that the !Kung describe. Martinus Drotsky, a famous Kalahari figure in his own right in the twentieth century, showed us the ruins of a stone structure at /Gam that he thought was Van Zyl's shelter.

Another party we think was that of Siegfried Passarge. He was in the Kalahari in 1897.[78] Old /Qui of Band 7 had seen white men at Kai Kai when he was a boy of ten or twelve; no Herero or Tawana were as yet living at Kai Kai. The white men had three ox wagons for their equipment and supplies, and they rode horses. They were always writing as we do, Old /Qui told us (n//au, "making marks"—the word used for drawing designs on ostrich eggshells or on the bark of trees). However, said /Qui, they did not ask questions of the Bushmen as we do; they just made marks by themselves. This must have been Professor Passarge. Who else would be so assiduously taking notes in Kai Kai in the late 1890's?

The 1905 inscriptions on the baobab trees were undoubtedly made by soldiers of the German-Herero War bivouacking under the baobabs. That war commenced in 1904 and continued into 1905. Herero fled from South West Africa into Botswana for refuge from extermination by the Germans. Soldiers pursued them to the border or where they thought the border was. Gray-haired Old Demi of Band 6, an unwilling witness to one of the battles, was caught in a crossfire. He demonstrated to us how he flattened himself behind a log. One German soldier was killed;

76. J. H. Esterhuyse, *South West Africa, 1880–1894* (Cape Town, C. Struik, 1968), p. 13.

77. George Silberbauer, *Bushman Survey*, Report to the Government of Bechuanaland (Gaberones, Bechuanaland Government, 1965), p. 114.

78. Passarge, *Die Buschmänner.*

the Herero fled away. No one noticed Demi lying perfectly still behind his log, his brown skin blending with the color of the sand and wood. This episode gave us a rough measure of the age of one old Bushman at least. Old Demi pointed to a young man, //Ao Wildebeest, saying he was as old as that young man at the time. //Ao already had three children. This places Old Demi probably in his twenties in 1905 and in his early seventies in 1951.

Wilhelm Mattenklodt, whose name is clearly inscribed on the biggest Gautscha baobab, was a German who escaped being put into a British prison camp in South West Africa in 1917 by fleeing into the veld. He was the author of *A Fugitive in South West Africa*.[79] His daughter is the widow of an esteemed member of our expeditions, our mechanic, the late Heinrich Neumann.

The date of the surveying of the border between Botswana and South West Africa was 1933; Berger and van der Berg may have been members of the surveying parties.

On two occasions, the !Kung told us, police from South West Africa mounted on camels had passed through the Nyae Nyae area. By gesture, the !Kung described the camels and the motion of their riders, leaving no doubt whatsoever as to what animals the men rode. Gao Beard, middle-aged in 1952, saw them marking trees at Gautscha when he was young. Many others saw them at one place or another. We think the dates of the camel riders were the 1935 and 1937 dates. The purpose of one of these police expeditions was to expel Herero who had brought cattle into the area from Botswana and were making a cattle post; the purpose of the other was to bring some fugitive to justice.

Another account from an old man at /Gam told of white men passing through who were looking for little stones. Why they should be looking for little stones, he could not imagine. We knew, however, for we had heard the rumor in South West Africa that Bushman girls had been seen in the Kalahari wearing diamonds hanging from their ears. There was another rumor about diamonds in circulation in South West Africa. People who simply could not believe that anyone would go into the Kalahari for the purpose of studying the filthy, thieving, murdering, wild Bushmen, as they considered them to be, decided that our real motive was to prospect for diamonds, and Laurence was asked surreptitiously several times if he had had any luck.

79. Wilhelm Mattenklodt, *A Fugitive in South West Africa*, ed. and trans. Oakley Williams (London, Thornton Butterworth, 1920).

In 1956 the contact of the Nyae Nyae !Kung with the outside world began to increase. Our expedition trucks, going out to Windhoek or Grootfontein for food and other supplies, had laid clearly visible tracks along the Eiseb Omuramba, and toward the north to the track laid down by the trucks of the Witwatersrand Native Labor Association. Late in 1955 and again in early 1956, white farmers came in trucks into the area, following our tracks, seeking labor for their farms, although it was illegal according to South West Africa governmental regulation to recruit Bushmen in that manner. The farmers persuaded several !Kung families to go with them and work for them. All the families we knew who went on that venture eventually returned to Nyae Nyae. We saw several in 1959. I mention some details of their story and their misadventures later. !Ungka said to me that Bushmen do not like to work.

It was also in 1956 that several families of Herero from Botswana settled in the Gautscha area, as they had on a previous occasion years ago when the camel corps was sent to expel them. The rains had been very good that year—all the big and small waterholes were well filled, and water stood in the pans for many weeks. The Herero, who overgraze their land till they denude it, were strongly tempted by the grasses in the Gautscha area, and since there was enough water for the cattle, they defied the border regulations and brought their herds across. They remained about a year.

Laurence Marshall made a brief visit to Gautscha at that time, although we did not have an expedition there. He found the !Kung greatly distressed, claiming that the Herero ill-treated them. And so they did when they wished to coerce the !Kung. Laurence reported the situation to the authorities, who, in 1957, sent a police corps, this time in motor vehicles, to persuade the Herero to return to Botswana.

How significantly the Herero presence affected the !Kung customs we cannot say; no deep study has been made. Two borrowings, however, were visible. The !Kung boys adopted drums (which we had not seen being used by Nyae Nyae !Kung before that time) and were playing them well and enjoying them when we visited in 1961. As the second borrowing, some of the !Kung, but by no means all, modified the shape of the shelters they build in the rainy season, making them look something like Herero huts, bigger and more rounded than the traditional crescent-shaped !Kung shelters.

In 1960, the government post was established at Tsumkwe to protect the !Kung from exploitation, now that a road was opened. At the post the !Kung learn Afrikaans and many other things that will help them to take their place in the larger world that surrounds them. Only government-appointed officials are permitted in the area, and studies and reports on the !Kung's transition have not been made public, to my knowledge.

I personally wish the !Kung could have remained as they were, remote, self-sustaining, independent, and dignified; but that is wishful thinking. Our modern society does not allow people to remain remote. Furthermore, many of the !Kung themselves want change; they want to have land and cattle like the Bantu.[80]

80. Megan Biesele has told me that many of the !Kung she knew in Botswana have expressed to her their wish to have cattle. In the fall of 1972, John Marshall was in Botswana. ≠Toma and his family and several others of the Nyae Nyae !Kung traveled across the border to see him. They too expressed the wish to have cattle.

2 *Environment and Settlement*

THE KALAHARI

The Kalahari Basin, a basin of sand which has been distributed by wind, has a mean high altitude of 3,000 feet, and it forms a part of the great plateau of southern Africa. It extends from the Orange River in South Africa through Botswana and eastern South West Africa into central Angola to the divide where the headwaters of the Zambezi, Cuando, and Okavango rivers rise. It takes up almost a third of the subcontinent. According to Wellington, from whom this information comes, it is probably the largest continuous sand surface in the world.[1] The Kalahari is a semidesert, not a true desert like the Namib. The rainfall is considerably higher in the northern portion than the southern portion, in which the Nyae Nyae region lies. Wellington has given figures of 6 to 10 inches as an average for the southern portion.[2] Richard Lee reports his measurement of the rainfall at Dobe in 1964 to be 6.9 inches, but tells us that higher averages are reported for Maun (18.6) and Ghanzi (18.5).[3] The rainfall is sufficient to sustain everywhere a covering of drought-adapted vegetation which supplies the Bushmen who inhabit the Kalahari the wherewithal to live. Conditions of great aridity prevail, however, and cause the most severe hardships that the Bushmen endure.

The desert is generous in its vegetation. It supplies the numerous species of edible plants that constitute the major part of !Kung diet. It supplies as well several species of succulent plants that add to the

1. John H. Wellington, *Southern Africa: A Geographical Study* (Cambridge, At the University Press, 1955) I, 52.
2. Ibid., p. 61.
3. Richard Lee, *Subsistence Ecology of !Kung Bushmen* (Ann Arbor, Mich., University Microfilms, 1968), pp. 92–93.

people's water intake. It supports the animals that the !Kung hunt. It supplies grass, wood, and reeds for shelters, firewood, and implements. The great dearth is surface water.

Robert Story says of the Kalahari (in a statement he gave me by personal communication which I published in my chapter on the !Kung in *Peoples of Africa*):[4]

> A lack of permanent water is probably the most trying of the difficulties which beset the Bushmen of the present day in the country which has ensured their survival, for while they have been dispossessed of their country and exterminated in the less arid parts, in the "Great Thirst Land of the Kalahari" they have been comparatively safe from their European and Bantu enemies. The austerity and hardships of the Kalahari are offset to some extent by its deep level mantle of sand, which prevents run-off of the rainwater and makes it readily available for plant growth. . . . This means not only that the sandy soil can support more luxuriant plants in greater variety, but also that storage organs are common among them, for drainage in sand is so rapid and thorough that shallow-rooted plants at least are in a stronger position if they are able to collect and store the water before it sinks into the deeper layers.
>
> Although some of the storage organs are poisonous, the Bushmen still have numerous edible bulbs, tubers and roots at their disposal. Thanks again to the sand, they can harvest these quickly and easily with wooden digging sticks which would be inadequate in a heavy or stony soil. Other storage organs which they do not eat because of bitterness or high tannin or fibre content are nevertheless important indirectly through being eaten by the various antelopes that are the Bushmen's meat supply.
>
> Hunting is easier as well, for as there could be few better tracking surfaces than the Kalahari sand and, as a wounded animal can thus be followed with very little risk of loss, hard-hitting weapons and careful aim are not necessary. Instead, the Bushmen use small poisoned arrows which have the advantage of being effective on any part of the body and of bringing death as certainly to big game as to small.

The rains of the Kalahari must not be thought of as a gentle fall over the whole country. The rains are of the summer thunderstorm type. The so-called big rains occur mainly in the months of January, February, and March. Little rains, which are only spatterings, or a few odd squalls, may begin in late September or October. They do little to refresh the land.

4. James L. Gibbs, Jr., ed. *Peoples of Africa* (New York, Holt, Rinehart and Winston, 1965), p. 246. The passage is republished with the permission of Story and the publisher.

The remainder of the year is rainless. The rains are spotty and unpredictable, watering the areas where the storm happens to occur, leaving others dry. The vegetation is indeed drought-adapted, surviving long periods without rain if the clouds hold it back. Local conditions of drought occur frequently, and there are many years of overall drought when the total rainfall is below the average. Lee, in his paper "!Kung Spatial Organization: An Ecological and Historical Perspective," gives a chart of the rainfall measured at Maun from 1922 to 1968. Lee says that the figures show the probability of drought to be two years in five, and of severe drought, when the rain is less than 70 percent of average, one year in four.[5]

In the southern Kalahari, no streams flow. The omirimbi[6]—shallow, ancient water courses hollowed out below the general surface of the lands—are dry. Bushmen depend on waterholes in which underground water wells up to the surface in outcroppings of the underlying rock. Waterholes are few and far between. Some are permanent; others are semipermanent, failing only in years of severe drought; still others are temporary, filling during the rains but drying before the end of the dry season. There are vast stretches of the desert which cannot be inhabited because there are no waterholes. The Nyae Nyae area is blessed with sixteen. The only other surface waters are the rain waters that collect in pans and pools and in the hollows of trees. They stand for a few weeks after the rains have finished, then seep away or evaporate, and the !Kung must depend again on the waterholes.

In appearance, the Nyae Nyae area is typical of most of the desert. The land is flat and monotonous. Outcroppings of rock form clusters of low hills in Botswana, the Mabela-a-pudi, Tsodilo, the Aha, and the Kwebe, but the Nyae Nyae area has no hills to lift the eye, nothing higher than the baobab trees and the extraordinary anthills the termites make, which may be twice as high as a Bushman. As one stands looking over the land, one sees around him clumps of sparse grass, pale gold most of the year, scattered, dull green bushes, and widely spaced trees, many the flat-topped acacias familiar in photographs of Africa. All the growth appears to be sparse nearby, but when one looks to the horizon, the vegetation appears to merge and one has the visual impression of being

5. Richard Lee, "!Kung Spatial Organization: An Ecological and Historical Perspective," *Human Ecology: An Interdisciplinary Journal* (New York-London, Plenum Press), 1 (1972), 131.
6. *Omirimbi* is the plural of *omuramba*.

surrounded by a low, dark rim. The rim seems near. Only the mind knows that the desert stretches on and on to vast distances.

Pans are a common feature of the Kalahari, but the group of very large pans in the center of the Nyae Nyae area is unusual. Those pans are part of the dry monotony till the big rains turn them into shallow, shining lakes, ankle-deep to knee-deep. Then they are an amazing feature in the otherwise featureless land.

Flocks of migrating geese, storks, cranes, and pelicans visit the pans, and once while we were there, thousands upon thousands of flamingos covered Gautscha Pan for days, dipping their pink feet, bending their

Grass, sparse trees, and bushes cover the flat land. In the distance, the trees and shrubs appear to merge and form a low, dark rim on the horizon. For many months the sky is cloudless. Then, as the season of the rains approaches, thunderheads begin to form. Three of the expedition's four trucks are seen in the foreground. They are laden with food and supplies, making the expedition as independent as a ship at sea.

necks in graceful ballet as they fed. But such splendid sights are fleeting. The water gradually dries up and the surfaces of the pans are again dry, whitish claylike mud, crisscrossed with cracks.

The glory of the Kalahari is in the sky that domes it. Nothing in the full circle of the horizon obstructs one's view of the sky and, living without a roof, one is in full and constant awareness of the ineffable beauty of dawn, sunset, and golden noon, moonlight so bright it sometimes makes rainbows in the clouds and, in the dark of the moon, the blazing stars in their slow progression through the night.

The !Kung are much aware of the sky. Their gods dwell in it—one where the sun rises, one where the sun sets. The spirits of the dead move about in it. The !Kung have names for many of the stars and a star lore.

There is nothing on the land higher than the mighty baobabs to lift the eye. This tree is the second largest of the Gautscha baobabs. Two boys, barely discernible, have climbed high on the middle trunk.

In the big rains, Gautscha Pan becomes a shallow, shining lake and everybody bathes.

They make practical use of the heavenly bodies, taking the time of day or night from them, and taking direction when they travel.

THE SEASONS

The !Kung differentiate with names six seasons of the year. Three are long and three are subseasons of about a month each, having some characteristic that distinguishes them. The !Kung have the concept of a year and a word for year, ‿guri. For them it is the round of the seasons that makes the year, not observations on the position of the sun or counted days or counted "moons." The !Kung do not realize that the sun moves between the summer and winter solstices. They think it always sets at the same spot on the horizon. There is no hill or roof peak to compare with the sun's position. The !Kung do not camp in exactly the same place repeatedly, so their position is always changing with respect to a baobab that might be a marker. Nothing calls their attention to the sun's movement. The seasons themselves are not given fixed lengths of time; the changes of the weather determine their advent and duration. However, allowing for the indefiniteness of informants and variation in weather, the seasons can be expected to fall, by and large, in the following months:

!gum	May–August	the coldest season; dry
!ga	September–October	the hottest season; dry
!gabu-!gabu	November	hot; little rains
!kuma	December	hot; little rains
bara	January–March	warm; big rains
//obe	April	warm; no rain or an occasional downpour

!Gum is winter; not a drop of rain falls from the clear blue sky. The nights are cold. Our expedition records show temperatures as low as 27°F; ice formed on our water buckets. The days are cold too; the fierce south winds are painfully cold for unclad people. I found the winter days of bright sunshine very pleasant when there was no wind, but even then I wore two sweaters and a leather jacket.

The !Kung appear to suffer more from cold than from heat. On the coldest, windiest days, the men standing in the wind clad only in breech clouts shiver violently. (I have never seen people shiver so violently.) Ordinarily the men do not wear karosses by day, but on the cold windy days of !gum they take out the karosses that they sleep in at night and wrap themselves in them. The women draw their karosses around them and the naked children creep into their parents' arms or wrap themselves together in bundles in someone's kaross. The people neither hunt nor gather. They huddle by their fires, their backs to the wind, and wait for more clement weather.

!Ga also is dry. The weather turns warm and suddenly it is hot; by October it is exceedingly hot. Our expedition records show air temperatures up to 115°F in deep, airy shade, and up to 126°F in the sun. The temperature of the surface of the sand in full sunlight in the hottest time reached 140°F. On such days the hunters complain that in the middle part of the day they cannot bear to walk in the sand. They seek shade, scrape out a shallow hollow, urinate in it, lie down on the moistened place, and dust a light layer of sand over themselves. They wait like this till the day cools, minimizing dehydration and saving their feet. If they must move, they hold leafy branches over their heads for parasols.

In the dry months whirlwinds and veld fires are features of the landscape. Most of the whirlwinds are only fierce little dust devils, but some are tiny tornadoes. In July 1953, when we were packing, preparing to leave the desert, a tiny tornado came through our camp and took our store tent up and away and with it not the remaining heavy cases of canned food but whatever else was left of our stores. I shudder yet to think that all my notes were spread out for filing and packing in a tent no more than twenty feet away.

Veld fires are a common sight. Bushmen set the fires to attract game. After a fire has passed, the grasses put forth green shoots and the game come to graze. The fires run raging before the winds till the winds shift and blow them back on themselves. We have seen around us as many as eight fires at a time. Some came crackling near, others were smudges on the horizon. Whirlwinds form in the burned-over areas, and the ashes rise like black pillars into the sky. Once we saw three such pillars near together, so tall they reached cool air above the earth and white clouds formed on their tops. We think we saw "a pillar of cloud" such as the Children of Israel may have seen: "And the Lord went before them by day in a pillar of a cloud, to lead them the way; and by night in a pillar of fire, to give them light . . ." (Exodus 13:21).

!Gabu-!gabu and !kuma (November and December) continue to be very hot. The !Kung expect windstorms and many dust devils. These are the months of the little rains. At first powder-puff clouds form and disappear in the clear sky. Occasionally a few drops of rain from them spatter onto the ground, leaving separate, polka dot marks in the sand and the fragrance of moist earth. The clouds gradually become larger and appear more frequently and a few short squalls occur.

As far as human beings are concerned, the little rains are insufficient to relieve the drought. They fill neither the dry waterholes nor the pans, so the people must still live by their permanent waterholes. By then, most of the plant foods within reach (that is, close enough for them to travel to, considering their water supply) have already been eaten or are so dried out as to be unpalatable. The people say that !ga is the time of hardship and thirst; !kuma is the time of starvation.

However, the season of little rains signals to the vegetation that the vernal time is coming. From their storage organs the sear, golden, crackling grasses begin to put forth green shoots, before even a drop of rain has touched them. Pink and white lilies suddenly appear full-blown.

With respect to the sun's position, bara is summer, but the temperatures are pleasant, cooled by the rains. Bara is the time of the big rains, which are usually violent thunderstorms. By January, the clouds have massed into thunderheads thousands of feet high. The torrential rain that pours from the towering clouds is cold, and occasionally it turns to hail. From a distance, the rain looks like a dirty gray curtain the cloud is dragging with it. Never once did we see a wholly overcast sky with gentle rain falling over a large area. The separate thunderheads are slowly driven by the winds hither and thither over the land, and like gigantic watering pots, pour out a deluge, drenching the land just under them, leaving other parts of the land without a drop. If one is under the storm, between shattering claps of thunder, one hears the rain being sucked into the sand with an ominous hiss. Lightning illuminates the clouds from within by incandescent flashes. Blazing bands zigzag from heaven to earth. Bushmen are sometimes killed by lightning. They seek shelter under trees, which are often hit.

When a torrential outpouring from the clouds is seen from a distance, the !Kung call it the "rain's hair."

Early in *bara,* all the vegetation suddenly revives; gold grasses turn green, dull gray-green trees and bushes brighten, flowers bloom. Pans and pools, small waterholes, and the hollows of trees fill with rain. The water frees the !Kung to move about throughout their territories and to travel wherever they wish. The plant foods are in their new growth and ripen rapidly.

//*Obe* comes in April at the end of *bara* between the big rains and the beginning of the winter dryness. There may be no rain in //*obe,* but if certain winds prevail, a few torrential rainstorms may occur. In any case, the pans and waterholes still hold water from the rains of *bara.* The weather is pleasant, neither hot nor cold. The plant foods have ripened and are at their best. Many kinds may be found. The !Kung say that //*obe* is the best of all the seasons.

TERRITORIES AND SOURCES OF WATER

Each band of !Kung is established in a habitable portion of the land in what I call a territory. The !Kung word for such a portion of land is *n!ore.* A !Kung speaks of his n!ore, his territory, as the place in which he lives or the place he comes from—it is the place to which he belongs. For a portion of land to be habitable, there must be a permanent or semipermanent waterhole at which the band of people who inhabit the territory base themselves in the dry season. There must also be areas of plant foods near enough to the waterhole for people to manage to go from one to the other in the dry season without perishing from thirst. A band's territory may include more distant sources of plant foods, the waterless mangetti groves, especially, which can be reached only when rainwater is still available in pans, temporary waterholes, or hollow trees. A combination of a permanent or semipermanent waterhole and plant foods reachable in the dry season is essential to a territory.

The size and shape of any area that could be called a territory varies enormously. The two principal fertile areas in the territory of Band 1 which sustain the people in the dry season are four miles and six miles respectively from the waterhole. The people of Band 1 go to gather at another place, Nama Pan, twenty miles south of Gautscha, during the rains and after, while the pan still holds water. The territories should not be thought of as resembling a jigsaw puzzle with edges fitting neatly together. They have no boundaries that could be depicted on a map by a clearly drawn line. Nevertheless, the !Kung define territories in ways that are suitable to them and clearly understood. The territory of /Ti!kay of Band 9, for example, they say is "the other side of the Gura baobabs." There may be a sort of no-man's-land between territories and even between fertile areas within a territory. One man said, "What good is ground that produces no food? One cannot eat it." Possession of the resources is what concerns the !Kung. (The !Kung concepts of ownership of the resources will be discussed in Chapter 5.)

We believe that all the habitable portions of the Nyae Nyae area are known and occupied, that no waterhole is yet to be discovered. !Kung hunters have traveled over the land for many generations.

During the season of the rains, in places where the passing clouds have poured out their torrents, water collects in pans, in pools in the little vleis, in small temporary waterholes, and in hollow trees. This surface water frees the people to go to gather in distant parts of their territories and to make long journeys to visit relatives and friends anywhere in the Nyae Nyae region. The smaller collections of rainwaters do not last very long after the rains cease, but water stands in the big pans for many weeks. The fortunate people of Gautscha, who live on the banks of the pan, delight in the water. Every day the children play in it, dancing and splashing in rhythmic patterns. Everybody bathes. In the dry season, the only sources of water are the waterholes and succulent plants. Several species of succulent plants occur in the Nyae Nyae area but none abound.

In the (roughly estimated) 5,400 square miles of the Nyae Nyae area are sixteen permanent or semipermanent waterholes that sustain the people through the dry season. At fifteen of these waterholes the nineteen bands that inhabit the Nyae Nyae area are based. No band lived by the big waterhole of Nama while we were in the area. It was deep in the rock and was filled with drowned animals that had fallen in while trying to reach water in their desperate thirst. The !Kung passed it by. Two good temporary waterholes prolonged the period in which hunters and gatherers could stay in the Nama vicinity but did not support them through the whole dry season. At four of the permanent waterholes, two bands were based, namely, at Gautscha, Deboragu, Samangaigai, and /Gam. (All waterholes and the bands based at them are listed in Table 3 in Chapter 5.) Like the plant food resources, the waterholes are owned by the bands.

According to the information given us by the !Kung, the waterholes called permanent had not failed, even in the most severe droughts, within the memory of the living people. I do not have histories of the water-holes or data to confirm the informants' statements. We were told that the following waterholes are permanent:

/Gam	Gautscha
Samangaigai	Deboragu
Tsho/ana	Kaitsa.

We think the big waterhole of Nama with the drowned animals in it is also permanent.

The waterholes called semipermanent rarely fail and do so only in years of extreme drought. The semipermanent waterholes, we are told, are:

West of Châssis	Kautsa
Tsumkwe	N!o !Go
Khumsa	/Gun/ga
Nam Tshoha	N//o!gau.

Those that failed in the drought of 1952–53, while we were in the field, were the waterholes south of /Gam: /Gun/ga of Band 14 and N//o!gau of Band 17. Three others in Botswana (east of /Gun/ga) failed in that drought: ≠Go≠gowe and Domn!a of Band 15 and ≠O //Gana of Band 16. Bands 14, 15, and 16 came to live at /Gam till their waterholes filled again in the next rains. Together with Bands 12 and 13, which are regularly based at /Gam, they made up the five bands that the /Gam water supplied. Happily for the !Kung, the semipermanent waterholes do not necessarily all fail at the same time. The more northern semipermanent waterholes had not dried in 1952–53.

The waterholes vary in size and productivity and keep their own balance with respect to the number of people who depend on them. Relatively abundant water allows large groups to congregate, scant water keeps groups small. At Samangaigai, Tsho/ana, and /Gam, the Bantu families who lived in those places had deepened the waterholes by blasting and digging. (No boreholes operated with pumps had been drilled till Claude McIntyre drilled one at Tsumkwe in 1960.) I have mentioned that the wonderful waterhole at /Gam, with conservative use, supplied the Bantu family, their herd of cattle, our expedition of fifteen people, and the five !Kung bands.

The /Gam waterhole was a hole about fifteen feet in diameter and twenty feet deep with a pool at the bottom. To take water from it was a three-man operation. One man would climb down to the pool, fill a

Miles and miles of dry sand surround this spot where a spring wells up, hardly more than a puddle, but, nevertheless, a semipermanent waterhole.

bucket, hand it up to a second man who stood on a ledge halfway up. He, in turn, would pass the bucket to a third man standing at the top who would pour the water into the cattle trough or into one of our drums, as the case might be, and throw the bucket back to the man at the pool.

Samangaigai and Tsho/ana had similar pools. The flow of water was not as strong as at /Gam but the demand was less, so they proved adequate.

The other thirteen permanent and semipermanent waterholes remained as nature made them, springs that came to the surface of the ground in outcroppings of limestone ridges or in pools or merely as wet places in the sand. The excellent Gautscha waterhole was the best of them all, a deep pool of clear water in the rock, about seven or eight by four feet, about three feet deep. Deboragu was a puddle in the sand at best, and when it was at its worst, Old /Gaishay said of it, "You will think there is no water, but scratch in the sand and wait and some will come." People dipped water from these natural waterholes with tortoise-shell dippers, or at Deboragu, when it was at its lowest, sucked up water with hollow reeds ("sip sticks").

Temporary waterholes fill during the rains and are expected to dry up before the end of the dry season. I happen to know personally of seven: I do not have a systematic count of them all. The seven, all small, were widely scattered from the Eiseb Omuramba to Thinthuma Pan. Hunters drink from the temporary waterholes when they pass by, and in several instances temporary waterholes relatively near fertile areas or mangetti groves prolonged the period in which people could gather at those places. Band 2 had a small temporary waterhole six miles from the mangetti grove they gathered in away in the west. Every other

The deep, clear Gautscha waterhole in the rock of the limestone ridge at the edge of the pan. A girl fills an ostrich eggshell with a tortoise-shell dipper.

day, as long as the water lasted, they sent their boys on the twelve-mile trip, back and forth, to carry water from the waterhole. When the waterhole dried, Band 2 returned to Gautscha.

The Nyae Nyae !Kung make conservative use of the water in their waterholes. They have no herds, and the only animals with whom they need share water are lions, hyenas, and the other smaller predators. The great antelopes do not depend on drinking regularly at waterholes. The !Kung take water for drinking, cooking, and washing themselves. They have no laundry to wash. On the whole, the !Kung have adequate water for drinking and for their other needs while they stay beside their waterholes. It is when they leave to hunt and gather and to travel during the dry season that water becomes a constant problem. The !Kung succeed in solving that problem. They know all about the water situation: where the water is, how much is available, how to manage time and distance away from water. We heard no stories of deaths from thirst among them. If they have to choose between lack of food and lack of water, they say that they stay by the water and leave the food.

Although the !Kung do not let themselves get into dangerous situations from lack of water, they often suffer from thirst, hunters especially. Hunters do not carry heavy ostrich eggshells filled with water, and they just endure thirst if they must. Gatherers also suffer from thirst when they are gathering far from water. In /Gam, for example, when the three bands from the south came to /Gam during the drought, the plant foods nearby were utterly inadequate to support them all. The people of each band made treks back to the areas of plant foods on which they regularly depend. Hunters do not carry ostrich eggshells filled with water, but gatherers do. They filled every container they had, bags made from the stomachs of animals, as well as their ostrich eggshells. Another container the !Kung use is their own stomachs. When hunters or gatherers are going to be away from water for an appreciable amount of time, they drink prodigious amounts of water before they start out, literally filling their stomachs till they are taut. When they return very thirsty from a long trip, they drink even more, it seems, gulping down incredible amounts of water.

The people from /Gam made their trek and gathered and ate as long as their water lasted. My impression is that they usually spent three or four days on these gathering trips, including the traveling time. They returned to the waterhole carrying whatever plant foods they had, stayed till those foods were eaten, and made the trek again.

Ostrich eggshells are the common water containers of the !Kung. A hole one-half to three-quarters of an inch in diameter is drilled at the tapered end of the shell through which the shell is emptied and filled. The hole is stoppered with grass. The beautiful creamy white shells are excellent containers. They are thick and not easily broken. Water does not spill or evaporate from them. Their only disadvantage is that they are heavy. The empty shells weigh about a pound. Those I measured contained thirty-six fluid ounces on the average, and weighed about three pounds when filled. Each family we observed had eight or ten shells. The number of shells a family has, I believe, is limited to the number they want to carry. Enough nests of ostrich eggs are found to supply the needs of the group. Surplus shells are broken and used for making the traditional ostrich-eggshell beads.

The person who finds and takes the eggs in an ostrich nest owns the shells. That person keeps any his or her family may need; he may give others away as gifts. Individuals own the shells as they own other artifacts. The shells are not family or communal property. We saw a few shells marked with designs. !Kung women are capable of creating beautiful and subtle designs in bead work in addition to the traditional bead designs seen in the ostrich-eggshell bead headbands and aprons, but apparently the !Kung, men or women, have not turned their creative imagination to drawing designs on ostrich eggshells. (Nowhere is their graphic design highly developed; music and dancing are their great arts.) The designs that were scratched on the shells were to make them identifiable to their owners, we were told. Men, women, and children may own shells, but mainly women own them, and it is women's work to carry most of the family's supply. The eight or ten shells the family possesses are all a woman wants to carry.

The !Kung also use water bags, which they make from the stomachs of animals. They tie one end of the stomach with a cord, pierce a series of holes in the other end, thread a flexible stick through the holes, and gather the edge of the stomach tightly on the stick. When the !Kung are encamped, they use these bags to bring water from the waterhole to the encampment. The bags are not satisfactory for carrying long distances; the water spills, drips, and evaporates. People also use wooden bowls to carry water from the waterhole to the encampment. But the !Kung depend mostly on the excellent ostrich-eggshell containers.

Succulent roots and melons supplement the water of the waterholes to some extent. The list of plant foods given in Chapter 3 mentions seven species of plants as being especially succulent. Three are remarkable: tsama melons (#47), !xwa (#16), and gwe (#64). These succulent plants occur here and there in the Nyae Nyae area, but they are not plentiful enough anywhere for bands to depend on them for any length of time. Nothing in the Nyae Nyae area compares to the situation we found in the central Kalahari where a group of eleven /Gwi lived for a month on a vast waterless plain at !Ai Ha !O Pan (ca. 23°1′ E, 22°25′ S) beside a huge patch of tsama melons, without any water at all. We had our own water supply in drums. We explained to the /Gwi that we could give them water and have enough for ourselves. They said cheerfully that they were accustomed to doing without and would not expect water from us. By rationing ourselves rigorously, we were able to spin out our supply and to spend a month with those gentle people. During that month, they depended for liquid on the tsama; they each ate eight or ten a day. We supplemented their food with moderate rations of mealie-meal porridge till our supplies of water and food were so nearly exhausted that we had to leave.

The /Gwi make use of liquid from the animals they kill. They squeeze the rumen of antelopes, handful by handful, and drink the odorous fluid they extract; they carefully collect the blood of any animal, cook it, and eat it. However, these /Gwi seldom kill an animal. Game is extremely scarce in the vast plain in which they live; weeks may elapse without their seeing any large animal. Furthermore, these /Gwi cannot engage in long, exhausting hunts where they have no water; they would become too dehydrated. They set snares and catch guinea fowl and an occasional little buck. We were with the /Gwi in July when the weather was comfortable. The worst of the year was still ahead of them. Before long the tsamas would all be eaten and the /Gwi would have to fall back to an area they reserve for that time of year, an area where they can gather tubers barely succulent enough to keep them alive. They lie still in the shade through the heat of the day, gather and set their snares in the morning and evening, and wait for rain. Compared to these /Gwi, the Nyae Nyae !Kung, all of whom had access to a waterhole, seemed to me well off indeed.

We had heard that Bushmen who are going on a long journey or going to gather plant foods in a waterless place sometimes make a preliminary trip halfway with ostrich eggshells filled with water. These they bury in the sand, carefully marking the place, and have the extra supply of water for the return journey. We did not observe this actually done, but informants demonstrated for us how they bury the shells.

The !Kung have no means of storing water in greater amounts than the water they carry in their ostrich eggshells.

Neither the !Kung nor the /Gwi, incidentally, had any other beverage than plain water. They greatly relished a gift of tea, coffee, or cocoa, but made no infusions of their own. They have no milk, of course, and they neither made nor procured any intoxicating drink.

SETTLEMENT AND FIRE

A !Kung encampment is called a *tshu /ko*. *Tshu* is the word for the shelters that !Kung build of branches and grass; /ko is the word for "place."

The !Kung have no permanent dwellings. Although a !Kung band, moving from one place to another to gather food and obtain water, returns season after season and year after year to the same waterholes and to the same areas in which their plant foods grow, the people do not reoccupy old camp sites—not, at least, until time and the winds have torn apart the abandoned shelters and blown away or covered up the piles of ashes from the old fires. The !Kung may settle near an old camp site, but they will make a new encampment, one that has never existed before. In that vast land there is plenty of ground for new camp sites. The !Kung do not want to kindle new fire exactly where old fires have been. New fire is associated with fresh hope, fresh chance for good fortune. To build new fires on old sites might nullify the fresh chance and invite misfortune.

The !Kung usually settle at some distance—half a mile or so—from their waterhole. This is discreet: lions, leopards, and hyenas share waterholes with the Bushmen, and the Bushmen think it wise to let the predators have the waterholes to themselves at night.

A place is selected that is relatively free from thorny bush and high grass. Soft, sandy ground is preferred; ideally there will be a tree or two for shade and bushes on which people may hang their belongings. When the site is selected the men put down their carrying-sticks and the bundles hung on them. From the pouches of their cloaks the women unload the ostrich-eggshell water containers and their other belongings. The band is settled.

After the bundles have been put down, the next act is to make fire. The process of making fire requires two fire sticks, called male and female, and a bunch of woolly grass for tinder. (//Galli grass or /gam grass is used.) The male stick, held vertically, is twirled rapidly in a small notch in the female stick, which is placed horizontally on the

The shelters of a !Kung encampment, made of the grass that surrounds them, merge with the landscape. These are the shelters of Gaú and his mother and sisters, Segment 3 of Band 2. The !Kung live mostly beside their fires, in front of their shelters rather than inside them.

ground, till the fine wood dust produced by the twirling is ignited by friction. The smoldering wood dust is quickly tipped onto the bunch of grass, which is picked up and gently blown on till the grass bursts into flame. The grass is then placed on the ground. Small twigs ready at hand are placed on the grass for kindling, and as soon as they are ignited pieces of wood are added.

The male stick is usually made of a hard wood, the female stick of a soft wood. *Catophractes alexandri* is often used for the male stick and *Grewia retinervis* for the female stick. Robert Story says of the *Grewia*: "The dry stems of this plant nearly always contain the tunnelings of grubs, and the tunnelings are packed with excreta in the form of a brown pith-like substance which forms a useful tinder. The Bushmen split the stems down the center, make a slight depression in the flat surface and use this as a socket for the fire-drill."[7] Another wood we observed used was baobab wood—for both sticks.

The male stick of one set I have is 28 inches long and just over ¼ inch in diameter. The female stick is 19 inches long, ⅜ inch in diameter. A notch is cut 1½ inches from one end of the female stick. The male stick must fit into the notch exactly.

When preparing to make fire, a man places the grass tinder on the ground and lays a knife on it. The end of the female fire stick which has the notch is placed on the knife blade at a right angle. A digging stick is laid across the fire stick near the other end and the man holds it down firmly with his foot. This keeps the female fire stick steady. The male stick is held upright, its end placed in the notch. The man twirls the stick between his hands with rapid motions of about an inch back and forth. He works his hands from the top of the stick to the bottom, strongly pressing the stick downward into the notch as he rotates it. He then slides his hands to the top of the stick without twirling or pressing so that his hands do not become too heated from friction, and repeats the twirling. The speed with which the man slides his hands up and starts twirling again is a crucial factor in success.

Frequently two men make fire together. As one pair of hands reaches the bottom of the stick, the second pair is ready at the top to keep the twirling continuous. The shortest time of twirling I observed was twenty-five seconds with two men working. They made their

7. Robert Story, *Some Plants Used by the Bushmen in Obtaining Food and Water,* Republic of South Africa, Botanical Survey Memoir, no. 30, Department of Agriculture, Division of Botany, 1958, p. 34.

downward twirl five times. The longest time, with one man twirling, was sixty-five seconds. The process looks deceptively easy when an adroit man is twirling. The men differ in ability. /Qui was so lacking in adroitness that he said he had given up trying to make fire and had thrown away his fire sticks. I understood his frustration. I did not once succeed in making a spark though I tried earnestly several times.

Making fire is the work of men. Men carry their fire sticks with them constantly in their quivers with their arrows. We were told that there was no law of avoidance that forbade a woman from using fire sticks if she needed to make a family fire or cooking fire, presumably in emer-

Dam of Band 2, husband of ≠Gisa, and ≠Gao, ≠Gisa's brother from Band 3 (visiting), make fire together. Notice Dam's haircut. The !Kung shave their heads from time to time, leaving on patches of hair in fanciful designs. The designs signify nothing; they are for decoration only. The shaving serves as a grooming process and discourages lice from inhabiting the matted peppercorns.

The wood dust is soon ignited by friction.

gency. However we never saw a woman use fire sticks. The women had no occasion to do so. They were never away from their men except during the days when they were on routine gathering trips. Ritual fire is another matter. Fire is deeply associated with !Kung ritual. Ritual fires must be freshly made by a man with fire sticks, not with brands from family fires. Women would have nothing to do with the making of ritual fire, and they must not go near the fire while the rituals are being conducted.

The making of a new fire in a new encampment has the aura of ritual, but the new fire is not strictly a ritual fire. Making the new fire is the responsibility of the oldest man in the band if he is still able to use his fire sticks; he may be helped by a younger man. When ritual fires are made after a death or severe misfortune or for changing bad luck to good in hunting, they must be made by an old man and they must be made with fire sticks. When we were observing and filming Band 1 settling in a new encampment, they took care that the oldest man made the fire with fire sticks in the traditional manner, but on other occasions the first fire was lit with matches, which were a gift from us. This was characteristic of the !Kung, who are flexible in most matters, even spiritual matters, though by no means in all.

While the old man makes fire, others go about picking up dry wood to lay on the new fire, and when it is burning well each family takes a brand from it to start his family fire, beside which the family will live. The original fire started by the old man is not regarded as a ritualistic, perpetual fire. If it is in a place convenient for the old man, he may settle by it and keep it going; otherwise he takes a brand, makes another fire for himself, and the first fire is allowed to burn itself out. Rarely is it necessary to make fire with the fire sticks a second time as long as the people remain in the encampment. They bank their fires with ashes during the day and usually find glowing coals on which to build the evening fires. If someone's fire does go out, he asks a neighbor for coals to start a new fire; almost always someone will have coals. There are no restrictions on women making new fires with old coals. Anyone may do so, man, woman, or child.

It always amuses me to speak of residence when I visualize the nomadic !Kung settling down for the night, like migrating birds in the bushes, or building their grass shelters for a longer stay, which will nevertheless be temporary. And it is a delightful insistence on precision to say that Lame ≠Gao lived (before he married in 1959) with his elder sister !U, not with his eldest sister, Di!ai, although the two sisters were accustomed to settle not more than two arm's lengths apart, because they liked to be able to hand things across from one household to the other without getting up. Yet the !Kung do have residence, and it does become clear precisely who lives with whom. One way this can be observed is to see whom the woman feeds with the plant foods she gathers: it was !U, not Di!ai, who fed ≠Gao.

The clearest visible indication of a family's location is the fire. One can see who lives at each. Always, summer and winter, every nuclear family has its fire, which is kept burning all night. The fire is the nuclear family's home, its gathering place, its rightful place to be. In a way, a fire is more of an unchanging home than is a house on a plot of ground, from which a family might depart. A fire-home is always where the family is. The family hangs its possessions in the bushes near the fire, sits around the fire, cooks at it, sleeps at it. At night, the light of all the family fires in the encampment forms the protecting wall that encloses the people, holding out the prowling beasts and the darkness. An old man once said to us, "Fire, water, and food hold our lives. We have been so created. Without fire we would have no light, no warmth; food could not be cooked. Even an old person can live by his fire. Someone will give him food and water, and he can be warm."

Fortunately for the !Kung, they live in a country that produces plenty of wood. Each family provides its own firewood. Both men and women gather it: they may pick up dry logs as they return from hunting or gathering trips, or they may go out from the encampment in the late afternoon to look for large branches and for dead trees, which the women can push over or the men chop down. They do not chop the logs or branches into sticks. For the fires that they keep burning all night they place the whole log flat out on the ground—perhaps three at a time— with their ends together, so spaced and tended that they produce a steady small fire with flames a foot or so in height. People push the logs in as they burn down; they awaken at night, from time to time, to do so. They like to draw near to a fire without being scorched or getting too much smoke in their eyes, so they keep the blaze small. Every day, to keep the space around the fire neat and pleasant for sitting or sleeping, the women clear away some of the ashes, scraping them up with their fire-paddles into a tortoise shell or an old scrap of leather, and deposit them in a pile at some distance from their dwelling place. The fires are customarily banked with ashes during the day, and the coals are fanned up only when they are wanted for cooking. The desert sun gives enough warmth on the clear dry winter days to make them comfortable unless a fierce south wind is blowing. If a family is away for more than a day, or if its fire goes out for some other reason, someone will give coals or brands to start the fire again. Or a man will twirl new fire with his fire sticks.

The families in a band always settle close together, and the brown and clustered encampment makes me think of a swarm of bees. Some people build their shelters actually touching each other; others may build shelters or place their fires ten or twelve feet apart.

Within the encampment, the families demarcate themselves consistently. The fires of the nuclear families that compose an extended family are always near each other, not scattered about among other families in the encampment. Adult dependents have their own fires near the families with whom they live. Visitors have their own fires near the families they are visiting. In other ways the settlement pattern is variable. The encampment can take almost any shape—roughly circular, oddly angular, or serpentine (but I never saw one look much like a square). Fires are not placed in a fixed pattern with reference to the father of an extended family, nor with reference to the points of the compass or to anything I know of except nearness together. A nearby bush to hang things on, a bit of shade, a relatively smooth and thorn-free spot on the ground determine the particular choice of place.

I have been referring to the settlement in terms of family fires rather than shelters because the fires are constant—the shelters are whims. The women may or may not build shelters (*tshusi*) for their families. (Women, being the gatherers, are associated with vegetation, and the shelters, built of branches and grass, are in their domain. Similarly, the making of leather garments is the work of men, since the skins from

N/aoka, the first wife of /Ti!kay, is beginning to lay armloads of grass on the frame of the shelter she is building. The light-colored object to the left in the photograph is a hide that her husband has scraped and tanned to make a kaross.

As often as not, the women do not bother to build shelters. Two families live beside this bush. The !Kung like to settle near together. The ashes of two extra cooking fires are discernible in the background.

which the garments are made are the products of the hunt.) A woman builds a shelter in a little less than an hour. The materials are always at hand—the Kalahari abounds in them. First she digs a row of from twelve to twenty holes, four or five inches deep, loosening the sandy soil with her digging-stick, scooping it out with her hand. The holes form a crescent. She then gathers some slender, flexible branches, pulling them from the bushes. The branches are five or six feet long and an inch or so in diameter. She stands a branch in each hole and tamps it down. When the branches are firmly in place she bends their tops together and weaves them into each other, thus making the frame of the shelter. Next she brings armloads of any nearby tall grass, which she lays on the frame, grass-heads down. She simply pats the grass into place, unless rain is expected and the winds are high, in which case she might bind the grass onto the frame with two or three long strands of sansevieria fibers (*Sansevieria scabrifolia* Dinter) or strips of bark, drawn horizontally around the shelter. The usual finished shelter is a half-hemisphere in shape, four or five feet high at its peak, about five feet wide on its open side, about three or four feet deep at the middle. During the rains some women built somewhat larger shelters that were more closed at the front.

The shelters may face in any direction of the compass and in any direction with respect to the winds, rains, and sun. They may be side by side, face to face, or back to back, according to the women's whims.

Unless it is raining, the women often do not bother to build shelters at all, even for the relatively long periods in the dry season when the bands must stay encamped near their permanent waterholes. Sometimes, if a woman has not built a shelter, she will put up two sticks to symbolize the entrance to the shelter, so that the family may orient itself as to which side of the fire is the man's side and which the woman's side. (The man's side is to the right of the observer facing the shelter, the woman's side is to the left.) Sometimes a woman does not even bother with the sticks.

The shelters are literally shelters—not dwellings. A family crowds into one during a downpour; it sits in the bit of shade it provides in hot weather. People may keep their belongings in them or on them, but they live very little inside them. A few sleep in their shelters, but for the most part life takes place outside the shelters, beside the fires. The fire is the home.

Other fires also appear in the !Kung encampment. Many are extra cooking-fires. Although there is a tendency (not a strictly observed custom) for the mother or father to cook in the late afternoon or early evening whatever food is available for the family, anybody (children included) may cook at any time. Especially when the hunters have been successful and the meat of a large animal has been distributed, people can be seen cooking little snacks all day long. For the most part they cook meat, nuts, and roots in the hot coals and ashes of their family fires, covering the food until it is cooked and then scraping it out with their fire-paddles and whacking off the ashes. They also have a few pots (Ovambo pottery or European iron pots acquired in trade with the Bantu) in which they boil meat or mangetti nuts or tsi. If the day is hot, they set these pots on little special fires away from the place where they habitually sit. Regularly the heads of the large game animals are cooked during the day in pits, piled over with hot coals, ashes, and earth.

As with the cooking-fires, there are more sleeping-fires in a !Kung encampment than there are families. Boys and girls, beginning at about the age of eight or nine, sleep at fires apart from their parents' fires. Several boys sleep together at a boys' fire; the girls either sleep with a widowed grandmother or some other widow, or have little fires of their own,

Dam and ≠Gisa roast two /ga roots on the coals (an age-old way to cook). Notice ≠Gisa's front apron bordered with beads.

Di!ai, wife of Gao, has been given a wildebeest head in the meat distribution.

not far from their parents'. In a large encampment there might be four
or five such extra sleeping-fires.

Finally, to complete this catalogue of the fires that appear in a !Kung
encampment, there are the fires that are built for the ritual curing dance
and for the performance of other rites. The dance takes place around a
fire built in the center of the dance circle. In addition, people who are
resting, or are for some other reason not dancing, sit at fires near the
dance circle. The rites that require special fires include the Menarcheal
Rite, the Rite of the First Kill (performed when a boy kills his first large
game animal), another hunting rite, a rite for a novice medicine man,
n/um k"xau ("owner of medicine"), and the rite for a child's first haircut.

An archaeologist of the future, examining a !Kung site, would be
hard put to estimate how many families inhabited it, with such a variable number of piles of ash from fires that had such a variety of purposes.

She bakes it in hot coals and ashes in a pit.

3 Plant Foods and Gathering

Vegetation supplies most of the resources for the life of the !Kung. Some of their needs it supplies in great abundance, giving all the people can use, all they want and more. Grass and branches for shelters; flexible, resilient wood for bows; firm, strong wood for digging sticks and carrying sticks; light, strong reeds for arrows and sip sticks; certain woods for quivers and fire sticks; fibers for cord; adhesive saps; resins for glue; light, soft wood that can be carved for musical instruments, mortars and pestles, bowls, spoons, and ornaments—there is plenty of material for these objects. Firewood, so important an item in !Kung life, is also available. Perhaps we should not call it abundant, but it is sufficient. One advantage of moving the encampments from place to place is that a fresh supply of firewood within reasonable distance can be obtained.

Certain trees and shrubs are hosts to the beetles from the larvae of which the !Kung make arrow poison, and certain pods and roots are poisonous and are also used in arrow poison. The poison material is not abundant but is sufficient to the population; no hunters that we knew or heard of lacked poison.

Vegetation also supplies a majority of the numerous medicines that are believed to have magical properties for protecting people from misfortune and, in particular, for curing sickness. Animal fat, especially eland fat, and, to a lesser extent, meat play a role in several of the rituals, but the rituals in which vegetation is used are the more numerous.

As to food, plant food provides the major part of the !Kung diet in quantity; meat is obtained only intermittently. Lee, calculating the food intake at one of the Dobe area camps, finds the ratio of meat to vegetables to be 25 percent meat to 75 percent vegetables.[1] Our rough estimates for the Nyae Nyae area were about the same. Meat is the highly desired food, but game is not abundant. In the Nyae Nyae area many days may pass between successful hunts. Meanwhile, the women provide the daily living by gathering plant foods. The family has the security of knowing that there will be something to eat.

The species of plants that yield some edible part known to the !Kung in the Nyae Nyae region must be about a hundred in number. In the lists that I have available (at the time of writing) of food plants collected by Story in the Nyae Nyae area in 1955 and 1958, and Lee in the Dobe area in 1963–1965, I count eighty-four reported by Story and eighty-five by Lee.[2] Each of those collections, made at different times in different places, includes a few species that the other does not have, indicating that the !Kung know more species than either list contains alone. I feel safe in assuming that about a hundred are known. We have a list of sixty-five of those plant foods which we observed or learned about in 1952–53. The list appears at the end of this chapter.

The numerousness of the species insures against their all failing at one time. If gatherers depended upon one principal species of plant food, this species might fail, as does occasionally a principal crop of agriculturists. A variety of nutrients is provided by the various plants, and monotony in diet is mitigated.

The number of species of plant foods is impressive. It must be realized, however, that all are not available to all !Kung. The territories differ. A food that is a staple in one may be lacking in another. Mangetti nuts (*Ricinodendron rautanenii* Schinz, called mongongo in Botswana) are notable in this respect (see the list of plant foods, #32). Band 1 has no mangetti nuts in its territory, whereas mangettis are a very important food for some !Kung. *Tsi* (#1), another important plant food, is extremely localized; in South West Africa it exists only in one locality in the Nyae Nyae area, south of Nama Pan where two large communities of the plant grow. Band 1 and others gather tsi, but not all the Nyae Nyae bands have rights to do so. Furthermore, many of the plant species make a negligible contribution in quantity to the people's diet for one reason or another.

1. Richard Lee, *Subsistence Ecology of !Kung Bushmen* (Ann Arbor, Mich., University Microfilms, 1965), p. 170.
2. Robert Story, *Some Plants Used by the Bushmen in Obtaining Food and Water*, Republic of South Africa, Botanical Survey Memoir, no. 30, Department of Agriculture, Division of Botany, 1958; Richard Lee, "!Kung Bushman Food Plants and Botanical Categories," unpublished ms.

They may be exceedingly rare in the area, or they may be perishable and of short season, or they may fail to yield in years of drought, or the edible part may be small and contribute little nourishment. The actual species of plant foods upon which the people depend throughout the year in their different localities are, therefore, relatively few compared to the hundred or so species known to exist in the area as a whole.

Our expedition made no nutritional studies. We have only the general knowledge that the roots, berries, and perishable seasonal fruits provide vitamins and minerals but are low in protein; they are low in calories as well. Mangetti nuts and tsi are high in protein and oils and calories, but neither is available to all !Kung and both are eaten only seasonally. Meat is thus a vital element to the diet as a contributor of protein.

My impression is that the Nyae Nyae !Kung at the time we were in the field had sufficient food of one kind or another—meat, mangetti nuts, tsi, other plant foods—to sustain them in health and vigor but not enough to fatten them. All are slender or thin. Doctors A. S. Truswell and J. D. L. Hansen of the University of Cape Town examined the !Kung in the Dobe area in 1964, and their observations, published in the *South African Medical Journal,* substantiate my impressions. They said they found little or no evidence of mineral or vitamin deficiency, they observed no kwashiorkor, edema, or pellagra, but that toward the end of the dry season protein intake became critical. They go on to say:

> Although they were not usually *malnourished,* the Bushmen's adult weights averaged only 80% of standard for their heights. [I assume that the standard referred to is that of a western industrial society.] Weight/height ratio declined with age in both sexes, and mean mid-triceps skinfolds were only 5–0 mm. in men and 9.4 mm. in women. Skinfolds increased significantly between the dry season and the examination after the rains. By these and other criteria the Bushmen were moderately *undernourished.*
>
> It appears that the hunter-gatherer diet of nuts, fruit, roots and meat is fairly well balanced in specific nutrients, but the Bushmen's problem is how to obtain sufficient total calories for the large amount of energy they have to spend walking from their waterholes to collect their food.[3]

3. A. S. Truswell and J. D. L. Hansen, "Medical and Nutritional Studies of the !Kung Bushmen in North-west Botswana: A Preliminary Report," *South African Medical Journal,* 32 (Dec. 1968), 1339.

THE !KUNG AS BOTANISTS

The !Kung are good botanists. They train themselves to be keenly observant, and they develop remarkable powers of visual memory. Story, in praise of them, says they unerringly distinguish among species even though the species closely resemble one another. It behooves them to be discerning; one species may be edible and one like it may be poisonous. They recognize the key characteristics of the species and are not confused by variations in individual plants. They are able to identify the plant not only in the season of bloom but in the dry season when merely a dead leaf, or a fragment of withered stem, or a bit of brown vine, thin as a thread among the grass stems, must suffice to tell them where the edible roots are to be dug.[4] Story illustrates their powers of observation and visual memory by telling of an incident in which he asked them to find a certain plant for him, *Raphionacme burkei* N. E. Br. (The !Kung name for the plant is *gwe*; it is called *bi* in several Bushman languages.) The plant has wide distribution in the Kalahari but is not common in the Nyae Nyae area. The storage organ is a source of water, not food. The part of the plant above ground is very inconspicuous, with stems about six inches long and small leaves that die back in winter. Story says: "How extraordinarily observant the Bushmen are was well shown when they were asked if they could find a specimen and demonstrate its use. One man guided the party for four miles across country, featureless except for clumps of trees, to a spot where he knew of one growing. It was found after a short search—nothing more than two or three small sticks among the grasses with the bark shredding into white silky fibres."[5]

The !Kung have names for the species of trees that surround them, for different kinds of grasses, for all the plants they use for implements and poison, and for all the food plants. In some instances, they have different names for the above-ground and underground parts of the plant if both are edible, and for the baobab tree they have different names for the tree, for the fruit, for the dried pulp of the fruit when it is scraped off and pounded to a meal, and for the seeds.

Their training in botany, like all !Kung training, is gained by participation and observation, not by formal schooling, and not apart from doing. It begins in early childhood. Mothers always carry their nursing

4. Story, *Some Plants*, p. 7.
5. Ibid., p. 39.

infants and young children with them on a gathering day. Visual impressions are implanted in the children. When the children can walk, they play at digging and picking and carrying the food in imitation of their mothers. They may also receive a little teaching.

An image of Di!ai with her two-year-old son, /Gaishay, comes to my mind when I think of this aspect of !Kung life. He was riding on her shoulder while she scanned the ground for signs of a root. When she saw the thread of vine in the grass that told her that a root lay below, she set him on his feet beside her, took the vine in her hand to show him, and began to dig. He held onto her and peered into the hole. When she pulled out the root, she held it out for him to see and told him its name. "/Dobi," she said, "/dobi."

In middle childhood, children participate in the gatherings—but only spontaneously and sporadically. Protective, lenient, and patient parents that they are, the !Kung believe in not taxing the children's strength and do not make them work at gathering. The children are often allowed to stay in the encampment if some adult members of the family are remaining there to keep an eye on them, and they play the day through instead of helping. When they do go with the gathering parties, however, between romping, eating berries, rolling about in the shade of a bush, and taking drinks of water from their mother's ostrich eggshells, they become interested in finding roots of their own and digging them out and thus participate to some extent. All in all, however, by the time the boys and girls are at an age the !Kung call "old child," dama n!a (early teen-age), they have spent much of their young lives at least in the presence of serious gathering. They are competent to find and recognize most, if not all, of the food plants, and are well on their way to being the experts the adults are. They complete their education as botanists during their teens and, as young adults, are fully competent.

WOMAN'S WORK AND RESPONSIBILITY

Gathering is primarily the work of women; hunting is the work of men. The roles are strongly cast. One woman said of gathering, "That is what women are made for; men are made to bring meat." However, men are not excluded from gathering, whereas women are totally excluded from hunting. Women never participate in a !Kung hunt. Furthermore, the !Kung believe that femaleness weakens the hunter's prowess and endangers his chance of success, and they practice certain avoidances for keeping femaleness apart from hunting. They believe that women must not touch bows and arrows, for instance. When they are menstruating, women are believed to exert an especially weakening influence on hunting. Men, on the other hand, are not believed to endanger the fertility of the land or the growth of the plant foods or the effectiveness of the gatherers. No such beliefs and no social regulations restrict men from gathering, and they do so whenever they wish. They are as competent as women in their botanical knowledge. Men always accompany the women if they are going to gather in distant places when they plan to stay overnight or longer and participate in gathering whatever plant foods they have come especially to get. Men always participate in gathering mangetti nuts or tsi and help carry the heavy loads back to the waterhole. However, when a band is encamped in the dry season by a waterhole, as Band 1 was at Gautscha, the regular daily gathering is the work of women. The men did not participate in it under normal circumstances.

Every able, adult woman is responsible for gathering for herself, her family, and her dependents. She may give to others as she wishes, but custom and expectation in !Kung society do not require that plant food be shared in a general distribution as meat is shared. This means that every able, adult woman must gather regularly. Unless she is sick or disabled, she must not expect to be supported by others. Failure to provide her share would be weakening to the group. For a woman to shirk or be lazy would be wholly unacceptable behavior in the society. The sanction of public opinion is very strong, and women do not shirk.

Women continue their gathering into old age, as long as they are able. The old men we knew, including Old /Gaishay of Band 4, Old Gaú of Band 1, Old ≠Toma of Band 2, and Old Demi of Band 6, had given up hunting. Though they were well and by no means decrepit, they apparently felt themselves not strong enough to hunt. Most of the old women we knew, on the other hand, spry and wiry as they were, gathered regularly. There were only a few who did not. One was the childless old blind woman in Band 9, N/aoka [9.15], who never gathered. Di//khao, wife of Old /Gaishay in Band 4, and an old great-grandmother in Band 10, Old Khokove, took their ease and gathered only occasionally.

When a person becomes genuinely dependent because of age or disability or is temporarily sick, he is provided for by close relatives. His firewood would be brought, meat would be given, someone would gather for him. The foremost responsibility belongs to relatives in the following categories: spouses, parents, and offspring, parents-in-law and son- or daughter-in-law, and siblings. All the old men I mentioned above had wives or daughters to gather for them. The old blind woman had her sister. The other two old women had daughters. It is rare to find someone living in a band without relatives in one or another of the above-mentioned categories, but it sometimes happens. One old man, the one old bachelor we knew, /Gaishay, had no one in the above categories of close relatives; all were dead. He was living with cousins; they gathered for him.

The women form gathering parties together. The !Kung do not like to be alone. If the band is small, the women usually all troop out together. In large bands, they break up into smaller parties. Visitors gather with the women of the family they are visiting. The formation of the parties is not fixed by rule but customarily kin gather together, mothers and daughters, sisters, cousins. Close friends may also gather together. Congeniality or lack of it plays a part. One party was habitually formed by two sisters, !U and Di!ai, and their cousins, another pair of sisters, //Kushay and !Ungka, daughters of old Gaú. The other women of Band 1, N/aoka, Gao's first wife, and her two married daughters, //Khuga and N≠isa, formed another party. Gao's two wives, N/aoka and Di!ai, disliked each other intensely, though in silence, and avoided doing things together whenever they could. When Band 2 was present or visitors from other bands, N/aoka and her daughters often joined gathering parties with friends or relatives among them. Sometimes the two pairs of sisters joined other friends, but more often they gathered by themselves.

GATHERING EQUIPMENT AND METHODS

The equipment used in gathering consists merely of a digging stick and containers to carry the food gathered. Men make the digging sticks for themselves and their wives. They break or chop off a branch of a suitable size about three or four feet in length; seven-eighths of an inch to an inch was the usual diameter. Rhigozum brevispinosum O. Ktze. is the preferred wood if it is available, Story tells us; other strong woods may be used. In making a digging stick, the men heat the bark of the stick over a fire, peel it off, scrape the stick smooth, and sharpen it at one end, not to a point in the center of the stick as a pencil is sharpened, but in one slanting plane. After a woman has been given a stick, she regularly

A woman digs a root.

sharpens it herself using her husband's knife or axe. !Kung digging sticks are not weighted.

When a woman or a man digs a root, the usual method is to squat or to sit on the ground with both legs outspread or with one bent and the other outspread for balance. The person begins by loosening the ground with slashing strokes at the spot where the vine or stem emerges, both hands on the digging stick, right hand high if chopping toward the left, left hand high if chopping toward the right. When the top ground is loosened, the person chops at it with one hand on the stick, and scoops out loosened ground with the other hand till the root is revealed.

The roots of the different species and the individual roots within a species lie at varying depths. The little onionlike !gewu (#20) may be finger-deep, others are hand-deep, fingertip- to elbow-deep, or armpit-deep. The minutes of digging required to extract a root also vary. An armpit-deep root may require fifteen or twenty minutes of digging. The soils in which the roots grow are sandy but are not the loose sands—loose as the sands of a seashore—in which our trucks stuck so often; they are relatively firm. If a root is more than armpit-deep, or is too embedded in hard soil, the woman is likely to abandon it unless she has the boys or men with her to squirm on their bellies at the side of the

A woman finds a /ga root (#6).

Women laden with their children, the food they have gathered, and wood for their fires return in evening light.

hole and scratch and tug at the root till they pull it out. A woman uses her time more advantageously in finding roots easier to dig. Digging, then standing up, picking up one's load and probably a child, moving on to find another root, digging again—this activity carried on for hours in the heat is strenuous work.

The !Kung methods of carrying are very effective for their purposes. The !Kung are mainly shoulder carriers. The men take all the weight of their loads on their shoulders; the women distribute the weight between shoulders and hips. In both methods, the pillars of their bones are bearing the weight.

Men have a supply of leather bags of various sizes. Some are made of the whole hide of warthogs, others are cut from any hides and neatly and firmly sewn with thread made of sinew. Fashioning and sewing the bags is the work of men, as the leather from which the bags are made is the product of the hunt. Men hang the loaded bags from their shoulders or on carrying sticks, carried on their left shoulder, balanced front and back. An assagai on the right shoulder crossed behind and thrust under the carrying stick distributes the weight to both shoulders. The men hold the sticks and assagai in place with their hands. A man may also have a loaded carrying net hung from both shoulders across his back. The carrying nets are lined with grass or a piece of leather to keep small objects like nuts or berries from falling through.

Women carry their loads in the pouches of their karosses. A kaross is the whole hide of a gemsbok. The forelegs are used as ties and are fastened firmly over one shoulder. A strong thong tied tightly around the waist allows the kaross to be pulled up a little over the thong to form a pouch. The women carry all their belongings, including all their ostrich eggshells, in these pouches when they move, and they put into them the heavy loads of food they collect on their gathering trips. A load is distributed as evenly as possible in the pouch, and the weight is shared between the woman's shoulder and her hips. She has both arms free for gathering and for lifting and carrying her child.

Richard Lee has made fascinating calculations of the weights !Kung women carry and the distances they travel. He says of the women he observed that, on each day of gathering, they walk from two to twelve miles round trip and that they carry 15 to 33 pounds of vegetable foods on the return trip. When the group moves from one area to another to hunt and gather, or to visit relatives or friends, a woman carries all her belongings, which Lee calculates weigh from 11 to 22 pounds (5 to 10 kg). He summarizes as follows: "Subsistence work, visits, and group moves require an adult woman to walk about 2,400 km (1,500 miles) during the course of an annual round. For at least half this distance she carries substantial burdens of food, water, or material goods."[6]

Lee goes on to say that the major burden the woman carries has yet to be mentioned—one or two children. He gives the average weights of forty !Kung children as follows:[7]

Age	Average Pounds	Age	Average Pounds
0–1	13.2	4–5	29.6
1–2	19.4	5–6	32.3
2–3	25.6	6–7	33.8
3–4	27.4	7–8	38.7

!Kung women nurse their children till the children are about four and have the children with them wherever they go. A woman constantly

6. Richard Lee, "Population Growth and the Beginnings of Sedentary Life among the !Kung Bushmen," *Population Growth: Anthropological Implications*, ed. B. Spooner (Philadelphia, University of Pennsylvania Press, 1972), p. 331.
7. Ibid., p. 333.

carries a baby from birth to two years of age. She carries a three-year-old most of the time. A four-year-old child may walk part of the way on a gathering trip, or when traveling he may be carried by his father. By the time a child is four, his mother may have another baby to carry. Lee has calculated that all in all during the child's first four years, his mother carries him about 4,900 miles.[8]

SOME OBSERVATIONS ON GATHERING

In the Kalahari some species of berries and roots are widely distributed, and hunters and travelers may come unexpectedly upon them, or upon a few melons or a truffle or two as they move over the land. But this is the extent of casual, unplanned gathering. People do not wander about hopefully searching for food. The plant foods that sustain their lives grow in certain productive areas in patches, clumps, communities, and groves, large and small. The !Kung know all the productive areas in their territories, and they know all about the plant foods within them, where the plants grow, when they ripen, what quantities to expect. The people plan their lives around those foods.

No territory has every kind of plant food in it, but each has some combination of the foods that sustain the people through the year. The productive areas may be miles apart, and they are at varying distances from the waterhole, but some of the plant foods must be near enough to the permanent waterholes for the people to sustain themselves in the dry season without dying of either hunger or thirst. Other productive areas in a band's territory may be more distant and may be reached only in the season of the rains, and for a time after, when water has collected in temporary waterholes, pans, hollow tree trunks, allowing people to move from their permanent waterholes.

The territory of Band 1 includes two vicinities—the vicinities of Gautscha Pan and Nama Pan, which is twenty miles to the south of Gautscha. I include the tsi communities south of Nama Pan within the Nama Pan vicinity. Band 1 gathers in the vicinity of Nama during the rains and after, while water still stands in the pan and small waterholes. In the dry season, this band is based at the permanent waterhole at Gautscha and gathers in that vicinity.

The pattern of gathering differs in the two vicinities. The patches and clumps of plants and trees appear to be somewhat more scattered

8. Ibid., p. 331.

in the Nama vicinity than in the Gautscha vicinity. In the Nama vicinity, when water is available the band breaks up. One family will go to a place where *sha* (#22) grows and will live beside the sha patch for a while. Another family will be at a place where something else grows. They move from one patch to another. In April when the tsi ripens, they all gather tsi. There is no water in the tsi area and people must carry water with them. They return with loads of tsi to Nama Pan, and so travel back and forth till the tsi crop is gathered and eaten.

In the dry season, when Band 1 is at the Gautscha waterhole, they depend mainly on two large fertile areas in which a number of different species of roots and berries grow. The areas are of major importance. Most of the plant foods of Band 1 gathered in the dry season come from them. One of the two fertile areas I speak of is four miles to the south of Gautscha along the trail to Nama Pan. The other area of major importance is six miles to the northeast of Gautscha Pan in the direction of Gura. These remarkable areas produce several different species of roots and berries and supply the dry season staples. Both produce more or less the same species but in different proportions. The Nama Trail area, for instance, has more /ga (#6) than the other; the northeast area has more n≠wara (#21) than the other. (A veld fire had passed over the northeast area and burned many of the dry leaves and stems that show where the n≠wara roots are. People could not find them that year in their usual quantities.)

The two areas produce the following species. Those marked with a dagger are of the utmost importance in the diet; they provide the larger part of the plant food nourishment. The others are important also but provide less in quantity (see the list of plant foods for descriptions):

Roots	Berries
/ama #4	/ore #27
!ama #5	†n≠a #30
†/ga #6	
!gwara!ai #9	
!gau #11	
≠go #14	
≠dau #15	
!xwa #16	
†n≠wara #21	
†/dobi #24	

In addition to the regular gathering in the two main fertile areas, the women gathered at other places where there were relatively small patches of plant food. One was a patch of n≠a berries (#30), another a patch of n/n berries (#28), another a patch of /ore berries (#27), another a patch of !gewu (#20). From somewhere leaves of !gwashe (#48) and //gwi_ja (#49) were brought two or three times. The baobab fruit, ≠m (#34), was eventually all picked up. Whenever people walked, they might come upon a glistening morsel of gum on a tree branch and pop it into their mouths.

Other foods eaten by Band 1 during the dry season were brought by visitors or hunters from outside Band 1's territory and were negligible in quantity. Visitors from the north brought some mangetti nuts, _//k'a (#32). Women of Band 1 were given about twenty nuts each as a present. Twice visitors brought morula nuts, _gai (#33). A few n!ana fruits (#40) were brought. Hunters on one occasion brought heart of palm, !hani (#39), and a few palm nuts. Early in November we made a trip in our trucks to the mangetti grove south of Samangaigai and brought back an unprecedented quantity of mangetti nuts to Band 1. Normally, without being taken in trucks, the people could not have gone to the mangetti grove in that season. They could not carry enough water to make the trip on foot, there and back. The nuts were a great boon to the people, but they interrupted our observation on normal gathering.

We have some observations, however, on normal dry season gathering in 1952 for !U and Di!ai, //Kushay and !Ungka. I take the first twenty-five days of September as a sample. Only two events slightly modified the gathering during those days. //Kushay and /Qui and their children were away for several days during this period, visiting at Gura with Band 8. !U gave birth to her daughter, !Ungka Norna, on September 4, and remained in the encampment for five consecutive days. She explained that it was for the sake of the baby, who she thought was ailing slightly. Di!ai gathered for her.

In the period of twenty-five days, Di!ai gathered during sixteen days, remained in the encampment nine days; !Ungka gathered fifteen days, remained in the encampment ten days; !U gathered twelve days, remained in the encampment thirteen days; //Kushay gathered seven out of the thirteen days she was present. Leaving out //Kushay because of her absence, the average of the other three women for the period is about 57 percent of days spent gathering as against 43 percent of days spent in the encampment.

A day of dry season gathering is arduous in the Gautscha vicinity. The walk to the Nama Trail area and back is eight miles, to the other area and back is twelve miles. Within the area the women zigzag around another mile or so looking for roots to dig. On one September day which we considered typical for that time of year, Di!ai and !Ungka gathered in the Nama Trail area. They set out while the morning was still cool and walked briskly for fifty minutes. They each began by picking about two pounds of n≠a berries from a clump of bushes near the area, eating berries as they picked. Then they went to the part of the area where they knew they could find /ga, n≠wara, /dobi, and !ama. That day Di!ai found thirty-four roots; thirty-four times she sat down, dug a root, stood up, picked up her son, walked on to look for another root to dig. She dug seventeen /ga, nine /dobi, two n≠wara, four !ama, one /ama, one !gau. Of those roots, one /ga was too immature to take; two /ga, four /dobi, and the /ama were thrown away after they were dug because they were too old, bitter, and pithy. One n≠wara and two /dobi were so deep in the ground Di!ai abandoned them in the holes after struggling with each of them for ten or fifteen minutes. This left twenty-three roots for Di!ai to carry back to the encampment, fourteen /ga, three /dobi, one n≠wara, one !gau, and four !ama.

Shortly after two o'clock, the women declared themselves ready to return. They had gathered all they could carry or all they wanted to carry. !Ungka had dug about the same number of roots as Di!ai. !Ungka had found less /ga but she had three n≠wara and three /dobi. She had found also a !xwa and a !gwara!ai. The women ate the !xwa and had a drink of water from their ostrich eggshells while they rested for about twenty minutes in the shade of a little thorn tree before starting back to Gautscha. (They had rested before and had a drink of water at noon-time.) After resting, they packed their loads into the pouches of their karosses, distributing the weight as evenly as they could around their bodies, tying the kaross, as usual, over the shoulder. The loads of roots and berries weighed about twenty pounds. Di!ai had her two-year-old son to carry also. Her heavy kaross, her ostrich eggshell, and the axe she carried to sharpen her digging stick were added weight. We figured that this thin little woman, four feet, ten inches in height, was carrying about fifty pounds on the return trip. In the oppressive heat of the latter half of the afternoon, the women were an hour and a half trudging the four miles back to Gautscha.

The two women had eleven people to feed that evening. They decided to pool their food and to plan supper for two days. That evening they cooked the roots they liked best, the n≠wara, /dobi, !ama, the !gwara!ai and !gau, leaving the dry berries and the fibrous /ga for the next day.

N≠wara and /dobi are cooked in the same way. /Dobi run from about eight to ten inches in length, three to four inches in diameter. N≠wara run somewhat larger, twelve inches long, four or five inches in diameter. Before these tubers are cooked, they are split in half, the center portion of the pulp, which is bitter, is scraped out and thrown away. A rim of pulp, an inch thick or more, adheres to the brown outside skin; this is the edible pulp. The halves of the tubers are roasted on the top of coals. When cooked, the tubers are cut into portions, as we would cut a Kranshaw melon, and the portions distributed to those who are eating together. The pulp is scraped off the rind and eaten. It is stringy even after long cooking and must be chewed a long time, but the !Kung consider both n≠wara and /dobi satisfying, desirable foods. The other roots are baked whole in hot ashes and coals. Any of the roots may be peeled and mashed in a mortar; frequently different roots are mashed together; berries may be mixed with them.

Old Gaú had caught a big lizard. He had boiled it for hours in a pot till it was a mush of bones and soft flesh. Everybody had a few spoonsful of this delicacy. The supper was considered a good one.

Such a day represents an optimum of dry season gathering in the Gautscha vicinity. Di!ai had only one child to carry; she might have had two. As the season advances and the people have consumed much of the year's plant yield, the roots become scarce and hard to find; more are dry and bitter. The women gather less in a working day. At the end of the dry season (December), while the people are still tethered to their permanent waterholes and the new growth of the vegetation is not yet available, the roots may become critically scarce. The !Kung we knew had not experienced situations in which people actually starved, according to their accounts to us, but they feel threatened in this season and they talk about starvation with dread. They call the season the time of starvation.

PLANT FOODS AVAILABLE TO BAND 1

A list of sixty-five plant foods is given below. These are the foods that were available to Band 1 while we were in the field in 1952–53.

The botanical identifications of the plant foods are taken from Robert Story except for five which Story did not have and which Richard Lee kindly gave me at a later date. The five are numbers 11, 12, 15, 27, and 48 and are marked with Lee's name. I wish to express my gratitude to both Story and Lee for their help and for their permission to use the identifications. Story was a member of our expeditions in 1955 and 1958. His publication, *Some Plants Used by the Bushmen in Obtaining Food and Water,* reports the collection made in 1955. Most of the identifications from Story are taken from that publication. Twelve come through personal communication and are from his later collections. Lee's collection was made in the Dobe area during the years 1963–1965. The correlation of our list with the lists of Story and Lee was made through the !Kung name for the plant. We observed a few more plant foods than I can enter on my list; I have had to omit them because I am uncertain of their identification.

The foods are listed according to the part of the plant that is eaten: underground part (root, tuber, etc.), berry, nut, fruit, leaf, gum. Within each category, the species are listed with the scientific names in alphabetical order. The numbers assigned are consecutive from beginning to end. However, if a plant has two edible parts, such as a root and a fruit, it will appear in two categories. In this case, the number first assigned to it is retained and repeated when the plant appears a second time.

The foods marked with asterisks (*) are the foods which were gathered in the dry season by Band 1; the double asterisk (**) marks the most important of those foods.

Plant Foods with Edible Parts Underground

The underground parts are roots, tubers, bulbs, storage organs, corms, underground stems, and one root parasite (#17). In referring to the underground parts in general, I shall call them "roots" in the sense in which we use the word when we say "root vegetables."

The roots are of the utmost importance to the !Kung diet in the Nyae Nyae area. Whereas many items of food, especially the fruits, are available only in the season of the rains and for a time after, the underground parts remain preserved in the ground throughout the year. In the territory of Band 1, they are the mainstay during the winter—the dry season.

In shape and size, the roots bear some resemblance to our common root vegetables or to our melons or fruits. Some look like large turnips, some resemble very big sweet potatoes in shape, others are like potatoes, or onions, or melons, or "flattened apples," as Story describes one. Many have hard, rough outside skins. The "water bottle," !xwa (#16), is very juicy, but many others are fibrous or woody. Most that I tasted were fibrous and lacking in flavor compared to our root vegetables.

Most of the roots must be cooked; a few may be eaten raw. They are usually baked covered with hot coals and ashes or roasted on top of a bed of coals.

!Kung Name	Botanical Name
1. n//n	*Bauhinia esculenta* Burch. The tuber of tsi (see section on seeds and nuts); tubers edible when sappy and young, boiled or roasted on coals; the old tubers, which may grow to thirty pounds, are too tough to eat; these tubers even when young are not a favorite food and are not gathered regularly.
2. //ore	*Brachystelma* sp. The tuber is eaten.
3. n!wi	*Ceropegia* sp. near *C. lugardae* N.E. Br. The above-ground parts of the *Ceropegia* are twining vines; the roots are edible, firm, not fibrous; found near Nama Pan.
4. /ama	**Ceropegia pygmaea* Schinz The tuber, the size of an apple, is edible, resembles !ama (#5); found near Nama Pan and Gautscha.
5. !ama	**Ceropegia tentaculata* N.E. Br. Tuber the size and shape of a flattened apple; grows near the surface of the ground; the !Kung say it is a favorite food because "it has a pleasant texture and a good taste"; it is not plentiful; found near Nama Pan and Gautscha.
6. /ga	***Coccinia rehmannii* Cogn. A climbing vine, tubers and fruit edible; tubers of varying size according to age, those dug near Gautscha were 6 to 12 inches long; the tubers have a rough skin; are juicy but fibrous and tasteless; relatively plentiful in the vicinity of Gautscha, an important food

!Kung Name		Botanical Name

in that area; one /ga serves two or three
people.

7. ⁻k'idwa

Coccinia sessilifolia (Sond.) Cogn.
   Vine and tuber similar to #6; tuber and
fruit edible; above-ground parts die back in
winter making tuber hard to find; grows in
vicinity of Nama Pan.

8. ≠gun//a

Corallocarpus bainesii (Hook. f.) A. Meeuse

9. !gwara!ai

Corallocarpus welwitschii (Naud.) Hook. f.
   Vine creeps over shrubs and low trees;
rootstock and fruit edible; rootstock grows
near surface of ground; easily pulled up;
gathered in vicinity of Gautscha; not common.

10. huru

Cucumis sp.
   The vine runs along the ground; the storage organ the size of a potato or smaller may
be eaten raw or cooked; is a source of liquid;
gathered in vicinity of Gautscha.

11. !gau   [Lee]

Cyperus sp. near *C. fulgens*
   A sedge with small onionlike bulbs gathered in the vicinity of Gautscha.

12. !goro   [Lee]

Dipcadi sp.
   Small onionlike bulbs gathered in rainy
season in the vicinity of Nama Pan.

13. n!umshe

Dipcadi sp.
   Small onionlike bulbs; the bulbs grow
near the surface but the above-ground parts
die back in winter and the bulbs are difficult
to find; gathered near Nama Pan.

14. ≠go

Eulophia sp. nearest *E. pillansii* Bol.
   A stemless plant with grasslike leaves;
corms the size of golf balls grow near the
surface; gathered in the vicinity of Gautscha
and Nama Pan; a favorite food but not plentiful; corms may be roasted or pounded raw
in mortar; sometimes eaten mixed with n≠a
berries.

15. ≠dau   [Lee]

Eulophia sp.
   Corms the size of small potatoes are juicy.
(Some people in Band 12 said they knew a
place where a lot of ≠dau grew and could

!Kung Name	Botanical Name

stay there several days without water, depending on ≠dau for liquid.)

16. !xwa

Fockea sp.

A very juicy storage organ which may be a foot in length, 5 or 6 inches in diameter, popularly called the "water bottle"; it is widespread and is an extremely important source of liquid for hunters, gatherers, and travelers. If they are in an area where !xwa are relatively numerous, people can live on them without water for a time; they are eaten raw, usually on the spot where they are dug; sometimes mixed with other plant foods; one mixture is cooked !ama, cooked !gwara!ai, raw ≠dau, raw !xwa.

17. hokxam

Hydnora sp.

The fruit of a root parasite that grows on *Combretum hereroense* Schinz; fruit resembles coconut, brown shell, white, watery pulp, delicate pleasant taste; not common; gathered near Gautscha.

18. //haru

Lapeyrousia cyanescens Bak.

Corm resembles a Jerusalem artichoke.

19. //geit'ama

Lapeyrousia odoratissima Bak.

Corm is juicy; eaten for water content.

20. !gewu

Mariscus congestus C.B. Cl.

A sedge; the stalks and leaves die back in winter; !Kung gatherers know in general where patches of the plant grow and dig around till they find the bulbs. They also find them by noticing that guinea fowl have been scratching at them; the bulbs, half an inch in diameter, are near surface; usually roasted in hot ashes; may be eaten raw.

21. n≠wara

**Trochomeria debilis* (Sond.) Hook. f.

Large storage organ (or tuber?) up to 8 to 12 inches long, 4 to 5 inches in diameter with hard brown skin and a long stem; grows armpit-deep; is difficult to dig. A very important food in the Gautscha vicinity.

22. sha

Vigna dinteri Harms

A twining vine; potato-sized swellings on

!Kung Name	Botanical Name

a long (2-foot) root are edible raw or cooked; they are soft; children and old people with poor teeth may eat them; an important and favorite food; it is gathered in the vicinity of Nama Pan. In 1953 the whole yield of sha had been eaten before the dry season set in.

23. tshũ   *Walleria nutans* Kirk

A small plant with grasslike leaves has a firm round storage organ about the size of a golf ball which grows near the surface of the ground; gathered by Band 1 in the direction of Gura and in the vicinity of Nama Pan.

24. /dobi   **unidentified

A climbing vine; a fibrous watery underground storage organ, resembles a large turnip in size and shape, has rough-looking but thin brown skin; grows elbow-deep and deeper. The tubers become woody and bitter when old and are thrown away; cooked like n≠wara (#21), split, on top of coals. An important food during the dry season in the Gautscha vicinity.

Berries

The berries listed below, except za (#25), are second only to roots in their importance in the daily diet of Band 1 in the dry season. There are many species. Story records six species of *Grewia* berries, Lee records nine. We remained in some confusion about the *Grewias* and only sorted out four species, though we doubtless saw more without making careful distinction among them. Two other species (not among the *Grewias*) are the fairly common za (#25), and n≠a (#30). N≠a is especially important in the vicinity of Gautscha. Za is not an important food. Some of the *Grewias* and n≠a are staples and are eaten practically every day.

Berries have advantageous and disadvantageous aspects. They are widespread and are an important food to hunters and travelers who come upon them and can gather them in passing. The *Grewias* are shrubs; n≠a is a small tree. The berries are visible and quickly picked from the branch by fingers deftly reaching in among the thorns; or the berries are knocked from the branches with digging sticks and are picked up from the ground. Still more important is the fact that the berries stay on the branch and are available in the dry season. Their disadvantageous aspects are that they are small, none more than half an inch in diameter, many less; they all have large stones, harsh skins—more roughage than nourishing pulp. Nevertheless, they assuage hunger and are available when more satisfying, nourishing food is lacking. They are eaten raw, stone and all, by people on the move. In the encampment they may be eaten that way but often they are soaked in water and pounded in a mortar; sometimes they are mixed with other plant foods. In any case, they are eaten stones and all.

!Kung Name		Botanical Name
25. za		*Boscia albitrunca* (Burch.) Gilg and Benedict
26. kamako		*Grewia* sp. near *Grewia bicolor* Juss.
27. /ore	[Lee]	**Grewia flavescens* Juss.
28. n/n		*Grewia flava* DC.
29. !gwa		*Grewia retinervis* Burret
30. n≠a		**Ziziphus mucronata* Willd.

Seeds and Nuts

1. tsi   *Bauhinia esculenta* Burch.

Tsi is the name of the seed of this plant. (N//n, see #1, is the name of the tuber.) The plant grows in open grassland in communities sometimes miles across. Two large communities lie between Nama Pan and /Gam. The plant is extremely localized; these are the only communities of it in the Nyae Nyae area. Perennial tubers produce annual vines up to 18 or 20 feet long that run along the ground. The round seeds, about ⅝ inch in diameter, are borne in pods. They are like nuts with a dark brown, very hard seed coat and a smooth white two-lobed kernel somewhat softer in texture than a hazel nut. They may be eaten raw, though the shells are hard to crack in that state. They are usually cooked in moderately hot coals and ashes. If put directly in very hot coals they explode. The baked or raw kernels may be eaten whole, or may be mixed with water and boiled lightly to make a porridge. Tsi is a delicious, nour-

!Kung Name   *Botanical Name*

ishing, satisfying food, rich in protein and oils
—a most desired and important food.

Although the tsi seeds can be kept for
years and remain edible, they function as a
seasonal food for the !Kung: the whole yield
is eaten in a matter of weeks. Tsi ripens in
April. All the !Kung who have rights to gather
it (Band 1 has such rights), plus relatives and
guests from other places, move to the area.
There is no water at the tsi communities.
People base themselves at Nama Pan, which
still has water after the rains, go from there
to gather, return to the water with loads of
tsi, feast upon it (you hear them cracking tsi
all night long), go again to gather, and so on
till the tsi is all eaten up, except obviously
for some that escape the gatherers' eyes and
grow to keep the communities alive.

Tsi, more than any other plant, is used in
rituals, notably the marriage rite, the first
menstruation rite, a child's first haircut, and
the *tshoa* rite.

31. ≠n≠dwa   *Bauhinia macrantha* Oliv.

Seeds from the pods are roasted in ashes,
peeled, and pounded into a meal; not common in the Nyae Nyae area; not an important
food.

32. _//k'a   **Ricinodendron rautanenii* Schinz

In South West Africa the tree, fruit, and
nut are popularly called *mangetti,* a corruption of a Herero word *omungeto;* in Botswana, the Tswana word *mongongo* is commonly used.

The nuts are a delicious, satisfying food,
highly nutritious in protein and oils, and,
along with tsi, the most desired of the plant
foods.

Mangetti trees grow in large groves on
enormous dunes of white sand. Their approximate location in the Nyae Nyae area is
indicated on Map 2. In addition to the six
above-mentioned groves, we learned that
there are others south of Tsho/ana along
the Botswana border. Nutritious, delicious,

satisfying as they are, mangettis are not a staple food in the Nyae Nyae area. Their importance is limited because they are not easily enough available. In the Nyae Nyae area not all the bands have mangettis. Band 1, for instance, has no mangettis in its territory. The bands that do have mangettis available have the eternal problem of water. The mangetti groves are all at a considerable distance from any of the permanent waterholes. All the groves are waterless except for the few gallons of rainwater that collect in the hollows of trees during the season of the rains. This rainwater supplements the amount of water people can carry with them in ostrich eggshells. Gatherers go to the groves, stay for a time, return to the waterhole with all the nuts they can manage to carry. In the dry season the trips are either impossible or so difficult that the rewards do not balance the expenditure of time and energy. People do better to dig their roots and pick their berries nearer their waterholes, and thousands of mangetti nuts lie on the ground ungathered.

The big flat-crowned mangetti trees have soft, smooth, light gray bark. The !Kung know the botanical fact that the trees are male and female, and that only the female trees bear. fruit. Mangetti trees bear abundantly. The fruits, the size of plums, fall to the ground and lie by the thousands under the trees. A tough outside skin protects them well, and fruits of previous years mingle with the fall of the current year. The nuts inside the fruits remain edible for more than one year, probably for several years, like tsi.

The gatherers pick up the fruit from the ground. They bend over, take the fruits they can reach, walk a few steps, bend again. People sometime ease their backs by picking up the fruits with their toes, lifting their foot toward the back, taking the fruit from their toes with their fingers. !Kung squatting fac-

!Kung Name   Botanical Name

ets, flexible joints, and excellent balance make this feat feasible for them; it even looks easy.[9]

Mangettis are eaten in a variety of ways, raw or cooked. The tough outside skin of the fruit surrounds a thin layer of pleasant-tasting pulp, crumbly when dry. Inside is the nut with a delicious white kernel in a shell that in some ways resembles an almond. The pulp may be gnawed off raw. The nuts may be boiled or baked in hot coals and ashes. In any case, the nuts must be cracked, and cracking them is an art. The shells are exceedingly hard. A novice bludgeons them into an inedible mess of shell fragments and flattened kernel. The !Kung crack them with anvil and hammer, either of stone or wood, deftly whacking them at exactly the right spot. One of my most vivid memories of a mangetti grove is the sound of cracking late into the night, beginning again at dawn.

On one occasion, for the sake of giving pleasure to the !Kung, we took a group in trucks, with a good supply of water, to the grove southeast of Châssis, a round trip from Gautscha of about seventy miles. A trip of this distance would not ordinarily have been attempted. People gathered and ate nuts for three days in the beautiful grove. In the end, they gathered more than they ate, and we returned with our truck laden with hundreds of pounds of nuts, which were shared with the people who had remained at Gautscha. This extra food interrupted our observations of Band 1's regular gathering for some days.

33. ‗gai   *Sclerocarya caffra* Sond.

Popularly called *morula;* not common in

9. The process of establishing squatting facets begins in childhood. Through continuous squatting, the posterior edge of the bone at the top of the tibia and that of the lower part of the femur, where the bones articulate at the knee joint, become eroded and form a sloping bevel—the squatting facet. People who have squatting facets can flex their legs more completely than people who do not have them. The !Kung squat with their buttocks against their heels and their weight on their heels. They often sit with their weight on the ground, their buttocks touching their heels and their knees up to their shoulders or behind their ears.

!Kung Name   Botanical Name

the Nyae Nyae area; both the flesh and seed
of the fruit are eaten; both are delicious.

Fruits

Some of the fruits listed below are found in one part of the Nyae Nyae
area, some in another. None is widespread and none is abundant in any
locality, as mangettis and tsi are abundant in their localities. The fruits
are a supplement to the diet of the people who are present to gather
them, contributing vitamins and refreshment, although they do not contribute much in quantity. They are perishable and are eaten only in the
season of their ripening.

Our knowledge of the distribution of the fruits is very limited. I list
those we observed Band 1 eating and say where the fruits come from if I
have that information, but I do not mean to imply that the fruits are
exclusive to those localities mentioned; they may be found elsewhere
as well.

The fruits we observed being eaten in the vicinity of Gautscha were
the fruits of three baobab trees, the little fruits of the relatively plentiful
/ga (#6), the less plentiful /horo (#36), !gwara!ai (#9), //goie (#45),
and a few dza dza (#44). In the vicinity of Nama Pan where Band 1 also
gathered, several fruits were available, among them ⁻k'idwa (#7),
!gwara!ai (#9), and n!o⁻shu (#41), which was relatively plentiful in that
vicinity. We observed the following additional fruits brought to Gautscha
from other vicinities. Visitors from Samangaigai brought n!ana (#40),
n!o (#43), and Annona Stenophylla subsp. nana (#35), each on one
occasion, as far as we know. Hunters twice brought palm nuts (!hani,
#39) and once the heart of a young palm. We saw mai (#37) and !goro-
shay (!oroshay?) (#42), when we were traveling in the northern part of
the Nyae Nyae area, also n!o (#43), mentioned before.

34. ≠m   **Adansonia digitata L.
                            The baobab tree; three trees grow at Gaut-
                            scha, and baobabs are found also at Gura and
                            Tsumkwe. The oblong fruits are 6 inches or
                            more in length, 3 or 4 inches in diameter. The
                            hard shell, which is covered with a green
                            pubescence, contains the seeds and a pithy
                            whitish substance that has the taste of cream

!Kung Name   *Botanical Name*

of tartar. The shells are sometimes used as water containers after being cleaned out. The fruit is gathered when it falls to the ground, but people also keep suitably sized sticks at the foot of the trees to throw at the fruits. The Gautscha people did not like baobab fruit very much and, if enough of something else were on hand, would leave it ungathered. However, the fruit keeps well, and by the end of the dry season it would all be eaten. The pithy substance is pounded to a meal mixed with water and made into a porridge. The seeds are roasted in ashes and pounded to a meal in a mortar or between stones. The pithy substance and seeds may be pounded together. Robert Story says the shoots from germinating seeds, young roots, and young leaves may be eaten. An additional contribution the baobab makes to the diet is a large edible caterpillar that feeds on its leaves. The trunks sometimes have hollows that catch rainwater.

35. —   *Annona Stenophylla* Engl. and Diels subsp. *nana*
A tree; the fruits, the size of large plums or small apples, are eaten raw or cooked; observed in the Samangaigai area.

6. /ga   *Coccinia rehmannii* Cogn.
A climbing vine; the fruits are about ¾ inch long; tubers also eaten; relatively plentiful in Gautscha area.

7. ⁻k'idwa   *Coccinia sessilifolia* (Sond.) Cogn.
A vine; fruits about 3 inches long, may be eaten raw or cooked; tuber also eaten.

36. /horo   *Corallocarpus sphaerocarpus* Cogn.
A creeping vine; fruits ½ inch in size; leaves also eaten.

9. !gwara!ai   *Corallocarpus welwitschii* (Naud.) Hook. f.
A creeping vine; fruit and rootstock eaten.

37. mai   *Dichapetalum cymosum* (Hook.) Engl.
The fruits of the plant resemble loquats with one or two big seeds; the pulp may be eaten, but the seeds and skin are poisonous;

!Kung Name	Botanical Name

the leaves of the plant are also poisonous—cattle and sheep sometimes eat them and die; grows in the vicinity of Tsho/ana and elsewhere.

38. tshaha

Diospyros chamaethamnus Mildbr.
Fruit the size of a golf ball is juicy and sweet.

39. !hani

Hyphaene ventricosa Kirk
Fruit of this palm is as big as a small orange, has a hard skin; the pulp is gnawed off it and off the stone to which it adheres or, if dry, is scraped off and pounded to a meal; the palm is rare in the Nyae Nyae area.

One day two young hunters returned without meat but with a load of fruit from a mature palm and the heart of a young palm. We do not know whether the heart was from the !hani or from its dwarf variant, which Lee tells us is lexically distinguished by the !Kung as //gun. The hunters had found the palms twenty miles north of Gautscha. They peeled off the bark, cooked the heart in a pit for a day covered with ash and sand, with a fire burning on top. They then sliced the heart and distributed it as if it were meat. The portions were divided and divided till every one had about a fist-sized lump, which was eaten in a twinkling. I thought of the time contrast—the long growth of even a young palm, the long chopping with the adzes, the long return walk, the long cooking, and the quick eating.

40. n!ana

Parinari capensis Harv.
Fruit the size of small plum resembling mai; has a large seed which is not eaten.

41. n!o⁻shu

Pentarrhinum insipidum E. Mey.
Young fruits green in color, about 3 inches long; may be eaten raw or cooked; old fruits are woody; leaves are eaten also; many n!o⁻shu near Nama Pan, relatively widespread.

42. !goroshay

Salacia luebbertii Loes. ex.descr.
Red fruit the size of a golf ball.

!Kung Name	Botanical Name

33. _gai

Sclerocarya caffra Sond.

Popularly called *morula;* the yellow fruits the size of a plum have a pleasant flavor; stones are cracked, kernels eaten.

43. n!o

Strychnos cocculoides Bak.

Fruit 4 inches in diameter, green when immature, brown when ripe in color; pleasant flavor with a hard outer skin.

44. dza dza

Typha latifolia L. subsp. *capensis* Rohrb.

A bull-rush; top part of male flower is eaten, and rhizome may be eaten, but the 'Gautscha people do not like either. They say the children eat the fruits of the few dza dza that grow by Gautscha Pan.

45. //goie

Ximenia caffra Sond.

The edible fruit, about 6 inches long, is pleasantly sour. When overripe it becomes wrinkled and mellow and resembles a prune in flavor. Seeds are charred in coals, pounded to a black powder, mixed with cooked fat, and rubbed on a person as a medicine for pains. Many people had charred //goie.

Melons

46. tsha

Citrullus naudinianus (Sond.) Hook. f.

Popularly called gemsbok cucumber; may be found here and there during the rains, but does not abound.

47. _tama

Citrullus vulgaris Schrad.

Popularly called *tsama* melon; a succulent melon up to 6 inches in diameter related to the watermelons but not as sweet; a refreshing food.

In the central Kalahari we observed tsama melons growing in vast communities. The /Gwi whom we observed lived for a month without any water but tsama melons. In the Nyae Nyae, tsamas do not abound. They occur here and there, not in large communities.

!Kung Name		Botanical Name

Leaves

36. /horo

Corallocarpus sphaerocarpus Cogn.
Stems and leaves are boiled (as well as fruit); they look like spinach.

48. !gwashe   [Lee]

*Dipcadi glaucum (Burch.) Baker
The leaves, which resemble tulip leaves, are eaten raw; they remain edible well into the dry season; observed them eaten in November.

41. n!o⁻shu

Pentarrhinum insipidum E. Mey.
Leaves, usually pounded to a pulp, are eaten raw.

49. //gwi_ja

*Talinum arnotii Hook. f.
In the season of the rains, leaves of this 8- to 10-inch plant, which look like spinach, are eaten raw, pounded in a mortar to a paste. Boys dug the tubers, which are up to a pound in weight, and made toy trucks of them in imitation of our trucks, complete with axles and wheels, steering wheels and headlights.

Gum

A number of trees exude drops of edible gum. The !Kung do not purposefully set out to gather gum, but it is a common sight to see someone, in passing, walk up to a tree and pick a morsel off. The best time to find gum, people say, is in the late afternoon when the drops glisten in the slanting sunlight. The gums do not add much in quantity to the !Kung diet but are enjoyed as a delicacy. Story reports the following species of trees that produce gum. The !Kung have a name for each tree but one word for all gum; it is gum, pronounced so that it rhymes with the German word dumm.

50.   Acacia detinens Burch.
51.   A. dulcis Marl. and Engl.
52.   A. fleckii Schinz
53.   A. giraffae Burch.

!Kung Name	Botanical Name
54.	A. heteracantha Burch.
55.	A. uncinata Engl.
56.	Burkea africana Hook.
57.	Combretum apiculatum Sond.
58.	C. coriaceum Schinz
59.	C. imberbe Wawra
60.	Terminalia sericea Burch.

The last five produce gum only rarely; the acacias are the more regular producers.

Pods from Two Leguminous Trees

These trees are found in the vicinity of Samangaigai. The leaves or seeds were brought to Gautscha by visitors. Members of Band 1 were observed eating them there on two or three occasions. They spoke also of getting them from friends or relatives when they visited in the northern part of the Nyae Nyae area.

61. tshow   *Dialium englerianum* Henriques

62. /gwi   *Guibourtia coleosperma* (Benth.) J. Léonard
     Popularly called *shiva*, presumably a Bantu name. This tree grows in great numbers in some places further north. For the !Kung in Tshimbaranda in southern Angola, it is a major source of food.

Sources of Water

The following plants are important as sources of water rather than for food value. The pulp is not eaten; liquid from it is squeezed into the hand and channeled into the mouth.

63. n!oru   *Ipomoea verbascoidea* Choisy
     Storage organ as large as a football.

64. gwe   *Raphionacme burkei* N.E. Br.
     The storage organ is about 5 pounds in weight, 6 inches in diameter; the pulp is shaved off in thin layers with a split stick. When squeezed, juice pours from it.
     The plant has wide distribution in the Kala-

!Kung Name	*Botanical Name*

hari; it is found but is not common in the Nyae Nyae area. In the !Kõ, //Gana, /Gwi, and Nharo languages, it is known as *bi*.

65. !hwi   *Sansevieria scabrifolia* Dinter

The juicy rhizome of the plant, Story says, is a source of water. We did not observe the !Kung drinking its juice, however, because they had plenty of water in the Gautscha waterhole. They use the fibers of the long, upright leaves of this plant to make cord.

4 Animal Foods and Hunting

ANIMAL FOODS

The animals of the Nyae Nyae area, taking the word "animals" in its widest meaning, supplied the !Kung with skins for all the garments of men, women, and children, skins for bags, bone and horn for several artifacts, sinew for bowstrings and other cord, cocoons for rattles, ostrich eggshells for water containers, and about 25 percent of their food (25 percent is Richard Lee's calculation).[1]

The literature on Bushmen reports that Bushmen have been observed to gorge themselves till they could hardly walk when plenty of meat was available. This we never observed. We have seen the Nyae Nyae !Kung eat hearty meals of meat when they have been long without, but not what we considered an abnormal amount. They cut meat in strips and hang the strips on branches to dry and can keep it for some time.[2] It is not uncommon for them to eat quite sparingly and to save bits for a coming journey or against a future day of hunger.

Charles Handley, collecting small mammals for the Smithsonian Institution and working with !Kung informants, found that they recognized and had !Kung names for fifty-eight species of mammals and sixty-four species of birds. The !Kung, for instance, have names for seven species of cats and for brown hyena, spotted hyena, and aardwolf, for silver fox and Delalande's fox, and so on and so on. Handley did not

1. Richard Lee, *Subsistence Ecology of !Kung Bushmen* (Ann Arbor, Mich., University Microfilms, 1965), p. 170.
2. Sometimes straight slices are cut. Sometimes long strips are made in the following manner: a slice is cut along the side of a slab of meat but is not completely severed. From the opposite direction, a second slice is cut and not severed, and so forth. When the meat is picked up, it falls into a segmented strip. Long leather thongs are cut from pieces of hide in the same manner.

elicit and count all the snake and insect names in the !Kung vocabulary, of which there must be a great number. The informants' knowledge of animals extends beyond the animals we saw in their area. From photographs they recognized roan antelope, as well as rhinoceros, zebra, and elephant, and gave the names for them. The last three are not present in the Nyae Nyae area now. The !Kung have one name for both zebra and horse, evidently having extended the name for an animal they knew to a similarly shaped animal they saw in the possession of Bantu or whites.

The !Kung do not eat many of the living things that exist in the

With adzes, the men are scraping a layer of fat off a hide that they are preparing for a kaross. The scraping motion is toward them. The scrapings are edible.

N/aoka, first wife of Gao, is shaking out an ostrich egg, preparing to scramble it in her Ovambo cooking pot.

Nyae Nyae area. They are indifferent to some of them, apparently simply not regarding them as food. I think of foxes, shrews, genets, four species of little wildcats, polecats, gerbils, bats, many snakes including cobra, many birds and insects. Perhaps if hunger were more acute than it is, the !Kung would catch and eat some of the creatures to which they are at present indifferent. Nothing in the nature of a taboo would prevent them from doing so.

There are other creatures that the !Kung do not eat, but not because of indifference. On the contrary, they were horrified and offended that I should even bring up the question of eating those animals. The very thought was abhorrent to them. They shouted vehemently that they would die of starvation before they would eat those bad things. The bad things include the predators and scavengers—lions, leopards, cheetahs, brown hyenas, spotted hyenas, aardwolf, wild dogs, and vultures. It did not occur to me to inquire about flamingos and chameleons, but, while they were on the subject of what they would not eat, informants spoke of them, saying those creatures were bad, bad, and no one would eat them. Mongooses, meerkats, and squirrels were spoken of also as bad, absolutely not to be eaten, but people spoke less vehemently about them than about the others.

Rats and mice, the !Kung said, used to be eaten, but a doctor at Runtu early in 1952 had given a message that had passed from Bushman to Bushman saying that the rodents should not now be eaten. (They may have been carrying some disease.)

We found that a number of people avoided certain foods because of personal distaste, not because custom required their avoidance. The smell of ostrich meat and honey badger meat is repugnant to some. It certainly was to me. Di!ai said the smell of ostrich made her vomit. Also, if people had happened to be sick after eating something, they might avoid that food henceforth, repelled by the memory of their discomfort, or believing that the food disagreed with them.

The !Kung also practice another system of food avoidances, different from the avoidance of the predators, and so on, mentioned above. The !Kung at times avoid eating many wholesome plant and animal foods that are regularly a part of !Kung diet in the belief that the avoidances protect the health and good fortune of the individual. According to this system of belief, the foods are avoided only during certain periods of life. For instance, men and women from the age of puberty till they are old enough to have had five children must not eat ostrich eggs; children and older people may eat them. (In a forthcoming volume, I shall describe these avoidances in detail.)

!Kung food avoidances do not include carcasses of animals found dead in the veld unless the animal is avoided for some other reason, provided the meat has not decayed. The animal may have been killed by predators or died from unknown causes. People consider it good fortune to make such a find, and one of their prayers to the gods asks that the hunters or the women, when they are out gathering, be led to find such easily procured meat.

The animal foods that we observed eaten by the !Kung are listed below. They are mammals, birds, reptiles, and insects. Those marked with an asterisk (*) provided most of the animal food consumed; these were the foods most frequently obtained. The unmarked foods provided little in quantity compared to the others, because of the small size of the creatures, or because the creatures were rare in the area, or, for one reason or another, difficult to catch.

None of the creatures eaten by the !Kung were abundant in the Nyae Nyae area. None were easy to procure, except the occasional grasshopper that hopped onto someone, and the thousands of termites that we saw, one time only, in nuptial flight. They fell like snowflakes onto the ground, shed their wings, and crawled about. The !Kung gathered them up in excitement and delight and ate them. The animals, large and small, were scarce.

Large Mammals

*eland
*wildebeest
*gemsbok
*kudu
hartebeest
springbok
*warthog
buffalo (rare in the area)
giraffe

Small Mammals

*duiker
*steenbok
honey badger
porcupine
aardvark
springhare
jackal (avoided by most !Kung, eaten occasionally by old women)

Birds

*guinea fowl
ostrich (and *ostrich eggs)

giant bustard (paouw)
*redwing partridge
hornbill
korhaan
geese ⎫
ducks ⎭ in migration, shot infrequently

Reptiles

*tortoise, Geochelone pardalis babcocki Loveridge
*leguaan and other lizards
python, observed eaten once
*puff adder
mamba
mole snake, Pseudaspis cana
//um (or //on?), an unidentified snake

Insects

termites, Isoptera, species not identified, known popularly as "white ants"
grasshoppers, observed once
ants called !kxon, observed once
caterpillars—(the larvae of the moths Nudaurelia bellina and Cirina forda

Insects, cont.

are reported by Story to occur in the area. Presumably the large caterpillars we saw eaten were of one or both of these species. We also observed the !Kung eating the larvae of the two moths the cocoons of which are used to make dance rattles. One of those is *Lasciocampid trabala*. The other is unidentified.)

We were told that the !Kung eat pangolins and bullfrogs if they find them; we did not happen to see them do so.

The approximate weights of the mammals, according to G. C. Shortridge, *The Mammals of South West Africa,* are:[3]

Large		Small	
eland	1200–2000 pounds	warthog	100–200 pounds
wildebeest	500– 600	duiker	30– 40
gemsbok	400– 450	steenbok	25– 30
kudu	500– 700	honey badger	20– 25
hartebeest	350– 400	porcupine	40– 50
springbok	80– 100	aardvark	140
warthog	150– 200	springhare	7
buffalo	1500	jackal	20
giraffe	1½– 2 tons		

We must not leave the subject of animal foods without the mention of honey. The !Kung with whom we lived delight in honey but seldom find it. Bees are not numerous in their arid land. I was present on only one occasion when Old Gaú found a beehive in a tree, smoked the bees out, received several stings, and took the honey. Honey is highly esteemed by the !Kung. They call the wife of the great God, the God who is the Creator of all things, Mother of the Bees.

We had an interesting experience with bees in another place. It so happened that when we departed at the end of one expedition from Gautscha, we camped at sundown miles to the west of Gautscha. Our camping procedure after a long day's drive was to have tea, then to do all the work of setting up camp. When Philip Hameva, our most excellent cook, friend, and helper, opened a water can to pour water to boil for tea, bees swarmed into it, thirsty, thirsty bees. They buzzed around and in seconds many had drowned. Elizabeth and I quickly got out our

3. G. C. Shortridge, *The Mammals of South West Africa* (London, William Heineman, 1934), passim.

wash basins, put grass and sticks in them for rafts, and filled them with water. The rafts were instantly covered with bees drinking. We continued to work surrounded by the bees, our hands in among them, making more rafts in more containers. Neither Elizabeth nor I nor any member of our party was stung. Our good fortune was still holding. These might have been the fierce African bees one reads about, instead of such exceptionally gentle ones.

HUNTING: A MALE ACTIVITY

Among the !Kung, hunting is exclusively the work of men, the dominant activity of their lives. Not only do !Kung women never join in the hunting, as women of the Pygmy net hunters do, but, as I mentioned previously, according to !Kung beliefs, women should remove themselves physically and ritualistically from hunting and observe certain avoidances in order not to weaken the male hunting power or nullify the hunters' good fortune by their femaleness.

!Kung men talk endlessly about hunting as they sit together repairing their equipment or poisoning their arrows. They recount over and over memorable episodes of past hunts, hear each other's news about recent hunts, and make plans. They often hold sessions with their divining disks (which I have called oracle disks) to learn what direction is likely to yield success and what the hunt may bring forth. (Oracle disks are described in a section below.)

With the rarest exceptions, all !Kung men hunt. Little boys play with tiny bows and arrows from the time they can walk and practice shooting throughout their childhood. At adolescence, they begin to hunt with their fathers. They learn the skills of tracking and stalking and begin to participate in actual hunts. They continue through their manhood till they are gray-haired old men who can no longer endure the exertion of the hunt.

A young man may not marry until he has killed a big game animal, proved himself a hunter, and had the Rite of the First Kill performed for him.[4] The pressure of group opinion upon men to conform to their society's expectation, to hunt and provide meat, is enormously strong. In the Rite of the First Kill, a scarification (one of several) is cut in the skin of the boy's chest and a magic substance rubbed into his body to insure

4. John Marshall's film, "A Rite of Passage," depicts the rite as it was performed for young /Ti!kay, son of Khan//a of Kai Kai.

that he will not be lazy, that his heart will say to him, "Why am I sitting here at my fire? Why am I not out hunting?"

We knew only one man who failed to hunt, the deviant old bachelor, /Gaishay, who was never given a wife.

LACK OF TERRITORIAL RESTRICTION AND LACK OF COMPETITION

!Kung hunting customs in the Nyae Nyae area do not require that hunters confine themselves to the territory of their own band in the search for game, and the ownership of the animals that are hunted is not based on territory. In !Kung concept the animals belong to no one till they are

Little boys play with toy bows and arrows from an early age. A woman avoids touching real weapons but may handle toys. Di!ai made a bow and arrow for her son.

shot, and they may be followed and shot anywhere. When an animal is shot, the hunters take the meat back to their people. If an animal is killed in a territory other than their own, the hunters give a present of meat to the owners of the territory should they meet them, but no tribute is obligatory.

The vastness of the country, sparseness of the population, and the fact that the animals wander anywhere are elements that combine to allow this freedom of hunting rights with respect to territory. Hunters can hunt for days without seeing another human being.

I must limit this observation to the Nyae Nyae area. There were indications that, among !Kung who were not so closely bound by kinship ties and friendship, or at least acquaintance, as were the Nyae Nyae !Kung, the situation might be different. Also, a denser population in an area might easily raise the level of competitiveness.

/Qui told J. O. Brew, who was questioning him, that once when he was visiting at Kai Kai he had gone hunting toward the east, far from the people he knew. A !Kung hunter from that territory met him and was angry and said, "Why are you coming to hunt in our area?" He almost started to fight, but an old man named !Kham ran up and stopped him, saying, "You must not fight for food. We are all looking for food. Nobody is going to fight about food." When /Qui was asked if he went there again, people laughed, for they knew what he would say. He replied simply, "I was frightened. I did not go to that side any more."

A hunt begins with the formation of a hunting party. The parties are usually composed of from two to four men. Men do hunt alone sometimes, but one hunter alone is at a disadvantage. If he kills a large animal, he has no one to help him carry the meat or to guard it from predators while he returns to the encampment to fetch help. Furthermore, the !Kung do not like to be alone. They much prefer companionship and cooperation in their hunting. Larger parties than four might be formed but seldom are, at least at the beginning of a hunt. It is more advantageous for small parties to start out and search for game in different directions than for the hunters to combine in larger parties. However, if it turns out that a big animal is shot, and if many people have congregated and more men are available, larger parties will gather to help in the tracking and especially to help carry the meat to the people.

Parties are formed freely and voluntarily and are ever changing. No categories of men are prohibited by !Kung custom from hunting together and none are formally required to do so. Men from different bands join each other, if they wish. No one is in command, but an informal leadership develops. Parties tend to form around certain good hunters. At Gautscha there were three nuclei: ≠Toma and Gao together in Band 1, Gao Beard in Band 2, and Short /Qui, the fabulous hunter, also in Band 2.

The groups that formed around these men habitually set off in different directions. The !Kung speak of hunting to this side or that side. The east and northeast were ≠Toma's and Gao's side. The west was Gao Beard's side. Short /Qui usually hunted to the south in the vicinity of Nama Pan. The hunting to one side or another was not a matter of strict rule. We saw no indication that the !Kung felt jealously possessive about the side to which they started out to hunt. The animals are so unpredictable that one direction offers as good a chance as another of finding them, and, once sighted, the animal can be followed anywhere. Furthermore, the hunting parties were not competing against one another. They were all looking for game, and if any party brought in a big animal, the meat would be shared with all the people assembled and all would benefit.

The meat of the big animals is shared according to a custom (see Chapter 9 and the social values of sharing, discussed there). The custom does not apply to small creatures that anyone may catch. Intermediate-sized animals, such as steenbok, duiker, aardvark, or warthog, would be divided among themselves by the hunters who brought them, and the men would be free to eat the meat with their own immediate families and make gifts of meat to others as they chose. No one wants to seem "far-hearted" or stingy in meat-sharing. No one would hoard large portions even of a relatively small animal, like a warthog. The hunters would give to relatives and friends close to them according to the amount of meat they had. That would be acceptable behavior. If the assembled community was very large, such as the assemblages we had at Gautscha, people would not expect that the relatively small amounts of meat be shared by all. It is expected, however, that the meat of the big animals be distributed so widely that everyone present receives a portion. There is every reason to distribute the meat widely. The big animals weigh hundreds of pounds. No one or two families could eat all the meat before it spoils, and, furthermore, the social value of sharing is inestimable. One has only to imagine the meat of a big animal not shared to realize that value. The custom of sharing is so strongly established in the minds of the !Kung, and is so faithfully followed, that it has all but extinguished the concept of not sharing.

HUNTING

The hunters of the Gautscha bands appeared to take little interest in snaring. Old Gaú, beyond hunting age, set snares frequently and caught guinea fowl and partridges. The boys also snared sometimes. Men in their prime, however, gave their time to hunting. Their principal hunting time and purposeful endeavor was given to the search for the big animals. Infrequently the hunters tried to dig out an aardvark, sleeping by day in its burrow, or to prod out springhare from their holes with hooks hafted to long flexible poles. They gladly shot duikers, steenboks, porcupines, geese, or paouw if they saw them. However, if they found spoor of the big animals fresh enough to encourage them, they would follow it and not deliberately search for the small animals.

The big animals most often hunted were eland, wildebeest, gemsbok, kudu, and warthog. These were the mainstays. Hartebeest and springbok were uncommon, buffalo very rare. Ostrich were common but hard to stalk, and I think during the time I was in Nyae Nyae area only one was shot. That ostrich was an enraged male that charged Short /Qui on an open pan where there was no refuge. Short /Qui, with perfect self-control, knelt facing the ostrich, his arrow poised. When the ostrich came within range, Short /Qui shot it in the heart.

Giraffe were numerous compared to other big animals. Hunters often saw them but did not often deliberately give their hunting time to following them. Giraffe are too wary; they do not put their heads down to graze, and they have such a vantage point from which to view the land and whatever moves on it that the men can rarely get near enough to shoot them. However, a hunter occasionally managed to kill one. John Marshall's film "The Hunters" shows such an occasion. The !Kung did not know that giraffe were royal game, protected by law in South West Africa. Bushmen were exempted from the game laws. Isaak Utuhili, the Tswana administrative chief in !Xabe, Botswana, had explained the Bushmen's exemption by saying, "The wild animals are the Bushmen's cattle." It was not until June 1953 that the Nyae Nyae !Kung were asked to comply in the protection of giraffe. Robert Morris, who was then the Native Commissioner at Runtu, made his first visit into the interior of the Nyae Nyae area at that time. He called a meeting, an *indaba*, the first the !Kung had ever attended, and, among other things, told them that giraffe were royal game, no longer to be hunted. After he left, the !Kung, young, middle-aged, and old, amused themselves by conducting meetings in imitation of the *indaba.* They made pronouncements in Morris' authoritative manner and called giraffe "Morrisi cows." The incongruous image that remark evoked made them roll on the ground in laughter.

The !Kung employ only one method of hunting. They do not join in large numbers to drive animals; they do not use pitfalls. Such methods would be of no use in their country. Wildebeest run in herds of about twenty or thirty; the other animals are seen singly or in herds of a few animals. The animals are widely scattered. The antelope, because they go without drinking for long periods, do not come regularly to waterholes. There are no migration routes in the Nyae Nyae area, no hunting grounds where animals tend to congregate. They roam anywhere in the vast land. The hunters start out from their encampment, choosing one direction or another, and begin their search. They may search for days covering many, many miles before seeing an animal, or seeing spoor fresh enough to be worth following. If they find nothing, they sometimes stay out overnight, continuing their search from the place where they stop. However, they usually return to their encampment to start out again next day. The hunting days are arduous and the hunters must endure thirst and hunger, for they do not burden themselves with heavy supplies of food and water.

When an animal is sighted, the critical moment of stalking and shooting is at hand. The hunters can shoot their delicate little bows and arrows with fair accuracy at twenty or thirty yards. Farther away they have much less chance of hitting.

John Marshall says in his sensitive paper "Man the Hunter" that the idea is to approach to within shooting distance as quickly as possible.[5] The hunters feel the longer they take, the longer the animal will have to decide what to do. Before they start their approach, the men lay down their hunting bags, quivers, and assagais, and carry with them only their bows and a handful of arrows. The men take cover behind bushes or trees if cover is available, but, for the most part, the country is open grassland and the hunters' approach must be made in the animal's full sight.

!Kung hunters do not disguise themselves by wearing the skins of animals or ostriches. In the ancient rock paintings, one sees what appears

5. John Marshall, "Man the Hunter," part I, *Natural History,* 67 (June-July 1958), 291–309; part II, *Natural History,* 67 (Aug.-Sept. 1958), 376–395.

Hunters make signs with their hands to let each other know without making a sound what animal they have sighted. On the left is the sign for wildebeest with widespread horns, on the right is the sign for hartebeest with the horns curved back.

to be an ostrich or a buck with human feet approaching game. The hunters nevertheless make themselves resemble animals by leaning over, their backs almost parallel to the ground, their arms held close to their side. Two men may run together in this way, one close behind the other. Often the men run forward when the animal they are stalking lowers its head to graze and then they stand perfectly still when it raises its head to stare. But John has seen a hunter continue to run forward to within twenty yards of a wildebeest that was watching him all the time.

The antelope do not take fright easily.[6] They stand watching the men for minutes at a time, apparently either shortsighted or puzzled by the

6. I think bitter thoughts about white sportsmen who kill these magnificent animals with their high-powered rifles for pleasure. I have myself heard such a remark as, "Had a fine season in Angola. Got my roan this year and the biggest elephant I've taken so far." Laurence and I were in the hunting area reserved by a safari company to which that speaker was referring. One of the rare roan antelopes standing at a discreet distance from us, alert but calm, watched us, as we sat in our jeep, long enough for Laurence to change a roll of film. A sportsman could have shot him as easily as he could shoot a cow in a farmer's field. My feelings about the animals Bushmen killed were in sharp duality. Even though in grief to see the animals die, I soon came to want the hunters to succeed, to make the kill, to have meat, more than I wanted the animals to go free.

A herd of wildebeest stares for a moment at two hunters creeping in the grass. Stalking is the most difficult part of !Kung hunting.

brown thing they see in the grass. As the men get closer they may creep forward on their elbows and knees or wriggle on their bellies. The animal at any point may decide that the brown moving thing is dangerous and gallop off in a wild flight before the hunters are near enough to shoot. But if the animal stands till the hunters are in range, the hunters, standing or kneeling, suddenly begin to shoot arrow after arrow as fast as they can. They take aim, but not long careful aim; they let fly, hoping that in the volley one or more of the arrows will hit an animal somewhere, stay imbedded, and let the poison work.

Many hunters wear a special belt which binds a number of arrows to their side at the waistline, fanned out so that the hunter can seize one with a swift gesture and place it in his bow.

If the animal they hit is in a herd and the whole herd bolts, as it naturally would, the men run after the animal as fast as they can to try to see which are the wounded animal's footprints. They return later, sometimes days later, to retrieve the arrows that fell short.

Once one or more poisoned arrows are in the animal, the hunters must track the animal until it dies. The little arrows do not inflict mortal wounds. It is the poison that kills when it enters the bloodstream. But the poison takes time to work. An animal the size of a wildebeest might

The herd takes off in wild flight. One of the hunters runs after it.

take two or three days to die, a smaller animal less time, an eland or giraffe perhaps more time. It would depend on the number of arrows shot in and their position in the body.

First the hunters must recognize the spoor of the wounded animal. If it was one of a stampeding herd, its spoor will be mingled with others and trampled on. But the !Kung have trained their power of observation and have learned so well what signs to look for that they track with uncanny ability. Their method then is to follow the spoor discreetly, not to startle the animal and make it run far, but to stay at a distance and hope the animal will lie down when it begins to feel sick. They must follow it closely enough, however, to prevent the ever-present predators from killing and devouring the weakened animal before the hunters do. When an animal is down and can run no more, if it is not yet dead, the hunters kill it with their assagais. John Marshall saw a group of four hunters throw their assagais into a downed wildebeest but fail to kill it. The problem was then to retrieve their assagais. Short /Qui ran and leaped over the wildebeest, avoiding its swinging horns, and pulled out his assagai as he leaped. He threw it again and gave the coup de grâce.

ANIMALS TAKEN

We do not have a significant record over a significant period of time of the man-hours spent in hunting or the amounts of animal food consumed. For one reason, our presence created unusual situations. John participated in the hunting with a camera not a gun. He wanted to influence the proceedings as little as possible, but his participation undoubtedly had some effect. On several occasions, for instance, he transported the meat to Gautscha by truck. The principal way we, as a whole expedition, modified the situation, I believe, was by attracting visitors. More people congregated at Gautscha than would ordinarily have been there, and everything was more complicated as a result. People normally visit each other in the Nyae Nyae area, but nothing suggested to me that they visited as often or in such numbers as when we were present. I have said that we were usually surrounded by about seventy-five people at a time. Another perusal of my notes reveals that I estimated at least a hundred on two

Crooked /Qui demonstrates the aim and the way the arrow is held and released. The !Kung use the primary release. /Qui has stuck his extra arrows into his breechclout (not the special belt some men wear) on his right side. If he were actually shooting at an animal he would have put down his rattly quiver.

occasions. People would stay for a time, disperse to go back to their own waterholes, or to go to different places to hunt or gather, and others would come. However, when a big animal was brought to be distributed, word would travel miraculously over the land. With so much coming and going, I believe that there was an exceptional amount of communication about the arrival of meat and that larger groups assembled than would ordinarily be expected.

None of our party wanted to curtail other studies to make a record of animal foods consumed, especially under those circumstances. I do, however, have a record for September and October 1952 of the large animals brought to Gautscha and distributed. As one can imagine, with the stir and excitement caused by the arrival of masses of meat, there was no danger of failing to take notice of the event.

The large animals brought to Gautscha during September and October 1952 were taken by hunters of Bands 1 and 2, with one exception. The wildebeest and wildebeest calf of October 20 were killed by visitors from Kai Kai on their way to Gautscha and brought to Gautscha for distribution. The large animals and the ostrich were given wide distribution, the warthogs only limited distribution. The animals were:

September 5	warthog	October 3	ostrich
13	giraffe	13	baby giraffe found dead, wildebeest
23	eland, warthog	20	wildebeest, wildebeest calf
		23	warthog
		29	eland

The number of animals taken is greater than the estimate made by Laurence and John Marshall. They had thought, basing their reasoning on the time spent in the long hunts, that the hunters of one band might expect to get between fifteen and eighteen large animals in a year. They were thinking only of the large antelopes, giraffe, and the rare buffalo, not animals the size of warthogs or smaller. Even if we eliminate all but the large animals, the number we record is greater than the estimate: two in September (giraffe and eland), three in October (two wildebeest and an eland). Data are lacking on which to base a significant comparison between a band in ordinary circumstances and the situation at Gautscha, but we are safe in saying that our presence did not result in deprivation. On the contrary, I think we observed a felicitous situation in which chance and endeavor combined to produce an unusual amount of meat. However, with so many people congregated to eat the meat, I am at a loss to know whether in the end the people ate more or less than they would have under ordinary circumstances.

THE HUNTS OF SEPTEMBER AND OCTOBER 1952

The giraffe hunt was a long one. Hunting parties had been out during the first days of September. On September 3, ≠Toma had tried to dig out an aardvark but failed. His baby daughter, !Ungka Norna, was born on the fourth. He stayed home that day but went the next and got a warthog. It was shared only with members of Band 1. On the sixth and seventh, ≠Toma, Gao, Crooked /Qui, of Band 1, //Ao of Band 2, and John (with camera) set out together. They returned the night of the sixth but stayed out the night of the seventh. On the eighth, they found giraffes. ≠Toma got an arrow into one of them, which ran off with the stampeding herd. The men tried to track it but proved that !Kung hunters are only human, not infallible. They lost its spoor. They could find the giraffe herd again, however, and this time Crooked /Qui made the shot.

The men tracked this giraffe for the remainder of that day and for four days more. On the twelfth, the giraffe was killed. It had traveled thirty miles in a great circle from the place in which it was shot. Several more hunters had become involved by this time and were present to help ≠Toma and his party cut up the meat and carry it to Gautscha. A large assemblage awaited them, and the distribution of the meat was made on the thirteenth. The meat was cut into strips, and it hung in every tree. The hunt of the giraffe which was brought in had been an eight-day affair. ≠Toma and others spent the ninth day, September 14, going back to the place where the giraffe had been shot to retrieve the arrows that had fallen short. They found eight.

People stayed on for four days enjoying the meat and the company of friends. They held two great dances that lasted till dawn and longer. On the eighteenth, they began to disperse, taking with them what dried meat they still had and pieces of hide. Hides are regularly eaten unless they are needed to make karosses or bags. The giraffe hide is too heavy to use and was all cut up and distributed.

On the eighteenth, a party of young hunters had gone out. They got no meat but found a young palm tree and brought the heart of palm, which they distributed as though it were meat. On the nineteenth and twentieth, ≠Toma and his party and another party from Band 2 hunted but got nothing. It was unusual to see the hunters managing the distribution of plant food. Instead of turning the palm over to the women to distribute, as I would have expected them to do, the two hunters who had found the palm cooked it in a pit until it was soft. Next, the two men sliced it lengthwise into eight slabs, each about 2½ feet long. Then, one by one, the people to whom the first distribution was to be made came up to the hunters. The first received a slab from one hunter; the next received a slab from the other hunter. In the end, eight people had come up, and each hunter had alternated with the other in giving out four slabs of the palm.

On the twentieth, Short /Qui with his wife, daughter, and mother-in-law, Old /Gasa, went to Nama. On the twenty-first, Short /Qui shot an eland, a warthog, and a duiker—all in one day, hunting alone! Short /Qui had the reputation of being the best hunter in the Nyae Nyae area and no wonder, with such accomplishment as this to his credit.[7] /Qui and the women carried as much of the meat of the warthog and duiker as they possibly could and returned to Gautscha to get help with the eland. Next morning before dawn, John took Short /Qui, ≠Toma, and others in a truck to the place where they could pick up the eland's spoor. The poison had worked with unusual rapidity, and they found the eland dead. They were barely in time to save it from jackals, hyenas, and vultures. The meat was brought to Gautscha in the truck on the twenty-third. Another wide distribution was made to another large congregation of people, who stayed eating eland for several days. Another dance was held. By the twenty-eighth, everyone had had enough of each other's company, enough meat, enough dancing, and there was a great exodus.

We were quiet in the encampment during the last days of September

7. Short /Qui is the /Qui Elizabeth Thomas tells about in The Harmless People, the /Qui who had the tragic accident in 1955. He was bitten by a puff adder. His life was saved by his people, who bound his leg with a tourniquet and cut and sucked the wound, but Short /Qui lost his foot from gangrene. Our expedition arrived at Gautscha just at that time. We took /Qui to Windhoek where his leg was operated on and he was fitted with a wooden leg. Our last present to him that year was a set of tools with which he could make more wooden legs as he needed to. He succeeded in adapting to the wooden leg and managed to hunt. John Marshall saw him again in 1957–58, Laurence and I in 1959 and 1961. He was well and smiling, and he had continued to hunt. In 1973, when John was making a film with the National Geographic Society in Botswana, the Gautscha people came to the border for a short visit with him. Short /Qui and his family were among them. He looked well, John said, but evaded giving a direct answer to a question about his hunting by making a joke. His wife now did the running, he said.

and first few days of October. ≠Toma, Short /Qui, and two or three other hunters were hunting intensely with John, who was trying to film any hunting scenes he could. On October 3, Short /Qui shot the ostrich —the one that charged him on the pan. The meat was brought to Gautscha and distributed by Short /Qui's brothers-in-law. Old women danced a dance of praise in Short /Qui's honor while weary Short /Qui slept on a pile of ostrich plumes. Hunters soon went out again, John accompanying one or another party. He and all the Band 1 hunters spent two days on a trip to get poison beetles. No meat was brought in till October 13, which proved to be a lucky day. John and Elizabeth traveling somewhere in a truck found a baby giraffe killed by predators. The meat was edible, and they brought it to Gautscha and distributed it. On that same day, the fabulous Short /Qui and his party brought in a wildebeest to Gautscha. Many people reassembled there, and for three days people ate and rested and gradually dispersed.

The next event was the arrival on October 17 of the party from Kai Kai, Khan//a and his family, including his teen-age son, /Ti!kay. They had encountered wildebeest as they traveled. Khan//a had shot a wildebeest calf, and his son had shot a full-grown wildebeest. This was the first large animal the boy had shot. A party was quickly formed to return to track the wildebeest. John went to film and brought the hunters and the meat back by truck on the twentieth. A moderate number of people were present. The meat was distributed and all got some. On the twenty-second, the Rite of the First Kill was performed for young /Ti!kay by his proud father and uncle and filmed by John.

Gao and his extended family had been away for many days. On October 29, they all returned laden with eland meat on the verge of spoiling from being carried in the sun too long. In addition, they had nineteen ostrich eggs. Many people came to eat eland meat, and, as it turned out when the eggs were opened, embryonic ostriches.

Members of the families of ≠Toma and Old Gaú had eaten some smaller creatures as well as their share of meat from the large animals. I did not keep track of the small creatures taken by other families, and may have missed noticing some in these families. Old Gaú had caught a lizard and snared a partridge and five guinea fowl. I gave a puff adder that had taken refuge under the canvas floor of my tent to Di!ai. She had told me she enjoyed puff adder meat. And /Qui caught a python near the encampment.

I cannot resist reminiscing about the python. It was distributed in a very special way. The python was not very large as pythons go, only a little over nine feet. /Qui and others thought the meat would be too little for a wide distribution and so decided to cook the snake for the children. /Qui and Old /Gam undertook the preparations. Old /Gam picked up the snake's bloodied, bashed head, drew it over her shoulder, and walked to the encampment dragging nine feet of snake behind her, her multitude of bangles swaying and bobbing. The sight gave me a turn. I knew /Gam as a dear, kindly, old grandmother, but she looked so weird, so preternatural that, although I was not the least afraid in my mind, my nerves automatically took fright and I was covered with tingles and prickles and gooseflesh. That peculiar reaction soon passed and we proceeded with the preparations. A pit was dug, a fire was built in it and allowed to burn down to coals. The python was eviscerated, trussed, placed on the coals, and covered with hot sand and ashes. There it cooked for about two hours. /Qui then took it out and skinned it, and he and /Gam removed the meat from the bones and put it into a big Ovambo pot to boil for another hour or so. At this point the children were summoned. They made a tight circle around a little fire, shoulder touching shoulder. /Qui broke the python's bones into segments and gave one to each child to lick. There they sat in the firelight, giggling, their eyes shining, their little pink tongues flicking in and out between the bones. When the boiled meat was ready, I was given the first helping. The rest was divided among the children and a few adults who eat python; not all do. Python meat is white, tasteless, and stringy, but not unpleasant.

EQUIPMENT

A full description of !Kung hunting equipment and the making of it is given in one of John Marshall's films, *!Kung Bushman Hunting Equipment.* I shall describe the bows and arrows here but only touch upon the other equipment briefly. A hunter carries a bag made of the whole skin of an animal; warthogs' skins were commonly used for bags. The bag is hung from the left shoulder. In it are carried a knife, an arrow belt, a carrying net, and a quiver made usually from the bark of the root of *Acacia uncinata.* In the quiver are the arrows. We were told that ten completed arrows would be few for a hunter to have, twenty would be many. A pair of fire sticks, a sip stick, a capped horn in which an extra supply of poison beetles is contained, an extra bowstring, cord made of vegetable fibers, and all the materials to make new arrows are also carried in the quiver. The hunter carries his bow run through slits in the straps of the hunting bag. He takes with him on a hunt his digging stick, his carrying stick, and his assagai. !Kung assagais have blades made from metal obtained in trade with the Bantu. The blades are hafted to long handles.

!Kung hunters have another tool in their hunting equipment, but they leave it in the encampment in order not to add its weight to the hunting bag when they are on a hunt. It is an arrow straightener, a stone about 5 inches long, about 2 inches wide, about 1½ inches thick. It has a neat groove cut lengthwise down the middle. A crooked arrow is warmed over the fire, its crooked portion is pressed into the groove and left to cool. This was the one stone implement I observed in use except for the stones the !Kung use as hammer and anvil to crack nuts and bones, the stones they use for sharpening metal knife blades, assagai blades, and arrow points, and the stones they use for weights to stretch their nets. All these others are untooled.

Bows can be made of any of several woods. *Grewis flava* is often chosen. A live branch about 40 inches in length is cut. It is tapered with an axe or knife at both ends. It is scraped till smooth, rubbed with fat, strengthened in several places with sinew bindings. The bowstring is a strong cord made by rolling together several strands of sinew. The sinews used for bowstrings are the long sinews from the legs of the big animals. The sinews are carefully taken out whole by the hunters. Giraffe sinews are especially valued. The bowstring is looped onto the bow at one end, wound around the other end several times, and fastened with a loop. A nub of wood bound on securely with sinew keeps the string from slipping down. The whole winding can be twisted one way or the other to loosen or tighten the string.

The design of the !Kung arrows is beautifully adapted to the materials used in the construction and to the fulfillment of the arrow's purpose, which is not to kill by inflicting a mortal wound but to convey a lethal poison into the bloodstream of an animal.

!Kung hunters make their own arrows; none are specialists. No two arrows are exactly alike in every proportion, though the general design is the same for all. The men identify their arrows by only slight differences.

The arrows are delicate and unfeathered. The smallest I measured was 18 inches in overall length; the longest was 26 inches. Most were between 21 inches and 23 inches. As I write I have before me the 26-

inch one; it weighs ½ ounce. A !Kung arrow has four parts: the shaft, the point, and two segments, one of bone, one of reed, that connect the point to the shaft.

The shaft is made of segmented, noded, hollow reed about ¼ inch in diameter. The shaft of a 21-inch arrow that I also have is 14 inches. The 26-inch arrow has a 19-inch shaft. *Pragmites communis, Andropogon gayanus,* or *Panicum* are the reeds used. The reeds grow in only a few places in the Nyae Nyae area. When the hunters happen to pass a clump, they gather extra supplies to keep on hand and to give to fellow hunters. One end of the shaft is cut at a solid node, and the node is notched to receive the bowstring. The other end is cut above a node and that end is hollow. Both ends are bound with sinew which is firmly stuck down with black gum from the root of a plant to keep them from splitting. The !Kung bind each end by holding the sinew taut and twisting the arrow.

We observed five types of arrow points. Three types are simple, un-barbed, tapered points, 3 or 4 inches long, made of bone, or wood, or a porcupine quill. The tapered points are used for birds and small ani-mals. They may be poisoned but are usually not. If a tapered point is poisoned it is carried reversed, its poisoned end stuck into the hollow reed of the main shaft till it is taken out for use. The remaining two types of points are barbed. They are made of bone (the leg bone of a giraffe is preferred for these bone points) or metal. The points are alike in form—a small triangular barbed point on a shank that is about 3 to 4 inches long. The point itself and its shank are one piece of bone or metal. The /Gwi in Botswana still frequently used barbed points of bone as well as metal. The !Kung much preferred metal to bone for their barbed points and were able to obtain sufficient metal by trade with neighbor-ing Bantu, so, although they could make exquisite barbed bone points like the /Gwi, they no longer bothered to do so. The metal points, as exquisite as the bone points, are fashioned from malleable scraps of metal or heavy wire and are hammered to shape against a stone used as an anvil with a stone used as a hammer, or with some of the metal tools the men obtain in trade. The bone or metal barbed points are the same in size and shape—½ to ⅝ inches long, about ¼ to ⅜ inches wide. Each man adopts a style in proportioning the little triangles and shaping the barbs which the !Kung call "ears." The points are sharpened on stone to a keen edge.

The shank is fastened to the reed arrow shaft by means of the two aforementioned connecting segments. Glue, a yellow gum from an acacia tree, is applied to the end of the shank, and the shank is inserted into the little reed segment. This segment, about 1 inch long, is made of a hollow piece of *Panicum*. It is bound all around with sinew to keep it from splitting. Before using the sinew, the men chew it till it is moist and pliable, or soak it in urine, or bury it in moist sand till it is soft. To begin binding an object, they hold the end of the sinew against the object, wind the sinew over the end two or three times to secure it. Then, holding the sinew steady and guiding it carefully, they twirl the object slowly around and around. The end that is left when they have finished the twirling is pressed down—not tucked under or glued down. When the sinew dries, it tightens and the end adheres.

The reed must fit the shank exactly, and when the glued end of the shank is inserted into it a firm connection is made. The second connecting segment is a piece of bone about 3 inches long which is shaped while it is fresh and not brittle. It is smoothed perfectly and tapered at both ends. One end, smeared with glue to make a firm connection, is inserted into the other end of the inch-long reed connecting segment. The other end of the bone piece, without glue, is inserted into the reed shaft. Both ends are tapered to fit the reeds exactly. The connection between the bone piece and the reed shaft is firm enough to hold the arrow together as it flies through the air but, once the arrow is shot into an animal, the connection is designed to give way and allow the shaft to fall off, if necessary. This is because of the poison. Should an animal run through brush or rub against a tree to knock the arrow out, the shaft would fall away but leave the poisoned point imbedded, giving the poison time to work.

When an arrow is prepared for poison, the shank behind the triangular point is wound with strands of moistened sinew which are glued down with yellow gum. When the sinew wrapping dries, it sets firmly and tightens. The poison adheres better to the sinew than to the bare shank.

The !Kung use three arrow poisons and often make a mixture of them. The poison they rely on primarily comes from the larva of beetles and their parasites. Three species of poison beetles and three of parasites have been identified by Dr. Charles Koch, namely:

Diamphidia nigro-ornata Stål, parasitized by *Lebistina subcruciata* Fairmaire

Diamphidia vittatipennis Baly, parasitized by *Lebistina holubi*
   Peringuey
Polyclada flexuosa Baly, parasitized by *Lebistina perinqueyi* Liebke.[8]

All these species look very much alike. The !Kung notice some of
the slight differences. They consider one species to be the females, another to be the males of a single species. The other differences they do

The arrow: the barbed metal point (left) has a shank 3 or 4 inches long, heavily
encrusted with poison. The point, the small reed connecting-piece (bound with
sinew), and the tapered bone connecting-piece are glued together and remain a
unit. The man is showing how the tapered bone connecting-piece comes apart
from the reed shaft, which he holds with his right hand. Some of the poison
larvae are seen in the background.

8. Charles Koch, "Preliminary Notes on the Coleopterological Aspect of the Arrow
Poison of the Bushmen," *South African Biological Society*, Pamphlet No. 20, 1958, pp.
49–54.

The larvae

not account for. The ones they think are females they consider to be the most toxic. Beetle poison is called *!oa*.

The beetles are monophagous. Although the trees and bushes that are hosts to them are fairly common, not all are infested; the beetles are not plentiful. For example, the hunters of the Gautscha area had to walk more than half a day to a certain morula tree which was infested. The hunters watch for new infestations as they travel about.

The beetles are taken when they are in the larva stage in cocoons buried two or three feet underground beneath the tree or shrub they feed on. The beetles mature at different times, and larvae can be found at any time of year. The hunters dig a lot of them at a time and keep a supply in a horn covered with a cap made of a scrotum. The larvae live a long time, and the hunters need replenish their supply only a few times a year. The hunters use the larvae to poison new arrows and to freshen the poison on old arrows from time to time. The poison on old arrows retains its potency for a long time if it is kept dry but needs to be freshened when it begins to flake off.

At the three poisoning sessions I observed, one man prepared a batch of poison from his own supply of larvae and shared it with one or more other men. This appeared to be an economical and advantageous way of doing it. Doubtless, the men take turns in making a batch of poison or give each other larvae to even things up. That is the !Kung way.

A man first of all carefully examines his hands for scratches or cracks. The poison is deadly when it enters the bloodstream, as deadly to man as to beast. The men warned me that it would blind a person should it get into his eyes. Whether this is so or not, I do not know. The men had no story to tell of an actual incident of anyone being blinded or of any accident to a man who was putting poison on his arrows. They are extremely careful. However, they had several stories of persons being accidentally wounded by arrows in other situations. Some died, some were saved. There is no known antidote, but if someone is present to apply a tourniquet and to suck the wound instantly, the wounded person may be saved.

A man poisoning his arrows. He has dotted the orange-colored drops from the bodies of several larvae directly onto the shank and is now applying with a stick the mixture of poison and an adhesive substance that he has prepared in a little bone dish.

On one occasion I observed ≠Toma and /Qui poisoning arrows. They each had two or three new arrows and ten or a dozen old ones on which the poison was becoming dry and flaking. They did not scrape the old poison off; new layers were applied over it in the same manner in which they were applied to the new arrows.

≠Toma spread out a number of larvae on a kaross. He first chose one of the smaller of two kinds, the kind that he believes are "female" and the most toxic. He broke away the brittle cocoon, took the larva out, and pulled off its front leg, which he called its "arm." From that spot exuded a clear amber-colored fluid. This ≠Toma dotted up and down the length of the sinew-wrapped shank of the arrow point, using two or three or four larvae for each arrow. He dotted the fluid most thickly just below the barbed tip but put none on the tip itself. The arrows would be altogether too dangerous to handle were the tips poisoned, especially when the hunters are shooting and reach quickly to take another arrow. As each arrow was dotted, it was stuck in the sand near a small fire to dry, awaiting a second layer of poison. The larvae were set aside.

The second layer of poison was prepared in a little bone dish, the socket of the knee joint of a large antelope. ≠Toma took ten or a dozen of the large larvae, opened them, and squeezed their insides into the dish. He then squeezed out the insides of the smaller larvae, those which had supplied the first layer of poison. ≠Toma happened to have on hand one of the other poison substances which the !Kung know, the pod of a tree called !gaowa. The tree is rare. ≠Toma knew of only one, which was far away, in the vicinity of Tsho/ana. The pod is not as toxic as the beetle larvae, but it adds a little to the strength of the poison mixture. The !Kung say that a small animal, the size of a steenbok, would die if it ate the pod. Its poison closes the throat, they say. With his knife ≠Toma scraped a few slivers of the pod. He then heated a leaf of sansevieria on the fire to soften it and twisted it to squeeze the juice into the mixture. Sansevieria is not poisonous; it adds an adhesive substance. When this mixture was well stirred with a stick, it was applied to the arrows with the stick as a coating all over the shank. The arrows were again set up to dry by the fire. Finally another layer of the mixture in the dish was applied.

Another arrow poison comes from the root of a plant in the asparagus family. It is called n/i !go. We saw it used at another poisoning session. The root is pounded and squeezed. The juice it emits is cooked till it has the consistency of wax. Some of the substance may be added to the beetle mixture. Like the !gaowa pod, it is not toxic enough to be effective alone but it adds to the strength of the mixture.

If a poisoned arrow strikes an animal's artery or the heart, death comes rapidly. But if the arrow penetrates perhaps only two or three inches into a fleshy part of the animal, a large animal may not die for two or three days; small animals succumb sooner. In the bloodstream the poison causes convulsions and paralysis. The meat of the animal killed by the poison and the blood itself may be eaten without harm.

One wonders how and when the !Kung learned that the larvae of three species of beetles and their parasites, buried in their cocoons two or three feet underground, were poisonous. Did a woman digging for roots happen to smash her finger and a cocoon at the same time with her digging stick? The !Kung say that the knowledge of poison came from the Creator. He gave the knowledge of planting crops and keeping cattle to the black people and the knowledge of poison to the Bushmen.

ORACLE DISKS

Sets of disks, usually made of leather, occasionally made of wood, are used by the !Kung for divination. The !Kung word for the disks is /xusi; I have called them oracle disks. The matters on which they are consulted are mundane not occult. The disks are believed to be capable of revealing recently past or current events and circumstances, and foretelling the near future. Hunting, with its results, was the subject on which the disks were most often consulted and the subject on which they made most revelations and predictions even when no definite inquiry was formulated. Hunting is much on the minds of !Kung men. The men consult the disks before starting on a hunt to ask what direction they should take to find animals. They carry the disks in their hunting bags and consult them for advice and encouragement during a hunt. The other subjects on which the men regularly consult the disks are the activities and conditions of absent relatives or friends. They also see in the disks what is to happen in their own encampment, such as the arrival of visitors.

The disks are made preferably of eland hide, but other heavy hide might be used or, rarely, wood. The disks of the sets I measured were round and graduated in size from 2⅛ inches to 2⅞ inches in diameter. They were about ⅛ inch thick. They are ordinarily used in sets of five or six. Larger sets, up to ten in number, are known, but ≠Toma said the larger sets were confusing and difficult to interpret. Most men prefer five or six. Each disk has its own identity and is recognized by its own peculiar irregularities or by designs scratched on the surface, or by bits of the animal's hair purposefully left on the hide to serve as identifying marks. The top and bottom sides of the disk must be distinguishable; a disk upside down has significance.

Each disk is named in one way or another, and to each disk either male or female sex is attributed. One set of names we heard attributed to a set of disks in order of size, large to small, was (1) Big Male Disk, /xu !go n!a, (2) Small Male Disk, /xu !go ma, (3) Big Female Disk, /xu di n!a, (4) Small Female Disk, /xu di ma, (5) Brown Hyena, !hau. The Hyena disk is female. In another set observed by Robert Dyson, the disks were called (1) Eland Bull, (2) Eland Bull, (3) Eland Cow, (4) Eland Cow, (5) Brown Hyena. Some men named their disks for various relatives, consanguineous or affinal. The owner of one set had given the first four disks his own name, his son's name, his wife's name, his daughter's name. His fifth disk was an unnamed male disk. He said he used this disk to represent non-Bushmen and the big carnivores, lions and leopards. His sixth was Brown Hyena. This man had left two tiny white tufts of the animal's hair on the hyena disk to represent breasts. The names by which the disks are identified do not necessarily have anything to do with the identities attributed to the disks when they are thrown; a variety of identities can be attributed.

There are no divining specialists among the !Kung. Any man may make oracle disks, own them, consult them at any time, and interpret them. But only men, not women, handle the disks. Women are not formally excluded from disk-throwing sessions as they are from some male rituals. They may listen to the men hold forth if they wish, but, disk throwing being the business of men, women do not ordinarily attend the sessions. On the other hand, all the men present in the encampment are likely to gather around when disks are being thrown. The man who throws the disks makes his interpretation of the cast and is listened to, but he is not allowed to pontificate. The men all read the disks with him and do not hesitate to express different opinions. They insist that some men can interpret better than others and, with banter and laughter, they call each other dunces and ignoramuses in disk reading. In all the many sessions in which I was an observer, the atmosphere was cheerful. The sessions revealed constant interest and concern with the hunt but not profound anxiety. Nor was great dread of evil apparent. The disks were not interpreted as revealing or foretelling anyone's sickness or death; nor was any grave disaster, such as severe drought, foretold.

The man who throws the disks sits down usually with a kaross spread out before him. He picks up his set of disks in order of size, stacks them into the palm of his left hand with the largest disk on the top. He cups his right hand over the stack, blows on his hands and bangs the edges of the disks down on the kaross before throwing, then he tips the disks out of his hands with a little toss and pulls his hands back quickly. As he tips the disks out of his hands he utters the word *fire, da.* The men could not tell me the significance of blowing on their hands, or banging the disks against the kaross before they throw, or of saying *da.* They could only say, "It is our custom." The disks are thrown so that they do not roll to a great distance; they fall within the space of about two feet more or less. From the position into which they fall with respect to each other the men interpret their message.

The men sometimes have in mind a definite inquiry and throw to see what information the disk can give them. Sometimes the men throw just to see what the disks have to say without formulating an inquiry. In some cases when the disks are very much spread out, the men see no meaningful relationships among them and say the disks have no news (n≠wa).

The reading of the meaning of the cast is apparently not governed by a complexity of fixed rules. The interpretations were a product of the imaginations of the men, who were, it seemed to me, as free to see in the disks whatever came to their minds as persons interpreting inkblots in a Rorschach test. The disks could represent any element of the men's inquiries: individuals; categories of persons such as strangers, visitors, non-Bushmen; animals; objects; or rain. They could indicate time and direction and good or bad fortune. (Direction in the cast is read as we read a map. North is up from the thrower, west on his left, east to his right, south toward himself.)

With a certain exception, to be mentioned, any disk upside down indicates "death" (⁻!khi or ⁻!hi), we were told. In any disk-throwing session I attended, when disk numbers one to four were upside down, the death predicted was that of a game animal, and the disks conveyed the cheerful news that the people would have meat.

The smallest disk, number five in a five-disk set, number six in a six-disk set, if right side up, could be used like any other disk to represent any person, animal, or object. When upside down, the disk could be called one of three names, Brown Hyena, Fire, or Sun. It was the disk usually used to represent the great meat-eating predators, lions and leopards, and non-Bushmen. As Brown Hyena, the disk does not represent an actual hyena; it is a sign of bad luck or something unfavorable. People called it "the strange one," and said it spoke for the //gauwasi, the spirits of the dead, and that it is a "death thing." The application of the word "death" (⁻!khi or ⁻!hi) or "death thing" is not limited to literal death in the !Kung language. Something that portends evil or grave misfortune may be called "death" or "death thing." (Falling stars, for example, are "death" or "death things." They portend evil and show that somewhere people are suffering and dying.) The Brown Hyena disk was an unfavorable sign, but, as I mentioned previously, the misfortunes predicated were only mild ones, failure in the hunt, John having trouble with his trucks, and so forth.

As Fire or Sun, although upside down, the disk is a favorable sign. (This role is not exclusive to the smallest disk. The largest also was sometimes called Fire or Sun.) To be interpreted as representing Fire or Sun, judging from the casts I saw, the disk must have fallen upside down and must stand apart from other disks. Sun can also be a sign indicating the direction in which the hunters will find animals, the direction from which visitors are coming, etc. I was utterly bewildered by this disk. I could not find out from informants what lore lay behind the names, Brown Hyena, Fire, or Sun, or if any factor other than their own whim determined which identity the men would attribute to the disk and whether to interpret it as a favorable or unfavorable sign. There must be some explanation to clarify this question, but I failed to find it.

The men know so much about the people and about the game and what is likely to happen that their interpretations are more likely to be right than wrong. No one seems to make a great issue of being right or wrong, however, and no serious blame accrues to the disks or to their interpreters for being wrong. And, as with divination anywhere, people tend to remember the prognostications that were coincidentally right while the wrong ones slip out of mind. I particularly remember the disks telling us on one occasion that John would return in precisely two days. We did not expect him for a week or more. On the afternoon of the second day when we heard the unmistakable drone of the distant trucks, ≠Toma came to me to say, "You see, the disks were right."

5 The Family and the Band

In their traditional social organization, the !Kung have only two groupings, the family and the band, the grouping in which families combine to
live together. The !Kung word for this grouping is n//abesi, which the
!Kung say means "the people who live together." In the Nyae Nyae region,
a few of the !Kung are employed by Bantu and live with their families in
what I call "groups" inside the Bantu kraals or nearby. I count these
!Kung as a part of the !Kung population. They preserve much of !Kung
culture; they intermarry with the other !Kung of the region. The only
difference between them and the !Kung who live in the traditional way
is that they obtain food and some cast-off clothes from the Bantu in
return for their services, and the group of !Kung in which they live comes
into existence by reason of their employment and not by reason of their
traditional band organization. At the time we were in the field, there
were three such groups in the Nyae Nyae area, and in the Dobe area, to
the best of our knowledge, there were six (see Table 3). Except for the
above-mentioned groups, all !Kung in the Nyae Nyae area live in bands.

POPULATION

In 1952, we estimated the !Kung population in the Nyae Nyae region to
be approximately 1,000 persons. An estimated 567 were in the Nyae
Nyae area, an estimated 432 in the Dobe area, adding up to 999. They
lived in thirty-seven communities counting bands and groups. (Band 8

This chapter is a considerably revised and somewhat expanded version of a
paper entitled "!Kung Bushman Bands," published in *Africa*, 30 (Oct. 1960), 325–355.
It is published here with the kind permission of the International African Institute.

A band walking, a brown sinuous line moving in the golden land. Gautscha
Pan (in the dry season) is in the background.

TABLE 3. Estimate of the !Kung Population in the Nyae Nyae Region

Band	Waterhole	K"xau N!a (K) or Leader(L)	Number of Persons
	The Nyae Nyae area, South West Africa		
Sixteen bands counted precisely or approximately			
1	Gautscha	≠Toma [1.16]L	26*
2	Gautscha	Gao Beard [2.9]K	38*
3	Kautsa and !Kabi	≠Gao [3.4]K	9*
4	Deboragu	Old /Gaishay [4.1]K	10*
5	Deboragu	Old N!aishi [5.1]K	8*
6	Nam Tshoha	/Ti!kay [6.12]K; Old Demi [6.4]L	12*
7	N!o !Go and Kaitsa	Old /Qui [7.2]K	16*
9	Khumsa	/Ti!kay [9.8]K	19*

Band	Waterhole	K″xau N!a (K) or Leader(L)	Number of Persons
10	Tsumkwe	Gao [10.4]K; ≠Gao [10.13]L	25*
12	/Gam	Gao [12.29]K	42*
13	/Gam	/Ti!kay [13.14]K; Old Debe [13.18]L	38*
14	/Gun/ga	/Ti!kay [14.9]K	28*
8 or 8A	Gura	Bo, Br of N/aoka [1.7]	47**
11	West of Châssis	Gao Hunchback K	35**
17	N//o!gau	—	25**
24	Tsho/ana	Debe L	9**

Three bands estimated

25	Northeast of 24	—	c.30
26	Samangaigai	/Ti!kay K	c.30
27	Samangaigai	Gumtsa K	c.25
		Total in 19 bands	472

Three groups estimated

1	/Gam		c.30
2	Tsho/ana		c.40
3	Samangaigai		c.25
		Total in 3 groups	c.95
		Total in Nyae Nyae area	567

The Dobe area, Botswana

Three bands counted precisely or approximately

15	Domn!a and ≠Go≠gowe	≠Toma [15.9]K	27*
28	/Gwia	/Ti!kay	32*
16	≠O //Gana	Zu/oa K	23**

Six bands estimated

18	Kai Kai		c.30
19	Kai Kai		c.35
20	Kai Kai		c.30
21	Kubi and !Gum !Guri		c.30
22	Kubi		c.25
23	!Xabe		c.30
		Total in 9 bands	262

Six groups estimated

4	Kai Kai		c.30
5	Kubi		c.30

Band	Waterhole	K''xau N!a (K) or Leader(L)	Number of Persons
6	!Xabe		c.30
7	Mahupa		c.25
8	Bahti		c.30
9	Khownwa		c.25
		Total in 6 groups	170
		Total in the Dobe area	432

Totals

Nyae Nyae area,	19 bands and 3 groups		567
Dobe area,	9 bands and 6 groups		432
Nyae Nyae region, 37 bands and groups			999

Average number of persons in the nineteen counted bands

16 counted bands in the Nyae Nyae area	387
3 counted bands in the Dobe area	82
Total	469

Average number of persons in each band: 24.6

* Counted precisely
** Counted approximately
c. Estimated

was in flux. We were uncertain whether it should be counted as one or two bands. Since the people were together when we visited them, we have put them in as one band.) Of these thirty-seven communities, nineteen bands and three groups were in the Nyae Nyae area. These included the whole population of the Nyae Nyae area at the time. In the Dobe area we encountered nine bands and six groups. There were other bands in the Dobe area which we did not see. Our estimation of the population of the !Kung in the area (432) must, nevertheless, have been in the proper order of magnitude, for Richard Lee's exact count ten years later was 433.[1]

In Table 3, I list the bands and groups, giving the places of their waterholes, the number of members counted precisely, counted approximately, or estimated, the name of the person who was called k''xau n!a

1. The figure 433 comes from Lee's Subsistence Ecology of !Kung Bushmen (Ann Arbor, Mich., University Microfilms, 1968), p. 27. In a later publication (Hunters and Gatherers Today, ed. M. G. Bicchieri, New York, Holt, Rinehart and Winston, 1972, p. 330), Lee raised the figure to 466.

MAP 2

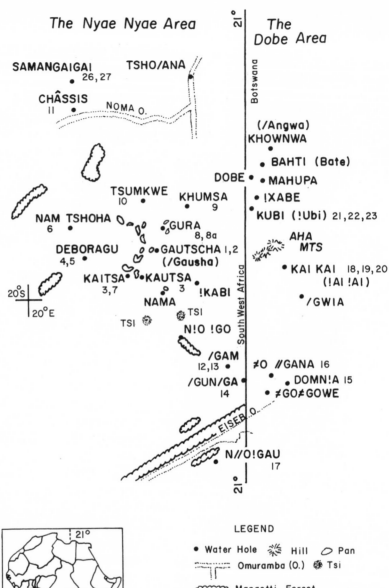

The Nyae Nyae Area

21°

The Dobe Area

Botswana

SAMANGAIGAI
• 26,27

TSHO/ANA
•

CHÂSSIS
11

NOMA O.

(/Angwa)
KHOWNWA
•

• BAHTI (Bate)

DOBE • • MAHUPA

TSUMKWE
10

KHUMSA
9

• IXABE

KUBI (!Ubi) 21,22,23

NAM TSHOHA
6

GURA
8,8a

DEBORAGU
4,5

GAUTSCHA 1,2
(/Gausha)

AHA
MTS

KAI KAI 18,19,20
(!AI !AI)

KAITSA KAUTSA
3,7

3
!KABI

NAMA

/GWIA

South West Africa

20°S
20°E

TSI

TSI

N!O !GO

/GAM
12,13

/GUN/GA
14

≠O //GANA 16

• DOMN!A 15

≠GO≠GOWE

E!SEB O.

N//O!GAU
17

21°

LEGEND

• Water Hole   ⁂ Hill   ⌀ Pan

⊤ Omuramba (O.)   ✹ Tsi

〰〰〰 Mangetti Forest

Numbers refer to bands in table 3.

This map indicates *approximately* the location of the waterholes at which the bands are based.

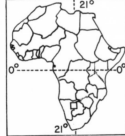

21°

0°

0°

21°

(big or old "owner") or the leader of the band, or, if I know neither of those, the name of some other individual whom we met.

The bands have been arbitrarily numbered for convenient identification. In Table 3, they are not listed consecutively in the order of their numbering, but instead have been grouped to make a distinction between the counted and estimated bands and between those in the Nyae Nyae area and those in the Dobe area.

The bands marked with a single asterisk (*) were counted precisely. Every member was seen. Those bands marked with a double asterisk (**) were counted approximately. Not all the members were present when we met the band, but we were given the names of the absent members and we consider the count to be approximately correct. The count given in both categories is that made during the period in which we first met the band. For all except Bands 24 and 28, that period was between August and December 1952. We met Band 24 early in January 1953, and we first met Band 28, the /Gwia band, in 1961.

Bands and groups marked *circa* (c.) were not counted precisely; only estimates were made. Either a few members of the band or group visited us or we visited the band or group but did not see all the members and did not gather precise information. In those cases we attribute the average figure of the counted bands, which we take to be 25, or, if we visited and saw the band or group, we attributed a larger or smaller figure according to our impression.

The figures in Table 3 differ slightly from those published in 1960 in the paper "!Kung Bushman Bands." There the total given was 986, here it is 999. One difference is the addition of the 32 members of Band 28. Other differences in the size of a few of the bands result from my having used a count made at a later period of time than the first count. Additional births and deaths had occurred, and, in two instances, segments of bands had moved from one band to another. Here I am taking out those changes and giving the first count for all the bands.

In Table 4, an analysis by age and sex is given of the members of the thirteen precisely counted Nyae Nyae bands, Bands 1–7, 9, 10, 12–15, with 298 persons. Table 5 gives the status of married persons in this sample. Table 6 gives the residence of married men, whether with their wives' kin or with their own kin.

In Appendix 1, charts of ten of the precisely counted Nyae Nyae bands (Bands 1–7, 9, 10, 12, with 205 members) give examples of large and small bands and show the relationships on which bands are formed.

In the charts and tables we indicate the roughly estimated ages of the people, arbitrarily placing them in the following categories:

old	(O)	from 50 onwards
adult	(A)	from 25 to 50
young adult	(YA)	from 16 to 24
child	(C)	from 8 to 15
young child	(YC)	from 0 to 7

The !Kung do not count their age in years, and we do not know how old they are. Our rough estimates of ages in years are based only on guessing. I am uncertain and tentative about all of those estimates.

The !Kung place people in general categories of old, n!a, and young, ma. Laurence at sixty-three and I at fifty-four were an old man (!hoa n!a) and an old woman (tsau n!a). Adults are called young men and young women (!hoa ma or tsau ma) when they are at the period of having their first three children. Just when adults cease to be called young and begin to be called old, I do not know. A teen-ager is called old child, dama n!a

TABLE 4. Analysis of Members of Thirteen Counted Bands by Age and Sex

	Old Adults		Adults		Young Adults		Children		Young Children		Total
	M	F	M	F	M	F	M	F	M	F	
Band 1	1	1	5	5	3	1	3	2	3	2	26
Band 2	1	3	6	7	4	2	4	1	7	3	38
Band 3	1	2	1	1	1				1	2	9
Band 4	1	1	2	2			1	1	2		10
Band 5	1	1	1	1	1	1		1		1	8
Band 6	4	2	1	1	3	1					12
Band 7	1	3	2	2		1	3	2		2	16
Band 9		3	3	4	1		3	2	2	1	19
Band 10		2	2	4	5	5	2	1	2	2	25
Band 12	1	4	6	8	4	4	5	7	2	1	42
Band 13	1	4	6	8	4	3	2	7	2	1	38
Band 14	1	2	6	6			7	5		1	28
Band 15	2	2	4	6	1	1	6	5			27
Totals	15	30	45	55	27	19	36	34	21	16	298

Summary:	Men over 15	87	Women over 15	104
	Boys under 15	57	Girls under 15	50
	Total males	144	Total females	154

TABLE 5. Marriage Status

	Males			Females	
O & A	married men		O & A	married women	
	with one wife	48		as one wife	48
	with two wives	8		as co-wives	16
YA	married men		YA	married women	
	with one wife	15		as one wife	12
	with two wives	1		as co-wives	2
			C	married girls under 15	3
O	widowers	3	O	widows	20
O	unmarried man		A	widows	4
	(the one old bachelor)	1			
YA	unmarried men	11	O	divorcee	1
			YA	divorcee	1
				spinsters	0
		87			107

NOTE: All women in the categories of old, adult, and young adult, a total of 104, are married, widowed, or divorced. In addition, three girls from the category of children (under 15) are married, making a total of 107 married females. The three girls were N≠isa [1.2], Xama [2.14], Baú [9.6]. (A fourth girl from the child category, N'ai [1.12], was not married at the time of our count in 1952. She was married a few months later, in May 1953.)

In addition to the three married girls mentioned, seven married girls in the young adult category had not yet borne children, making a total of ten young married females without children. Among the total of twenty-seven young adult males, eleven were still unmarried and no boys from the category of children were married.

TABLE 6. Residence of the 72 Married Men in the 13 Counted Bands

1. Men in residence with wives and wives' kin:		
with no kin of man present in band other than his offspring	23	
with some kin of their own present	10	33
Men in residence with their own kin:		
with no kin of their wives present other than offspring	18	
with some kin of their wives present	14	32
Total		65
2. Men (and their wives) in residence with		
a married son who is with his wife's kin	2	
Man (and his wife) in residence with		
a married daughter who is with her husband's kin	1	3
3. Residence undetermined		4
Total married men		72

(plural *divi n!a*). Between the age at which a child walks well and the beginning of the teens, a child is called young child, *dama ma* (plural *divi ma*). A baby is called *dama ma tsema*, little young child. The !Kung refer more specifically to the ages of children in terms of their physical development. They refer to a child's first beginning to smile, the closing of the anterior fontanelle, a child sitting up alone, walking alone, the first and second teeth coming in, a girl's breasts beginning to bud, a girl's first menstruation, a boy's voice changing. They say of a boy or girl who has reached full growth that the young person "sees his or her head's place." The more specific age of young adults is measured by the time required for them potentially to have had one, two, or three children, not by the actual birth of the children. The !Kung need to measure age more specifically than merely to place people in young and old categories, because many of their rites and avoidances are related to age. Girls, for example, must avoid eating certain foods from the time of first menstruation till they are old enough to have had one baby. (The rites and avoidances will be described in a forthcoming volume.)

Average Number of Living Offspring; Size of Families

!Kung families are small. In preparing the paper "'!Kung Bushman Bands" for publication in *Africa,* I made a count of living offspring of a sample of 68 living women from ten bands. They had 164 offspring, an average of 2.41. In that count, I had included births from dates later than 1952. In making a new count, I am taking a sample of 79 living women from the thirteen precisely counted Nyae Nyae-bands and limiting the data to the period in 1952 when the first count of those bands, as listed in Table 4, was made. I have omitted from the count 14 women for whom data are lacking, 8 married girls who were still young and had not yet borne a child, 2 women who had borne children (I do not know how many) but whose children were all dead. I omitted also the one old woman, Old N/aoka [9.15], who had never borne a child. The remaining 79 women had 171 offspring, an average of 2.16.

I commend to the reader a fine demographic study by Nancy Howell, "The Population of the Dobe Area !Kung," a chapter in *Kalahari Hunter-Gatherers.*[2] She devised a method of reckoning the age of Bushmen and

2. Nancy Howell, "The Population of the Dobe Area !Kung," in *Kalahari Hunter-Gatherers,* ed. Richard Lee and Irven DeVore (Cambridge, Mass., Harvard University Press, 1976).

has compiled meaningful demographic data. No demographic study of the Nyae Nyae area has been made, but I believe that if one were to be made the findings would be very similar to those Nancy Howell presents for the Dobe area. Among much else, she tells us that the average age of the girls first menstruation is 16.5, the average age of mothers when their first child is born is 19.5, the modal length of the interval between births is about four years.

Among the many factors that may contribute to the small size of !Kung families, low fertility is one. Nancy Howell says, "Over the whole reproductive span, ages 15–49, women averaged 4.7 live births for the cohort born 45–49 years ago, and 5.2 for the cohorts born more than fifty years ago. The variance of the number of live births is small for the !Kung; the maximum number of live births is only nine. This level of fertility is considerably lower than any other population known that is practicing natural fertility."[3]

Other factors that keep !Kung families small are infant mortality and the practice of infanticide. I have no statistics on the number of deaths by natural causes of children born to the mothers in my sample. My impression is that many mothers had lost children by natural causes in the first, second, and third years of the children's lives. Before we first met her in 1951, !U had lost two, one at one year of age and one at three years.

I have neither figures nor impression of the number of instances of infanticide that occur. Nancy Howell reports a very low incidence, six in five hundred births.[4] No one spoke to me of infanticide till I asked, but when I asked, informants responded—both men and women. All the women I spoke to claimed that they had never had to "throw down" a baby. /Kao is the word they use; it means "to throw down," "to hurt," "to go from" (Bleek, Dictionary, p. 408). They said, however, that they knew that sometimes a woman had to do this.

In the minds of the !Kung, spacing their children three or four years apart is the necessity that makes them practice infanticide. They know of no contraceptive or abortive methods. Low fertility and long lactation help to prevent frequent pregnancies in some women. (The !Kung say that women who do not become pregnant easily have "good backs." I think this phrase refers to buttocks. Breasts are associated with nursing,

3. Ibid., p. 145.
4. Ibid., p. 147.

not with sex; they are left bare. Buttocks are associated with sex and are kept modestly covered.) However, some women resort to infanticide in order to space their children.

A woman goes into the bushes apart from the encampment to give birth, either alone or with her own mother. A n/um k"xau does not attend her except in the rare instances of a very difficult birth. If she decides not to keep the baby, it probably never breathes. I did not have the fortitude to learn more. I have the impression that the !Kung do not feel that they commit a sin or a crime when they practice infanticide, but I believe that it is very disturbing to them nonetheless. When they talked about it with me, they never once spoke concretely or directly of the act itself but had much to say about the necessity for it.

We believe that the meagerness of the resources of food and water puts pressure on the !Kung to keep their population in balance. This, however, does not seem to be the conscious concern of the !Kung when they speak of infanticide. They spoke of the nourishment of the children as the primary reason; they spoke in explicit detail. They want children, all the children they can possibly have, but, they explained, they cannot feed babies that are born too close together. They said Bushman children must have strong legs, and it is mothers' milk that makes them strong. A mother had not enough milk to sustain completely two infants at the same time. They believe a child needs milk till he is three or four years old at least. The !Kung have no milk from cows or goats and no cereals to feed an infant, and they say that even if they supplement the feeding by chewing their tough meat, harsh roots, and nuts and feed the infant premasticated food from their own mouths (we have seen them do this), they cannot successfully feed two infants this way. Neither thrives, both may die.

A second grave concern for these nomadic people is the carrying of the children. When traveling, the men carry all their belongings and whatever food they have in skin bags hung on carrying-sticks. The child of about three to six years—the "knee child"—rides on one of his father's shoulders or astride both, his legs around his father's neck. Vibrant and at ease at the same time, the children ride with exquisite balance, rarely needing to hold on to their fathers' heads. On the long treks, the mother is laden with all her worldly goods, perhaps including several ostrich eggshells filled with water, and such roots and berries as she may have. These and her infant she carries in the pouch of her kaross. On the shorter daily trips to gather food, the mother carries the baby in her

Khuan//a carrying her two young children

kaross, and for most of the way the "knee child" as well on her shoulders. Strong though they are, to carry a third child and the food they gather would be practically impossible for those small women. Children of about seven and upward walk along with the adults.

We may note that the number of males and females in the population does not differ greatly. In the thirteen counted bands, there are more women than men; old women apparently outlive old men. Among the young, there are more boys than girls. In the counted bands, there are 57 boys, 50 girls, and 8 more young adult males than females. However, in the formerly mentioned sample of 164, it so happened that the number of boys and girls was even. There appears not to be a marked preference for children of one sex over the other.

THE FAMILY

Of the two groupings in !Kung social organization, the family and the band, the family—in its nuclear form—is the primary grouping. It is not an independent residential group—no nuclear family lives alone—it is primary in the sense that it is the building block, the unit which combines with other similar units to form extended families and bands.

Sometimes a strong extended family, composed of three or four nuclear families, lives alone, constituting a band in itself. More often, nuclear and extended families combine in larger numbers to form the bands.

The family in either of its two forms, nuclear or extended (which I shall define presently), is both cohesive and stable. The family's existence as a unit and its cohesiveness are visible in the way the members settle near together in an encampment and in the way they sit by their fires. These characteristics are clearly visible also when bands disperse and families go to different places temporarily to gather food or to visit relatives: then one sees whole families separating from other families, each a unit in itself.

Bride Service

Marriage is the subject of Chapter 8, but because bride service is an important factor in the structure of the family and determines for many people the band in which they live, I shall discuss it here. Two points should be mentioned in passing. A !Kung band is not per se an exogamous unit. Marriage prohibitions are based on kinship, and although a marriage between two members of one band is not a usual occurrence, no rule of exogamy prevents such a marriage provided no consanguineous or affinal ties exist that prohibit it. The other point is that the !Kung practice polygyny. Their marriage prohibitions and their polygyny are discussed in Chapter 8.

!Kung society, rigorously and without exception, requires that all men go to live with the parents of their brides and give them bride service. Should his bride's parents be dead, the man goes to whatever relatives she lives with and serves them.

Bride service is required in any marriage, in first marriages arranged by the parents when the boys and girls are young, in subsequent marriages when a widower or a divorced man remarries, and in instances when polygyny is practiced and a man takes more than one wife.

The service a man gives is hunting. The great concern of the !Kung is food; they talk about it constantly and explain bride service in terms of meat. They say: "Our daughter's husband must give us meat. We are old, or we shall soon be old [whether this is actually true or not]; we need a young man to hunt for us; we need karosses." These are their refrains. They want meat, and they also want the boy to feed his bride while she is young, believing that this unites the two. People also say that they want to see the young man grow to maturity and to make sure that he is able and responsible and that he will be kind to their daughter.

A man is responsible for the support of his parents and their dependents, and when he marries he becomes responsible as well for the support of his wife's parents and their dependents. Any or all of these relatives may choose to live with him, and if they do, he will hunt for them. If he moves from one band to another to give bride service, or for any other reason, he takes with him those who need or want to accompany him. In a polygynous marriage when a man gives bride service for a second wife, he takes with him his first wife, his children by her, and all her relatives who live with him. Thus, bride service brings whole segments of bands to join other bands. For example, both Gao of Band 1 and Gaú of Band 2 married their second wives in early middle age, when the two men had quite large families attached to them. Gao brought his first wife, N/aoka, two daughters by her, their husbands and children, and a teen-age son into the band of his second wife, Di!ai. Gaú brought his first wife, Be [2.26], three sons by her, his mother, Old /Gasa, and two sisters with their husbands and children.

The duration of bride service is indefinite. The people say it should be long enough for three children to be born. In first marriages, when the young girls have been married for several years before their first menstruation, ten or more years might elapse before three children could be born. I believe that in subsequent marriages the time requirement may not be as long or as strictly adhered to as in first marriages when the brides are young. Nothing precludes the couple's visiting the husband's people during bride service.

After his obligations are fulfilled, the man is considered to have the right to return to his own people, taking his wife and children and dependents. However, he is not required by social rule to return. The couple may stay on with his wife's people. For various reasons, they may find it more advantageous or agreeable to do so. In several instances in which the men had remained with their wives' people, the men had no people to return to. Their families were dead or their bands had dispersed because of insufficient resources. This was true of ≠Toma, Crooked /Qui, /Gao Music, and Dam [2.32]. In other instances, the couples made the choice of living with the wife's people because the women were so reluctant to leave that the men conceded to them. In other instances, the relative scantiness or plentitude of resources determined the choice. Also, the feelings and preferences people had for each other might determine the choice of residence.

As of 1959, Gao, originally of Band 4, had lived for nine years with his second wife's people in Band 1. We think his remaining in Band 1 was not in response to the time requirement of bride service, or not entirely so. He was free to return to his father's band (Band 4) at any time, but these particular people in Band 1 liked living together. The attachment between the two sisters, Di!ai, Gao's wife, and !U, ≠Toma's wife, was very strong. The two brothers-in-law, ≠Toma and Gao, were also attached. Each was the other's favorite hunting partner, and their apparent harmony and enjoyment in their relationship was notable. Incidentally, there was no question of the family returning to the band of Gao's first wife, N/aoka. Her people had disbanded and left the area in which they had formerly lived. The area was far to the west, near Epata, where N/aoka's people had been loosely attached to a group who worked for Herero.

Required bride service and the choice of staying on with the wife's people combine to account for the fact that about half of the adult men are living with their wives' bands. The ratio we find in Bands 1, 2, 3, and 4 is consistent with larger samples in our study (see Table 6). In those bands there are twenty-five married men. Eighteen of these are living with their wives' people. Of the eighteen, eight have taken residence in their wives' bands, and ten are in bride service and may in the future choose either to stay or to return to their own bands. The remaining seven of the twenty-five men had chosen to return and are in residence again with their people. When I say that a man has taken residence in his wife's or his own band, I mean only that he has chosen for the present. The vicissitudes of life might lead him to make another choice in the future.

Composition of the Family

Although the family is a stable unit, it fluctuates in composition, passing from one phase to another. It does so in a continuum, repeating the same phases through the generations. There are two phases, the nuclear and the extended phase. The nuclear phase itself may have two or possibly three phases; the extended phase may have two.

In its simplest nuclear phase, a !Kung family is composed of a man and his wife. It is then augmented by such children as are born to them. The family may have some dependent of the husband or wife living with it—a dependent parent or grandparent or sibling; an uncle or aunt who has no offspring of his or her own to live with; an orphaned nephew or niece or grandchild.

Since bride service brings the young husband to live in the bride's family, one does not find a young nuclear family living independently unless it should happen that the bride's parents were dead. In such circumstances, the couple would live beside and somewhat under the authority of some of the bride's people, but this is not a normal family phase. In normal conditions, the new nuclear family, the bride and groom, live in the extended family of the bride's father.

I include among nuclear families those in which the man has two wives, but I consider them to be in a later phase than the first, as the first marriage is arranged with just one wife (at least this was so in all instances that I knew).

When the daughters marry and the young husbands come to give

The family of ≠Toma and !U is an example of a nuclear family. Left to right they are ≠Toma, Tsamgao, /Gaishay, and !U holding !Ungka Norna. !U made sketchy shelters. This one (left) has been almost blown away.

bride service, the family becomes an extended family. In this (earlier) phase, the unmarried daughters and unmarried sons of the bride's original family are present. The married sons have left their family to live with their brides' parents.

In the second extended phase, the married sons may have returned, with their wives and offspring, from bride service to live again with their own parents. The married daughters with their husbands and offspring may continue to live with their parents or may go to live with their husbands' people.

The father of an extended family is the head of that family. He has authority over his sons-in-law during the time they live with him as well as over his own offspring. His authority is not formally defined, is not supported by structured sanctions, is not expressed dictatorially.

The family of Gaú and his two wives—Be, his first wife, on his right, Khuan//a, his second wife, on his left. Be's three sons are in the photograph. Khuan//a is holding her young son.

His authority is a matter of attitude and is sanctioned by group expectation and opinion. Sons-in-law comply, do what is expected of them, fall in with the father-in-law's plans—which for the most part are plans that the son-in-law will go hunting. We did not observe any examples of conflict between a son-in-law and father-in-law during our field work. If a son-in-law were displeased, he would be more likely to mope than to argue or refuse to do what his father-in-law expected of him.

When the father of an extended family dies, that particular extended family headship ends and the extended family breaks up. Family headship, I believe, is strongly associated with males. A widowed mother continues to live with one or another of her offspring and his or her spouse, and has full claim upon their support, but she is in the role of dependent, not head of family. The nuclear families of the married

The extended family of Gao Hunchback of Band 11. Gao's three sons-in-law are in the foreground, his wife and daughters and their children are in the background. Gao is on the right with his hand against his face.

daughters and sons are independent of each other. Families of siblings may live together in the same band, but as families one has no authority over another. If they are no longer involved in bride service themselves, and their offspring are not yet married, these families again become independent nuclear families. When the offspring marry, these families become new extended families.

The various phases of the !Kung family are exemplified in Bands 1 and 2. The family of ≠Toma, the leader of Band 1, is an independent nuclear family. The family of Gao of Band 1 is extended in the earlier extended phase. His two married daughters by N/aoka, his first wife, namely N≠isa [1.2] and //Khuga [1.4], are present with their husbands. Also present are N!ai, the daughter of Gao's second wife, Di!ai (by Di!ai's former husband Gumtsa), and N!ai's husband, /Gunda. (We count /Gunda present in Band 1 if we take a date after May 22, 1953, which was the date of his marriage to N!ai.) The family of Old ≠Toma of Band 2 is in the later extended phase. His married son, //Ao Wildebeest, with his wife and child (he had three—two died), has returned to live in the extended family relationship with his father. The daughter of Old ≠Toma, //Kushay, is no longer a part of his extended family. She lives with her husband, Gao Beard. This presents a fine distinction, for they all live in the same band and usually settle no more than fifteen or twenty feet apart. Yet, they do not reside as one extended family. Gao Beard's bride service is long since completed, and he is no longer under the family authority of Old ≠Toma. Old ≠Toma has with him his wife, Old /Gam, his two unmarried sons, the tall young /Gunda [2.18] and /Gao [2.19], as well as his married son, //Ao Wildebeest.

Both Gao Beard and Old ≠Toma said explicitly that they liked living together. Furthermore, one can see this arrangement as being advantageous to both. Gao likes Old ≠Toma. Furthermore, he gains three young men to hunt with him, //Ao Wildebeest, an excellent hunter, and his two younger brothers. The two boys were just beginning to be competent hunters. The arrangement is advantageous to Old ≠Toma and Old /Gam as well. Gao Beard is a good provider and they like living with their daughter, //Kushay. She is an attractive, fair-minded, even-tempered, competent woman and a good daughter to them.

Men and Women

Women make an enormous contribution to !Kung life. They are so much in demand as mates that none remain unmarried. Young men wait for years for girls to whom they are engaged to grow up; widowers and divorced men seek wives; many men want two wives. As food gatherers, women provide more of the family's food than the men do with their hunting. In their role as mothers, women contribute more to the care of the children than men do as fathers. Fathers are with their children when in the encampment, but fathers do not take their children hunting. Women do take their children with them when they go to gather and have the principal care of them throughout the days during all the years of their childhood. When I think of the contribution women make to !Kung life, I think also of their nursing each baby for three or four years. They supply the major part of the sustenance of their people and contribute in every way to the common life.

Nevertheless, their preciousness as mates and the magnitude of their contribution do not put women forward into a dominant position or a position of leadership in the society. Men come forward into that position. Women in some ways and to some degree lean upon their men, look to them for protection, depend on them.

!Kung women are encouraged to be gentle and compliant by the fact that in their love of peace the !Kung like quiet, modest women. Overbearing, strident, demanding, or nagging women would disturb not only their own husbands but the whole encampment, and group disapproval would be expressed.

Women appear to acquiesce in their role and expect to be the followers. In their dealings with us, they were notably more circumscribed, less outgoing, than the men. Women were more apprehensive of strangeness and strangers and drew back from new experiences, such as riding in trucks. As informants, they held back. Some said explicitly that they feared they would not know the correct answers to my questions. Others made the sweeping statement that men know more than women do. In our frequent conclaves, when we tried to explain our purposes, asked the !Kung for their cooperation, and made plans together, the women did not take part. They said we must ask the men; the men must decide. One woman said, as if by way of explanation, "Men can do everything, they can shoot and make fire."

The society does not structure the dominance of men with offices or rules that give men power over women. In this connection, it is to be noted that men give bride service, leaving their own people to live with and hunt for their wives' people. The forward position of men does not result in the subjugation of women. !Kung women are not subjugated, and they are by no means subservient. Although the women expect the men in the final analysis to be the decision makers and the leaders, they nevertheless express themselves fully and have a place in family discussion and in making family arrangements. Mothers and fathers share authority over the children. No formalized modes of obedience are required of women. Women do not wait on men. Food is shared equally by men and women. Women are not excluded from any space in the encampment nor from activities or rituals except those related to hunting and the boys' initiations. Women are not ill treated.

Once I saw a woman hit her husband. Gao Beard's young second wife, //Kushay II, hit him on the head with her digging stick when she was thwarted and sorely vexed. But I never happened to see a man attempt to coerce or punish a woman by physical force. That is not to say no !Kung man ever did strike a woman, but to do so is by no means common practice. Differences are resolved by talk. Relatives and friends may intervene in quarrels between the husbands and wives and help them to stop the quarrel. Or a man and wife may separate if they cannot resolve their differences. For a man to beat or to browbeat a woman is not the !Kung way.

Instead of being domineering, the men's role is one of protection and support. Women go out from the encampment alone for days of gathering, but never to more distant places where they would stay overnight, or longer, without the men accompanying them. The men always help in gathering of tsi or mangetti nuts and help to carry the heavy loads.

I believe that the men's forward position derives principally from two factors. One is their physical strength. !Kung men are small and slender, but they are wiry and vigorous. When they swing their weapons, their bags of possessions, and their children onto their shoulders and stride out in front of the women, the image they present is one of strength and leadership. I believe that the following women, laden with their babies and their heavy loads, are borne up by the strength of the men and take heart in it.

The hunt, I believe, is the other principal factor that gives men in !Kung society the position they have. !Kung society accords the hunt great importance and, for the !Kung, hunting is entirely a male affair. Women are wholly excluded from hunting and from taking part in the several hunting rituals that the men perform. The !Kung hold a belief (expressed in some of their avoidances and in the hunting rituals) that femaleness and success in the hunt are in opposition, that femaleness negates hunting prowess. Therefore, for example, women must avoid touching arrows. Men must avoid having intercourse with their wives at certain times, and the !Kung believe that if a man's wife is lactating, he must carefully avoid letting her milk touch him. The milk, they believe, would destroy his hunting powers. Women must not be nearby when the hunting rites are being performed.

Women bring most of the daily food that sustains the life of the people, but the roots and berries that are the principal plant foods of the Nyae Nyae !Kung are apt to be tasteless, harsh, and not very satisfying. People crave meat. Furthermore, there is only drudgery in digging roots, picking berries, and trudging back to the encampment with the heavy loads and babies sagging in the pouches of the karosses; there is no splen-

did excitement and triumph in returning with vegetables. The return of
the hunters from a successful hunt is vastly different. The intense crav-
ing for meat, the uncertainty and anxiety that attend the hunt, the deep
excitement of the kill, and, finally, the eating and the satisfaction engage
powerful emotions in the people.

One time when the people had been many days without meat and
were anxious about the hunters' success, an eland was killed, and the
hunters were sighted moving toward the encampment in a dark, lumpy,
bobbing line in the golden grass, their carrying sticks loaded with meat.
We heard the sound of voices in the encampment rising in volume and
pitch like the hum of excited bees. Some people ran toward the hunters,
others crowded together at the edge of the encampment, some danced
up and down, children squealed and ran about, the boys grappled and
tussled together. I think also of the time the women danced a dance of
praise for Short /Qui and his ostrich. I venture to say no women have
been greeted in this manner when they returned with vegetables, and I
believe that the value put on hunting and the satisfaction in its success
accrue to the enhancement of men's position in !Kung society. Men, the
!Kung say, are "masters of meat," "owners of hunting."

A song expresses the people's feeling about meat. The song tells
how the God, //Gauwa, favored the hunters, led them to find game, gave
them luck, and they brought meat to the people. Afterward a man said to
the women:

> You must sing well.
> We are happy now.
> Our hearts are shining.
> I shall put on my rattles,
> And put on my headband,
> And put a feather in my hair
> To explain to //Gauwa how happy we are that he
>   has helped us and that we have eaten.
> My heart is awake.
> When we do not have meat
> My heart is sad from hunger,
> Like an old man, sick and slow.
> When we have meat my heart is lively.

I should like to point out, furthermore, while considering the position of men and women among the !Kung, that men have the forward
position in the religious life of the people. Women perform some rites,

including rites for the protection of their children's health, and the Rite of First Menstruation, and women may participate in a rain rite. (The last is not an important rite and is not often performed. It was extremely interesting to me to find that the !Kung do not have an important rain rite and that !Kung women perform no rites over their gathering.) Men, on the other hand, perform more rites than women do and take a leading position in the most important rites, namely, the rites for success in the hunt, and the extremely important initiation rite for boys, the Rite of the First Kill, which is based on hunting and which must be performed before a boy may marry. Furthermore, in the great rite that overshadows all others, the curing dance, men are the curers, the n/um k"xausi; "owners" of the magical "medicine," n/um, who go into trance and protect and cure the people. Women participate in the curing rite, in synchronization with the men, but in the secondary role of music makers who help the n/um k"xausi, but who themselves do not have the role of curers in this rite.

THE BAND

The band (n//abesi), the grouping above the family, is the unit in which families combine to live together in groups of viable size, and the unit through which rights to the resources of water and plant foods are held.

!Kung bands have an entity that is visible to the eye. When the band encamps, the members cluster their fires together. If more than one band inhabits a territory and the bands encamp near the same waterhole, or if bands are visiting and are encamped near their hosts, the bands maintain a distinct separation. We had an unusually good opportunity to observe this particular characteristic during the drought of 1952 when five bands encamped themselves around the /Gam waterhole. Again at Gautscha, when several bands visited at a time, we observed their separateness. At /Gam, the encampments were a mile or so apart. At Gautscha, the distance between them varied very much. For example, the two bands that belong to Gautscha, the bands we numbered 1 and 2, encamped half a mile apart at one time, a hundred yards at another time, and at still another time they were only about twenty feet apart. Even though the separation was small, it was visible.

Although the composition of a band is fluid—marriage takes individuals from one band to another, and whole families move from one band to another, bands split or disband completely and new bands form

—many of the bands have existed as entities for a long time. Some have names that were given by the old old people, we were told, names that have been known as long as anyone could remember. The names express something about the land in which the band lives. One of the interpreters, Frederick Gaeb, a Bergdama, who always gave a flourish to his remarks, said that the !Kung name /Gausha, which has been corrupted to Gautscha, meant "we are a salty people who live in a salty place."[5] !Gui!oma, the name of Band 12, refers to the sand dune where that band often camps. N!ao !Kei, the name of Band 14, means "Kudu Neck" and refers to a feature in the landscape where they live which resembles a kudu neck. A person will identify himself by the name of the band to which he belongs, saying, "I am a Kudu Neck man," or "I am (a) !Gui!oma 'owner,' " mi o !gui!oma k"xau.

Bands are to be seen in their entirety only infrequently. In the time of the rains, when surface water can be found, the families that compose the bands take the opportunity to separate, to hunt and gather in different places and to make journeys to visit relatives. They are more likely to be together in the dry season when they must stay within reach of their permanent waterhole, but even then, people separate to gather and hunt. Much of the time some of the members are away, different people are visiting, and the assemblage of people keeps changing.

Visiting has very important functions in !Kung life. The !Kung visit a great deal. They visit relatives and friends, but mainly relatives. They visit for many reasons, for the pleasure of seeing people they like to be with, for change of scenery, to take gifts, to receive gifts, to arrange marriages, to take news of marriages, births, and deaths, for solace in

5. Gautscha was not a very "salty place," but on the pan there was a spot where salt exuded. It was the only salt spot we ever came across in all of our travels in the Nyae Nyae area. The Nyae Nyae people are accustomed to living without salt. They relished an occasional gift of salt from us and ate it like candy but did not sprinkle it on their food. The "salty" Gautscha people apparently ignored their salt spot. No one went to it till we asked Tsamgao, ≠Toma's son, to show it to us and to show us what they did. Tsamgao agreed and prepared for the trip taking one of our empty tin cans, filled with water. He led us for what I guessed to be about an eighth of a mile out into the pan and began to search around for the spot. When he found the footprints of a small buck which had apparently been digging at the hard, cracked, mud crust of the pan at a certain spot, Tsamgao broke the crust and tasted the sand below. He had found the salt spot. He made a shallow scoop in the surface of the sand and filled his water tin with the sand he scooped up. When it was thoroughly wet, he made balls with it which he left to dry on a pad of grass. In the afternoon he went back for his salt balls. They were unimpressive, consisting of much more sand than salt. Tsamgao gave one to an old woman who put it away among her belongings. The others were abandoned and soon crumbled away.

grief, and to participate in rituals. For example, at the ritual of a child's first haircut, the person for whom the child is named should be present. If tensions arise, people may separate for a time and visit elsewhere to benefit by change and rest from each other. N/aoka, the first wife of Gao in Band 1, separated herself frequently from Gao's second wife, Di!ai, and visited her brother in Band 8. The custom of visiting helps to keep the resources of the area equally distributed. If a band's waterhole fails temporarily or its food resources are low, the members of the band visit relatives who are better off. The Nyae Nyae !Kung travel from one end of the area to the other on their visits and frequently exchange visits with !Kung from the Dobe area. Every year old N/aoka walked the fifty miles to Kubi in Botswana and made a long visit to her eldest son, Gao. The families of ≠Toma and old Gaú visited ≠Toma's sister in Kai Kai every year, and she and her family visited them in Gautscha.

No higher grouping unites the bands into a structured unit such as a tribe with a paramount chief. No band has higher status than another and none has authority over another. The bands are autonomous.

The separateness of the bands, the fact that they are not organized into a higher unit, does not function as a strongly divisive force among the people. For one reason, membership in bands is not rigidly fixed. On the contrary, families and individuals often move from one band to another. Furthermore, the population as a whole is homogeneous, bound by ties of consanguinity and affinity, and, as I explained when discussing the region of Nyae Nyae, much interaction and much visiting give many of the people face-to-face acquaintance. If they are not actually acquainted personally, as most are, they can at least place everyone in his family connections. And, although they maintain a visible separateness in their dwelling, when different bands happen to be encamped near each other the members of bands may intermingle in their activities any way they wish. No social rules set the bands apart in that respect. The men may hunt and the women may gather together in voluntary companionship. They may sit at their tasks together. A man will share his arrow poison with a friend from another band as readily as with a member of his own band, and when bands are encamped near each other, they are sure to join in their great ritual curing dances.

How long the bands have lived where they do is not known. The !Kung make no point of tracing their ancestors into the deep past, and ancient heritage is not a concern. Only the relatively recent past and the forebears of two or possibly three ascending generations and the current occupancy of the territories concern them. If the !Kung at the time they originally established themselves in territories were as discreet and as averse to fighting as they are now, the process of establishment was probably a peaceful one. Quarrels occur between individuals and families, but our informants had no memory of a war between bands for possession of resources or for anything else for that matter, nor had their parents or grandparents told them of any such conflict. The bands' establishment in their territories continues to be peacefully observed. The bands do not encroach upon one another. The !Kung have other ways of managing their affairs.

Relationships on Which Bands Are Formed

!Kung families join together and form bands on the basis of consanguinity and affinity. Families are linked by the same relationships that form the nuclear family, the consanguineous relationships of parent and offspring and siblings and the affinal relationship of husband and wife. One of these relationships links every individual to a family, and one of these relationships links each family to another family in a band, in a chain-like manner. Clusters of related families which form segments of bands are linked to other segments also by one of the nuclear family relationships. In the few instances in which an individual's name appears in the charts without the connecting links being shown, it is because I do not know the links, not that they do not exist.

Stated in another way, parents and offspring, siblings, and husbands and wives always have a right to live together. For instance, when a person enters a band by marriage, he has a right to bring his parents and siblings with him if it should suit them to come. His parents and siblings may have relatives attached to them by one of the nuclear family bonds, and they may bring those relatives into the band with them. To illustrate what I mean, Segment 3 of Band 1 comprises Gao's extended family, which includes his first wife, N/aoka, two daughters by her, their husbands and children, a teen-age son by her, his second wife, Di!ai, a son by her, her daughter by another husband, and the daughter's husband. One sibling bond links that segment with Segment 1, the family of !U and ≠Toma; the bond is the sister bond between Di!ai and !U. Old Gaú's extended family, Segment 2 of Band 1, is linked to Segment 1 and Segment 3 by a sibling bond also. Old Gaú's deceased wife, /Khoa, was the sister of !U's and Di!ai's deceased father, Debe. In Band 2, a parent-offspring bond links old ≠Toma's extended family with the family of Gao Beard: Gao Beard's first wife is Old ≠Toma's daughter. A sibling bond links Old ≠Toma's extended family with Segment 3, namely Gaú's cluster of families which includes his mother and his two sisters with their husbands and children. Gaú's second wife is the sister of Old ≠Toma's wife.

It amused me occasionally to work out the chains of relationships between individuals as well as to notice what relationships held the segments of the bands together. Take, for example, /Qui [1.3], son of /Gao Music, and /Qui [1.24], husband of Old Gaú's daughter, //Kushay: /Qui [1.24] is to /Qui [1.3] mother's brother's second wife's deceased father's deceased sister's daughter's husband.

The continuing force of the relationships of parent-offspring, sibling, and husband and wife may bring into residence in a band uncles and aunts with nephews and nieces, cousins with cousins, grandchildren with grandparents, and parents-in-law with sons-in-law or daughters-in-law. Old /Gaishay [3.8] and Old ≠Gisa [3.9], who lived with their cousin, ≠Gao [3.4] in Band 3 and later with Gaú (≠Gao's brother) in Band 2, are examples. Their deceased mother and ≠Gao's and Gaú's deceased father had been siblings. The childless old woman, N/aoka [9.15] in /Ti!kay's band, was the sister of /Ti!kay's wives' mother, /Goishay. N/aoka stayed on with her nieces when /Goishay died. A grandparent bereft of offspring could live with a grandchild. But the presence together of people in the above-mentioned relationships comes about because of the original parental or sibling relationship, not because !Kung society has established patterns of avuncular or cousin or grandparent-grandchild residence.

In one instance, the name-relationship (described in Chapter 6) provided a substitute for consanguinity or affinity as a means of entering a band. Old //Kushay [12.12], a woman from Band 13 whose consanguineous kin were all dead except her grandson, Gao [12.11], lived with her friend, Old Baú [12.13] in Band 12. Old //Kushay's daughter had died. She had been the second wife of /Ti!kay [13.14]. Old //Kushay could have stayed on with her son-in-law after the death of her daughter, but she disliked her son-in-law's first wife, //Aha, a bad-tempered, selfish woman. She disliked her so much that after her daughter died she left Band 13 and went to live with Old Baú, taking her grandson with her. Although she had no consanguineous or affinal ties in Band 12, this was acceptable because //Kushay's deceased daughter had also been named Baú.

Informants said that if a person had no relationship that would allow him to enter a band, he would have to live alone. This is a hypothetical and almost inconceivable situation among !Kung. No one lives alone in the Nyae Nyae area, and no one knew of a person who had no relative whatsoever with whom to live.

Kxai K''xausi

The band that inhabits any given territory is formed around a core of people who are established as belonging to that territory. They are called the kxai k''xausi ("owners") in the territory (n!ore): they are the "owners" of its resources. The people from other bands in other territories who join the band of a given core of people directly by marriage or through some chain of consanguineous or affinal relationship I shall call incoming members. Incoming members have rights to the resources of the particular band during the time they are members of it, They do not retain the rights to that band's resources if they leave the band. The rights of the kxai k''xausi to the resources are inalienable.

I rather awkwardly paraphrase the words kxai k''xausi as "owners who possess." Kxai means "to possess." K''xau means "owner," si is the plural suffix. The word k''xau is used with respect to the ownership of artifacts and of resources. It also is used with respect to immaterial things and the mastery of a skill. Men who are curers are "owners" of medicine; a person who sings well or tells stories well is an "owner" of singing or storytelling.

The kxai k''xausi of a territory have their position as "owners" through inheritance reinforced by their presence in the territory. At some time their forebears became established in the territory and the position is passed on through the generations.

The territory to which an individual kxai k''xau belongs may be that of his father's people or that of his mother's people. Whichever territory his family is established in and identified with will be his n!ore. If the person leaves to live elsewhere through marriage, or changes residence for some other reason, he will identify himself as having come from his n!ore. A Gautscha person will say mi o /gausa k''xau.

Band 1 provides illustration. !U, of Band 1, is a kxai k''xau of the Gautscha territory. Her mother was, before her, and her grandparents before her mother. ≠Toma, her husband, is an incoming member in Band 1. He comes from /Gam. ≠Toma and !U have lived all their married life in the Gautscha territory. Their children were born to the Gautscha territory and are growing up in it. They are well established in it, having never lived elsewhere. They are examples of persons being established in the territory of their mother's people.

The !Kung use the expressions to "hold strongly" or to "hold weakly."[6] A person "holds" his n!ore strongly if he remains in it ("sits" in it, they say). He holds his n!ore weakly if he lives for long periods away from his n!ore or if he shifts around, living in one band and then another in different territories. ("What kind of business is that?" exclaimed ≠Toma, putting a value judgment on such behavior.) !U's elder brother, Gao, who lived all his married life with his wife's people in Botswana in Band 21, "holds weakly" his Gautscha n!ore to which he was born. His mother, N/aoka, and his siblings, Di!ai, !U, and Lame ≠Gao, "hold" Gautscha very strongly, the family having been represented there by some of its members for three generations without interruption. (The family may have been there longer. I could trace only two ascending generations above !U's.) Gao has the right to return to Gautscha, and if he did, he would be recognized as a Gautscha k"xau along with the rest of his family and his children would be regarded as belonging to Gautscha. However, he does not return and so he holds his n!ore weakly. When Gao dies, if his children have never come to live in the Gautscha territory, they will not be recognized as Gautscha people and their potential hold on Gautscha will fade away.

≠Toma holds his n!ore in /Gam even more weakly than Gao holds Gautscha. ≠Toma's parents died; his sister went to live with her husband's people in Kai Kai; the band she and ≠Toma had lived in disbanded. ≠Toma has no people to return to who are established in a /Gam territory. The original establishment of his family there is being forgotten, his identification as a /Gam k"xau is fading. For ≠Toma's and !U's children identification with /Gam has already faded away. They are recognized as belonging to Gautscha, not /Gam. ≠Toma himself says that although he knows he is an incoming member to Band 1 and to the Gautscha territory, he has been there so long that he feels like a Gautscha "owner."

In Band 1, Old Gaú, his two daughters, and two sons are another branch of the family who are kxai k"xausi in the Gautscha territory. Old Gaú's mother (now deceased) and !U's mother were sisters.

---

6. I am indebted to John Marshall for the expressions "hold strongly" and "hold weakly" given me by personal communication.

Gao and his first wife and their offspring were incoming members to Band 1, as were their offspring's spouses. Gao's n!ore is Deboragu, his band is Band 4. In spite of having lived nine years (by 1961) in Band 1, Gao held strongly his own n!ore. Gao's father, mother, and two sisters with their husbands lived there. He visited often and took his children with him. They were recognized and identified as Deboragu people. Gao's first wife, N/aoka, had come from the vicinity of Epata away to the west. The band she belonged to before her marriage had disbanded completely. She had no relatives in the Epata vicinity to return to, and her hold and her children's hold on the n!ore near Epata has faded away. Her children are examples of those who take their place in a n!ore through their father.

Suppose a family has lived for years in the, wife's territory, long enough to be established and identified as being kxai k"xausi in it, and then has moved to the husband's territory. Where do the offspring belong? Potentially, they could be kxai k"xausi in either. If they had relatives living in a band established in the territories whom they could join and if they had kept up their identity with the territories by visiting and being recognized as belonging, I think they could choose to settle in either or to move from one to the other. Informants gave me the impression, however, that they rarely, if ever, feel the duality of belonging to two bands. Adults seem to have made up their minds and feel clearly to which band they belong. Children feel they belong to the band in which their parents settle. Posing hypothetical questions to the !Kung is never rewarding. Old Demi dismissed the hypothetical complications I was trying to raise by saying, "Everyone belongs somewhere, and everyone knows where he belongs."

The families of the !Kung who lived in groups employed by the families of Musindjan and Kavasitue in /Gam and Moremi in Tsho/ana were held together by the same relationship I have been speaking of, though the families as a whole are not linked to other families as the families in a band are. Possibly one or two members of the family would be actually employed. Their families, extended or nuclear, would come to live with them in the same ways they would if they lived in bands. The families were supported by the employed members. There were no unattached persons in the Nyae Nyae area—except one family which, if not utterly unattached, was on the very edge of being so. It was the family of !Kham, the lame man.

!Kham as a young man had been crippled by a bone disease which had left both his legs withered. The boy, Lame ≠Gao, the only other

cripple we met among the Nyae Nyae !Kung, had apparently suffered the
same disease; but only one of his legs was withered and he limped with
a cane. !Kham propelled himself by lifting himself by his hands, holding
on to two forked sticks taller than himself, and swinging his whole body
forward between his sticks. He could not hunt. His tiny wife, Be, the
smallest of the !Kung women we measured, gathered for !Kham and
herself and (as of 1952–53) their four diminutive children. The children
were diminutive but appeared to be well and lively. (!Kham and Be had
six children by 1961.) People in the bands they visited gave them meat.
This family was the most peripatetic we knew. They appeared to spend
most of their lives on the move. They made journeys of a hundred miles
traveling back and forth between /Gam and Tsho/ana and visiting all
the N//hwã!ai bands in between. They made themselves useful by
carrying messages and gifts from one person to another and brought
the news and gossip of the countryside. They appeared to be welcome
visitors. Be was self-effacing, discreet, quiet—no trouble to anyone.
!Kham had apparently attained a remarkable degree of resignation to
his affliction and was an agreeable, gentle person, also self-effacing,
though less retiring than his wife. Their hold on a group and a place to
belong was the most tenuous we knew. They were not established in a
n!ore in which their families had been established before them. Neither
!Kham or Be had a living parent or sibling. !Kham's closest relative was
a cousin in /Gam, his father's brother's daughter, a woman named Di!ai.
She and her husband were among the group employed by Kavasitue and
Musindjan. They were no longer themselves kxai k''xausi of a n!ore nor
closely connected with any who were kxai k''xausi. Be's connections
were with the group employed by Moremi in Tsho/ana. I do not know
who her people were but I hope she had more relatives than !Kham. My
feelings about Bushmen who have become landless and unattached are
very concrete and personalized when I think about !Kham and his family.

Ownership of Resources

Each group of kxai k''xausi who compose the core of a band "own"
exclusively the resources of plant food and water of their territory. By
that I mean that the resources are not owned communally throughout
the Nyae Nyae area. One band does not have rightful access to another
band's resources. Visitors and travelers from other bands must be invited or ask permission to partake of the resources. The plant foods are
owned with strict definition and jealous concern. The water in the water-

holes is owned but not so exclusively or with so much jealous concern. The permanent and semipermanent waterholes refill themselves. The plant foods, once they are gathered and eaten, do not grow again till the next growing season.

I believe the bands' ownership of the resources is strictly recognized and adhered to. The !Kung bands of the Nyae Nyae area have not encroached upon or fought each other for the fertile areas in which the plant foods grow within the memory of the living people. The informants had no tales to tell of fighting in the past. Visiting being a common practice, it is better to visit than to fight. Encroachment on the fertile areas of one band by another band would be like stealing, and stealing is a dangerous and exceedingly rare crime among the !Kung. One chilling tale was told of a killing. A man took honey which was not his. When a man finds honey in a tree or a nest of ostrich eggs, it is the custom for him to mark the find with a bunch of grass stuck into a forked stick or a crotch of a tree to indicate that someone has found the treasure and will be back to get it. A man stole such a find of honey, and the man who had first found it killed him for doing so.

It is to be remembered that a person's footprints are as well known as his face. This undoubtedly has something to do with the sanctions which so effectively prevent the society from stealing. There is a woeful song which the !Kung sing when the mood to lament is upon them. It expresses how they would feel if they were to go to their tsi patch and find footprints there and the tsi all picked and gone.

The !Kung have several different concepts of ownership. Artifacts are owned outright by an individual. There is, as far as I know, no communal ownership of property in movables. Artifacts are not even family property. Each arrow, each bag, each bead is owned personally by an individual man, woman, or child. In gift-giving, one individual specifically gives something he owns to another individual, who then becomes its owner.

Another concept of ownership, I believe, applies to the meat of the big animals. The person who owns the meat and is responsible for its distribution in the process of meat-sharing does not own it exclusively and personally as artifacts are owned. John Marshall suggests that to say he controls the meat comes nearer to the concept and that the verb for this kind of ownership is //ei.[7]

7. John Marshall, personal communication.

Resources of plant foods and water are owned in still another way. The verb that applies to that type of ownership is *kxai*.[8] This is the word that appears in the designation *kxai k"xausi*. The ownership the word denotes again is not an exclusive personal ownership. It might better be called "a nonexclusive right to the use of the resources," to use John Marshall's phrase.

A kxai k"xau of a given territory inherits the rights to the resources from his (or her) parents (father or mother) who were kxai k"xausi in the territory before him. The rights are inalienable. A person who leaves the territory in which he is a kxai k"xau to live as an incoming member in some band elsewhere retains the right to return to his own territory throughout his lifetime, should he wish to do so and should circumstance make his return feasible. Even if the band in which he grew up has disbanded, a person retains his inherited rights to the resources. ≠Toma is an example. ≠Toma retains rights to the tsi that grows between /Gam and Nama. The band into which he was born belonged to the /Gam waterhole. Its members were related to members of Bands 12 and 14 of /Gam which have rights to the tsi. ≠Toma's people also had rights to the tsi.

No one lives at the tsi patches. There is no water near. The people who have rights to them go each year to gather when the tsi seeds ripen. ≠Toma takes the whole of Band 1 with him. Short /Qui in Band 2 also has rights to the tsi. The band into which he was born is Band 12 of /Gam. His brother still lives in Band 12. Short /Qui goes to gather tsi taking with him the members of Band 2 with whom he now lives. There they meet the members of the /Gam bands who are owners of the tsi and the incoming members of those bands. Many people gather tsi.

Incoming members of a band share equally with the kxai k"xausi of the band while they are members of the band. No one in a band has the right to withhold resources from another member of the band, however the member has come into the band, whether born to a kxai k"xau or by direct marriage to a kxai k"xau or by being related in some chain of relationship to a member. No one has the right to take a larger share than others. The only difference between kxai k"xausi and incoming members is that the latter do not retain rights to the band's resources if they leave the band.

8. John Marshall, personal communication.

Individuals apparently respect each other's rights on the whole. We were told that there is sometimes strife and conflict between members of a band over plant foods or gathering plans, but we observed no quarrels. However, we heard of one in the past that ended in bitter tragedy. Two men at /Gam quarreled about their plans and arrangements to make a gathering trip. One was Tsamgao, the father of ≠Toma. The young son of the other man became frightened for his father and wanted to protect him. He took a poisoned arrow from his father's quiver and shot and killed Tsamgao.

Once plant foods are gathered, they belong to the person who gathers them. Custom requires and allows the person to share with his or her own family, and the person may give presents of plant food as he or she wishes, but no patterned, wide distribution is required. Even if some of the band go to gather mangetti nuts or tsi and others remain in the encampment, the nuts or tsi beans are not distributed widely in a standardized way, as meat is. Each gatherer owns what he or she gathers and may share it with whomever he or she pleases. Custom and rules of politeness require that a person share with his or her visitors. Visitors may be invited to join gathering parties as a courtesy.

The waterholes are owned by the kxai k"xausi as the fertile areas of plant food are owned, but less exclusively. Water, like the animals, seems to be thought of as belonging more to mankind than to individual bands, and the ownership of waterholes entails more the managing than the withholding of water. I cannot imagine a !Kung withholding water from another !Kung.

Travelers and visitors should ask permission before taking water because, someone said, the owners know how much there is and how it should be managed. But one of the listeners laughed at this and said, "If you are very thirsty, you have no time to ask permission."

We were told that at /Gam people no longer know how to behave properly, as they did in the good old days, and now they take water without asking permission. Doubtless the Bushmen feel that their own system is superseded where the waterholes have been more or less dominated by the Bantu.

At the small waterholes, which fill during the rains and dry up at some time or other during the rainless months, the situation is different. We saw small waterholes marked with bundles of grass thrust into forked sticks. This was to tell visitors or travelers that the owners of the waterholes were in residence, as it were, and were counting on the water.

We believe that in these circumstances water would not be taken unless it were known that it would be all right to take some.

Situations are not likely to arise where permission need be refused. The !Kung know where the others are, or are likely to be, at a given time, and they know how much water is available. If Old Debe [13.18], leader of Band 13 at /Gam, sets off with his band down the Eiseb to their mangettis, and is depending on a waterhole that produces a pint in the sand after digging, large groups of friends are not going to visit him and use up his water at that time. An odd hunting party from a neighboring band passing by would know whether or not it was all right to take some water and would not take his last drop and leave without telling him. If necessary, they would all go back to the permanent waterhole. They manage better than to get themselves into desperate situations.

Hollow trees in mangetti groves are an important source of water. Mangetti trees grow on immense white sand dunes. There are no waterholes in any of the mangetti groves we know, and all are so far from water that they present a constant water problem. During the rains, however, hollow trees fill with water. That water supplements the water people can carry with them, and trips to the groves are possible.

The hollow trees appear to be owned, and people other than the owners do not take water from them. /Ti!kay of Band 9 owned a tree with a very large hollow, a tree that he said he inherited from his father. People dipped water from the hollow as if it were a little well. They used tin cans we had given them tied to strings, but they could have used their own water bags. When we went to the mangetti grove, the water in that tree, with sparing use, was enough to supply twenty-five people from Bands 1, 2, and 9 for four days.

K''xau N!asi

In Nyae Nyae !Kung bands, there is a man, a member of the kxai k''xausi group, who is called k''xau n!a or simply k''xau. In k''xau n!asi, si is the plural suffix, n!a means "old" or "big," k''xau means "owner." I thought at the time I was first working up my material, and when I wrote the article "!Kung Bushman Bands," that "headman" was an appropriate paraphrase for k''xau n!a. I have come to realize through talks with other students of !Kung culture, through additional studies made by John Marshall, and through more work on my own notes and more thinking on my part, that "headman" was a misleading and unfortunate paraphrase.

Although I said that the k''xau n!a did not have political authority, the word "headman" is so imbued with the connotation of political authority of some kind that I should not have used the designation, and I hereby retract it.

I retract the word "headman" and furthermore report a change in my understanding of his position in the band in two respects. First, I believe I formerly gave the k''xau n!a too much emphasis as a nucleus of the band when I said that the chains of relationship that bind the members of the band together link them with the k''xau n!a. They do, but I made it seem that the link with the k''xau n!a was all important. I did not make it clear that the links that all the kxai k''xausi have with each other are equally important in binding them together in a band. If there were no k''xau n!a in a band, the band would be held together just as well by the other relationships.

Secondly, I believe that I was both mistaken and inept in saying it was the k''xau n!a's responsibility and principal duty to integrate the band's utilization of its resources, to plan which area within the territory the band will move to, at what time, and in what order they will consume the plant foods. I believe the statement ascribed too much authority to the k''xau n!a. It implies that the k''xau n!a has authority to permit members of the band to go to gather in this or that place or to prohibit them from going. He does not have the authority. I think I was more nearly correct in the modification I made of the statement which was that "the seasonal patterns of the band's movements follow long-established customs and usually cause little if any controversy. Nature herself dictates most of the seasonal plans; her pattern is known to all. Though the !Kung do not have a council of elders, everything is talked over, and the actual plan adopted is more likely to be a consensus than the decision of the k''xau n!a."

What a k''xau n!a does is to give focus to the ownership of the resources of plant foods and waterhole that his band lives on. He personifies that ownership and gives it a voice. He does not have stronger claim to the resources than the other kxai k''xausi or the incoming members of his band. He cannot withhold the resources from them nor do they feel that they receive the resources through his bounty. All members of the band have the same right to partake of the resources, and they share alike. The k''xau n!a represents the ownership in his person, and as the position is passed from father to son, it expresses continuity of ownership from generation to generation. When people outside a band ask permission to take water or plant foods that belong to the band, it is the k"xau n!a they should ask.

We were told that if a person were found taking the plant foods of the band when he had no right to do so, it would be the duty of the k"xau n!a "to chase him away." How he would do so is left to the imagination. As people do not encroach upon plant foods where they do not have rights of their own, or where they may properly visit, this contrary-to-fact image is very funny to the !Kung.

Mostly informants spoke of the position of a k"xau n!a in terms of water. In explaining who was and who was not a k"xau n!a in a band, informants would say, "So and so is the man you should ask for water, he is the one who has the say over the water," or "he is the master water."

In conducting their affairs in general, the members of a band are not under the control of the k"xau n!a. It is not his function to instigate or organize hunting parties, gathering parties, trading trips, visits, the making of artifacts, gift-giving, nor does he have any authority in making marriage arrangements. Individuals and families instigate and conduct their activities independently, and when plans and arrangements must be coordinated, this is done by people's talking together and reaching consensus. So much of !Kung activity follows long-established custom that there is little about plans and arrangements that is likely to be controversial, and consensus is easily come by. The k"xau n!a does not rule in these matters; he does not give or withhold permission. Neither is he a judge called upon to determine guilt or to inflict punishment upon a wrongdoer. In instances of wrongdoing or to avenge a wrong, group opinion is expressed in talking. Group opinion acts as a sanction and group disapproval as a punishment. Furthermore, a person who is personally wronged by another may take his own revenge. If the wrong is very great and fierce anger flares, as it may in instances of adultery or stealing, the wronged person may kill the wrongdoer, or the two may fight and either or both be killed.

We do not know who were the original k"xau n!asi of the bands. The !Kung hold only a shallow past in memory. A band must originally have formed around some man who had rights to the resources of the territory, and he would have been its first k"xau n!a. The rule is that the position passes from father to son at the death of the father. Primogeniture prevails. The eldest son becomes k"xau n!a. However, if the eldest son leaves the band and remains away, the position would be taken by the next eldest son who remained in the band. If the eldest son was away only temporarily and returned, he would fill the position again. A man who moves away from his band does not carry the designation of k''xau n!a with him. He is called that only in his band where he is a kxai k''xau. Band 1 offers an example of an elder son remaining away. Gao, the elder brother of Di!ai, !U, and Lame ≠Gao lives with his wife's people in Botswana. Their younger brother, Young Lame ≠Gao, is k''xau n!a in Band 1.[9]

If the k''xau n!a who dies has no son, or no son remaining in the band, the designation passes through a daughter, presumably the eldest who remains in the band, to her son. We find an example in Band 10 of the position of k''xau n!a passing through two generations of women, a daughter and granddaughter whose husbands were both incomers to the band, and eventually passing to the old k''xau n!a's great grandson, a young man, married, but with as yet no children in 1952.

The !Kung do not have lineage, but a patrilineal inclination can be detected in the way the Nyae Nyae !Kung use the designation k''xau n!a. Women among the Nyae Nyae !Kung were not called k''xau n!a. Although women are just as much "owners" in the kxai k''xausi group as men, and the daughter of a k''xau n!a passes the designation to her son, should her father have no sons or none that remained in the band, the daughter herself is not called k''xau n!a.

The position of k''xau n!a is not especially advantageous to the individual. Among the !Kung each person does his own work, carries his own load, and shares meat. The k''xau n!asi are as thin as the rest. No regalia, special honors, or tributes mark them out. In common with all !Kung we know, they do not want to stand out or be above others by having more material things than the others, for this draws unfavorable attention to them and arouses envy and jealousy. We often observed the care people took to avoid invidious distinction. On one occasion even food was refused. ≠Toma refused a buck that John Marshall had shot for him as a parting gift when our expedition was leaving. He asked John to give it to someone else, saying he was afraid of the jealousy people

9. I have a correction to make about Lame ≠Gao's age. Through inadvertency on my part, the article "!Kung Bushmen Bands," p. 350, says that Lame ≠Gao was about nine years old. This error passed under my unseeing eyes in typescript and proof. My own notes say I thought he was in late teens, and Richard Lee figures that he was born about 1935, which would have made him seventeen in 1952. By 1959, lame though he was, he had killed a buck and was married to a charming girl named Xama in Kai Kai.

would feel if he were more favored than they. We were told that instead of feeling himself privileged, a k'"xau n!a is likely to feel that he must be more generous than others in gift-giving. This is one of the problems of a k'"xau n!a, one informant said.

Leadership

A k'"xau n!a may or may not be a leader in his band. If he is too young or too old or lacks personal qualities of leadership, the people may turn quite informally to some other man for leadership—go to him for advice, ask his help, and fall in with his plans. A leader has no authority and receives no honors or rewards. We overheard two men talking together about this one day. "All you get is the blame if things go wrong," they said.

We observed three instances in which the k'"xau n!a was too young, and one in which he was too old and weak to be a leader. In each of these bands, leadership had fallen to another man in the band who had the personal qualifications for it. In Band 1, Lame ≠Gao was still too young to be a leader. We were interested to observe that the leadership of Band 1 had not fallen to the oldest man of the band, Old Gaú, though he was much respected and was not decrepit. It had fallen to ≠Toma, undoubtedly because of his personality. ≠Toma is a man of uncommon intelligence, decisiveness, and force, skill in hunting, perception in human relations, and probity. Not only do members of his own band look to him, but neighbors and visitors do also. We looked to him for advice and support in making all our plans and decisions.

Not understanding anything about kxai k'"xausi or k'"xau n!asi when we first attached ourselves to Band 1 in 1951, we assumed that ≠Toma was a "headman" because he behaved as we expected a "headman" to behave, although the question was never made explicit and ≠Toma never claimed to have authority. It was not until 1952 when we began to learn about kxai k'"xausi and k'"xau n!asi that we discovered he was an incoming member to Band 1 and that his outstanding leadership resulted from his personal qualities, not at all from his position in the band.

Size of Bands

People group themselves into bands of a size that is adjusted to the conditions of the several territories and to hunting-gathering activities.

Of the nineteen bands in the Nyae Nyae area, at the time of our count in 1952, Band 5 was the smallest with eight members in one extended family composed of three nuclear families. Four other bands were small, two of them with nine members, the others with ten and twelve members respectively. I am omitting consideration of Band 8 with forty-seven members, because I know little about the band and think it perhaps should be counted as two bands. The remaining thirteen bands had between sixteen and forty-two members with an average of twenty-nine, which is near the general average of about twenty-five.

The resources available in the territory strongly affect the size of the band or bands that are based on them. Some resources are so scant that only small bands can form around them. The waterholes of Bands 4 and 5 limit the number of people who can depend on them. Band 4's waterhole is the one about which old /Gaishay said, "Sometimes you will think there is no water but scratch in the sand and wait and some will come." The splendid waterhole at /Gam allows large bands to form (large by !Kung standards), but the plant foods in the /Gam vicinity are limited, and some are so distant from the water that the /Gam bands suffer considerable deprivation in the dry season. Nowhere in the area are resources of both plant foods and waterholes so abundant that they can support very large aggregations throughout the year. (The tsi bean communities can support large aggregations, but only temporarily when water permits and until the year's yield of tsi seeds is all consumed.) For the Nyae Nyae !Kung to spread themselves out into the several territories of the area in moderate-sized aggregations is the best arrangement.

Other factors besides resources mitigate against the bands' becoming very large or very small compared to those we observed. The need for mutual support limits smallness. We were told of several bands in the past that had become too small to be viable due to death or people leaving the band. The bands had broken up and remaining people had joined other bands. ≠Toma, Crooked /Qui, and /Gao Music in Band 1 had grown up in such bands. Dam [2.32] in Band 2 was in the same situation.

One nuclear family alone is not enough to sustain the arduous hunting-gathering life of the !Kung. The mutual support of a larger group is needed. There is also the need for companionship; the !Kung abhor loneliness. A mood song called the Song of the Old Stump expresses the feeling of a hunter who got separated from his companions and found himself alone when evening came. In the dusk he saw a man in the distance. He ran to him shouting, glad that there would be two together by the fire that night. When he came near, he found only an old stump.

Women gatherers also need a group. Technically women do not require help in digging and picking plant foods. Each gathers for herself, each carries her own load. They need each other's support, however, when they are sick or old, and they need companionship. I believe to gather day after day alone would be insupportable for a !Kung woman, and I imagine that even co-wives together could hardly bear the gathering life without other companionship. Living in bands of several families together suits the !Kung.

Bands 3, 4, 5, and 6 were at the limit of smallness. Bands 3 and 4 happened to be quite strong, however, for small bands. Each had two able hunters, and in Band 4 a young boy was beginning to hunt. Each band had three women to gather together. Bands 5 and 6 were not as strong. Band 5 had two able-bodied hunters, ≠Toma [5.5] and /Qui [5.8], a son and a son-in-law of Old N!aishi, but the two did not get on well together and the son-in-law made long visits back to his father's band at Samangaigai. The others of Band 5 visited much of the time in Band 2, with N!aishi's daughter, /Gasa [2.5], wife of /Qui [2.4].

Band 6 was the weakest. Seven of its twelve members were old. The old men were beyond hunting age, though the women could gather. We imagined that the band would soon have to break up. Meanwhile, Old Demi told us he liked to live at Nam Tshoha. Although the water was scant, the plant food was good, and he still had his unmarried sons, Khan//a [6.5] and Gao [6.6], to hunt for them. The place was beautiful and they were all peaceful together, Demi said.

Factors in addition to the limitation of resources in the various territories mitigate against largeness of bands. In the two instances in which the waterhole is shared by two bands, Gautscha and /Gam, the two bands do not merge. In the dry season when people must remain within reach of their permanent waterhole, Bands 1 and 2, both based at Gautscha, could join and encamp together. They have relationships that would allow them to do so. N/aoka, mother of !U in Band 1, and Old ≠Toma in Band 2 are brother and sister. However, these bands do not choose to merge. The irascible Gao Beard is jealous of ≠Toma, and everybody believes that things go better when they stay apart. Friction in relationships must often be a cause for separateness; the larger the band the more opportunity for friction to develop. Also, apart from the question of friction, the !Kung may just prefer not to have to relate in daily life to substantially larger groups than we observed. They do not have to. Nothing prevents them from splitting apart, except that an extremely small group is not viable. People may be based in the same territory, but they do not have to live together; witness Bands 12 and 13 at /Gam, Bands 1 and 2 at Gautscha.

New Bands

A new band can be formed at any time that circumstances permit and people desire to form one. The new band would have kxai k''xausi members who had rights to the resources of the territory. It would have a mature man to head it; he would be its k''xau n!a. It would have enough families to make it a band of viable size.

We did not see the formation of a new band, but we thought for a while that we might do so. We thought that Short /Qui might go to live with his people in the vicinity of Nama. He had been spending a lot of time there and had great success in hunting. No band was living at Nama at the time. The deep waterhole full of drowned hyenas and jackals was not usable, but the small waterhole supported Short /Qui's group. We waited to see if they would settle there. The tragic loss of Short /Qui's foot from the puff adder bite in 1955 put an end, we think, to that possibility.

Mobility and Stability

The possibility of families' moving from one band to another to adjust to resources, or to relieve tensions within a band, or for any other reason, exists to the benefit of !Kung society. I do not want to give the impression, however, that there is constant breaking up of bands and shifting of members from one to another. Forces of stability are also at work. Except in extreme drought, the resources remain relatively constant. Only a few bands in the shallow past that the !Kung hold in memory had broken up because of failure of their waterholes. With considerable flexibility as to which relatives decide to live together, a good many people have the opportunity to join the band of their choice. The families often separate temporarily to visit other bands and to gather in different places during the rains, but my impression is that they then tend to keep their band membership for long periods.

Marriage causes most of the moves that take place. During the period from the beginning of our 1952 expedition to the end of our 1955 expedition, several young men married and left their bands to go into bride service in their wives' bands. One whole family changed its band membership because of a divorce. Among the N//hwā!ai bands (that is, Bands 1–7, 9, and 10) this was the only family to change its band membership during that period. We could not follow the northern and southern bands beyond the period in which we counted them and do not know how many families among them may have changed bands. We have no reason to suppose, however, that they would be less stable than the N//hwā!ai bands. The family I am speaking of moved twice, out of Band 3 into Band 7 for bride service, out of Band 7 back to Band 3 at the divorce. It was the family of Gao [7.12], brother of ≠Gao who is k"xau n!a of Band 3. (These two brothers are brothers also of Gaú in Band 2 and of the sisters ≠Gisa [wife of Dam] and N/aoka [wife of Short /Qui], offspring of Old /Gasa.)

Gao married Doīn, the daughter of Ti//khao [7.7], as his second wife, and took his first wife, Di!ai, and their three children to live in Band 7. It seemed to us an unlikely union, and we were not surprised that it broke up. Gao was of mature age (having had three children), Doīn was young, very pretty, very willful, and she made no secret of the fact that she did not like Gao. She said he had a big black belly, and she did not like big black bellies. We wondered what there was about Gao that was so attractive to Doīn's parents and came to the conclusion that it was his power as a n/um k"xau. He was an exceedingly ardent curer who went into deep, impressive trances. Old /Qui, Ti//khao's father, had been a famous n/um k"xau in his day, but he was very old. (He died late in 1952 and Ti//khao, his son, became k"xau n!a of Band 7.) Ti//khao was not a good curer or trancer, and Band 7 without Old /Qui would not have the protection of a powerful n/um k"xau, so, we think, they wanted Gao for that reason. But it was not reason enough for a marriage, and the marriage dissolved.

Interrelationship

As I stated previously, !Kung society has no wider social structure, such as a tribe with a paramount chief, that organizes the separate autonomous bands into political unity. The separate bands, as whole units, do not engage together in any organized way in economic, ritualistic, or other activities. Whole bands may come together, but it is through the interaction of their individual members that they do so, usually through visiting.

The interaction of the !Kung population as a whole in the Nyae Nyae region is governed by a kinship pattern. This pattern is based on and extends from the numerous actual kinship bonds. Intermarriage, by preference and custom, within the region, for unknown generations, has bound the people together across band demarcations. Counting only parents, offspring, and siblings, we find, for example, that persons of Band 1 have one of these primary relatives in seven other bands, those of Band 2 in thirteen other bands, those of Bands 3 and 4, each in five.

These are the closest bonds and the ones on which residence is patterned. But the !Kung also interact with their collaterals, especially in their own and adjacent generations—uncles and aunts, cousins, nephews and nieces. Furthermore, !Kung society has taken a form out of the concepts of kinship and cast it upon the relationship of people who have no known consanguineous or affinal ties. It is what we call the name-relationship. The !Kung apply kin terms to persons who have the same names as their consanguineous kin or affines.

The applying of kin terms means to the !Kung that they are not strangers but that they belong together and should accord to each other polite, respectful behavior, as they would to kin or affines, and take care not to give offense. Methods by which the !Kung help to keep peaceful relations amongst individuals within a band, methods such as meat-sharing and gift-giving, which I shall describe later, are employed also with name-relatives and have worked for peace in interband relationships. Our informants never heard of a fight between bands in the Nyae Nyae area, even from the old, old people.

6 The Kin Terminology System

My method of studying !Kung kin terminology was first to gather genealogical material.[1] After I had gathered a considerable amount and was

This chapter was first published as a paper, "The Kin Terminology System of
the !Kung Bushmen," in *Africa, 27* (Jan. 1957), 1–25. It is republished here with the
kind permission of the International African Institute.

1. In the hope of improving the clarity and emphasis of the paper, revisions have
been made in the wording of several passages and a major revision has been made
in the order in which the material is presented. The section on the joking relationship has been moved forward. The section on the homonymous method of applying
kin terms has been moved back. It now follows the section on affines. In that position, it can describe the application of terms by that method as it affects both consanguineous kin and affines.

The information presented is the same except for two corrections, a few omissions,
and the amplification of several points. One correction deals with an error regarding
the application of terms to secondary affines. A second correction is made in a statement regarding great-grandchildren. I said on p. 19 of the paper published in *Africa*
that we did not meet any !Kung who had a great-grandchild. However, when the data
on the composition of bands were all charted and thus made clearly visible, I realized
that three living old people were great-grandparents: Old Khokove [10.9], Old /Gai-
shay [4.1], and his wife Old Di//khao-! Gun≠a [4.2]. I have added in the section on
the naming of children the statement that, although it is not customary for children
to be named for the sibling of their grandparents, we know at least one who was so
named.

Several changes in spelling have been made. One is in the word for "mother." I
thought I had heard "d" in the word and had spelled it *"dai."* Most other researchers
who have worked with the !Kung language, however, have spelled it *"tai"* or *"taie."*
Since to my ear the sound is so nearly in the center between these two consonants, I
am changing my spelling to accord with the one most general in the literature. A
tilde has been added to the term tun!ga making it tũn!ga. The terms formerly spelled
!umba and !undai are now n!unba and n!untai in conformance with the Harvard
Group's spelling.

The omissions are of minor importance. Most are covered elsewhere, but one is
not. It is a brief reference and a long footnote to Dorothea Bleek's paper on kin
terms. I prefer not to give the space to the subject here but to refer an interested
reader to the paper itself. The paper is: "Bushmen Terms of Relationship," *Bantu*

able to place in their web of relationships all of the people whom we knew well and many whom we had come to know slightly, I began to ask people what kinship terms they used for each other. There are twenty terms in all, nine applied to males, ten to females, one to both males and females. The terms for parents, offspring, and siblings were easily learned. But the terms for lineal kin, except father, mother, son, daughter, and all collaterals, except siblings, threw me into confusion. (Henceforth, throughout the chapter I shall use abbreviations for the English kinship terms: Fa [father], Mo [mother], So [son], Da [daughter], Br [brother], Si [sister], FaBr [father's brother], FaBrSo [father's brother's son], and so forth.) I found that different persons used different terms in a given relationship. One of three terms might be applied to a grandfather, one of two of these same terms to a grandson, one of two terms to a grandmother or granddaughter. One of three terms might be applied to a male collateral and one of three to a female collateral. The terms might be applied to kin on either the paternal or maternal side. A relative age distinction and a distinction man-speaking and woman-speaking complicated matters. I did not know for some time what factor determined, for instance, whether a person applied the term a, b, or c to his FaFa or MoFa, or the term a, b, or d to his FaBr, MoBr, or some other collateral. When I asked, I was usually told, "It is our custom," but one informant gravely explained that "God created people and told them what terms to use for each other. Parents have taught their children ever since what terms to use." It was ≠Toma who at last figured out what it was I did not understand and told me what he had assumed everyone knew, that the term "followed the name." In other words, there is a factor, which I finally called "the factor of the name," that under certain circumstances determines what term the individual uses. I began afresh to gather information to understand this factor, and eventually I learned that there are two aspects to the !Kung system of kin terminology, and two methods by which the terms are applied. In one aspect, people are classified by their consanguineous or affinal relationships to each other, and terms are applied on that basis; in the other, which takes precedence wherever it is applicable, people are classified with others if they are named for

---

Studies, 2(2) (Dec. 1924), 57–70. See also her "Comparative Vocabularies of Bushman Languages," University of Cape Town Publications of the School of African Life and Languages (Cambridge, At the University Press, 1929). The !Kung material collected by the Bleek family was from informants who came from north of Lake Ngami and was collected in the years 1879 and 1880 (ibid., p. 3).

Three figures have been added (Figs. 1, 3, and 11) and some of the tables have been rearranged.

or happen to have the same names as those others—here the name is the factor that gives them their terminological position. I call the former of these two methods the *generational* method; the latter I call the *homonymous* method.[2]

Some further comments about the factor of the name are appropriate here.

The !Kung invariably name their children for relatives; therefore, the names are repeated over and over from generation to generation.

The !Kung believe that the name is somehow a part of the entity of the person; when one is named for a person one partakes of that person's entity in some way. A distinction is made between being named *for* and having the same name *as* a person. If one has not been named for a person but happens to bear that person's name, one partakes of the entity of that person also, but to a lesser degree. Informants could give no further elucidation of this belief. In either instance, having the same name is a force that binds people together.

In my opinion, the homonymous method of applying kin terms stems from this belief. If ego is named for A, he partakes of A's entity and, to some extent, he shares A's position—that is, he has kin terms applied to him in certain instances as though he were A. And he applies terms to others as though they were the persons they were named for.

In addition to the belief that the entities of persons who bear the same names merge in some way and to some degree, the !Kung also have an underlying assumption that, since children are named for relatives, persons who are not relatives but who have the same names may have had forebears in the forgotten past who were consanguineous or affinal relatives. This assumption, I believe, lies at the basis of the *name-relationship,* in which the application of kin terms is extended by the factor of the name to persons who have the same names as ego or his consanguineous kin and affines, although the possible distant relationships which might exist between such persons and ego are no longer traceable.

Except in the phrase "kin terms," I do not use the word "kin" in the wide sense that includes both ego's consanguineous kin and persons who come into relationship with him through marriage. I use the designation "affines" for the latter and reserve "kin" or "consanguineous kin" for the former, including lineal and collateral blood relatives in this designation. When no distinction need be made between consan-

2. Douglas Oliver, who kindly read and criticized the manuscript, helped me with many excellent suggestions for which I am most grateful. Among his suggestions were the terms "generational" and "homonymous."

guineous kin and affines and it is convenient to combine them because
I am applying a statement to both, I refer to them as ego's "relatives." I
must stress the point that I distinguish between *relatives* in this sense
and *name-relatives;* name-relatives have neither consanguineous nor
affinal ties with ego, and come within the categories of persons to whom
ego applies kin terms by virtue of their names.

THE GENERATIONAL METHOD

Before proceeding with a description of the application of kin terms by
the generational method, a description of the joking relationship and
some general principles with respect to the terms should be given.

The Joking Relationship

Every relationship in which kin terms are applied is one in which joking
is either permitted or forbidden; every kin term carries its joking status
(which will be given when the terms are set forth). The application of
kin terms is so extensive that it comes to involve the whole population
of the Nyae Nyae region, with the result that a !Kung, by the rules of the
system, is specifically permitted or forbidden to joke with every other
!Kung he knows.

Joking is in the foreground of people's awareness. It came up constantly in our talks about kinship. The !Kung were apparently not always
assiduous in teaching their children the exact biological position of their
kinsmen (whether a given man was FaBr or MoBr, for instance), and
a person would not always know *why* he applied a certain term to someone, but he would know that the term he used was proper, and he would
know the proper joking status to observe; that would have been well
taught him by his parents. The !Kung, I believe, take satisfaction—perhaps I should say they take security—in knowing proper behavior and
conforming to it. This is true of their behavior in the joking relationship.
It was disturbing to them not to have a clearly established joking status
with the members of our expedition. This was one of the reasons for their
quickly giving us !Kung names.[3] Through the names we took our place

3. It was ≠Toma who bestowed names on our family. He gave me his mother's
name, Di//khao, and I was called Di//khao N!a (Old Di//khao) by all. Laurence was
named Tsamgao N!a for ≠Toma's father. Elizabeth was named Di!ai for !U's sister, I
think at Di!ai's request. ≠Toma gave John his own name.

in their scheme of things, and everyone knew whether or not he must refrain from joking with us.

The jokes that are permitted among persons who have the joking relationship, and are avoided among those who do not, are sexual jokes and insults. Anyone may make jokes that are not sexually tinged. Persons who have the joking relationship constantly use it and enjoy it. Men accuse each other of having genital organs of excessive size or abnormal condition (castration or circumcision), or of being excessively preoccupied with sexual intercourse, unable to leave their wives long enough to go hunting. (Only a mad person would say that to a man unless he had the joking relationship with him, we were told.) We noticed that the !Kung do not call each other sons of bitches or base their insults in any way upon ancestry. Men accuse women with whom they may joke of being lazy, useless, slovenly, wanton, or ugly ("Your figure looks like a man's" [is as tall as a man's]). A man may accuse a woman of gadding about, visiting a great deal, and not being home when her husband wants her; or, worse, a man might accuse a woman of eating all the plant food she gathers and bringing nothing home to her family. The women retaliate, perhaps accusing the men of being worthy only of castration or of unfaithful wives. Frequently a man joking with a woman calls her "my wife." The implication is that they have sexual relations together; the !Kung find this pretense very funny. A boy might say "my wife" or "I am going to marry you" to a girl with whom he could joke, implying that they had had or would have sexual relations; but it would be considered neither proper nor funny to say such a thing to a very young girl, regardless of whether the boy and girl had the joking relationship.

To make blatantly insulting jokes with old people is not proper. The deference due to aged persons is expressed in the joking relationship by a moderate tone, and the joking relationship between an old person and a considerably younger one, especially between grandparents and grandchildren, becomes a cozy, friendly intimacy without the sexual emphasis.

Laughter, often uproarious, follows the jokes. A particularly telling sally brings out shrieks and howls. Everyone around hears the jokes and joins in the laughter. People are forbidden to address jokes to those with whom they do not have the joking relationship, but they are not forbidden to laugh at jokes addressed to those persons by others.

There may be occasions when someone takes advantage of the joking relationship to vent his animosity and to hurt someone in anger. I believe that Gao Beard and /Ti!kay have been known to give a bitter flavor to their joking. But this, the !Kung said, is not the custom. When people are quarreling, they said, they do not use the joking words.

A !Kung told us that joking was not only amusing, it was useful in that it taught people, young men especially, not to lose their tempers, but to have poise, instead, in their social relations. I thought that joking served many good purposes, and that the laughter provided for all an outlet for feelings of hostility and a certain amount of release from tension imposed by social restraints.

Though the !Kung enjoy the joking relationship, I had the impression that their primary concern lay with the prohibition against joking. They say that they _koa the person with whom they may not joke and _koa the joking. The verb _koa means to respect (as a !Kung respects his mother-in-law), to avoid (as one avoids joking with a mother-in-law or avoids saying aloud the name of the gods), and it also means to fear (as one fears a lion). It would be madness, the !Kung say, for one to joke with someone with whom he did not have the joking relationship.

When I was beginning to learn about the joking relationship, some of my questions sounded to the !Kung like obscenities, and to have them come from the mouth of a sedate, middle-aged woman threw people into paroxysms of laughter. I remember the howls that arose when I asked if one could joke with a daughter. ≠Toma, when he could get his breath, said he knew I was only beginning to learn the !Kung ways, and he wanted me to know he did not blame me when I said such bad things.

The pattern of the joking relationship emerges basically as follows. In the nuclear family, ego avoids joking with his parents and his offspring. Among siblings, according to a cross and parallel pattern in which a sex differentiation is made, a male jokes with his brother, but not with his sister; a female jokes with her sister, but not with her brother. Among other lineal kin and collaterals, the pattern is one of alternating generations; no sex differentiation is made. Ego avoids joking with his uncles, aunts, nephews, and nieces, who are, respectively, of his parents' and his offspring's generations. He jokes with his cousins, who are of his generation. He jokes with his grandparents and his grandchildren, who are in generations alternate to the generation of his parents and offspring.

Affines fall into a similar pattern. Ego's spouse's parents are like his parents; ego avoids joking with them. His offspring's spouse's parents are like himself; he jokes with them. His offspring's spouses are like his offspring; he avoids joking. Among siblings of spouse, as among siblings, a sex differentiation is made and a cross-parallel pattern obtains. Ego takes the same position as that of his spouse.[4] A man jokes with his wife's sister and avoids joking with her brother, as his wife does. A woman jokes with her husband's brother and avoids joking with his sister, as her husband does.

Sex is not the differentiating factor with respect to the joking relationship among groups of consanguineous kin and affines other than ego's siblings or his spouse's siblings. Ego's joking status is the same with both persons of a married couple among kin and affines. In other words, if ego refrains from joking with an uncle, he also refrains from joking with the uncle's wife. A man jokes with his brother and with his brother's wife. He refrains from joking with his sister and his sister's husband, and so forth. However, in the name-relationship (see "The Homonymous Method," below), ego assumes his status with the name-relative, male or female, individually on the basis of the individual's name, and he does not necessarily accord the same status to the husband and wife.

Informants, trying to explain the joking relationship to me, had an additional statement to make about the prohibition of joking. They said that just as they must not joke with their own parents or offspring, they must not joke with both a person and that person's offspring. When the homonymous method is in operation and persons may be taken out of their biological, generational position and given their terminological position through their names, configurations of terms can occur, theoretically, in which ego might joke with a person and his offspring. (I did not confirm this point with actual tests.) The homonymous method is never applied to the nuclear family, nor to primary affines, so in those categories, ego never jokes both with a person and his offspring. It does not follow that if ego does *not* joke with a person he *must* alternate the gen-

4. I formerly used the expression here that "the point of reference is the spouse." The interpretation that "ego takes the same position as his spouse" with respect to joking with siblings appeals to me and I believe throws more light on the cross and parallel pattern. The interpretation comes from Johannes Fabian, from his paper "!Kung Bushman Kinship: Componential Analysis and Alternative Interpretations," *Anthropos*, 60 (1965), 694, 697. He makes his interpretation as follows: "Spouses occupy the same position in the kinship system." I do not find that an appropriate statement for the whole system, including the homonymous method of applying terms and the name-relationship, but it fits the position of both spouses with respect to the parents, siblings, offspring, and primary affines of each. They parallel each other in the joking relationship. (See Fig. 3 as well as Fig 1.)

erations and joke with the offspring of that person—he may *avoid joking* with both, as, for instance, a man avoids joking both with his sister and with his sister's offspring, and a woman avoids joking with her brother and his offspring.

The generational aspect of the pattern was not brought out by !Kung informants and did not become clear to me until I worked over the material. !Kung informants showed no interest in generation as such. What a !Kung says, when he associates his relatives with each other in the pattern I have called generational, is that they are "like" each other. He considers his parents' siblings to be "like" his parents, his sibling's offspring to be "like" his offspring, his cousins to be "like" himself. That they are alike because they occupy the same "step or stage in the succession of natural descent" (as Webster defines "generation") apparently does not concern the !Kung. Instead it was the joking relationship they spoke of, and they pointed out the parallel position of their kin in its terms.

Joking is reciprocal; if ego jokes with A, A jokes with ego.

In Figure 1, the pattern of the joking relationship is shown.[5] A rectangle calls attention to the nuclear family. Throughout in ego's generation and in the first ascending and descending generations, the pattern of joking is parallel to the pattern in the nuclear family. Only among ego's lineal kin in the generation of great-grandparents, grandparents, grandchildren, great-grandchildren is the joking relation established by the generational method. To persons in those generations, other than lineal kin, the joking relationship would be determined through the name-relationship.

Some General Principles Regarding Terms

1. Terminologically, no two persons may be simultaneously interrelated in more than one way. Persons may change their terminological relationship by marriage or, under some circumstances, by having their names changed, but when this occurs the old terminological relationship is supplanted by the new.

2. The relative age of any two persons applying kin terms to each other is always recognized and indicated by means of the term used, except in a few instances among affines. Relative age is determined by

5. James Fox, who kindly read this chapter, suggested the $+$ $-$ scheme and the general form of Fig. 1. I wish to express my thanks to him.

3	2	1	Ego's	1	2	3	Generation
╎	+	╎		╎	+	╎	Lineal kin
			*⃰╎ · *+				Siblings
			*╎ · *⃰+				Spouses of siblings
		╎	+	╎			Cousins, uncles, aunts, nephews, nieces
		╎	+	╎			Spouses of the latter
			+				Ego's spouse
				╎			Ego's spouse's parents
		╎	*⃰+ · *╎				Ego's spouse's siblings and their offspring
			*+ · *⃰╎				Spouses of ego's spouse's siblings
				╎			Parents of the latter
		╎					Ego's offsprings' spouses
			+				Parents of the latter

+ Joking allowed

╎ Joking prohibited

* Same sex as ego

⃰* Opposite sex from ego

No asterisk means no differentiation is made between sexes.

The rectangle calls attention to the kin in the nuclear family.

Fig. 1.   Ego's joking relationship

order of birth. The concept of relative age is inherent in the terms for father, mother, son, daughter, elder brother, elder sister, and younger sibling. In other instances, the term that the older person applies to the younger is a diminutive.

3. Unless it is specifically stated that the information given pertains only to a male ego or only to a female ego, it is to be assumed that it pertains to both.

4. The abbreviations "m.s." and "w.s." following the kin terms mean "a man is speaking" and "a woman is speaking." If no indication to the contrary is given, it is to be assumed that the term is the same, man-speaking and woman-speaking. (For the sake of avoiding possible ambiguities, I have occasionally used both abbreviations together— "m.s., w.s."—instead of simply omitting them.)

5. When I use English kin terms in my description of the !Kung system, these terms have their English meanings. Thus "grandparents" includes FaFa, MoFa, FaMo, and MoMo. The terms "uncle" and "aunt" include siblings of both of ego's parents and the spouses of those siblings. The !Kung make no distinction between paternal and maternal cousins, nor between cross and parallel cousins, so one can conveniently use the term "cousin" to include FaBrSo, FaBrDa, FaSiSo, FaSiDa, MoBrSo, MoBrDa, MoSiSo, MoSiDa. When I use the terms "nephew" and "niece" I include BrSo, SiSo, BrDa, SiDa.

6. If ego has the joking relationship with persons to whom he applies a given term, this will be indicated by *yes*; if not, by *no*. (The abbreviations "m.s." and "w.s.," when used in reference to the joking relationship, have the same meanings as in paragraph 4 above.)

Terms Applied to Consanguineous Kin by the Generational Method

I distinguish three categories of terms applied to consanguineous kin by the generational method. (A !Kung calls his consanguineous kin *mi jusi*, "my people.") The first category comprises *parent-child* terms; the second category, *sibling* terms; and the third category comprises five terms which I refer to as *generational* terms, two pairs with an alternate, woman-speaking, to one of them. The designation "generational" is a choice of the ethnographer, not a !Kung designation. I consider "generational" appropriate, because ego applies one or the other of these pairs of terms across a whole generation of kin, excepting his parents, children, and siblings.

The parent-child terms appear in Table 7.

TABLE 7. Parent and Child Terms

English	!Kung	Joking
Fa	ba	no
Mo	tai	no
Mo (vocative)	aiya	no
So	!ha	no
Da	≠khai	no

The terms applied to parents and offspring have no diminutives or alternates. They are applied by ego only to his biological parents and offspring. The terms are *fixed* in these relationships in the sense that no other terms can be applied to the biological parents or offspring, and the terms, as they appear in Table 7, are applied in no other relationships. However, these terms do appear in combination with other elements as parts of the terms for stepparents and stepchildren and as parts of two affinal terms, n!unba, n!untai.

The terms for stepparent and stepchild are given in Table 8.

TABLE 8. Stepparent and Stepchild Terms

English	!Kung	Joking
Stepfa	ba-tsu	no
Stepmo	tai-//ga	no
Stepso	!ha-tsu	no
Stepda	≠khai-//ga	no

The sibling terms are three in number; they are given in Table 9.

Table 9. Sibling Terms

English	!Kung	Joking
elder Br	!go	yes m.s., no w.s.
elder Si	!kwi	no m.s., yes w.s.
younger Br	tsī	yes m.s., no w.s.
younger Si	tsī	no m.s., yes w.s.

The sibling terms are used for both full and half siblings. These terms are fixed to the sibling relationship in the sense that no other terms replace them under any condition; but unlike the parent-child terms which are applied in no other relationship, the sibling terms are applied in relationships other than those of biological brother or sister, as will be explained. One extension of the application of sibling terms is made by co-wives in polygynous marriages; they term each other *!kwi* (elder Si) or *tsī* (younger Si), unless they have the same name, in which case they term each other *!gun!a* and *!guma* (terms which will be described presently). Megan Biesele has given me another term used by co-wives for each other and used also in referring to co-wives, *!gwa⁻di*.

The generational terms are applied to lineal and collateral kin (other than those related to ego by parent-child or sibling ties). They are given in Table 10.

TABLE 10. Generational Terms

Applied to Males	Applied to Females	Joking
tsu	//ga	no
!gun!a (or tūn!ga w.s., alternate to !gun!a)	tūn	yes

The pairs of generational terms are reciprocal. If a male ego applies the term *tsu* to a mạn, he is termed *tsu* by that man. Or, if a male ego terms a woman *//ga,* she terms him *tsu.* It is the same with the *!gun!a-tūn* pair.

The above statements about reciprocation are subject to the qualification that when the terms are used in reciprocal pairs, an older person addressing a younger person uses a diminutive form of the term.

TABLE 11. Generational Terms and Diminutives

Generational Term	Diminutive
tsu	tsuma
//ga	//gama
!gun!a	!guma
tūn!ga w.s.	toma w.s.
tūn	toma m.s.

Table 11 gives the generational terms together with the diminutive forms applied reciprocally by older persons to younger persons. Henceforth, to avoid extra complexity in the text and figures, I shall, for the most part, omit the forms the older person applies to the younger, asking the reader to bear in mind that they would be used.

In three instances the diminutive is made simply by adding the suffix *ma* ("small" or "young") to the term. In the other two instances the term is modified in forming the diminutive.

With respect to the *tsu-//ga* pair of terms, an older man termed *tsu* by a younger man or by a younger woman terms both the younger man and younger woman *tsuma*. An older woman termed *//ga* by a younger man or by a younger woman terms the younger man *tsuma*, the younger woman *//gama*. In respect to the *!gun!a-tūn* pair of terms, an older man termed *!gun!a*, or *tūn!ga* w.s., by a younger man or by a younger woman terms the younger man *!guma* and the younger woman *toma*. An older woman termed *tūn* by a younger man or by a younger woman terms the younger man *!guma* or *toma*, the younger woman *!guma*.

Ego applies the terms *!gun!a* (or *tūn!ga* w.s.) and *tūn* to persons in his own generation and in generations alternate to his own; he has the joking relationship with anyone to whom he applies these terms. (Women commonly use *tūn!ga* for their grandfathers rather than *!gun!a*, but *!gun!a* w.s. does occur.) Ego applies *tsu* and *//ga* to persons in generations adjacent to his own or alternate with these latter, and he avoids joking with them.

!Gun!a means "big [or old] name"—*!gu*, "name," *n!a*, "big" or "old." The diminutive form is *!guma*, "small [or young] name." In kin terms, *!gu* occurs only in combination with either *n!a* or *ma*, never alone. With the exception of the words *!hoa*, "man," used as the term for husband, and *tsau*, "woman," used as the term for wife, all the other terms, so far as I know, are specific kinship terms with no application other than that of designating certain kin or affinal relationships.

Another term comes from the word *!gu*; it is ⁻*di !guma*. ⁻*Di* means female, *!guma* is the same word as above, meaning small or young name. ⁻*Di !guma* is applied m.s. and w.s. only to women who have the same name as one's mother and is an alternate to *//ga* in this one sense. It is rarely used, and I have omitted it from the figures.

By standing sticks in the sand to represent persons and ascribing identity to them beginning with known, near kin, we were able to describe the relationships of siblings of grandparents, siblings of great-grandparents, and second and third cousins. Informants clearly recognized the blood ties in those relationships. Their marriage regulations prohibit marriage with second and third cousins, as well as first, because of blood ties. Nevertheless, these more remote kin are considered to be in a category different from the nearer kin to whom kin terms are ascribed as in Figure 2. I did not feel that the categorization was formal or that clear, consistent lines were drawn. People's feelings in this respect would depend probably on circumstances; a kinsman with whom one had lived or had visited often, whose name one knew, would be considered nearer than a kinsman one had never seen. By and large, however, people did not think of the more remote kin as being a part of the constellation of persons who were their very own people, the people to whom they belonged. They use the phrase "my people" for those related to them as in Figure 2 and say they are people who "own" each other (ju-s-a e!ka kxei akwe, "people who own each other"). They make a distinction between people who own each other and more distant kin. "We name our children for our people," they say. "Those people [the more distant kin] would name their children for their people."

In summary, the parent-child and sibling terms and the generational terms, as they are applied to consanguineous kin by the generational method, are set forth in Figure 2. Terms are not attached by the generational method to consanguineous kin more remote than those shown in this diagram. Terms would be applied to more remote kin through their names in the name-relationship.

Terms Applied to Affines

I distinguish three categories of affines: those I call "primary," those I call "secondary," and another category that I call "spouses," which comprises persons who are married to ego's kin or secondary affines but who are not primary affines. A !Kung calls his affines mi twisi.

Once established, an affinal relationship is considered to be indissoluble even though the person through whom the relationship with ego was brought about be dead or divorced. For example, should ego's brother die, his brother's wife remains in affinal relationship with ego, and the application of a kin term and the joking status with her continue to be the same as if ego's brother were alive.

Primary Affines. I designate as "primary" certain affinal relationships that have a factor in common, namely, that terms applied in these relationships are fixed, as the parent-child and sibling terms are fixed in

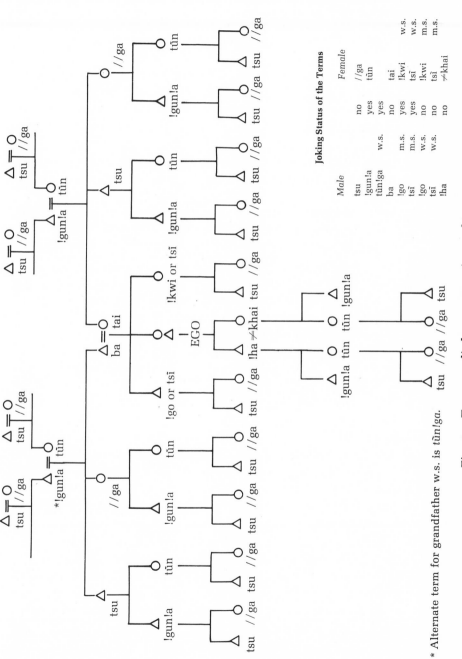

Joking Status of the Terms

Male		Female	
tsu	no	//ga	no
!gun!a	yes	tūn	yes
tūn!ga	w.s. yes		
ba	no	tai	no
!go	m.s. yes	!kwi	m.s. w.s.
tsī	m.s. yes	tsī	w.s.
!go	w.s. no	!kwi	m.s.
tsī	w.s. no	tsī	m.s.
!ha	no	≠khai	no

* Alternate term for grandfather w.s. is tūn!ga.

Fig. 2. Terms applied to consanguineous kin

those relationships: nothing changes them. The homonymous method is not practiced. When a person comes into one of the primary affinal relationships with ego, ego drops whatever term he used previously and adopts the term that is linked to the affinal relationship, even if the person's name is the same as ego's.

The primary affines parallel ego's nuclear family and, together with it, form a group of close relatives, which I believe can be thought of as the core of the !Kung kinship system. Characteristic of this whole core is the fact that terms are fixed specifically in the relationships—in the affinal as well as the parent-child and sibling relationships. Nothing changes the terms. The homonymous method of giving terminological position to the relative according to his name does not operate. The fixed, specific terms set this core of relatives apart from ego's other relatives to whom he applies terms. To his other lineal and collateral kin and his secondary affines (to be described later), the generational terms are applied (tsu-//ga, !gun!a-tūn), and they may be applied through the factor of the name by the homonymous method.

Twenty-two affinal relationships are primary in the above sense. They are: the spouses of ego's siblings; ego's spouse; the parents and siblings of ego's spouse, and the spouses of those siblings; the spouses of ego's offspring, and the parents of those spouses.

Of the terms used for primary affines, three (!go, !kwi, and tsī) are the sibling terms. A man explained the use of the term !go for WiSiHu by saying, "That man and I married sisters. We are therefore like brothers." The same sort of analogy could be made for using the term !kwi for HuBrWi.

Two generational terms, tūn and tūn!ga, are applied to affines as well as to consanguineous kin. Tūn is applied to kin m.s. and w.s., to affines by men only; tūn!ga is applied to affines m.s. and w.s., to kin by women only.

Three pairs of terms are applied exclusively to affines: !hoa ("husband") and tsau ("wife"); ≠tum and /utsu; n!unba and n!untai.

The affinal terms are reciprocal in pairs and the pairs maintain consistency in joking. For example, a man terms his SiHu tūn!ga; to that man ego is WiBr, who is also termed tūn!ga. A woman terms her SiHu tūn!ga. She is WiSi to him and is termed tūn by him. A man terms his WiFa ≠tum; he is DaHu to that man, also termed ≠tum. To a woman HuFa is ≠tum; she is SoWi to him, termed /utsu. Ego and WiSiHu are !go and tsī to each other, and so forth. Relative age is recognized as in all application of terms. A diminutive is used by the older person for the younger, except that ≠tum is often used when the diminutive ≠tuma would be strictly correct.

Table 12 shows how the terms are applied.

!Hoa and tsau are the two affinal terms (mentioned earlier) which, along with !gun!a ("big [old] name") and !guma ("small [young] name"), are the only !Kung terms that are words rather than terms specific to kinship. !Hoa is the !Kung word for "man," and tsau the !Kung word for "woman." As kin terms they are used only between husband and wife.

The terms !hoa and tsau have no forms that indicate relative age. The indication of relative age is inherent in the sibling terms !go (elder brother), !kwi (elder sister), and tsī (younger sibling). The terms /utsu, n!unba, and n!untai have diminutive forms made with the suffix ma, used by the older person for the younger: /utsuma, n!u̇nbama, and n!untaima. However, among affines the use of diminutive forms is not strictly adhered to. Even though the forms exist, they may be ignored. The diminutive of ≠tum, ≠tumma exists but is consistently ignored in the relationships of HuFa, WiFa, and DaHu. HuFa and WiFa are presumably older than ego, but DaHu is presumably younger. I have no explanation for this exception. ≠Tumma is occasionally heard among name-relatives. Tūn!ga m.s. has a diminutive form (tūn!gama m.s.), but tūn!ga w.s. has a modified form as the diminutive, that is, toma w.s. The modified form of tūn m.s. is toma m.s. Toma is the form used for the diminutive of tūn m.s.

As to the joking relationship: !hoa, tsau, n!unba, and n!untai allow joking; ≠tum and /utsu do not. Tūn!ga w.s. allows joking; tūn!ga m.s. does not.

The pattern of the joking among affines has a form that matches the pattern of joking among ego's parents, offspring, and siblings, as seen in Figure 1. Ego is prohibited from joking with primary affines in the generation of his parents and offspring. In the sibling category, a "cross" and "parallel" pattern obtains among ego's primary affines as among his siblings. Ego jokes with a sibling of the same sex and with the spouse of that sibling. Ego does not joke with a sibling of opposite sex nor with the spouse of that sibling. In the case of ego's spouse's siblings, ego takes the position of his spouse; as his spouse does, ego jokes with the spouse's sibling who is of the same sex as the spouse and does not joke with the spouse's sibling of the opposite sex from that of the spouse. Husbands and wives are paired: thus, a male ego jokes with his WiSi and WiSiHu

TABLE 12. Terms Applied to Primary Affines

Affinal Relationship	Applied to Males		Affinal Relationship	Applied to Females	
	Term	Joking		Term	Joking
Ego's Generation					
Hu	!hoa	yes	Wi	tsau	yes
SoWiFa, DaHuFa	n!unba	yes	SoWiMo, DaHuMo	n!untai	yes
Generations Adjacent to Ego's					
HuFa, WiFa, DaHu	≠tum	no	HuMo, WiMo, SoWi	/utsu	no
Sibling Category					
SiHu	tũn!ga m.s. / tũn!ga w.s.	no / yes	BrWi	tũn m.s. / /utsu w.s.	yes / no
WiBr	tũn!ga	no	WiBrWi	/utsu	no
WiSiHu	!go or tsi	yes	WiSi	tũn	yes
HuBr	tũn!ga	yes	HuBrWi	!kwi or tsi	yes
HuSiHu	≠tum	no	HuSi	/utsu	no

but not with his WiBr or WiBrWi; a female ego jokes with her HuBr and HuBrWi but not with her HuSi or HuSiHu.

Figure 3 shows the primary affines, the terms applied to them, and the joking relationship among them.

Secondary Affines. I call "secondary" a group of more remote affines— the parents, offspring, and siblings of ego's primary affines. !Kung families visit each other a great deal, and a person is likely to have close and frequent contact with many of his secondary affines as well as with his primary affines.

Secondary affines are:

1. Parents and siblings of BrWi, SiHu
   Offspring of the above siblings
2. Offspring of WiBr, WiSi, HuBr, HuSi
3. Parents and siblings of WiBrWi, WiSiHu, HuBrWi, HuSiHu
   Offspring of the above siblings
4. Siblings of SoWi, DaHu
   Offspring of the above siblings

Terms are not fixed in the secondary affinal relationships as they are in the primary affinal relationships. The factor of the name is operative in secondary affinal relationships, and if there were reason for the term to be applied on the basis of the name, this would be done. In all probability, the persons who become ego's secondary affines at the time of his marriage have been, prior to the marriage, ego's name-relatives. If this is the case, as it was for my informants, ego continues to apply to these persons the terms he applied in the name-relationship, adding to these terms either *n!unba* or *n!untai*: that is, *tsu-n!unba*, *//ga-n!untai*, *!gun!a-n!unba*, *tūn-n!untai*, *!go-n!unba*, *!kwi-n!untai*, and *tsī-n!unba* or *tsi-n!untai.*

Although it is strictly correct to use the combined terms for secondary affines, many people drop one or the other part in addressing each other. It is especially common to drop *n!unba* or *n!untai* when addressing children or young persons.

The name-relationship is so extensive that it is very unlikely that ego's secondary affines would not previously have been his name-relatives. If, however, it were to happen that ego had no term to apply to a secondary affine on the basis of the factor of the name, he could fall back on the generational method and apply a term according to its pattern.

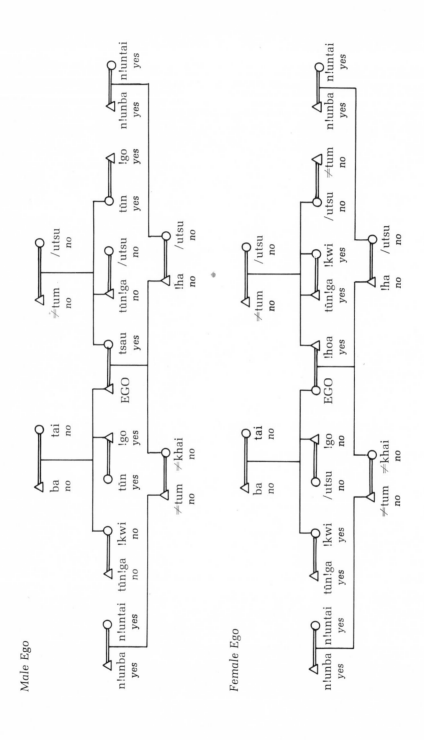

Fig. 3. Ego's nuclear family and primary affines

The terms applied by the latter method are the generational terms, the *tsu-//ga* and *!gun!a*—or *tūn!ga* w.s.—*tūn* pairs. The affinal terms *n!unba* or *n!untai* would probably be added except when the terms were applied to young persons and children. The sibling terms are not applied to secondary affines unless the homonymous method is in use and requires them. The terms *!gun!a* and *tūn* are applied to the persons with whom ego may joke, *tsu* and *//ga* to persons with whom he avoids joking.

I had difficulty at this point in clarifying the statements of my informants as to the pattern of the application of the terms. Actually, informants applied terms to their secondary affines on the basis of names, not by the generational method, and it was hard for them to figure out what term they would use if they were not to use the one they do use. They are not accustomed to working things out theoretically, and I, in my attempt to do so, misconstrued what was told me, applied the wrong principle, and constructed a diagram that was wrong (namely, Diagram 8 on p. 17 of my article as originally published in *Africa*). I wish to express my thanks to Ward Goodenough for his careful study of the diagram and for his kindly calling my attention to an inconsistency in reciprocation within it. An inconsistency is a signal of error; the !Kung system has no inconsistencies.

My misunderstanding lay in the matter of alternation of joking by generations. I thought informants were telling me that there *must* be that alternation, that if ego applied *tsu* or *//ga* to a secondary affine and did not joke with that person, it would follow that he would apply the *!gun!a-tūn* terms to that person's offspring and joke with them. But this proved to be a mistake. The system does not work that way. Ego may avoid joking in both the generation of the parent and the offspring.

Further study of my notes and more careful thought lead me now to believe—in fact, make it seem obvious—that the consistent and proper pattern of applying terms to secondary affines is essentially the same pattern that we see applied to primary affines, which in turn is analogous to the pattern of joking among consanguineous kin. All secondary affines in his parents' generation ego would term *tsu-n!unba* and *//ga-n!untai*. He would apply these same terms to all in his offspring's generation, probably omitting the *n!unba* or *n!untai* part of the term. Among secondary affines who are the siblings of primary affines, the primary affine is the point of reference. With the sibling of his primary affine who is the same sex as the primary affine, ego would maintain the same joking status (be it joking or not joking) that he maintains with his primary affine. He would take the opposite position with the primary affine's sibling whose sex is the opposite of that of the primary affine. Thus, for example, a male ego would joke with his BrWiSi since he jokes with his BrWi, and he would refrain from joking with his BrWiBr. Since the sibling terms *!go, !kwi,* and *tsī* are not used in these relationships, the term applied by a male ego to BrWiSi would be *tūn-n!untai,* to BrWiBr *tsu-n!unba.* A female ego would avoid joking with BrWiSi since she does not joke with BrWi, and to her BrWiSi she would apply the term *//ga-n!untai;* she would take the opposite position with BrWiBr, whom she would term *!gun!a-* (or *tūn!ga-*) *n!unba.*

I shall spare the reader diagrams of all the permutations of these terms m.s. and w.s. and give only two samples in Figure 4.

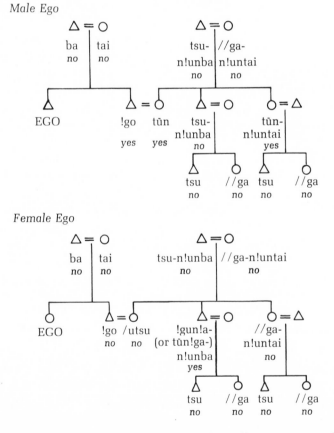

Fig. 4. Examples of terms applied to secondary affines: parents, siblings, nephews, and nieces of Ego's sibling's spouse

Spouses of Relatives. When a person marries one of ego's kin or affines, ego drops whatever term he may have previously used for that person and adopts the term appropriate to the spouse of his kin or affine. Ego applies a term that gives him the same joking relationship with both members of the married couple.

The terms have already been given for married couples among lineal kin (great-grandparents, grandparents, parents) and among the primary affines, and need not be repeated. It remains to give the terms that are used for the spouses of uncles, aunts, nephews, nieces, cousins, grand-children.

These terms are given in Table 13.

TABLE 13. Terms Applied to Spouses of Kin and Affines

Terms		Joking
Applied to Males	*Applied to Their Wives*	
tsu—FaBr or MoBr	//ga	no
—nephew	/utsu	no
!gun!a—cousin or grandson	tūn	yes
tsu-n!unba	//ga-n!untai or /utsu	no
!gun!a-n!unba	tūn-n!untai	yes
!go or tsī	tūn m.s. /utsu w.s.	yes m.s.
		no w.s.
Applied to Females	*Applied to Their Husbands*	
//ga—FaSi or MoSi	tsu	no
—niece	tūn!ga m.s. or tsu	no
	≠tum w.s. or tsu	no
tūn—cousin or granddaughter	!gun!a	yes
//ga-n!untai	tsu-n!unba or ≠tum	no
tūn-n!untai	!gun!a- (or tūn!ga- w.s.) n!unba	yes
!kwi or tsī	tūn!ga	no m.s.
		yes w.s.

THE HOMONYMOUS METHOD

Before proceeding with a description of the application of kin terms by the homonymous method, several points about the naming of children should be made.

1. It is the duty and the right of fathers to name their sons and daughters.

2. Children are named at birth. Although a father may change his

child's name if he wishes, this is rarely done. Most people keep the same name throughout their lives.

3. The !Kung have no surnames.

4. Names are sex-linked; hence men and women never have the same name.

5. According to !Kung kinship regulations, parents and child must not bear the same name. The !Kung said it would be "madness" for a man to name a son for himself or a daughter for her mother. In gathering genealogical data, I encountered no deviation from this rule.

6. Children are always named for relatives, either consanguineous or affinal. They are named for relatives in the first or second ascending generation. The relatives may be living or dead. The father may or may not have the joking relationship with the relative for whom he names his child.

7. A man invariably names his firstborn son for his father (i.e., the child's FaFa) and his firstborn daughter for his mother (the child's FaMo). If he has more than one wife, he names the firstborn son and daughter of each wife for his father and mother respectively. Thus half siblings, though they are not named for each other, often bear the same name, having been named for the same person. I believe that the !Kung adhere strictly to this rule. When in the band charts the oldest son or daughter to appear does not bear the FaFa's or FaMo's name, it may be assumed that a child who did bear that name has previously died. My records of dead children are not complete. Sometimes when a firstborn child dies, the father gives his father's or mother's name to the next son or daughter born, but this is not required by the rule.[6]

A man often, but not invariably, names his secondborn son for the child's MoFa and secondborn daughter for her MoMo. Fifty-one percent of the !Kung in my records are named for their grandparents.[7] Subse-

6. An example: the mother of Gao Beard is Old Xama. Gao gave her name to his first daughter by his first wife (a child who died), to his second daughter by his first wife, and to his first daughter by his second wife. Both his wives, incidentally, are named //Kushay.

7. We wondered if !gun!a came into the system with the homonymous method and speculated that perhaps it originally used to be applied only to the person for whom ego is named. It is not strictly a kinship term, being composed of translatable words, "big or old name." We think it may have been superimposed upon tūn!ga (which probably comes from the same root as tūn). Tūn!ga may originally have been applied to grandfather, man-speaking as well as woman-speaking, and later !gun!a may have become associated with grandfather because so many men are named for their grandfathers. Megan Biesele, who has great mastery of the !Kung language, has assured me that the "u" in tūn!ga is nasalized, whereas I had been uncertain myself. I have added the tilde.

quent children, I was told, are usually named for the siblings of their father or mother, or for the spouses of those siblings. These are the usual namings, but children may be named for other relatives: I know of two children, for example, named for their parents' cousins. It is not their custom, !Kung informants told me, to name children for the children's great-grandparents or for the siblings of the children's grandparents. However, this last custom is not observed with fidelity: I know of at least one child named for his grandmother's younger brother. There may be more. My genealogical records are not full enough with respect to the dead for me to trace every naming.

8. The names are repeated over and over from generation to generation. They run in families. There are relatively few names in use—we recorded 48 men's names and 41 women's names, as follows:

Women's Names		*Men's Names*	
//Aha	Khuan//a	//Ao	N//ami
//Asa	//Khuga	Bo	N≠amshi
Baú	Khwo//o	Dam	N!ani
Be	Khwova	Debe	N//ao
Di!ai	//Kushay	Demi	N/oshay
Di//khao	N!aba	!Gai	N//u
Doĭn	N!ai	/Gaishay	N/unu
/Gam	N/aoka	Gao	Obi
//Gao	N≠isa	/Gao	//Oshay
/Gasa	N!oshay	≠Gao	/Qui
!Ghia	Sa≠gai	Gaú	Sao
≠Gisa	Sebe	/Gishay	Tame
/Goishay	≠Ta//ai	Gumtsa	Ta//ne
!Gun≠a	Tsaba	/Gunda	/Ti!kay
//Haru	Tshi!ko	/In!ao	Ti//khao
//In	Tshua	Kali	≠Toma
//Insa	!U	!Kham	Tsa
Khabo	!Ungka	Khami	Tsamgao
Kharu	Xama	Khan//a	/Tuka
/Khoa	Zuma	Khon/u	Tushay
Khokove		Kuara	/Tushi
		≠Ñ	Twey
		N!aba	Zo/oa
		N!aishi	Zu!ko

We met personally 18 men named /Qui, 23 named Gao, 19 named /Gaishay; 13 women named //Kushay, 18 named /Khoa, 16 named N≠isa, and so forth.

Nicknames are in common use especially among men. I have heard that women, too, have nicknames, but apparently much less commonly than men. I personally was not aware of a nickname being used for a woman. Men's nicknames are usually bestowed by their peers. In at least one instance, however, a man had been given a nickname at the time he was named. He was /Qui Shoulder. There was nothing notable about his shoulders, but he had been named for a man called /Qui Shoulder. The nicknames usually refer to physical characteristics of the individual, though some refer to traits of character and some to events. The following are examples:

Gao Feet
Gao Beard
Short Gao
Gao Thumb
/Gunda Chubby
Bo Black
/Gao Knees
/Qui Stomach (because he ate so much)
/Qui Shoulder
/Qui Crooked
/Qui Short
/Qui Navel
/Qui Collarbone
//Ao Fat Chin

The nickname of ≠Toma was ≠Toma Word. It referred to his wisdom, his understanding of people and their actions and feelings, and his outstanding ability to guide people by talking with them and to persuade them to do the right things. /Qui Navel was sometimes called "I refuse I refuse" because of a tendency to hold back and take a pessimistic view rather than an optimistic one when some plan was proposed. //Aa, the son of Old ≠Toma, was called //Ao Wildebeest, because the morning after he consummated his marriage he went hunting and killed five wildebeest.

Nicknames are bestowed by a man's companions, but the men themselves adopt epithets that praise their prowess in hunting. /Ti!kay praises himself by calling himself "Sharp Edge of the Arrow Point"—//Kai //Ha N!e ("arrow point, edge sharp"). ≠Toma praises himself by calling himself N!ao //Gumsi, "Bow Muscles." /Ti!kay said simply that they call themselves by these names because they are very good at shooting.

Several women and girls we knew had two names, Di//khao-!Gun≠a and Khwo//o-/Gasa, for example. I did not learn of a man who had two names, although many had nicknames. The women may commonly use either one or the other of their double names or both together. I was told that the mother or other relatives or friends often seek to influence the father's choice of names for a child, and that sometimes they succeed. The second names of girls, I was told, were frequently given as a result of some relative's insistence. The second names may be of non-related persons. ≠Toma, for example, gave my name, Lorna, to his daughter as her second name. Her first name was !Ungka, after ≠Toma's sister. !Ungka-Lorna was always called Norna. (The !Kung do not have "l" in their alphabet.)

The Homonymous Method of Applying Kin Terms to Consanguineous Kin and Affines

The homonymous method, when it is applicable, is superimposed upon the generational method of applying kin terms. The factor of the name comes into operation. Relatives (both kin and affines) may be classified terminologically with the relatives for whom they are named, and terms are applied accordingly.

In describing the homonymous method, we must make a distinction between a person's being named for another and his fortuitously having the same name as another. In this section, we shall be discussing the former situation; in the next section, on the name-relationship, the latter.

When it is applicable, the homonymous method takes precedence, and ego applies terms by it rather than by the generational method. I must stress the fact that terms are not applied by the homonymous method in all relationships. As we have seen, they are not so applied in the relationships of parents, offspring, and siblings—ego applies terms by the homonymous method to persons named for the above relatives, but not to those relatives themselves. The terms applied in those relationships are fixed to the relationship; the factor of the name does not change them. Also, in the relationships of primary affines, terms are not applied by the homonymous method.

When two persons apply terms to each other by the homonymous method, it is the older person who determines what term shall be used between them. The above rule requires us to keep in mind that ego's terminological position should be thought of from two points of view.

(a) Relatives older than ego classify ego with the person for whom he is named, and they apply terms to ego in accordance with their homonymous patterns; ego reciprocates with the terms called for by the terms they use for him. (b) In his turn ego establishes the terms he uses for relatives younger than himself. He classifies them with the persons for whom they are named and applies terms to them in accordance with the terms he would use for those persons; they reciprocate appropriately.

Ego's relatives for whom his younger relatives may be named fall into five categories:

(1)   ego's parents and offspring
(2)   ego's siblings
(3)   ego and his spouse
(4)   other kin
(5)   affines

(1) Parents and offspring. Some of ego's nephews and nieces would be named for ego's parents. His brothers, for instance, would name their firstborn sons and daughters for the children's FaFa or FaMo (i.e. the parents of ego and his brothers). Some of ego's cousins might also be named for ego's parents. Some of ego's grandchildren might be named for his sons and daughters. The terms *ba* and *tai*, *!ha* and *≠khai*, as I have said, are used only for the biological parents and offspring. The generational terms which have the same generational association and joking status as the terms for parents and offspring are *tsu* and *//ga*, and these are the terms ego uses for relatives named for his parents and offspring.

In some instances, the terms applied by the homonymous method turn out to be the same as those which would be applied by the generational method. This is true of the terms applied to the nephews and nieces named for ego's parents; *tsu* and *//ga* are the terms used according to both methods in these instances. Cousins would be termed *!gun!a* or *tũn* by the generational method; however, if they are named for ego's parents, the terms applied must be *tsu* or *//ga*.

(2) Siblings. If a relative is named for ego's sibling, ego applies sibling terms to the relative, and ego has the same joking position with him that he would have with his sibling.

(3) Ego and his spouse. Relatives may be named for ego and his spouse. *!Gun!a* is the term used for a male named for himself; but the term would be in its diminutive form, *!guma*. A male named for ego would be younger than ego. That male would reciprocate by calling ego *!gun!a*.

When the generational method of applying terms was described, we saw *!gun!a* applied m.s. and w.s. to males only. *Tūn* was the corresponding term applied to females. When the homonymous method is used, a female ego applies the term *!gun!a* (or rather its diminutive *!guma*) to a female named for her. That female reciprocates by calling her *!gun!a*.

The terms applied to persons named for ego's spouse are also *!gun!a* (or *tūn!ga* w.s.) or *tūn*. The affinal terms *!hoa* and *tsau* for husband and wife are used only for ego's actual spouse. Persons named for the spouse, who is terminologically of ego's generation, have the generational terms applied to them that classify them with ego's generation and give them the joking relationship. The term *tūn* is applied to the wife of a male whom ego terms *!gun!a* (or *tūn!ga* w.s.). *Tūn!ga* is the term applied to the husband of a woman whom a female ego terms *!gun!a*. (In this situation, *!gun!a* is not used; in other words, it is not an alternate to *tūn!ga* here.)

The term *!gun!a* has other applications. Ego applied it to the person *for whom he is named,* and also to anyone, related or not, who happens to have the same name as his, and to relatives *named for him*—with two exceptions: (a) Siblings. Although they are not named for each other, they frequently have the same name, being named for the same person. If ego and his sibling have the same name, the sibling terms are retained, taking precedence over the term *!gun!a*. (b) Primary affines. As I have mentioned, if the primary affine and ego happen to have the same name, or even in the unlikely situation of ego's being named for a man who became his primary affine, the term *!gun!a* would be dropped and the affinal term used. The same is true for a woman applying the term to the woman she is named for, to females named for her, or to females having the same name as hers.

(4) Other kin. I believe that the basis of the homonymous method is ego's classification of relatives by their names with himself and his spouse, his parents, offspring, and siblings, but classification by this method is not limited to these categories. Other kin as well are classified by their names. When some relative is named for another of ego's kin, ego applies the same term to him that he applied to the kinsman.

Furthermore, ego continues to apply terms to relatives in the descending generation who are named for those whom he has classified by name. For example, he applies the term *tsu* to A because A was named for his (ego's) father; he continues to apply the term *tsu* to relatives who are named for A.

(5) Affines. Consanguineous kin of ego's may be named for his pri-

mary or secondary affines. Ego's son and ego's brother, for example, would in all probability name some of their children for their wives' parents or siblings. When one of the generational or sibling terms is used for the affine, ego uses that same term for the kin named for the affine. The exclusively affinal terms, as I said previously, are not used for kin. For kin named for ego's ≠tum, /utsu, n!unba, or n!untai, for example, ego would use the generational term that corresponds in generation and joking status with the affinal term, namely, tsu, //ga, !gun!a, and tūn.

Some of ego's secondary affines would be named for his primary affines and some, possibly, for his offspring. These children would be ego's secondary affines, and ego would apply generational terms to them which correspond in joking status to the term he applies to the person for whom they were named.

The correspondence of the affinal terms with the generational terms is shown in Table 14.

Diagrams will be given to illustrate the homonymous method of applying terms, but they do not illustrate a typical family. No Bushman family we knew in 1952–53 had as many living children as in Figure 7, to say nothing of Figure 11. ≠Toma, helping me one day to construct one of these hypothetical illustrations, laughed and said, "Who is this who has so many children? Is it an ostrich?"

In the figure, letters represent names. A person who is designated by the same letter as a person in a generation above him has been named for that person. The naming in the diagrams is customary. Children are named most often for their grandparents, the siblings of their parents, and the spouses of those siblings.

Figures 5 and 6 illustrate the application of terms between ego's !gun!a and ego, and between members of the !gun!a's family and ego. All ego's kin in these two diagrams are assumed to be older than ego, and they, as the older persons, establish the terms they use for ego according to their homonymous pattern. They would apply the diminutives, and what we see in the diagrams is ego's reciprocation with the form of the term appropriate to the older persons.

In Figure 5, ego is named for his FaFa, C. His FaFa and FaMo term ego !guma. He reciprocates calling them !gun!a and tūn. A and B, siblings of C, term ego tsi, younger sibling, because he is named for their sibling; ego reciprocates giving them the sibling terms. E and F term ego tsuma because he is named for their father; ego calls them tsu and //ga.

In Figure 6, ego is named for his FaBr, D. Ego's grandparents term

TABLE 14. Correspondence between Affinal Terms and the Generational Terms Used for Ego's Kin Named for Affines

Affine for Whom Kin Is Named	Applied to Males		Applied to Females		
	Term Ego Applies to Kinsman Named for Affine	Joking	Affine for Whom Kin Is Named	Term Ego Applies to Kinsman Named for Affine	Joking
!hoa	!gun!a w.s. or tûn!ga w.s.	yes yes	tsau	tûn	yes
n!unba	!gun!a m.s., w.s. or tûn!ga w.s.	yes yes	n!untai	tûn	yes
≠tum	tsu	no	/utsu	//ga	no
tûn!ga m.s.	tsu m.s.	no	tûn	tûn	yes
tûn!ga w.s.	!gun!a w.s. or tûn!ga w.s.	yes yes			
!go or tsi	!go or tsi	yes m.s. no w.s.	!kwi or tsi	!kwi or tsi	no m.s. yes m.s.

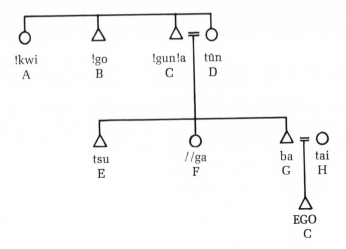

Fig. 5.   Application of terms by homonymous method

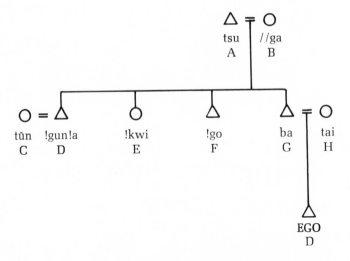

Fig. 6.   Application of terms by homonymous method

him *tsuma* because he is named for their son. His FaBr, D, terms him *!guma*. His father's other siblings give him the sibling term for younger brother, *tsī*.

Ego makes a secondary application of the terms that he originally applies to members of his *!gun!a*'s nuclear family. Ego applies terms to persons who are named for the latter and continues during his lifetime applying to persons descending from his *!gun!a's* nuclear family the same terms that he applied to the persons for whom they were named. Figure 7, which shows terms applied to cousins, illustrates this point.

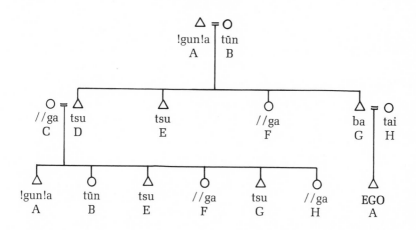

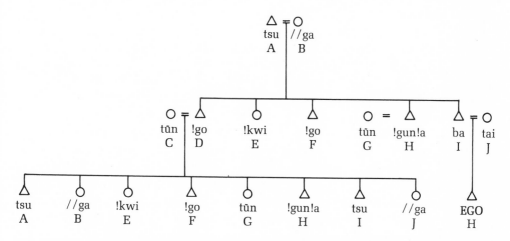

Fig. 7. Application of terms by homonymous method

In Figure 7, it is assumed that ego is older than his cousins and that he establishes the terms he applies to them. (The terms would be in the diminutive forms.) In the first instance, ego is named for his FaFa, in the second for his FaBr. Ego's FaBr, D, has named his children for his parents and siblings.

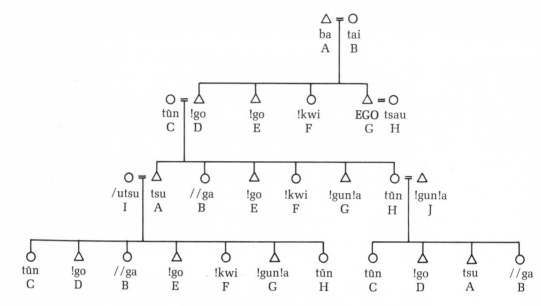

Fig. 8.   Application of terms by homonymous method

Figure 8 shows what terms ego would apply to nephews and nieces, children of his brother D, if the children were named, as they customarily would be, for ego's Fa, Mo, his siblings, and himself and his spouse. The illustration also shows the terms and the names carried, linked together, into the descending generation.

In Figure 9 it is assumed that ego is a woman. The illustration shows what terms she would apply to her grandchildren if their father, ego's son C, followed the customary pattern in naming them. Ego, being a woman in this illustration, uses the term !gun!a for her granddaughter A, who is named for her. (I remind the reader that, for the sake of brevity, I omit the diminutives which are to be found in Table 11. Actually, ego would use the form !guma for her granddaughter.) Ego's grandson B is named for ego's husband. !Hoa is the term for the actual husband. The term !gun!a (or tun!ga w.s.) is used by a woman for someone named for her husband.

I have been assuming up to this point in the illustrations that ego is named for someone on his father's side of the family. What has been said about the paternal side is applicable to the maternal side when ego is named for someone on that side.

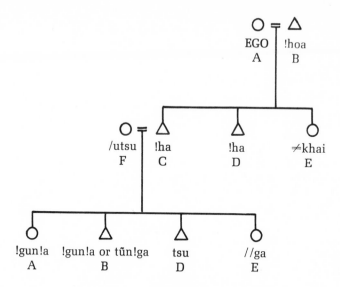

Fig. 9.   Application of terms by homonymous method

The side (either paternal or maternal) that does not include the person for whom ego is named is referred to here as the *off-side*. The terms applied by the generational method are applied to ego's off-side kin, unless a person is terminologically taken out of his biological generation through the factor of the name. Grandparents on the off-side are always termed *!gun!a* (or *tũn!ga* w.s.) or *tũn*. These are the generational terms applied by the generational method. Ego is not named for anyone on the off-side and, therefore, occasion does not arise in which ego would be required to term his off-side grandparents *tsu* and *//ga*.

Figure 10 illustrates the application of terms on the off-side. In the diagram it is assumed the ego, E(3), is named for his FaBr, E(1). Ego is of the younger generation with respect to his uncles and aunts; he is assumed to be older than his cousins. Ego's maternal uncles H and J(1) retain the "adjacent" generational term *tsu* for ego; the factor of the name requires no other. Ego's maternal uncle E(2) applies the term *!gun!a* to ego because he and ego have the same name.

Whereas ego applies the term *!gun!a* to anyone either named for him or merely fortuitously having the same name as his own, in other relationships a distinction is made between being named for someone and merely having the same name. In Figure 10, it is to be noted that,

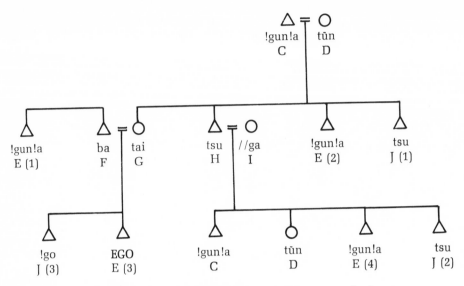

Fig. 10. Application of terms by homonymous method

although ego has a brother named J(3), he does not apply the sibling terms to J(1) or J(2). J(1), ego's uncle, being in the ascending generation, establishes the term used between them; his term for ego is the "adjacent" generational term *tsu*. As J(2) is named for J(1), not for ego's Br, ego uses the "adjacent" generational term *tsu* for J(2). He would use the sibling term for someone named for his brother.

Figure 11 gives examples of ego's kin named for affines and his affines named for kin and the terms he would apply.

There is one further complexity that may beset the student of !Kung kin terminology in his effort to follow the names and the terms. Names may be changed, and, when they are, the person is reclassified and the kin terms applied to him or her are changed accordingly. One blazing hot day I heard Old Xama call her little granddaughter //*gama* (diminutive of //*ga*). I felt the whole system, which had caused me so much difficulty, begin to swirl and dissolve into formlessness, for the child was named for Old Xama and, if I understood the system at all, Old Xama must call that child !*guma* (diminutive of !*gun!a*). I fanned myself with my helmet, kept my voice low, and asked Old Xama if I had heard correctly. "Oh yes," she said. "Little Xama's name has been changed." Old Xama's son, Gao Beard, the other day when his sister Di!ai was visiting,

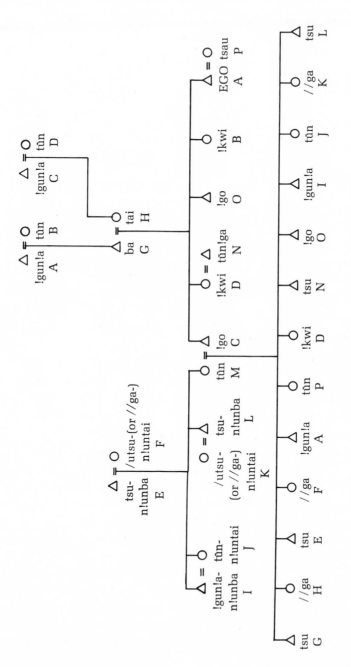

Fig. 11.　Application of terms by homonymous method

had decided to give his sister's name to his daughter instead of Old Xama's. Now she and her little granddaughter were //ga and //gama to each other. Old Xama said she was very disappointed. I was not. I took a deep breath and went on to the next task.

The Name-Relationship

Generational and sibling terms are applied to persons who have no consanguineous or affinal ties with ego if they have the same names as ego or his kin or affines. I refer to this aspect of the !Kung system as the name-relationship.

Among name-relatives, as among consanguineous relatives, it is the older person who classifies the younger with respect to his (the older's) kinship constellation. The older person uses the diminutive or other modified form of the term for the younger person; the younger person uses the unmodified form for the older. Throughout this discussion, it will be assumed that ego is the older person.

One of the factors in the name-relationship is an ancestral list of names to which terms are linked. Each !Kung has his own individual list to learn, taught to him by his parents and by the person for whom he is named (his !gun!a). No one could tell us exactly how the list is compiled, or exactly how the association between names and terms was made. One surmises that the forebears whose names are on ego's list were great-grandparents and their siblings and the siblings of grandparents and so on, or perhaps persons of still earlier generations. Name-relatives who have these names may have had some distant consanguineous connections with ego. Ego no longer knows, but the old people knew, and in following their teaching, ego knows he is following his proper homonymous pattern. Every informant had such a list and told us what term he linked with every name we knew. Some had more than one term linked with a name. ≠Toma used the term tūn for women named Khwova who came from the /Gam region and !kwi for Khwovas from the north. His parents, he said, told him to do this.

There is a system of applying terms to name-relatives. Ego invariably applies the term !gun!a to any name-relative who has the same name as his. Furthermore, ego applies terms to the Fa, Mo, So, Da, siblings, and spouse of a !gun!a who is a name-relative with the same name as his, as he does in the case of the person for whom he is named. However, this application of terms is carried no further. He does not apply terms to persons named for these name-relatives, and he does not apply terms to the nuclear family and spouse of a person he happens to term *!gun!a* in the name-relationship unless the *!gun!a's* name is the same as his.

Ego applies the term *tsu* to any male name-relative who has the same name as his Fa; *//ga* to any female name-relative who has the same name as his Mo.

There are gaps in our knowledge at this point; confusion in the data was not resolved. I think, but am not certain, that next in order comes the ancestral list taking precedence over siblings, children, and spouses as a source of terms to apply to name-relatives. I think the terms applied to name-relatives derive mainly from the ascending generations (except for the term *!gun!a* when it is applied to persons with the same name as ego's). An illustration will make this clearer: Take a man named Bo (whose nickname is Djo, "black"). Unless Bo is ego's name (in which case ego would term him *!gun!a*) or unless Bo is ego's Fa's name (in which case ego would term him *tsu*), ego would give Bo Djo the term he had for Bo on his ancestral list. Even if Bo were the name of ego's Br, he would not give him the sibling term because this Bo Djo was not named for his Br. Even if a female ego's husband were named Bo, she would use the term she had linked with Bo on her ancestral list, not the term she uses for males named for her husband (*!gun!a*), because this Bo Djo was not named for her husband. I am certain that the ancestral list takes precedence over ego's children as a source of terms for name-relatives. For instance, if ego is accustomed to apply the term *!gun!a* to men named Bo according to his ancestral list, and if he chooses to name a newborn son Bo, he will not change his term for men named Bo from *!gun!a* to *tsu*.

I have been assuming that the name occurs on the ancestral list. If a person should come along whose name was not on ego's ancestral list but whose name was the same as that of one of ego's consanguineous kinsmen or affines, ego would apply to that person the term that he applies to the consanguineous kinsman or affine. (In the case of an affine, ego would use a generational or sibling term corresponding to the affinal term, not the affinal term itself. The correspondence in terms is the same as that shown on Table 14.) I know of no rule to prevent a name-relative's being classified with any consanguineous kinsman or affine should his name not be on ego's ancestral list.

Supposing a name did not occur on ego's ancestral list but did occur several times among his contemporary consanguineous kin and affines, the question arises as to which kinsman or affine would be the one with whom ego would classify a person of that name. I have no precise data on this point, but I think that consanguinity takes precedence over affinity and the near over the more distant relationship.

As I have said earlier, the spouses of kin and affines are always paired terminologically with the kin, but this is not true of name-relatives with the exception of one who has the same name as ego. Ego establishes the name-relationship with each member of a married couple individually. It was in this connection that I learned of an aspect of the !Kung system that has not yet been mentioned.

Informants told me that ego may apply a term to the parents and children of an individual name-relative on the generational basis if he has no term established by his ancestral list. If ego's term for a man is !gun!a, he may apply the term tsu to that man's Fa and So, observing the same alternation of the terms !gun!a and tsu that is apparent in Figure 1. In this connection informants told me furthermore that "boys follow their fathers, girls follow their mothers," meaning that a son is classified with respect to his father and a daughter with respect to her mother. I think ego would apply terms in this way only if the parent or child of the name-relative had a name for which ego had no term. The !Kung in the Nyae Nyae region had so many name-links that I did not find people applying terms to parents and offspring of name-relatives in this manner.

Richard Lee found that the !Kung many times discussed and negotiated the terms that one would use for another, and that there was much fun to be had from these negotiations. (Lee tells me this by personal communication.) In his field notes (also given me by personal communication), Lee comments upon the change that takes place in a lifetime in the matter of applying terms. He says, "When you are young you play a passive role; others older than you control the terms they apply to you. Eventually you control the terms you apply to others younger than you. Learning the system is a lifetime affair. Your universe evolves as you grow older. As you pass through marriage, the birth of your children, and the marriage of your children, you add new names and new twists to your application of kinship terms."

Use of Kin Terms in Reference and Address

All !Kung commonly use kin terms in referring to and addressing each other. In some relationships persons must avoid using each other's names in address and are restricted to using kin terms or respectful modes of address in place of the names (see Chapter 7); but I have the impression that kin terms are used more often than names even among persons who need not avoid each other's names.

The same terms are used in both reference and address, with the exception of the term *aiya* (mother), which is used only in address. (*Tai*, the term for mother that is used in reference, may also be used in address.) The possessive pronoun *mi*, "my," regularly precedes the term in reference; it may or may not be used in address. Before the term *ba*, the *i* of *mi* is dropped, so that the sound of the phrase is *m ba*. Sometimes terms and names are combined, especially in reference, as in, for example, *mi tūn Khwova*.

Children may use the terms in the same manner as adults, saying *mi !gun!a, mi tsu*, and so forth, but in address they often double the term and omit the possessive pronoun: *ba ba, tai tai, !go !go, !kwi !kwi, tsu tsu*. It is not the custom to double the vocative term for mother, *aiya* (nor to precede it with the possessive pronoun), nor to double the terms *!gun!a* or *tūn!ga*. The !Kung had no explanation for this, but common sense suggests that while doubling a monosyllable like *!go* is easy enough, doubling a two-syllable term like *!gun!a* is just too cumbersome.

Both adults and children add *o* when they call from a distance: *m ba o, aiya o, tsu o*, or *mi tsu o*. A child might call the double term, *tsu tsu o*. Not infrequently they add the *o* when speaking normally, as well as when calling. The *o* shows respect, they say.

The Name-Relationship as a Factor in Social Consolidation

The !Kung have developed to the full the practice of applying terms on the basis of names, making it so flexible and expansive that they manage to apply a kin term to everyone they meet, or almost everyone. /Qui had never in his life met a !Kung for whom he had no kinship term until one time he was visiting in the vicinity of Tsho/ana. There he met four !Kung from outside the region, from the north. They had names that were not commonly used in the Nyae Nyae region and /Qui had no term for them. This had made him uneasy. Ta//ne was one of the names. ≠Gao of Band 3, who had affinal connection with /Qui, said that he had a *tsu* named Ta//ne, and he and /Qui nodded together in agreement that they would work out a term for /Qui to give Ta//ne, should they meet again.

In their personal encounters, it is very helpful to the !Kung to apply a kin term. They are nonaggressive and apprehensive of strangers;

strangers are ju *dole*. But when two people can apply kin terms to each other, this puts them on another level of relationship. They are not complete strangers; they have a sense of belonging.

When we were staying at Tsho/ana, Gao of Band 21, the brother of !U, went on an errand for us to Khadum. Khadum is not in the Nyae Nyae region, but lies not far to the north. The !Kung in the Nyae Nyae region are not accustomed to travel out of it; in fact very few have ever done so. Gao had never been to Khadum before. The !Kung who lived there at once called him ju *dole*. He was in haste to say that he had heard that the father of one of the people at Khadum had the same name as his father and that another had a brother named Gao. "Oh," said the Khadum people in effect, "so you are Gao's !gun!a," and they took him to their fire and gave him a present of edible gum.

The !Kung have no structured social units larger than the band of kin and affines who live together, but within the Nyae Nyae region, in which the name-connections and the application of kin terms extend through the whole population, the name-relationship serves to give them common identity and a sense of belonging together. The people are not ju *dole* to each other; the name-relationship makes them feel they are one people.

The !Kung of the Nyae Nyae region do not include all !Kung speakers or even all speakers of the central !Kung dialect in their feeling of being one people. Although none that we know had ever been to Karakuwisa or Nurugas, they know that the !Kung there speak the same dialect. However, the Karakuwisa and Nurugas !Kung are distant, and they are ju *dole* to the Nyae Nyae !Kung. The people of Nyae Nyae say they hear that the people of Nurugas put a strange poison into the pipes they give you to smoke that makes you become as thin as a stick and then die. I felt that this statement made apparent their suspicion and fear of strangers and also pointed up the great value of the name-relationship, which enlarges more than any other single factor the group of people with whom they feel some sense of belonging.

7 Reserved Behavior

As I described in Chapter 6, the !Kung avoid sexually tinged joking with certain categories of relatives and name-relatives. A number of additional avoidances are also practiced with persons who fall into these categories of relationship, and respectful modes of address are used with them. With a few exceptions (mostly for children), these avoidances exactly parallel the joking relationship—if a person avoids joking with another he also practices the other avoidances with him and uses respectful modes of address. Taken all together, the avoidance of joking, the additional avoidances, and the use of respectful modes of address form one large complex of behavior that I call "reserved behavior."[1] The !Kung standards of modesty also seem to me to belong to this complex.

The demands of reserved behavior are mild, moderate, and practical in all cases. No exaggerated action or excessive inconvenience is required. Essentially, I believe, reserved behavior is a set of conventions that act in a formal, almost token way to demonstrate constraint. Reserved behavior requires, for example, that people keep at a distance from each other, avoid joking with each other, and avoid addressing each other by name. The conventional behavior is the opposite of intimate. I believe its purpose is to manifest and reinforce in everyday life the sexual constraints imposed by the !Kung belief in the extended incest taboo. Moderate as these demands are, they are taken seriously by the !Kung and are rarely disregarded, so far as I know. The !Kung say they fear to joke with someone they should not joke with. They fear also to disregard the other avoidances, although they say that should they do

1. Some remarks on polite behavior as distinct from reserved behavior are to be found in Chapter 9.

so no punishment would be inflicted by the gods, the forces of nature, or society. "Nothing would happen," they say—except that they would incur the disapproval of the group: "People would laugh." Group approval is a powerful sanction to the !Kung. They need approval and want it, and to win it they readily conform to the proprieties.

MODESTY

The !Kung are modest in the presence of anybody, not just the persons to whom they accord reserved behavior. Nevertheless, I think it is possible to interpret their modesty, like the avoidance of joking, as demonstrating the restraint required by the incest taboo. The !Kung live close together, without privacy, without walls, constantly in each other's sight, and they are likely to be regularly in the presence of relatives to whom the incest taboo applies, before whom any visible expression of sexuality would be improper. From this, I believe, their modest behavior has developed.

The !Kung constantly kiss their babies, but adults do not embrace or kiss in public view. They conduct their sexual intercourse with extreme discretion.

They are exceedingly careful to keep their genitalia covered. The men are never without their breechclouts. When I several times dressed a very bad boil in Short Gao's groin, he took such precautions to keep himself covered that I could hardly manage to bandage him properly. His friends thought this very funny and leaned over us snickering and joking. The women wear a modesty apron hanging from their waists in front and a small skin tied around their waists, hanging down in back or drawn up between their legs, in addition to their large karosses. They tuck their garments around them when they sit, and they sit in modest posture. Their breasts are bare; breasts are associated with nursing, not sex. Buttocks, however, are definitely associated with sex. A common position for sexual intercourse is for the man to lie at the back of the woman. The word "back" is part of the vocabulary of sex. If it is said that a woman has a "good back," it means that she does not become pregnant too often. We wanted the women to take off their karosses and back aprons so that we could observe the presence or absence of steatopygia among them. We also wanted them to take off their karosses, as they customarily do, when they danced the Eland Dance of the first menstruation rite for us. In both instances they were highly offended and vehemently refused to do what we asked.

!Kung modesty is expressed also in their habits of urinating and defecating. All but young children who are not yet trained go well away from the encampment and squat behind bushes or in tall grass out of sight, thus combining cleanliness with modesty.

AVOIDANCE OF NAMES

To use a person's name in direct address connotes intimacy to the !Kung.[2] Adults who have the joking relationship may address each other by name, but people who do not joke—people who _koa each other (respect, avoid, fear each other)—avoid this. Children's names are not avoided by adults or by other children. One does not begin to avoid using a person's name until that person is·old enough to have children of his own.

In general, the same restriction applies to the use of a person's name in reference, but here a fine distinction is made between speaking of a person's name and speaking of the person by name. When informants gave me genealogical information, they did not hesitate to say the names of any of their relatives, dead or alive, but they would frame their replies so that they were talking about the relative's name rather than about the relative himself. Speaking of his father, an informant would say "My father's name is [or was] Tsamgao," but he would not say "Tsamgao is [was] my father."

A !Kung avoids referring to dead people by name, regardless of whether or not he accorded them reserved behavior in life. A dead person is referred to as !kwa ju. Ju means "person." Our interpreter, Kernel Ledimo, did not know how to translate !kwa. He said that it seems to be a word the !Kung use when they want to avoid saying "dead" (⁻!khi); he thought its equivalent in English might be "late" ("the late Mr. So-and-so").

Avoiding their names shows respect for the dead, but the !Kung have another reason as well. The dead become //gauwasi ("spirits of the dead") and live in the sky with the gods. The gods and the spirits of the dead dislike hearing their names uttered. "Who is calling my name?" they say. Their displeasure is drawn to the speaker, and they might show it by sending a sickness to him.

The !Kung use the avoidance of names not only to express their re-

---

2. /Qui observed that the use of first names has the same connotation for us: he noted that some members of our staff called me Madame, some Mrs. Marshall, and that my children called me mother or mom, and that only my husband and some expedition members called me Lorna.

serve toward people they *koa;* they also show respect to their elders (whatever the relationship) by avoiding their names in direct address. Children do not address adults by name; adults do not address by name persons appreciably older than themselves. I did not find precise rules defining the age-boundaries.

The forms of address that are used when a person's name is avoided are discussed below. With one exception (in the use of pronouns), these forms are applicable both when one is according reserved behavior to a person and when one is simply showing respect.

FORMS OF RESPECTFUL ADDRESS

A common way to avoid using someone's name is to use a kin term instead. Kin terms are always permissible and respectful. It is my impression that kin terms are used not only as part of reserved behavior or to show respect for one's elders, but as ordinary forms of address between persons who have the joking relationship and are of the same age.

People also frequently use descriptive phrases, such as "mother of my wife," "father of my daughter's husband," and so forth.

The language of the !Kung includes both familiar and respectful second-person-singular pronouns. The familiar pronoun, *a,* is used in addressing any child, and is used between persons who have the joking relationship, regardless of disparities in age. It is also used between brother and sister until they grow up, when they change to the respectful pronoun. The respectful pronoun, *i,* is used only between persons who accord each other reserved behavior. It is not used to show respect for one's elders, whom it is perfectly appropriate to address using the familiar pronoun, provided one may joke with them.

The respectful second-person-singular pronoun, *i,* is also the pronoun used for the second-person plural, both respectful and familiar.

The !Kung use several terms in respectful address. One term is *mama.* It is applied, man-speaking and woman-speaking, to any adult and is commonly used. It implies respect, but respect mingled with warmth and intimacy, not the respect that requires reserved behavior and keeping one's distance. It is so often used for grandparents that I thought at first it was the kin term for grandparent. It is used when the speaker wishes to express affection, approval, gratitude. It is also used when one wishes to ingratiate himself mildly with the person he addresses to make the person feel pleased and responsive, especially if one is about to ask him for a gift.

N!ao is a respectful term that is applied to old men. It is commonly used by anybody for any old man. The term (like all the respectful terms mentioned here) stands alone in address—that is, it is not combined with a kin term or a name. It is often used in addressing the high God, ≠Gao N!a. A !Kung might pray, "N!ao, let the rain fall."

The respectful terms n/iha and gaoxa (to be discussed in a forth-coming volume) are applied to the deities and to men who are above others in status, such as a district commissioner or a Tswana chief. The egalitarian !Kung have no offices of high status and accord no one re-served behavior because of his status, but especially respected old men might be called n/iha. N!ao, however, is more commonly used.

A respectful term that may be used for any old person, male or fe-male, is ju n!a. An old woman may be called tsau n!a. Other respectful terms for women are !gao dima n!a (or !gao dima ma) and koli di. We were told that a woman who had many possessions could appropriately be addressed as !gao dima (n!a or ma would be chosen, depending on whether she was younger or older than the speaker). We heard koli di used to refer to the wives of the gods, but were told it could also be applied to women.

The !Kung practice teknonymy. When they avoid using a person's name, they may substitute the name of the person's youngest child. ≠Gao [1.28] was the youngest child of /Qui and //Kushay; people addressed /Qui as ≠Gao ba and //Kushay as ≠Gao tai. ≠Toma was Norna ba, !U was Norna tai.

We asked informants how they would address persons who had no children. If the person is young and unmarried or is recently married and is not yet expected to have children, this form of address is not applica-ble, since children and young people are called by their own names until they have a child. However, if a person is old enough to have children but is childless, people address that person as they do Old N/aoka [9.15]. Old N/aoka was the only woman we met who had never borne a child. She was the old blind sister of /Goishay [9.14], who was the mother of /Ti!kay's wives. We asked what people called Old N/aoka when they avoided her name, and were told that they called her "mother of !Kham" or "mother of //Gao" (!Kham tai or //Gao tai). Informants explained that !Kham and //Gao were the names of N/aoka's husband's parents. If N/aoka and her husband had had a child, N/aoka's husband would have named the child for his father or mother, and therefore they use those names for N/aoka.

Our attempts to learn what the !Kung considered to be the reasons for using the name of the youngest child brought forth one of the !Kung circular responses. (We had many such responses to our inquiries.) Informants said that when they wish to show respect they address a person by the name of his youngest child because using the name of the youngest child shows respect. Our informants went on to explain that the older children are older, that is why people use the name of the youngest.

Even if the offspring is an adult with children of his own, his name is used in respectful address to his parents. And even if the youngest offspring is dead, a person would be addressed as the father or mother of that offspring. However, since the names of the dead are not spoken, the form of address in this instance is *!kwa ju ba* or *!kwa ju tai*.

There is one circumstance in which the use of teknonymy in address presents a problem to the !Kung. The !Kung believe that if a person is absent and there is any cause for anxiety, his name should not be spoken, whatever his relationship to the speaker. Similarly, if a speaker longs for an absent person's return, he will not speak the person's name. The avoidance is observed strictly for absent children, not so strictly for adults, unless the speaker is especially anxious about the persons who are away and longing ardently for their return. I was advised not to say the name of my husband and son when they were away, especially if they were a few days later than expected in returning from a trip to Windhoek for food and, in imagination, I was picturing the truck sunk deep in a huge aardvark burrow with broken axles, or broken steering mechanism, or the main frame cracked (all of which experiences we had and had found most inconvenient and time-consuming). For me to say their names would cause them to feel more uneasy than they otherwise would, the !Kung explained. Instead of saying the name, one refers to the absent person by a descriptive phrase that identifies him and the word *!uma*, that is, mi *!hoa !uma* or mi *!ha !uma* ("my husband or my son" [gone?]). *!Uma* was not a word our interpreter knew, and he could not work out a translation.

One should never say the name of an absent child. To do so would make the child cry and make his heart *xobo*. *Xobo* means to jump, beat hard, or quiver. It is what the heart does if one is suddenly startled. *Xobo* is also the word for the feeling one has when one sees a dearly loved person who has been long away or the feeling that lovers have when they meet. "Mi !xa xobo," a !Kung says.

A SITTING AVOIDANCE

The !Kung like to be close together. When women and girls sit together they tend to huddle, touching one another shoulder to shoulder, knee to knee, ankles overlapping. Boys and young men sit this way also, but to do so is not so common among old men. Men and women often sit in separate groups. They may also sit in the same group, fairly close together, but they will not huddle so close as to be touching each other. In general, men and women maintain some degree of separation in sitting. This separation is not due to reserved behavior, but rather to the !Kung belief that it is dangerous for men to sit where women have sat previously, and vice versa. They believe that if the genitalia of a man were to touch a spot on the ground that a woman's genitalia had touched (regardless of whether or not the men or women were clothed), his prowess as a hunter would be destroyed. A woman whose genitalia touched a spot on the ground where an old man had been sitting would suffer disorders of her urinary tract and would pass blood in her urine. Women avoid sitting where old or young men have sat, but to sit where old men have sat is the more dangerous. At the family fire men sit on one side (to the right of a person facing across the fire toward the opening of the shelter), women on the other.

None of the !Kung are prevented by this belief or by the rules of reserved behavior from touching each other in many other ways. They cut each other's hair, groom each other's heads for lice, lean over each other to rearrange ornaments that are out of place, rub each other with fat.

There was so much physical contact that it was hard to see where reserved behavior came in at all. Informants explained it, however. They said that propriety permitted them to sit in the lap or even between the legs of a !gun!a, but they must not assume such a position with anyone they could not joke with. They demonstrated the proper distance that should be maintained: one must not sit closer to a tsu or a //ga than about eighteen inches, they claimed; a mother-in-law and father-in-law should keep a distance of about three feet between themselves and their son-in-law or daughter-in-law. The !Kung may not always have been as scrupulous about keeping a distance of eighteen inches as they were when we asked them to demonstrate what was proper, but the idea of practicing constraint in physical contact with people whom one "respects" is definitely present.

AVOIDANCE OF ENTERING SHELTERS

People who "respect" each other also avoid entering each other's shelters. A son's wife or daughter's husband would strictly avoid entering the shelter of his or her parents-in-law. A brother and sister, we were told, must be equally strict in this practice after they are married and have built shelters of their own. These remarks of informants imply that people in other relationships need not take this avoidance very seriously —and no wonder. If the shelter is supposed to symbolize a place in which to find privacy, in which one would be hidden, or a place for sexual activities, it is the merest token of a symbol. As often as not the shelter is not there at all. If it is, it may be half blown away by the wind. When fully constructed it is a half-hemisphere in shape, only about five feet long and three feet deep, with the whole interior space open to view. The !Kung do not sleep in their shelters nor live in them by day. They sleep and live by their fires. Still, this avoidance indicates that the !Kung do hold shelters as a symbol for demonstrating reserved behavior.

AVOIDANCE OF ASKING FOR FOOD

Reserved behavior requires that people who practice it refrain from asking each other directly and overtly for food. They give food to each other and receive it from each other as freely as do people who have the joking relationship, but apparently asking for food directly implies too much intimacy.

A SPEAKING AVOIDANCE

This avoidance differs from the others discussed as part of reserved behavior in that it is required only in the relationships of parents with their offspring's spouses.

For the first few years after the marriage of a son or daughter, the parents and the son's wife or daughter's husband must avoid speaking directly to each other. When three children have been born to the son or daughter, or enough time has elapsed for three children to have been born, the avoidance is eased and these affines may speak—not every day, we were told, but every third day or so. They should speak only about things that are necessary to discuss. They never are free to exchange gossip or huddle together in long intimate talks.

Customarily a married son or daughter settles next to the parents, their fires and shelters only a few feet apart. They often build their shelters so that these are actually leaning on each other.

The speaking avoidance under these circumstances does not impose excessive inconvenience. Both families overhear each other's conversations, and if, say, a man wants his son-in-law to know something, he simply says it to his wife or his daughter loudly enough for the son-in-law to hear. Unless one were informed one might not know that they were practicing a speaking avoidance.

The interactions of people who accord each other reserved behavior are not constrained in any way except in the avoidance of joking and the practice of the other avoidances just described. The !Kung build their shelters and place their family fires close together, they hunt, gather, fetch water and wood, make artifacts, sing, dance, share food, and exchange gifts with the people they "respect"—with whom they are reserved—as readily and freely as with people they do not "respect" and with whom they may joke.

8 Marriage

My study of !Kung marriage regulations is based on data derived during the year 1952–53 from a sample of 353 !Kung.[1]

TABLE 15. Marriage Status of a Sample of 353 Persons

Married men (9 of whom had 2 wives)	88
Wives of above men	97
Old widowers	3
Old bachelors	1
Old widows	24
Young widows	2
Young divorced women	2
Unmarried boys, adolescent and younger	78
Unmarried girls, adolescent and younger	58
Total	353

As we examine the !Kung rules of exogamy we find that the band is not an exogamus unit as such. Actually, most members of the band are so interrelated by consanguinity or affinity that the marriage regulations strictly prohibit their marrying, but there might very likely be some in a band between whom marriage would be permissible, such as, for instance, a man and his wife's sister or the widow of a deceased brother.

The !Kung have no unit that is strictly endogamous. Those of the

This chapter is a revised version of a paper, "Marriage among !Kung Bushmen," first published in *Africa, 29* (Oct. 1959), 335–365. It is republished here with the kind permission of the International African Institute.

1. They were the 298 members of the thirteen precisely counted bands, listed in Tables 3 and 4 of Chapter 5, and 55 persons from other bands with whom we had considerable contact.

Nyae Nyae region almost all marry among themselves within the region, not because a formulated social rule definitely prohibits their marrying outside, but because they almost never go out. They do not like strange places, strange situations, or strange persons, and have no way of feeding themselves when away from their own territory unless they are visiting relatives or friends who give them food. In utterly strange country, they would not know where the plant foods grow, and, if they found any, they might not be allowed (by the owners of the plant foods) to gather them. Nevertheless, a few Nyae Nyae !Kung have married other !Kung outside the region, and two !Kung women we know at /Gam are married outside their own race, to Tawana men, with acceptance and ease of relations all around. Numerous !Kung women in Botswana are married to Herero or Tawana, but among the Nyae Nyae !Kung such marriages are rare.

Prolonged intermarriage within the region has woven the !Kung together, and much visiting among kin develops acquaintanceships and friendships that unite the whole Nyae Nyae !Kung population. They are not aliens or strangers to each other, they are *jū /wāsi*.

MARRIAGE PROHIBITIONS: THE INCEST TABOO AND ITS EXTENSION

!Kung marriage prohibitions apply to first marriages arranged by parents for young couples and also to additional marriages contracted later in life. A man may remarry if his wife dies, and he may take a second wife at any time. A woman may remarry if her husband dies or if divorce makes her available for remarriage. In those situations, marriage is prohibited in certain relationships as it is in first marriages.

Extramarital sexual relations are considered wrong in the same categories of relationships in which marriage is prohibited.

Once a person has come into affinal relationship with ego, that relationship remains fixed, and marriage prohibitions continue to apply to the affine even though the person through whom the relationship was established be dead or divorced. For example, a man is prohibited from marrying his son's wife even though his son be dead, or the couple divorced.

It is to be assumed that ego in the following description is either male or female and that the marriage prohibitions, of course, apply to the appropriate sex.

Marriages are forbidden in !Kung social organization on the basis of incest only. In common with nearly all mankind (excepting the Pharaohs and a few other rare examples), the !Kung incest taboo prohibits marriage or sexual relations between Fa and Da, Mo and So, Br and Si. The incest taboo is extended beyond the nuclear family to certain additional categories of persons, and marriage and sexual relations with them are also rigorously forbidden by !Kung social law.

The !Kung did not express the belief that inbreeding produces inferior offspring and must for that reason be avoided. Also, the thought that incest has been avoided by mankind because it would be exceedingly disruptive to the internal cohesion of the nuclear family comes to the mind of the analyst of social forms, not to the minds of !Kung informants. The same might be said of the social advantage of marrying outside the nuclear family and thereby weaving a supporting web of kinship with many other families and bands. The !Kung apparently do not think of incest in these terms. They feel a deep, internalized, pervading horror of incest, which they do not try to explain. Incest with parent, offspring, or sibling is unthinkable. "Only dogs do that—not men." "It would be madness (di)." "It would be dangerous, like going up to a lion." Many refused to speak with me about such "bad things."

The !Kung extend the incest taboo to certain categories of persons outside the nuclear family, because they hold that the relationships resemble the relationships of the nuclear family. They believe it would therefore be incestuous for persons who have those relationships to unite in marriage. A man will say explicitly, for instance, that he must not marry this or that woman because it would be "like" marrying his mother, daughter, or sister. In all, the !Kung prohibit marriage with four categories of persons. The categories are: (1) members of the nuclear family and certain other consanguineous kin; (2) certain affines; (3) stepparents, stepchildren, stepbrothers, stepsisters, and the close kin to ego's mother's co-wife (for example, ego's mother's co-wife's sister who is "like" his MoSi); and (4) certain name relatives.

Categories 1 and 2. Kin and Affines

In Table 16 are listed the consanguineous kin with whom ego's marriage is prohibited. The !Kung consider uncles and aunts parallel to parents (they are "like" parents); nephews and nieces are parallel to offspring; cousins are parallel to siblings.

TABLE 16. Consanguineous Kin with Whom Ego's Marriage Is Prohibited

Kin	Male	Female	Joking
Parents	ba	tai	no
Siblings of parents	tsu	//ga	no
Siblings	!go, tsĩ	!kwi, tsĩ	{ yes, same sex / no, opposite sex
Cousins, 1st, 2nd, 3rd	!gun!a	tũn	yes
Offspring	!ha	≠khai	no
Nephews, nieces	tsu	//ga	no

I made considerable effort to determine whether or not I should in-clude second and third as well as first cousins in the categories of per-sons with whom marriage is prohibited. It was difficult to make sure that the relationships were clearly understood. As I said previously, we stood sticks in the sand to represent persons and tried to demonstrate the several varieties of cousins. We would say, for instance, "This is your father, this is his brother, these are your father's brother's children. Here are your children. May your children marry his children? May your grandchildren marry his grandchildren? I was convinced that in-formants did understand the relationship, and they said that second and third cousins, as well as first, should not marry. ≠Toma, I suppose con-templating the questions we asked and wondering why we asked them, remarked that we "red" people, as he called us (indeed we were quite red under the desert sun), might marry our cousins, but the jũ /wãsi would consider it wrong to do so.

Finally, among kin, it goes without saying that the !Kung do not marry grandparents or grandchildren. Close consanguineous ties and discrepancy in age between ego and those relatives combine to make the idea practically unthinkable. Informants were slightly offended that I should bring up such a ridiculous question. Someone said that those old people were already dead, and ≠Toma stated huffily that it was not his wish to marry a baby.

The affines with whom ego's marriage is prohibited are listed in Table 17. !Kung informants see parallels with the nuclear family among affines as among kin. The parallels of parents of spouse with ego's par-ents and of spouse of offspring with ego's offspring are clear. The thought of marriage or of sexual relations with the above-mentioned affines, I believe, is as horrifying to the !Kung as the thought of such relations with

TABLE 17. Affines with Whom Ego's Marriage Is Prohibited

Affine	Male	Female	Joking
Spouses of parents' siblings	tsu	//ga	no
Parents of ego's spouse	≠tum	/utsu	no
Parents of BrWi and SiHu	tsu-n!unba	//ga-n!untai	no
HuSiHu WiBrWi	≠tum	/utsu	no
Parents of offsprings' spouses	n!unba	n!untai	yes
Spouses of offspring	≠tum	/utsu	no
HuBrSo WiSiDa	tsu-n!unba	//ga-n!untai	no

parents or offspring. We learned of no instance of the taboo being broken.

Informants were able to give explanations, as they see them, for prohibition of marriage with the following affines. Why, we had asked, is marriage with WiSiDa and HuBrSo specifically prohibited? ≠Toma explained that a man often marries his WiSi if his wife should die, or as a second wife. His being her potential husband makes him "feel like" her husband even though he is not married to her. As a result, his WiSiDa seems to him like his own daughter. Similarly, a woman is a potential wife of HuBr, so HuBrSo is like her So.

Marriage with a SiHuFa or BrWiMo seems improper to the !Kung, because a woman's marriage with a SiHu (as second wife or if her SiHu is a widower) or a man's with a BrWi (if the death or divorce of the brother makes the marriage with BrWi possible) is highly appropriate, and the parents of these affines, therefore, seem to ego "like" his spouse's parents.

Among the affines ego must not marry are SoWiFa, DaHuFa, SoWiMo, DaHuMo. Marriage with one of these would turn ego's So and SoWi, Da and DaHu into stepbrothers and stepsisters, which would be most awkward.

Marriage is prohibited with HuSiHu and WiBrWi, termed respectively ≠tum and /utsu; ego avoids joking with them as he avoids joking with HuSi and WiBr. Informants had no verbalized explanation for the prohibition of marriage with these affines as they had for some other prohibitions. They simply said marriage with them would be wrong. In other words, the incest taboo is extended to them. I think symmetry in the avoidance of joking is the factor through which the incest taboo is extended. Among siblings and their spouses, and among spouse's siblings and their spouses, the prohibition of joking and marriage are seen as

TABLE 18. Marriage and Joking in the Sibling Category

	Male Ego				Female Ego		
Ego's Siblings and Their Spouses							
Br	!go* or tsi*	BiWi	tún**	Br	!go or tsi	BrWi	/utsu
Si	!kwi or tsi	SiHu	tún!ga	Si	!kwi* or tsi*	SiHu	tún!ga**
Ego's Spouse's Siblings and Their Spouses							
WiBr	tún!ga	WiBrWi	/utsu	HuBr	tún!ga**	HuBrWi	!kwi* or tsi*
WiSi	tún**	WiSiHu	!go* or tsi*	HuSi	/utsu	HuSiHu	≠tum

No asterisk indicates that marriage and joking are prohibited.
* Joking is allowed.
** Opposite sex makes marriage possible, and marriage and joking are allowed.

coinciding. Opposite sex making marriage possible, ego may marry the affines with whom he may joke and is prohibited from marrying those with whom he avoids joking (see Table 18). I think that, furthermore, the terms *≠tum* and */utsu* reinforce the feeling among the !Kung that marriage with HuSiHu and WiBrWi would be wrong. These terms are strongly associated with the incest taboo and marriage prohibitions; they are the terms applied to parents of spouse and spouses of offspring.

The kin and affines with whom marriage is prohibited are shown in Figure 12. I have added to Figure 12 the affines whom ego may marry in order to complete the affinal categories and show the balance in joking.

In summary, the !Kung formulate and verbalize marriage regulations in three generations, namely, (1) ego's and (2) the first ascending and (3) the first descending generations. Marriage with kin in the other ascending and descending generations, great-grandparents, great-grandchildren, grandparents, grandchildren, is not specifically allowed, but specific prohibitions are not formulated, because to the !Kung these relatives do not fall within the range of potential marriage partners.

The prohibition includes all the primary affines (see Chapter 6) except BrWi, WiSi, SiHu, and HuBr, with whom marriage is allowed. In addition to the primary affines, two categories of secondary affines are included, WiSiDa and HuBrSo and the parents of BrWi and SiHu.

The joking relationship and the marriage prohibitions are not en-

Fig. 12. The kin and affines whom Ego may or may not marry

FaBr, MoBr	tsu	FaBrWi, MoBrWi	//ga	BrWiFa, SiHuFa	tsu-n!unba				Fa	ba
FaSi, MoSi	//ga	FaSiHu, MoSiHu	tsu	BrWiMo, SiHuMo	//ga-n!untai				Mo	tai
Cousins 1st, 2nd, 3rd	!gun!a (m)*†			BrWi	tũn m.s.**	Br	!go m.s.*			
	tũn (f)*†			BrWi	/utsu w.s.	Br	!go w.s.			
				SiHu	tũn!ga m.s.	Si	!kwi m.s.			
				SiHu	tũn!ga w.s.**	Si	!kwi w.s.*			
				BrSo, SiSo	tsu				So	!ha
				BrDa, SiDa	//ga				Da	≠khai

tirely coincident among the kin and affines we are discussing. In no category is marriage allowed when joking is prohibited, but in two categories marriage is prohibited while joking is allowed, namely, among cousins and among the parents of offspring's spouse.

Categories 3 and 4. Stepparents and Name-Relatives

The third category to which the marriage prohibitions are extended—ego's stepparents, and so on—needs no further elucidation.

The fourth category comprises certain name-relatives. Ego should not marry (1) anyone who has the name of his parents or offspring; (2) the parent, offspring, or sibling of opposite sex of anyone who has the same name as ego; (3) anyone who has the same name as ego's spouse's parent or ego's son's or daughter's spouse. ≠Toma explained that if he married one of those persons, it would "sound as though" he had married his parent, offspring, or one of the above close affines.

DEVIATION FROM THE RULES

The !Kung deviate from their marriage prohibitions to some extent, and they have a gradation of feeling about the severity of the offense when a marriage rule is broken. Incest with the nuclear family or parent of spouse or spouse of offspring would be horrifying, but a man's marrying

				WiFa ⎱ HuFa ⎰	≠tum			
				WiMo ⎱ HuMo ⎰	/utsu			
Wi	tsau**	SoWiFa ⎱ DaHuFa ⎰	n!unba*†	WiSi HuSi	tūn** /utsu	WiSiHu HuSiHu	!go* ≠tum
Hu	!hoa**						
		SoWiMo ⎱ DaHuMo ⎰	n!untai*†	WiBr HuBr	tūn!ga tūn!ga**	WiBrWi HuBrWi	/utsu !kwi*
		SoWi	/utsu			WiSiDa	//ga-n!untai
		DaHu	≠tum			HuBrSo	tsu-n!unba.

No asterisk indicates that marriage and joking are prohibited
 * indicates that joking is allowed
** indicates that opposite sex makes marriage possible and that marriage and joking are allowed
*† indicates that joking is allowed but that, in instances in which opposite sex makes marriage possible, marriage is prohibited

someone in the name-relationship with the name of his mother would be hardly frowned at.

On the whole, the !Kung conform strictly to the regulations among consanguineous kin and primary affines. None of the persons whose genealogical records we gathered (about 175) had married lineal kin or collaterals through first cousins. However, informants told about two !Kung men in Botswana who had married their cousins: the discussion suggested that the cousins were first cousins, but I do not know whether they were cross or parallel cousins. What was interesting was the attitude of the informants. They said that the men should not have done this, but there was no talk of madness or danger or expressions of horror, such as we had observed when incest was spoken of at other times. No punishments, social or divine, had been meted out, according to the informants. Some said they thought it was not too bad a thing for a man to do, especially if the woman were a FaSiDa, who is not, they said, so much like your sister as a MoSiDa is. I believe that the system's allowing joking with cousins, although it prohibits marriage with them, may mitigate the force of the incest taboo and accounts to some extent for the tolerance toward the breakers of this rule.

How much deviation there is in marrying second and third cousins I do not know. I soon gave up trying to gather data on kin more remote than first cousins, because informants so often did not know the names and I could not rely on the information. I imagine there is considerable deviation in these categories.

One account came to our ears of a man who had violated the incest taboo with his stepdaughter. He was /Gunda Legs, and he lived with Band 9. He is dead now. What he did was so outside the good and the normal that it could be accounted for only by madness. He had drunk the milk of a young gemsbok doe, the people told us, and this is what had made him mad. Something came from his forehead and went in and out, a sort of swelling. After that he fell in love with his stepdaughter, N≠isa, and married her, and both she and her mother were his wives at the same time. The people "laughed at him" so much because he had made such a horrifying "mistake" that he took his stepdaughter and lived apart from his band—the only instance we know of a man and woman living alone. They had a son, ≠Toma, who died young. When /Gunda's madness waned, he sometimes came back to his people; he would go again when his madness returned. People said they did not understand why N≠isa went with him. They mocked her, saying that she was *dole* ("bad") and that it was "nonsense" to fall in love with one's stepfather. Our informants laughed uneasily when they told about these people, as they laugh when they tell of vultures eating their meat, or of being chased by fierce bees when they try to take a honeycomb. There came to my mind a penetrating remark made by //Kushay, the wife of /Qui, which might, I thought, be applied to N≠isa. //Kushay had said, "When a *jū wā* girl goes against the customs of her people and people talk about her and say she is bad, she is very unhappy. She would hear the people talking and be ashamed and would come to them angry." Or, I thought, go away because she was ashamed.

Deviations occur frequently, I think, in the fourth category (name-relatives). Two men we met had married women whose names were the same as the men's mothers' names. A man named /Ti!kay married the daughter of another /Ti!kay, and there were other such instances. /Qui said he proposed to do this himself. The girl's family had flatly refused, but he was going to keep on trying. ≠Toma said he would not do this, but he sees some people doing these things. There are not enough women whom one may properly marry, he said with a grin, and he would be in favor of changing the marriage prohibitions among name-relatives so that a man need avoid only ugly women.

APPROVED MARRIAGES

No marriages are compulsory in !Kung society.

Marriage is allowed with anyone to whom the incest taboo is not extended. It appeared to me that there were three degrees of approval of marriages: preference, permission, and toleration. Once a marriage has taken place, no differentiation is made.

The joking relationship is the differentiating factor between the preference and mere permission which the society accords. In preferred marriages the man and woman are name-relatives who have had the joking relationship before marriage and have applied to each other the terms *!gun!a* and *tūn*. This makes the marriage seem altogether right.

Marriage is permitted between name-relatives who apply the terms *tsu* and *//ga* to each other and avoided joking before marriage, provided the incest taboo is not specifically extended to them; and, in the same way, marriage is permitted between name-relatives who apply to each other the terms *!go*, brother, *!kwi*, sister, or *tsī*, younger sibling.

Marriage is tolerated, though it rarely occurs, as I mentioned before, with persons to whom the name-relationship and the application of kin terms is not extended; that is, persons of other races, persons of other Bushman language groups, or other !Kung outside the Nyae Nyae region.

To contract a marriage with someone with whom one must not joke brings in a touch of the anomalous, and that deprives the !Kung of the perfect symmetry and consistency which so content them and make them feel secure in rightness. This society tolerates the anomaly, for obviously it must not forbid marriage in too many categories, and adjusts the joking status by giving to husband and wife the joking relationship as soon as marriage takes place.

Though neither the sororate nor the levirate is compulsory, marriage is highly approved with the wife of a deceased brother or the husband of a deceased sister. A man is expected to take care of his BrWi should she need his care, even though he is not required to marry her. Marriage with a WiSi or HuBr is also highly approved. Ego has had the joking relationship with these affines.

A marriage arrangement which the !Kung consider especially good is called *!oa ku*. This means that an exchange is made between two bands: a boy and girl from one marry a girl and boy from the other. *!Oa ku* is not a common practice. Bands as units have no authority in the arrangements of marriages, which is the duty of parents, as I shall describe presently, and parents do not make the exchange between bands a major factor in their choices. If it happens to come about, however, the people are glad because each band thereby gains a person to replace the person lost, and the bonds between the bands are strengthened.

POLYGYNOUS MARRIAGE

In first marriages, which are arranged by the parents when the boy and girl are still young, the boy is given only one wife. At least this was so in all the instances we knew. Only rarely is a girl given in her first marriage to a man who already has a wife. In instances in which this happens the girl is likely to be the younger sister of the first wife, but not necessarily so. Most polygynous marriages are contracted by the individuals themselves, not by their parents, when the man and the woman have passed their first youth and when widowhood or divorce has made a woman available for remarriage.

I have the impression that many !Kung men favor polygyny as the ideal form of marriage. Many men among our !Kung informants said they aspired to having more than one wife. They pitied Laurence Marshall because the laws of his land forbade his having several, which they considered him able to afford. One said he would not want to live where there were such nonsensical rules. Not all !Kung men, however, wanted more than one wife; some said explicitly that they did not.

The number of wives a man may have simultaneously is not limited by social rule. However, despite many men's saying they would like to have more wives, most had only one. There is no great excess of women in the population and in this egalitarian society in which all possessions are carried by the owners and in which possessions pass from one to another in a stream of gift-giving, no man has appreciably more wealth than another to give him advantage. Nor does any man have status which entitles him to special privileges in obtaining wives. An agreeable personality and the ability to hunt are to a man's advantage. The determining factor in the contracting of polygynous marriages, however, is the feelings of the man and woman who marry.

At the time we were in the field only nine men in a sample of eighty-eight had two wives; none had more than two. However, we heard of one man, /Ti!kay's father, then dead, who had four, and /Qui's father had had three.

Marriage to the same man gives co-wives the joking relationship, and they do not observe the sitting or the name avoidance, though they may have observed those avoidances and may have avoided joking before marriage. Co-wives apply the kin terms !kwi or tsi (sister) to each other, or, if they have the same name, they apply the terms !gun!a and !guma. Megan Biesele has given me another term that is used by co-wives for each other and is also used in reference to co-wives, !gwa⁻di.

The !Kung, though they do not institutionalize the sororate, say it is a good idea to marry sisters because they are not so likely to be jealous of each other as other women are. Of the nine pairs of co-wives we knew, three pairs were sisters, another was a pair of half sisters.[2] None of the others had traceable consanguineous ties. The !Kung's claim that sisters tended to have more harmonious relations than other pairs of co-wives seemed to be confirmed by any observations we could make. The two attractive sisters who were /Ti!kay's wives appeared to have a particularly close, harmonious relationship. I thought it never more apparent than

2. In the paper previously published, I wrote that only two of the nine pairs of co-wives had traceable consanguineous ties. Further work in my notes brought two more pairs to my attention.

when they lay down to sleep, / Ti!kay in the middle, a wife on each side, on cold nights both very close to him.

The first wife is supposed to have a somewhat more highly esteemed and dominant position than a second wife. She is supposed to have the right to tell a second wife what to do, and a young second wife should fetch water and wood for the older wife, but I never saw this done. No property or other material advantage is given a first wife, and no important social advantages accrue to her. It appeared to me that first wives were often at a disadvantage. Among the people we knew, the husbands favored their younger second wives—with two exceptions: / Ti!kay favored his first wife, the elder sister, and Gao Beard favored his first wife. Both were good-tempered, intelligent, able women. They appeared to take care of the girls who were their co-wives rather than to be served in any way by them. Other older first wives seemed sometimes to be dejected. One told me her husband always took the young second wife with him, and, to her deep humiliation, sometimes left her, the first wife, to stay for a time with one or another family in the band, although she said to him, "Why do you shame me so?"

Megan Biesele tells me that she knew some co-wives who lived beside different fires and built separate shelters. However, all the co-wives we knew shared one shelter and one family fire. The little shelter of branches and grass that the women build, a half-hemisphere in shape, is only about five feet wide on the open side, about three to four feet deep at the center, and perhaps four to five feet high at the peak. In it and in front of it, beside their one fire, the two wives live, share their man, share the food they gather, share the work of fetching water and wood, nurse each other's babies, and cooperate in whatever degree of harmony their spirits can attain.

The degree of harmony varies. A few men said that the jealousy of co-wives could be so unbearable that they would not marry a second wife, but one said it made him feel good to have two women fighting over him. // Aha [13.13], the second wife of / Ti!kay [13.14], at / Gam (his first wife had died) was an example of an extreme. She was still a young woman herself and, with her fierce jealousy, had driven / Khoa [12.10], the pretty young third wife, wailing into the night, back to her family's fire. / Ti!kay used to sit for hours upon hours singing soft, sad, sweet laments for / Khoa, but she did not return to live with him.

The expression of disharmony, especially in wrangling, upsets everyone, as all expression of discord does. Although co-wives may be jealous and may irritate each other in various ways, !Kung society encourages them to mold their conduct to acceptance. Group disapproval is expressed by talk and also by song. We were told that a song called "Two Baús" was composed about two loudly quarrelsome co-wives. When they heard this song strummed on the //gwashi or hummed here and there in the shadows of the encampment at night, they mended their ways.

The behavior of N/aoka and Di!ai, the wives of Gao, was more typical than that of //Aha, or the two Baús, and also more typical than the behavior of the very congenial sisters, /Ti!kay's wives, N/aoka and N!ai. Both N/aoka and Di!ai were approaching middle age, Di!ai somewhat younger than N/aoka. N/aoka had two married daughters and a teen-age son when Gao married Di!ai. It was apparent to all that the two women disliked each other, but they managed to preserve a decent semblance of harmony by self-control, silence, avoiding each other as much as possible in the small space in which they lived by their fire, and by separating often—going with different groups of relatives and friends to gather plant foods, to fetch water, or to visit.

On the whole, the women with whom I discussed polygyny did not express enthusiasm for it, and they gave me the impression that, in general, !Kung women prefer not to be co-wives.[3] They did not expound the social advantage that polygyny affords women—that women have abundant opportunity to marry or to remarry, should they be widowed or divorced, and few remain long without the support of a husband. None suggested that an old wife might welcome the assistance of a young second wife in the work of gathering and fetching water and wood. They just said they did not want to be second wives, and they told of protests and quarrels that attended the husbands' proposals to take second wives. One woman, who belonged to the group that worked for Musinjan and Kavasitue in /Gam, threatened openly to leave her husband if he turned into reality what appeared to be his persistent fantasy of having a second wife. She said he was not a good hunter and could not support her adequately as it was. She showed us her kaross, the lower portion of it so worn it was like lace, and complained with vehemence that he failed to provide her with a new one.

3. I did not talk directly with the co-wives. I knew about their feelings on the subject of polygyny. I thought it best not to do so. In several instances, the tension between the co-wives was quite apparent. I especially did not want to be a factor in bringing the difficulties in their relationships explicitly into words and perhaps increasing animosity.

MARRIAGE BY CAPTURE

Marriage by capture was mentioned fairly frequently by the !Kung in conversation. Elizabeth, our daughter, and I questioned a number of informants about it, and we are convinced that wives are not actually acquired by this means at present. Perhaps they were in the past. The !Kung are a present-oriented people who make no concerted or consistent effort to retain their history and teach it to their children, and we obtained no significant data on their past customs. Nowadays the idea of capturing wives appears to be enjoyed by the men as a fantasy. The remarks of one /Gaishay from /Gam illustrate what I mean. He weighs, at a good guess, about ninety pounds, and he looks like a miniature Mephistopheles. With a gleam he told me that if he wanted to take another wife he would go to her encampment, seize her, throw her over his shoulder, and run off with her. That is the way jũ /wãsi do, he said, and he wished I could see him do so. I also wished that I could.

ARRANGEMENTS FOR MARRIAGE

First marriages are arranged by the parents of the bride and groom; second marriages are also arranged by the parents, if the couple is still young. Adults, when both have been married before, may contract subsequent marriages themselves.

Although !Kung society recognizes bilateral descent, there is a slight paternal emphasis—seen, for example, in the fact that the father names all of his children. The mother and father seem, however, to have equal authority in the choice of a mate for their child. By and large, it appears that the father and mother talk things over and come to agreement. If they do not agree, it appears that the strength of personality of one or the other, the opinions of relatives, and various circumstances have weight in the decision.

Either the parents of the boy or those of the girl may take the initiative and go to the other parents with the proposal. A go-between is not required, though it is possible that a friend will sometimes act as such. The parents visit and talk, and, if they all agree, the arrangement is thereby settled. They normally give each other gifts in honor of the occasion.

Property does not enter much into the consideration of the parents in arranging marriages for their children. No property settlement is made, no bride-price paid, no dower given, though at the time of the wedding a few gifts are exchanged.

Food and water must, one imagines, weigh in the parents' thinking when a marriage is being arranged, and these may sometimes be determining factors. However, there is a considerable amount of equalization in these supplies. In the Nyae Nyae area each band has access to a supply, and the resources balance out in various ways. The affine who marries into the band, as long as he lives with the band, has a right to the water, to the hunting, and to the gathering of plant foods, as members born to the band have.

I think that the standards parents apply and the assets they seek in choosing mates for their children have to do primarily with the kind of security that is attained through human responses and relations. Friends may want their children to marry because they know and trust each other. Or a family may want to increase its kinship bonds—and thereby its security—with certain bands, for any number of reasons (among them could be food, water, or a desire to have supporting friends in a certain area).

Merging with such desires, and to be balanced with them, is consideration of the characteristics of the families concerned. The !Kung want their boys and girls to marry into upstanding families, among people who are "able to feed themselves," who are "not lazy and not thin." Substantial people are called "heavy" people among the !Kung. They do not want "far-hearted" in-laws who are ungenerous in food-sharing and gift-giving. !U said she would take particular note of parents' generosity in giving bead ornaments to their children: she would not want a daughter of hers to marry among people who were stingy in that. Proper observance of the avoidances and other social regulations is an asset in in-laws, for they can then be assumed to have taught their children how to behave properly.

The individual's characteristics are also a concern. Parents of boys hope the girls to whom their sons are engaged will grow up to be good-looking, because, they say, a man takes pride in a beautiful wife. Old Xama, the mother of Gao Beard, said she had wanted for her son a light-skinned girl with good teeth who was not too thin and not too tall, but most important of all is a sweet temper, she said. A mother hopes, she said, that the girl will not be lazy or wander about visiting at night at other people's fires "like a bitch." The girl should observe the avoidances and the menstruation and other taboos, and she should in every

way behave like a well-brought-up girl. However, since the girls are engaged when they are very young, I suppose the parents of the boys can
only watch the girls grow and hope for the best.

Girls would not want a man "as tall as a giraffe," we were told. They
would seek smaller husbands. !U's first husband (/Gao [13.17]), from
whom she was divorced, is so tall that people laugh and say, "Did his
mother have a dream with a //gauwa?"[4]

The girls themselves, all twitters and giggles, told me what they ad-
mire in the boys. They like a good hunter like /Gunda; and they like hand-
some teeth and a wide smile like young Tsamgao's; and straight, slender
legs like //Ao Wildebeest's; and a fluid, swift walk like /Gao Music's.
They hate a big black belly like Gao's. (Gao [7.12] was the middle-aged
man in a band distant from Gautscha, to whom the young /Doin [7.11]
was married.) The parents of a girl want the boy to be responsible, kind
to their daughter, and, above all, a good provider—which means a good
hunter. They want him to make his arrows straight, to shoot swiftly and
accurately, to be able to run down an eland, and, most of all, they want
a son-in-law whose heart says to him, "Why am I sitting lazily here by
the fire? Why do I not get up and go hunting?"—and who, in obedience
to his heart, and the group's desire, and the magic that has been rubbed
into his scarifications in the Rite of the First Kill, gets up and goes.

Boys are always considerably older than girls before their parents
betroth them. We never knew the precise age of any of the !Kung because they reckon time from one season to the next, not in years, and
do not keep track of a person's age by any measurement. Boys appear to
be usually around twelve to fourteen or fifteen before they are betrothed.
At this age their fathers begin their serious hunting training by starting
to take them on the long hard hunts for the big animals that supply the
people's meat.

As for girls, wives are in such demand in this polygynous society
that the parents of boys have their eyes upon every girl baby and may
say to the parents of an unborn infant, "If it is a girl, let us have her for
our son." It is not unusual to betroth the girls when they are between
two and five or six, but betrothal may be made at a later age. The boys
wait patiently for long years for their fiancées to grow up.

We wondered what would happen if, when the time at last came
for the marriage, the boy or girl should refuse the parents' choice. It

4. A //gauwa is a spirit of the dead.

appears that he or she seldom does. A boy is usually too eager to get a wife. To refuse the betrothed might mean he would have to wait for years and years again for a girl baby to grow up. The girls are usually too young to protest, but it sometimes happens that one does. !Kung parents are exceedingly protective and permissive with their young children and take great delight in them. The same protectiveness and permissiveness were apparent in parents' lenience with respect to their girls' betrothals. They complied with the girls' wishes.

The marriage may take place when the parents agree. The age of the young people varies greatly. For the girl, there is no definite age requirement. The girl need not, for instance, show physical signs of maturity. By the time the important Rite of the First Menstruation is performed, the girl may have been married for years. Baú, who was married in 1951 to Tsamgao [9.5], ≠Toma's cousin, did not have her first child for six years. N!ai was married to /Gunda in May 1953. She menstruated for the first time in May 1959. To be married as young as that is not at all unusual, but we have known several girls to be somewhat older.

The parents explain that when the girls marry young they "get used to" their husbands. I am sure there is a great deal in this, and I am sure it strongly affects the relations of husbands and wives, but I had insufficient opportunity to observe eight- or nine-year-old brides with teen-aged husbands, and insufficient means, through interpreters, to grasp the nature of their relationships. What is the young husband like to a girl child? The friendly, gentle old man, Old Demi, said to me, "They enjoy their youth together."

The young couples are expected not to have sexual intercourse until the girls are "big enough," informants said, and the boys must not force the girls. If a girl complained to her parents and the parents took her back and sent the young husband away, he might have to wait for years again for another bride to grow up. The !Kung are prevented by their incest taboos and their modesty from speaking freely about sex, and I learned nothing about the actual sexual practices of the young couples. N!ai and her young husband /Gunda had only one good kaross between them; they slept together bundled in it, feet to feet. Baú and Tsamgao slept quite apart—at different fires—when we observed them in 1952. In 1953 they slept at their own fire, apart, she inside the shelter, he outside. Apparently no established custom patterns their sleeping. Individual adjustments are made.

The boys before they marry must have proved themselves to be hunters, and they must have performed over them the most important rite in the life of a !Kung boy—the Rite of the First Kill. The killing of birds or small animals does not qualify him for the rite: the animal he kills must be one of the great antelopes or a giraffe or buffalo, any one of the large animals killed for meat. When the boy has killed one of these, he is ritually scarified by his father or by another kinsman if his father is dead. The rite is performed twice for each boy. For the first male animal he is scarified on his right side and for the first female animal on his left side. Charred meat and fat, turned to magic by the rite, are rubbed into the several lines of vertical cuts on his face, arms, back, and chest; the purpose of this is to give him the will to hunt, good sight, and accurate aim, and also to enable him to find the animal and to prevent him from being seen by the animal. The rite is both a solemn celebration and a magic force to increase and strengthen the boy's power to hunt. It also carries with it the right to marriage and attests the boy's readiness.

Marriage does not necessarily follow immediately upon this rite; years may elapse, but the way is prepared and readiness is proved. And once more the act of hunting is ritually linked with marriage. At the time of the wedding, the boy must bring to his bride's parents an animal that he himself has killed. The meat he brings must not be eaten by the bride.

A boy who never killed any large meat animal would not be given a wife, informants said. This was why the strange old deviant /Gaishay had remained a bachelor.[5] For reasons no one understood he could not hunt; he gathered plant foods like a woman. Gossip had it that twice he had tried to drag a woman against her will into his shelter, but had not succeeded. Informants remarked, "Women like meat."

As John Marshall shows in his film, *The Hunters,* the primary sources of physical life—sex and food—are involved. In !Kung concept they are linked together, and, as they pertain to men, their duality is lifted to oneness in the being of the man, who is the sexually powerful male and the provider, the hunter. Power as a male and worthiness and dignity are associated with hunting and not with the failure to hunt. With bride service the bride's people can capture at once the sexual and the hunting powers of the young man.[6]

---

5. /Gaishay had poor vision when we knew him as an old man. Carleton Coon has suggested (*The Living Races of Man* [New York, Knopf, 1965], p. 262) that possibly he was color-blind and that this was the disability that made him unable to hunt. It is a plausible explanation. I wish the idea had occurred to one of us when we were in the field. We might have been able to test his color vision.

6. Bride service is discussed in detail in Chapter 5.

THE WEDDING OF N!AI AND /GUNDA

N!ai, a pretty little girl with a quick responsive smile, was married on May 22, 1953, at Gautscha. The bridegroom, /Gunda, was about sixteen, we judged, and the people said he was the best young hunter among the boys of the territory.

N!ai's age has been a matter of interest to me. As I have said, we do not know the ages of the !Kung in years and I do not have confidence in my guesses. Having read Nancy Howell's demographic material and having talked to Richard Lee on the subject, I believe I have guessed the children younger than they are, possibly unconsciously influenced by their size compared to American children. I guessed that N!ai was about eight when she married. I now think she was more likely about ten, but still that is a mere guess. At the time of her marriage, she was forty-seven inches tall. As a fully grown adult, she is fifty-seven inches tall. When

N!ai and her young half-brother, /Gaishay. The photograph gives an idea of N!ai's size and age at the time of her marriage.

she was married her breasts had not begun to bud. She did not have her
first menstruation till May 1959. As of September 1961, when I last saw
her, she still had not borne a child. She had her first child early in 1962
and when John Marshall saw her late in 1972, she had five children—
an extraordinary number in extraordinarily quick succession for a !Kung
girl. It should be noted that she had been living at the administrative post
at Tsumkwe with the McIntyres much of that time and had received food
from them.

N!ai's mother, Di!ai, had divorced her former husband, Gumtsa, the
father of N!ai, and was now the second wife of Gao in Band 1. /Gunda's
mother, Khuan//a, had divorced /Gunda's father, Bo. Khuan//a was
now the second wife of Gaú in Band 2. Both Gumtsa and Bo had remarried. Gumtsa lived at Kubi, Bo lived with Band 8.

The two mothers had betrothed their children some time previously.
We heard that Di!ai had had her eye on the strong young /Gunda, saying, "We must get this boy for N!ai. He will take care of her and will
hunt for us." Di!ai had gone to Khuan//a to propose the betrothal.
Khuan//a said "Yes, this is very good." The mothers exchanged gifts.
Khuan//a gave to Di!ai a necklace of five strings of ostrich-eggshell beads
which reached to the umbilicus (shorter strings would have been inap-
propriate), and Di!ai gave other beads and copper-wire ornaments to
Khuan//a.

Gumtsa, N!ai's father, heard about the betrothal. He had hoped to
arrange a marriage between N!ai and someone of his choice at Kubi.
One day in November 1952 he came to Gautscha to complain that he had
not been consulted and to protest against the betrothal. He wanted to
take N!ai to Kubi with him. Tension rose. N!ai cried and looked very
frightened. The members of both Bands 1 and 2, although theoretically
they had no authority in the matter, all expressed themselves and poured
torrents of talk over the affair. Mostly they were supporting Di!ai in her
steadfast refusal to yield N!ai, saying that Gumtsa had not fed N!ai, had
not so much as sent her a gift, and should not now come and interfere
in her betrothal. After four days of this, Gumtsa gave up and went home.

Meanwhile the affair, like a spoon stirring in a pot, brought to light
another tension. Some of N!ai's relatives began to express objection to
her betrothal, not because they wanted her to go with her father, but
because they were angry with Khuan//a, the mother of the bridegroom.
Possibly older stresses underlay the episode, but what brought them to
light was an affair about a knife. N!ai's stepfather, Gao, had given a

present of beads to one of his relatives. He was expecting a return gift to be made in due time, and it had seemed that there was a knife making its way to him in the ever-flowing currents of gift-giving. However, Gao's wife, Di!ai, and her sister, !U, claimed that Khuan//a had got possession of the knife and had given it instead to one of her relatives. Feelings flared up one day and a talk ensued. (The talk is described more fully in Chapter 9.) !U began it, declaring in a voice that could be heard across the encampment that Khuan//a was a grasping, stingy woman. Gaú loved Khuan//a so much, !U sniffed, that he spoiled her and let her have power over his belongings. !U had no doubt that Gaú would soon find himself very poor. !U disapproved of N!ai's marriage to the son of such a woman but said that she would reconsider her position if the knife that had been diverted by Khuan//a were now given to Gao, as had been expected.

It never was, but gifts of ostrich-eggshell beads and a blanket were given and Gao declared himself satisfied. N!ai's mother wanted the marriage so much she was ready to overlook the matter of the knife, and they all started again in peace.

Nothing more happened about N!ai's wedding until the morning of May 21, 1953, when we noticed the two mothers together building the wedding shelter. They had placed it between the two encampments, about twenty-five feet from the fire of the bride's family. The shelter was slightly larger and more nearly round and much more carefully built than the usual skimpy structures.

Next morning N!ai's mother asked me if I would bring the wood for the bride's fire. I knew it was because her back ached, not to honor me, but I felt honored anyway and brought the wood.

All that day N!ai sat at a short distance from her family's fire. N!ai was covered, head and all, with a big gemsbok kaross of her mother's. She wore her usual beads, but no special regalia brightened the somber gray-brown of the old kaross.

Just as the sun was setting, N!ai, without speaking to her mother and stepfather, walked alone over to another fire, seven or eight yards away. The big kaross was still pulled over her head and trailing behind her. She went to this fire because it was the one beside which she had slept, with her mother's widowed cousin, !Ungka, since she had reached the age when girls and boys leave off sleeping beside their parents. Her old kinsman, Old Gaú, was there. She sat down opposite him. He paid no particular attention to her, and they did not speak.

By then the sun had sunk below the horizon. N!ai uncovered her head but kept the kaross tied around her waist and over one shoulder in the way karosses are customarily worn.

Presently two girls came to N!ai. They had waited till twilight was deepening into darkness because, it was explained to us, people sleep at night and a wedding is a "night-thing." One of the girls was N≠isa, wife of Gao Music. The other was Xama, daughter of Gao Beard. The attendants were not selected for their precise relationship to the bride. They were the only young kinswomen of N!ai's who were present in the two bands. The girls sat down and chatted with N!ai for a moment and then stood up and, giggling and chattering, took N!ai by the arms. N!ai drew back. Then Xama pulled N!ai's arms over her shoulders and bent over taking N!ai onto her back so that her feet did not touch the ground. Xama carried N!ai in this position to the wedding shelter, laid her down inside, to the left of the opening as one entered, in the dark shadow, and covered her over with the kaross. There N!ai remained. We did not see her again that night.

It is the custom for the parents to take brands from their own fires to light the wedding fire of the bride and groom. Presumably this was done, though I did not see it. When the girl arrived, the fire was burning and a young man, a cousin of the groom, was tending it. The two girls sat down by the fire on the women's side.

In the encampment of Band 2, about twenty or thirty yards to the west, a group of boys had come to /Gunda to attend him. They were all the young boys in Band 2 of approximately /Gunda's age: two cousins (MoSiSo) and three of the sons of Gaú (/Gunda's stepfather) and Be (Gaú's first wife). The boys made a show of catching /Gunda, and they held him by the arms for a moment, laughing and talking. Then they formed a line with /Gunda following at the end, walked to the wedding fire and sat down on the men's side. /Gunda sat behind the line of boys, in a deep shadow, to show, we were told, that he was "ashamed" and that he respected ("feared," _koa) the wedding shelter.

One of the boys began to play, not their ritual music of the curing dance nor the Eland Music of the menstruation rite, but "songs of the //gwashi"—little melodies these people compose about happenings in their lives, about pleasures or distress, about their moods. Accompanied by a //gwashi (a five-stringed pluriarc), they sing these melodies for hours upon hours in the afternoons when they are resting or in the evenings by their fires, and they played for hours that night at the wedding fire.

Soon young guests from both encampments, the children with whom N!ai played, began to arrive. All of them were younger than the boys who attended /Gunda and the girls who carried N!ai. The youngest guest was the ubiquitous little ≠Gao, a four-year-old boy who never missed anything. No adults came.

One boy brought four mangetti nuts with him and roasted, cracked, and ate them himself. That was all that appeared by way of a feast. Di!ai said that they would like to have given the children something to eat but there was nothing in the encampment that night. Even if the others had had something to eat, the bride and groom would have had to abstain. They must not talk or eat in order to show that they are "ashamed." The young guests seemed to enjoy themselves, nevertheless, and they were still singing and chatting when I left at midnight.

On the morning after the wedding, the wedding party posed for a photograph. /Gunda is on the right, N!ai on the left of the opening of the shelter, and four of the young wedding guests are present. The boy beside /Gunda is playing a //gwashi.

Soon after sunrise the following morning—/Gunda had already departed—N!ai's mother went to the wedding shelter and sat down beside the embers of the night's fire. N!ai stood shivering beside her in her little genital apron and the duiker skin that women wear around their buttocks and up between their legs, but stripped of her kaross. Her mother had brought a little fat (eland fat, if they had it, would be used) and a bit of powdered red stone, one of the red earths (/gam !gai gwoie). mixed with fat. She rubbed N!ai all over with the fat, and drew a line on her forehead and a circular design on her cheeks with the red powder mixed with fat. Over in /Gunda's encampment, Gao, N!ai's stepfather, presented /Gunda with a blanket.

This completed the wedding rite.

N!ai was a lively child who loved the dancing and singing games the girls play. She often danced alone, tapping her bare feet on a stone in rapid rhythm or making a game of printing a design in the sand with tiny steps. She liked babies and as often as not had her infant half brother or some very small cousin tied to her back. That morning she appeared to turn into a housewife as though it were her next blithe step. When the women went to gather plant foods, she put on her own little duiker-skin kaross, took her digging stick, and went with them. At the end of the day, when they returned in the slanting sunset light, she had two big roots. She went straight to her own fire, blew on the embers, added wood, and sat down. Her digging stick and three ostrich eggshells full of water were her household goods. These she arranged beside the shelter. /Gunda came and sat down opposite her. She smiled at him and set the roots in the ashes to cook.

It had been said in talks with informants that before the wedding the bridegroom must bring to the parents of the bride an animal that he himself has killed; but no animal had been brought—there had not been a scrap of meat in the encampment for days. I asked Di!ai about this. "Oh, that," she said in effect. "Yes, he should give me an animal, but we thought we would have the wedding first and that /Gunda would then come with us when we leave tomorrow to gather tsi. He will hunt from that place and get us some meat."

The ritual elements in the wedding rite, so far as I observed, were as follows: (1) carrying the bride; (2) covering her head; (3) waiting till the sun has set before taking her to the wedding shelter; (4) the fact that the shelter is specially built and set apart from the others; (5) anointing the bride with fat; (6) painting a design on her forehead and cheeks with

N!ai with the design of red powder on her face; the mark of a bride

powdered red stone; and (7) lighting the wedding fire with brands from the fires of the bride's and groom's parents.

Apart from the third and seventh, all of these elements occur also in the Rite of the First Menstruation, a more elaborate and prolonged ritual with which the !Kung wedding rite is apparently connected. The design on the face is the same; the girl must not walk on ground from the instant her first menstruation begins to the end of the period, when she is washed and anointed with both eland or other fat and the oil of the tsi. When the girl is taken to her special shelter or moved out of it to urinate or defecate, a kinswoman carries her on her back. Her head is covered with a kaross, whether she is sitting in the shelter or being carried out.

Our endeavor to bring to light the meaning of the ritual elements yielded little. The meaning or origin of the design on the face, I am convinced, was not withheld but was instead lost to memory, lore, or myth. "It is our custom" was all the people could tell me.

The carrying of the bride to the marriage shelter suggested to me the ritual of the feet not touching the ground, a ritual frequently observed, according to Frazer, by menstruating girls. The !Kung, however, had no such interpretation of it. They think that carrying the girl is meant to suggest that she is reluctant to go to the arms of her bridegroom. To be proper, she should feign modesty and shyness even if she is eager to go and should show her reluctance to be separated from her own family. When the attendants take hold of the bride and groom by the arms and pull them a little they also symbolize the overcoming of reluctance and modesty, and perhaps there is even a vestige of bride-capture in that gesture. But I was not convinced that there might not have been another meaning to the carrying, no longer known, that related the bride to the menstruating girl being carried to and from her shelter.

The !Kung say that the sun is death-giving. When the three months of life-giving rains are past, the sun dries up the water pools; it kills the fresh leaves and fruits, dries the roots and berries, and would scorch the people if they did not find shade. They pity the morning star, the kuli /gaishay, which crosses the sky all day ahead of the sun, because it has no branches to carry for shade and cannot turn aside to rest under a tree. The sun is a "death-thing," ⁻!khi tshi, and the bride is shielded from it. A wedding, they say, is a "night-thing," /du tshi.

The most important element of behavior with respect to kinship in the wedding rite is the avoidance of the parents. Any kinswoman (preferably a young one) who is tall enough and strong enough, whether she herself is married or not, and whether or not she has the joking relationship with the bride, may carry the bride and any may attend her. Only the mother absolutely must not do so. The groom's father must not attend him. Neither pair of parents goes to sit by the wedding fire, for they must not sit near their son's wife or daughter's husband, nor speak to them. Guests of mature years might go and sit by the wedding fire only if they have the joking relationship with both the bride and the groom. Very young guests, such as we saw at N!ai's and /Gunda's fire, may go, whether or not they joke with the bride and groom, because the avoidances are not stringently observed with young children.

EXTRAMARITAL SEXUAL RELATIONS

Murdock points out that "Our own culture includes a blanket taboo against fornication, an over-all prohibition of all sexual intercourse outside of the marital relationship." He goes on to say that our society is highly aberrant in this and that "from available evidence it seems unlikely that a general prohibition of sex relations outside of marriage occurs in as many as five per cent of the peoples of the earth."[7]

!Kung society has an overall prohibition against any sexual relations outside of marriage, with one exception. It makes no requirements such as sexual hospitality or *jus primae noctis*. It makes no provision for sexual access to certain categories of kin or affines outside of marriage, such as BrWi. Premarital unchastity, unchastity of widows, and prostitution are not among their social conventions. But /kamheri, though not required, is either fully permitted or tolerated as not a very bad thing; I never reached certainty as to which of these attitudes the society adopted.

/Kamheri means that two men may agree to exchange wives temporarily, provided the wives consent. This is regarded as a concern of the couples involved rather than a concern of society as a whole. One man said, "If you want to sleep with someone's wife, you get him to sleep with yours, then neither of you goes after the other with poisoned arrows."

No actual instance of /kamheri came to our attention, and we failed to find out if it is now practiced. One man in /Gam lent his first wife to an unmarried friend, one of the gossips told us, because he was in love with his second and did not care any longer for the first; but this was a mere deviation from the rules, not an instance of /kamheri.

We heard of several instances of adultery, in addition to the irregular sexual union mentioned above. No instances of rape were recounted. Fornication must be very rare, because there is practically no one with whom to commit it. Almost all females are married, except for very

7. George Peter Murdock, *Social Structure* (New York, Macmillan, 1949), pp. 263, 264.

young girls and leathery old grandmothers. Adultery is the usual form for irregular unions to take. Adultery, however, is sharply limited by several deterrents. One deterrent is the incest taboo, which forbids extramarital sexual relations with tabooed categories of kin as it does marriage with persons to whom the taboo is extended. The same internalized sanctions induce obedience to this rule as to the marriage regulations. The same gradation of feeling probably exists, and I expect that people comply strictly with respect to consanguineous kin and close affines; no doubt, just as in the choice of marriage partners, they are less strict with respect to name-relatives.

Ease of divorce must exert a modifying influence on adulterous unions. If a married couple really want to change mates, nothing need deter them but the general difficulty of extricating themselves from the web of responsibilities that marriage entails.

In a sense, the impossibility of maintaining secrecy exerts a control over extramarital relations. There is no privacy in a !Kung encampment, and the vast veld is not a cover. The very life of these people depends on their being trained from childhood to look sharply at things and to take into their attention what they see. They must observe the most minute marks on vegetation to distinguish from the matted grasses the almost hair-thin brown vine stems that come up from the edible roots. Hunters memorize visual impressions and are able to follow the tracks of an individual animal in the midst of a large herd in a way that seems to us miraculous. They register every person's footprints in their minds, more vividly I am sure than we do faces, and read in the sand who walked where and how long ago.

The !Kung value control of anger. They uphold self-control as an ideal, train themselves to exercise it, and reward it with approval. Despite this, volatile tempers sometimes flare and burst out of all control. And always at hand are the little poisoned arrows. They are formidable weapons. There is no antidote for the poison; at least our !Kung informants said they know none, and they told us of tragic deaths from the poison which would have been averted had they had an antidote.

Adultery, so exceedingly provocative of anger and vengeance, could be very dangerous under these conditions. Anger turns upon the adulterer. We were never told about a woman who had been killed or even very severely punished, but a husband is considered to be quite within his rights by !Kung rules of conduct if he kills a man who sleeps with his wife. However, the adulterer may fight back. With poisoned arrows both men might be killed. Fighting is so dangerous it is feared by the !Kung with a pervading dread.

Nevertheless, although prudence counsels against it and anxiety may attend it, adultery does occur. During the years from 1951 to 1958, five instances in our sample came to our knowledge. When it did occur, the most clearly observable behavior was the attempt on the part of related persons and other members of the band to help resolve the situation in order to avoid fighting and discord, for fighting, like fire, may spread and consume much before it is quenched.

A husband and a young widower had quarreled and almost fought over the young widower's attentions to the wife. The fight had been averted by the husband's running away. He came to Gautscha where we were with Band 1. When I saw him handling his weapons, his face contorted with emotion, visions possessed me of the two men, both angry and afraid, shooting each other in nervous self-defense, writhing, bleeding, and dying in agony, and I was as filled with the fear of fighting as any Bushman. But before sundown that day the affair was resolved in the following fashion. ≠Toma, a relative of the young widower, undertook to use his influence and went and brought the young widower and the wife to Gautscha. ≠Toma had two motives. He wanted peace, as everybody does, and he wanted no disgrace in his family, which the affair would bring, for the young widower and the wife were sexually taboo to each other, albeit in the mildest and most extended way. ≠Toma is an able man, and he succeeded. The pair agreed to his behests. When they arrived at Gautscha the wife went directly to her husband and, to our surprise, in a few minutes they left the encampment with their child and came over to our camp, where they settled themselves right in our cleared camp space. Presently the young widower came too, with his three children, and settled himself beside the others. Under our wings they had less fear of each other's flares of temper, and tensions relaxed. In a day or so the young widower left. Peace prevailed. The wife was still with her husband in 1958. We did not see them after that.

When John Marshall was with Band 1 in 1957–58, a young unmarried man took to sleeping with a young woman about his age, who was the second wife of an older man in another band. Nobody seemed to expect a great deal of this young woman, who was thought not to have very good sense, and she was not blamed nearly so much as the young man was. His family railed at him quite openly. "People get killed doing that," said his sister. Eventually the young man stopped the affair—influenced at least in part, John thought, by the group's openly expressed disapproval. Furthermore, the young man decided it would be best to go to the woman's husband and say he was sorry. The older man said the younger was right to come directly to him and that they should not fight. He gave his wife a mild thrashing instead.

Then a close relative of the young woman roused up the whole matter again by claiming that when the young man "insulted" the woman he insulted him as well. This man was the k"xau n!a of another band. Although in a cool moment he could speak eloquently and philosophically about the evils of fighting, he was an erratic person, self-centered, frightfully jealous, shrewd to see that no one got more than he, quick to take offense. A third man, a relative of the young man who had started the affair, shouted out that the k"xau n!a was a troublemaker not to leave well enough alone. The k"xau n!a thereupon foully insulted the young man's relative, who shouted back that the k"xau n!a was not fit to be a k"xau n!a. The latter, now in a rage, called out that the young man's relative "lied to his own arrows." John said that some of the people flattened down on the ground or got behind things at this point. But two half sisters of the k"xau n!a threw themselves on him, pulled him away, and sat down beside him, holding his arms. He quieted down, and the other man also sat down and was quiet. As the tempers cooled, peace took hold once more and, John says, the matter did not flare up again, at least during the remaining weeks he was there.

In some societies, it would be incumbent upon such kinsmen as these to express anger, whether feigned or felt, and make a show of fighting to satisfy the conventions of honor. We observed no episodes, other than the one just related, that raised the question of such a custom. John was strongly of the opinion that the emotions were genuine and that the k"xau n!a's temper, which we had all experienced two or three times before, had released itself once more and that a fight had been averted only because people wanted peace and harmony most of all.

OFFSPRING OF EXTRAMARITAL UNIONS

Girls are usually married before they are old enough to have children. But, we asked, what would happen if a girl had a baby before she was married? People said the parents would go to the father of the child and say he must marry their daughter. Did they know anyone who had done this? No.

Suppose that a child were conceived in adultery and it were known with certainty that the father was not the woman's husband, what would happen to that child? we asked. The baby would be kept by its mother, of course, informants said. After they had talked things over among themselves, one said and others agreed that they thought that if the woman's husband fed the child for years while it grew, he would be justified in keeping the child, and the biological father should not try to take the child away.

There is such a child now, born under conditions of change. Late in 1955 or in 1956, white farmers came into the Nyae Nyae region to recruit labor for their farms. In South West Africa the recruiting of labor is under government control, and it was illegal for the farmers to' take Bushmen in this way. Nevertheless they did, having succeeded in persuading several families to go with them. Sometime later, these families tried to run away from the farms to return to Nyae Nyae. They told us that they were followed by two white men and a white woman on horseback with guns, led by a "tame" Bushman tracker. These people forced some of the !Kung to return to the farm. Under a barrage of threats and with pointed guns, they seized some of the !Kung children. The mothers and some of the men followed the children. In the fracas, others of the !Kung got away. Husbands and wives were separated. When the South West Africa authorities learned on which farm these !Kung families were, they acted to restore them to their bands and fined the farmer, but two years had passed. One girl had had a child by one of the !Kung men. Once they were all restored to the Nyae Nyae area, the girl went back to her own husband with her baby and was with him in 1958. The people said the baby's biological father, as well as the baby's mother's husband, should do something nice for him. Perhaps when he receives his first assagai—a very proud moment for a boy—it will be his begetter who gives it. But we do not know what the future holds for these people or where they will be by then.

TERMINATION OF MARRIAGE AND REMARRIAGE

Widows and widowers are not treated in any special way because of their status.

If her husband dies, a young widow usually returns to her own parents or lives with one of her own siblings; but if her people are dead, or if it is her own preference, she may stay on with her deceased husband's people. It is the duty of her HuBr to hunt for her if she needs his support.

Several possibilities are open to a young widower: rarely he might stay with his deceased wife's parents or siblings; more likely he would return to his own parents or siblings. If he marries again, he goes into bride service with his new bride. In any case, a man is responsible for his deceased wife's parents and young siblings, and if they depend on him for support he must take them with him. They would be likely to prefer, however, to live with an adult son, daughter, or sibling of their own, if they have any.

Old widowers or widows whose own parents are dead usually live with either a son or daughter, or perhaps with their own sibling—as they wish.

The surviving spouse is free to marry again within the regulations of the extended incest taboo, which applies to all marriages.

Parents would arrange the subsequent marriage of a boy or girl whose spouse died. Adults may make their own arrangements directly. My impression was that persons might be considered fully adult somewhere in their middle or late twenties. An adult man takes the initiative and asks the woman to marry him.

No restriction of time is put upon the remarriage of a widower, but a widow should not remarry until one rainy season has passed. She is then considered "clean" and may marry again. ≠Toma said, "The rain washes (n//um) the death away from the widow." N//um is the gesture of wiping a dish clean with one finger. /Ti!kay said that some men wait for a rainy season to pass before marrying a widow, but that others would be pleased the husband was dead and, without waiting, say, "This is my chance." One interpreter understood that the widow had to take off her kaross and spend a night out, letting the rain fall on her, but ≠Toma said this was not what was meant. That would be very uncomfortable, he said. It would make her shiver and might make her sick. The rainy season's passing is what cleanses the woman. When she is about to go to her new husband she prepares herself by washing in the ordinary way.

Unless a woman is quite old she does not remain long unmarried. One man said, "Even if a widow is thick and tall but is a good woman, some man will want her." Widows may marry as second wives of married men, or they may marry widowers, divorced men, or bachelors. The two young widows and the two divorced women who were unmarried in 1953 had remarried in 1955. Only the very old widows remain unmarried.

There are so few unmarried women that widowers have difficulty in finding wives. The young widowed musician, /Gao Music, was an example. He was first married to a younger sister of Gao whose name was N≠isa. She had died and /Gao Music then married Gao's daughter, also named N≠isa, when she was approximately ten or eleven years old, about the age of his own son, /Qui. /Gao was patiently waiting for her to grow up. Only one of the old widowers had succeeded in finding a wife by 1957.

The children of a widowed parent are kept by that parent. A widower may leave his children with a woman relative, but they remain his. Orphaned children go to live with relatives, without any formal adoption. (Formal adoption does not exist in !Kung society.) There is a tendency for the !Kung to feel that the boys belong eventually to the father's side of the family, the girls to the mother's. This concept came to our attention several times, but we did not find it to be a rigid social rule. The relative who is expected to take the children if they are young is the MoSi. But the FaSi might be nearer or more able for one reason or another to take them; if she were, she might do so. FaBr would be the relative most likely to take half-grown boys, but again MoBr might be the one. Failing these, some other relative would take them. When it came to arranging marriage for orphaned children, informants said that the father's eldest brother would have the most authority. We were told that stepparents do not have authority in making marriage arrangements.

Divorce may terminate a marriage. The couple may divorce without formality, by mutual consent, or simply by one spouse's leaving the other. I use the word "divorce" for convenience, although no legal action takes place. If parents of a very young couple withheld consent this might influence the couple, but the parents' consent is not a requirement. No property entanglements present difficulties, for there is no dowry or bride-price to be resolved. The only property a !Kung owns personally consists of artifacts, and these are never owned in common by man and wife. Every artifact belongs to an individual who takes his property with him in case of divorce.

Divorce does not change people's status in the community in any way. They are free to remarry without restrictions.

Young children of divorced parents remain with the mother. As they grow to adolescence, the girls usually stay with their mothers; the boys may go to their fathers or stay with their mothers or spend some time with each.

Divorce is never obligatory, and the grounds are not formalized; the desire of the couple concerned is the determining factor. A condition such as sterility, for example, or a wrongdoing such as adultery, might

or might not lead to divorce, depending on how the couple felt about
it. Mistreatment or failure to provide would certainly be considered
justification for divorce, should they ever occur, but justification is not
necessary. "A wife can get tired of loving her husband," we were told,
"and just tell him to go away."

We learned of only nine divorces in our sample. The middle-aged
Khuan//a, the mother of the bridegroom /Gunda, had left her first
husband, Bo, to marry Gaú [2.25], son of Old /Gasa. Another middle-aged
woman left her husband because he was on the point of marrying a
second wife. Jealousy between the two young wives at /Gam, lamented
in song by the young husband, had been the cause of a third. The whims
of young girls caused others. One girl, married to a considerably older
man, hated him though he was good to her and gave her ornaments for
her hair. She cut off her hair and threw it, ornaments and all, into the
fire. She thrust her head into the ashes and made herself filthy. In another instance, the girl took offense the first night of her marriage and
left her husband the next day, to his painful chagrin. The divorce of
Gao of Band 3 and Doïn of Band 7 was another. The lenient and patient
parents of these girls arranged other marriages. Di!ai of Band 1, now
the wife of Gao, was divorced from two former husbands in her youth.
And !U, while still very young, had been persuaded by ≠Toma to leave
her tall young husband from /Gam and to marry him.

Our data on the frequency of divorce are too scant to be significant.
We have merely the impression that there seems to be some tendency for
couples to separate while they are young but that, on the other hand,
there is considerable stability in marriage once a compatible mate is
found. At least, no divorces occurred between 1952 and 1959 in eight
of the bands of our sample.[8] We lack data on the others.

Although the !Kung do not consider divorce reprehensible, they de-
plore it. Divorce is untoward, disruptive; it can cause trouble. Anything
other than peace and harmony in human relations makes the !Kung
uneasy.

On the whole, we have the impression that there was a notable
freedom from quarreling between husbands and wives. The instances
of strife that I have mentioned were breaks in their predominantly peaceful, well-adjusted human relations.

8. The eight bands were Bands 1–6, 9, 10. We did not see all of the individual members of these bands, but we saw some and were told the news of the others.

9 Sharing, Talking, and Giving: Relief of Social Tensions

This chapter describes customs practiced by the !Kung which help them to avoid situations that are likely to arouse ill will and hostility among individuals within bands and between bands. Two customs which I consider to be especially important and which I describe in detail are meat-sharing and gift-giving. I discuss also the ways in which manner-liness, the custom of talking out grievances, the customs of borrowing and lending, and of not stealing function to prevent tension from building up dangerously between members of a group and help to bring about peaceful relationships.

The common human needs for cooperation and companionship are particularly apparent among the !Kung. An individual never lives alone nor does a single nuclear family live alone. All live in bands composed of several families joined by consanguineous or affinal bonds. The arduous hunting-gathering life would be insupportable for a single person or a single nuclear family without the cooperation and companionship of the larger group. Moreover, in this society, the ownership of the resources of plant foods and waterholes and the utilization of them are organized through the band structure, and individuals have rights to the resources through their band affiliation. Thus, the !Kung are dependent for their living on belonging to a band. They must belong; they can live no other way. They are also extremely dependent emotionally on the sense of belonging and on companionship. Separation and loneliness are unendurable to them. I believe their wanting to belong and be near is

This chapter is a slightly revised version of a paper first published in *Africa*, 31 (July 1961), 231–249. It is republished here with the kind permission of the International African Insititute.

actually visible in the way families cluster together in an encampment and in the way they sit huddled together, often touching someone, shoulder against shoulder, ankle across ankle. Security and comfort for them lie in their belonging to their group free from the threat of rejection and hostility.

Their security and comfort must be achieved side-by-side with self-interest and much jealous watchfulness. Altruism, kindness, sympathy, or genuine generosity were not qualities that I observed often in their behavior. However, these qualities were not entirely lacking, especially between parents and offspring, between siblings, and between spouses. One mother carried her sick adult daughter on her back for three days in searing summer heat in order for us to give her medicine. N/aoka carried her lame son, Lame ≠Gao, for years. Gaú clucked and fussed over his second wife, Khuan//a, when she was sick. When !U had a baby, her sister, Di!ai, gathered food for her for five days. On the other hand, people do not generally help each other. They laugh when the lame man, !Kham, falls down, and they do not help him up. !U's jealous eyes were like a viper's on one occasion when we gave more attention to her husband, ≠Toma, than to her, because he was much more ill than she. And, in the extreme, there was a report from the 1958 Marshall expedition of an instance of apparently callous indifference in one band on the part of some young relatives to a dying old childless woman, an old aunt, when her sister with whom she lived had died.

Occasions when tempers have got out of control are remembered with awe. The deadly poisoned arrows are always at hand. Men have killed each other with them in quarrels—though rarely—and the !Kung fear fighting with a conscious and active fear. They speak about it often. Any expression of discord ("bad words") makes them uneasy. Their desire to avoid both hostility and rejection leads them to conform in high degree to the unspoken social laws. I think that most !Kung cannot bear the sense of rejection that even mild disapproval makes them feel. If they do deviate, they usually yield readily to expressed group opinion and reform their ways. They also conform strictly to certain specific useful customs that are instruments for avoiding discord.

TALKING AND TALKS

I mention talking as an aid to peaceful social relations, because it is so very much a part of the daily experience of the !Kung, and because I believe it usefully serves three particular functions. It keeps up good, open communication among the members of the band; through its constantly flowing expression it is a salutary outlet for emotions; and it serves as the principal sanction in social discipline. Songs are also used for social discipline. The !Kung say that a song composed specifically about someone's behavior and sung to express disapproval, perhaps from the deepest shadow of the encampment at night, is a very effective means of bringing people who deviate back into the pattern of approved behavior. Nevertheless, during our observations, songs were not used as much as talking. If people disapprove of an individual's behavior, they may criticize him or her directly, usually putting a question, "Why do you do that?," or they may gossip a bit or make oblique hints. In the more intense instances what I call a talk may ensue.

The !Kung are the most loquacious people I know. Conversation in a !Kung encampment is a constant sound like the sound of a brook, and as low and lapping, except for shrieks of laughter. People cluster together in little groups during the day, talking, perhaps making artifacts at the same time. At night, families talk late by their fires, or visit at other family fires with their children between their knees or in their arms if the wind is cold.

There always seems to be plenty to talk about. People tell about events with much detail and repetition and discuss the comings and goings of their relatives and friends and make plans. Their greatest preoccupation and the subject they talk about most often, I think, is food. The men's imaginations turn to hunting. They converse musingly, as though enjoying a sort of daydream together, about past hunts, telling over and over where game was found and who killed it. They wonder where the game is at present, and say what fat bucks they hope to kill. They also plan their next hunts with practicality. Women (who, incidentally, do not seem to me to talk as much as men in !Kung society) gave me the impression of talking more about who gave or did not give them food and their anxieties about not having food. They spoke to me about women who were remembered for being especially quick and able gatherers, but they did not have pleasurable satisfaction in remembering their hot, monotonous, arduous days of digging and picking and trudging home with their heavy loads.

Another frequent subject of conversation is gift-giving. Men and women speak of the persons to whom they have given or propose to give gifts. They express satisfaction or dissatisfaction with what they have received. If someone has delayed unexpectedly long in making a return gift, the people discuss this. One man was excused by his friends because his wife, they said, had got things into her hands and made him poor, so that he now had nothing suitable to give. Sometimes, on the other hand, people were blamed for being ungenerous ("far-hearted") or not very capable in managing their lives, and no one defended them for these defects or asked others to have patience with them. The experiences of daily life are a further topic of conversation. While a person speaks the listeners are in vibrant response, repeating the phrases and interposing a contrapuntal "eh." "Yesterday," "eh," "at Deboragu," "eh," "I saw old /Gaishay." "You saw Old /Gaishay," "eh, eh." "He said that he had seen the great python under the bank." "EH!" "The python!" "He wants us," "eh, eh, eh," "to help him catch it." The "ehs" overlap and coincide with the phrase, and the people so often all talk at once that one wonders how anyone knows what the speaker has said.

Bursts of laughter accompany the conversations. Sometimes the !Kung laugh mildly with what we would call a sense of humor about people and events; often they shriek and howl as though laughter were an outlet for tension. They laugh at mishaps that happen to other people, like the lions eating up someone else's meat, and shriek over particularly telling and insulting sexual sallies in the joking relationships. Individual singing of lyrical songs accompanied by the //gwashi, snatches of ritual music, the playing of rhythmical games, or the ritual curing dances occupy the evenings as well, but mostly the evening hours are spent in talk.

As far as we know, only two general subjects are avoided in conversation. Men and women do not discuss sexual matters openly together except as they make jokes in the joking relationships. The !Kung avoid speaking the names of the gods aloud and do not converse about the gods for fear of attracting their attention and perhaps their displeasure.

A talk differs from a conversation or an arranged, purposeful discussion. It flares spontaneously, I believe from stress, when something is going on about which people are seriously concerned and in disagreement. I think that no formalities regulate it. Anyone who has something he wants to say joins in. People take sides and express opinions, accusing and denying, or defending persons involved. I witnessed one such talk only, in 1952. It occurred over a gift-giving episode at the time of N!ai's betrothal and involved persons in Bands 1 and 2, who were settled near together at the time. Khuan//a, the mother of /Gunda, N!ai's betrothed, had diverted a gift—a knife—that people thought was making its way to Gao, the present husband of N!ai's mother. Instead of giving it to him at the time when an exchange of gifts was in order, she gave it to one of her relatives. N!ai's mother's sister, !U, sitting at her own fire, began the talk. She let it be known what she thought of Khuan//a, in a loud voice, a startling contrast to the usual low flow of talk. Di!ai, N!ai's mother, sitting with her shoulder pressed against her sister's, joined in. People went to sit at each other's fires, forming little groups who agreed and supported each other. From where they sat, but not all at once and not in an excited babble, they made their remarks clearly, with quite long pauses between. Some expressed themselves in agreement with !U as she recounted Khuan//a's faults and deviations, past and present. Khuan//a's family and friends, who had moved to sit near her, denied the accusations from time to time, but did not talk as much or as loudly as !U. Khuan//a muttered or was silent. !U said she disapproved of her sister's daughter marrying the son of such a woman but would reconsider her position if Khuan//a gave the expected gift to Gao. The talk lasted about twenty minutes. At that point Khuan//a got up and walked away and the talk subsided to !U's mutterings and others' low conversation. In a few days Khuan//a gave Gao a present, not the gift in question, but one which satisfied Gao, and, as they said, "they all started again in peace."

There is a third form of verbal expression which might be called a "shout" rather than a "talk," but as far as I know the !Kung have no special name for it. It is a verbal explosion. Fate receives the heat of the remarks in a "shout."

We were present on two such occasions, one in 1952, the other in 1953. Both occurred in response to the burning of shelters. In both instances little children, whose mothers had taken their eyes off them for a few minutes, had picked up burning sticks from the fire, had dropped them on the soft, dry, bedding grass in the shelters and, at the first burst of flame, had sensibly run outside unscathed. On the first occasion, the two children, who were about three years old, were frightened and were soothed and comforted by their mothers and other relatives. They were not scolded. On the second occasion, Khuan//a, the two-year-old granddaughter of Old ≠Toma and /Gam, had set fire to her grandparents' shelter. She was not apparently frightened at all and was found placidly chewing her grandfather's well-toasted sandal. She was not scolded either.

What was especially interesting on both occasions was the behavior of the people. They rushed to the burning shelters, emitting all at once, in extremely loud, excited voices, volcanic eruptions of words. The men made most of the noise, but the women were also talking excitedly. No one tried to do anything, nor could they, for the grass shelters burned like the fiery furnace. I asked the interpreters to stand close to one person at a time and try to hear what he said. People were telling where they had been when the fire started, why they had not got there sooner. They shouted that mothers should not take their eyes off their children, that the children might have been burned. They lamented the objects which had been destroyed—all in the greatest din I have ever heard humans produce out of themselves. It went on for about eight or ten minutes in bursts, then tapered off for another ten. While Old ≠Toma's shelter was burning, he and his wife, /Gam, the great maker of beads, sat on one side weeping. After the shouting had subsided, a dozen or more people set about looking for Old ≠Toma's knife blade and arrow points and picking up what beads they could find for /Gam in the cooling ashes. The two instances of "shouts" provided examples of the vehemence which vocal expression can have and vividly illustrated the !Kung way of venting emotion in words.

There is still another kind of talk, not conversation, that I consider to be an outlet for tension and anxiety. It occurs in varying degrees of intensity. People say aloud what is on their minds. For instance, whether it is actually so or not, someone may be reiterating that he has no food or that no one has given him food. The remarks are made in the presence of other individuals, but the other individuals do not respond in the manner of a discussion or conversation.

An example of such talk is the following monologue of !U that John Marshall recorded one evening when !U and !Ungka were sitting alone by !U's fire. !U said musingly, more to herself than to !Ungka:

Di!ai was given something by Di//khao N!a [Lorna Marshall]. She strung them and wore them. I want Di//khao N!a to give me the same. Please give me something to drink. Next time she will give me some beads to wear. Di//khao N!a will give me a scarf. //Kushay and I were working for Di//khao N!a. She gave each a scarf is what I say. I am asking her to give nice things to /Gaishay [!U's son]. Di//khao N!a does not favor me. I have been asking these things, Do you not know you are our chief? Di//khao N!a's heart is far from me. When she goes away, she will give me a scarf and beads. When she goes away, I want her to give me a scarf and beads. Why does she not let us speak? Di!ai and !Ungka have been asking things from Di//khao N!a, but she does not give them things. This is what I say. I was hurt by falling from a truck. My back and body are sore. I am sick. That is why I don't go out for plant foods, because I am sick. I want my mother [she means Di//khao N!a here] to give me some, and she does not give me any. I want !Ungka to get me some; she does not. I am lying down sick. I am starving. If my mother, /Naoka N!a, were here she would give me some plant foods. She is not here. So I am starving. Di//khao N!a and Tsamgao N!a [Laurence Marshall] do not favor me. They do not give me food. Only mealie meal. That is what I am living on. Why does not Di//khao N!a give me some fat? My ankle is sore. If she gave me fat my ankle would be better and I could go out for plant foods. Tsamgao N!a wants me to go to the mangetti trees. I do not think I shall be able. He wants me to go to the mangetti trees. It is far. This is what I say. The place is far. The people who stay there are not people who favor others. Not sympathetic. They do not give food. When they see people from a far place coming to their place, their hearts do not feel good. I do not want to go. I do not like to go to far places. When a person follows people to a far place, she gets tired. She does not get enough food for herself. I have told this to Tsamgao N!a, but he does not understand what I am saying. I ask my mother, Di//khao N!a, to tell him. People are to stay in their own country to get food. If they go to another place, the people there are not pleased. My mother, Di//khao N!a, does not tell Tsamgao N!a. Going to a far place—I am not pleased with it. This is what I say.

In an extreme instance we saw a woman visitor go into a sort of trance and say over and over for perhaps half an hour or so in ≠Toma's presence that he had not given her as much meat as was her due. It was not said like an accusation. It was said as though he were not there. I had the eerie feeling that I was present in someone else's dream. ≠Toma did not argue or oppose her. He continued doing whatever he was doing and let her go on.

All these ways of talking, I believe, aid the !Kung in maintaining their peaceful social relations. Getting things out in words keeps everyone in touch with what others are thinking and feeling, releases tensions, and prevents pressures from building up until they burst out in aggressive acts.

ASPECTS OF GOOD MANNERS

In !Kung society good manners require that, when !Kung meet other !Kung who are strangers, all the men should lay down their weapons and approach each other unarmed. The first time ≠Toma approached us, he paused about thirty or forty feet away from us, laid down his bow, arrows, and assagai on the ground, and walked toward us unarmed. After we were accepted and given !Kung names, we were no longer strangers and we never observed the practice again.

Good manners require that visitors be received courteously and asked to sit by the fire. The woman whose fire it is may welcome the visitor by taking a pinch of the sweet smelling sã powder, which she carries in a little tortoise shell hung from her neck, and sprinkling it on the visitor's head in a line from the top of the head to the forehead.

Good manners in eating express restraint. A person does not reveal eagerness or take more than a modest share. When a visitor comes to the fire of a family who are preparing food or eating, he should sit at a little distance, not to seem importunate, and wait to be asked to share. On several occasions we gave small gifts of corned beef to be shared with a group. The person who received the food from us would take only a mouthful. Once an old man who received the meat first only licked his fingers. The lump of food would be passed from one to another. Each would take a modest bite. The last person often got the most. I found it moving to see so much restraint about taking food among people who are all thin and often hungry, for whom food is a source of constant anxiety. We observed no unmannerly behavior and no cheating and no encroachment about food. Although informants said that quarrels had occasionally occurred in the past between members of a band over the time to go to gather certain plant foods, and although we observed expressions of dissatisfaction, no quarrels of any kind arose over food during our observations.

The polite way to receive food, or any gift, is to hold out both hands and have the food or other gift placed in them. To reach out with one hand suggests grabbing to the !Kung. Food may also be placed on the ground in front of the person who is to receive it.

Good manners in general should be inoffensive. Any behavior which is likely to stir up trouble is regarded with apprehension and disapproval by the !Kung. In view of this, the joking relationship has its interesting side. Men and women who have the joking relationship insult each other in-a facetious way and also point out actual faults or remark on actual episodes which embarrass a person. Everyone joins in the uproarious, derisive laughter. All this is joking and one should not take offense. The !Kung say this teaches young persons to keep their tempers.

In contrast to the joking is their care in other aspects of conduct to avoid giving offense. ≠Toma said, for instance, that if he were forming a hunting party and a man whom he did not want asked to join him, he would be careful to refuse indirectly by making some excuse and would try not to offend the man.

Gossip which can stir up trouble is discouraged. People do gossip but usually discreetly, in low voices, with near and trusted relatives and friends. It is best to mind one's own business, they say.

People are expected to control their tempers, and they do so to a remarkable degree. If they are angry, aggrieved, or frustrated, they tend to mope rather than to become aggressive, expressing their feelings in low mutters to their close relatives and friends. ≠Toma told us that he had lost his temper twice when he was a young man and on one occasion had knocked his father down. On the other he had pushed his wife into hot ashes. It had so frightened him to realize that he could lose control of himself and behave in this violent way that, he said, he had not lost his temper since.

MEAT-SHARING

The !Kung custom of sharing meat helps to keep stress and hostility over food at a low intensity. The practical value of using up the meat when it is fresh is obvious to all, and the !Kung are fully aware of the enormous social value of the sharing custom. The fear of hunger is mitigated: the person with whom one shares will share in turn when he gets meat; people are sustained by a web of mutual obligation. If there is hunger, it is commonly shared. There are no distinct haves and have-nots. One is not alone.

To have a concept of the potential stress and jealousy that meat-sharing mitigates in !Kung society, one has only to imagine one family eating meat and others not, when they are settled only ten or fifteen feet apart in a firelit encampment and there are no walls for privacy. The desert does not hide secret killing and eating because actions are printed in its sands for all to read. The idea of eating alone and not sharing is shocking to the !Kung. It makes them shriek with an uneasy laughter. Lions could do that, they say, not men.

Small animals, the size of duikers or smaller, and birds belong to the man who shoots or snares them. Tortoises, lizards, grasshoppers, and snakes are picked up incidentally by anyone and belong to the person who picks them up. That person may share his find only with his or her immediate family or with others as he or she chooses, in the way plant foods are shared. ≠Toma says that if he has only a small creature, he and his family eat a meal and give a little to anyone who happens to be nearby at the time. As I said in Chapter 4, the custom of meat-sharing applies to the big animals which are deliberately hunted by hunting parties: eland, kudu, gemsbok, wildebeest, hartebeest, springbok, warthog, and ostrich.

The composition of the hunting party is not a matter of strict convention or of anxious concern. Whoever the hunters are, the meat is shared and everyone profits.

When the kill is made, the hunters have the prerogative of eating the liver on the spot and may eat more of the meat until their hunger is satisfied. If they are far from the band, they may eat the parts that are especially perishable or most awkward to carry, like the head, and they sometimes eat the cherished marrow. They then carry the animal to the band in its parts, bones and all, or, if the animal is very big, they leave most of the bones and cut the meat into strips. The strips dry to biltong quickly and thus are preserved before they decay, and they can be hung on carrying sticks and transported more easily than big chunks. The blood is carried in bags made of the stomach or bladder.

The gall bladder and testicles are discarded at the kill. Eventually the picked bones and horns are thrown away. (The !Kung make only a few artifacts of bone and horn; the artifacts last a long time and seldom need replacing.) Sinews are kept for making cord. The hide would be skinned off whole and tanned if it were suitable for a kaross and someone wanted a new kaross at the time. Otherwise, the hide is dried, pounded up, and eaten. Hides are quite tasty. Feet are picked of every tissue; gristle is dried and pounded. Soft parts, such as the foetus, udder, heart, lungs, brains, and blood, are often given to old people with poor teeth. Intestines are enjoyed and desired by all. The meat of the rump, back, chest, and neck is highly appreciated. Nothing is wasted; all is distributed.

The owner of the animal is the owner of the first arrow to be effectively shot into the animal so that it penetrates enough for its poison to work. That person is responsible for the distribution. The owner may or may not be one of the hunters.

Hunters have arrows which they acquire in three different ways. Each man makes arrows for himself, shaping the points (usually now of metal, but still possibly of bone or wood) with some slight distinction so that he will know them from the arrows of other men. Secondly, arrows are given as gifts. The man who made the arrow or had himself acquired it as a gift may give it to someone else, either a man or a woman, consanguineous kin, affine, or friend. Thirdly, people lend arrows to one another. The status of the arrow plays its part in the distribution of the animal killed with it. There is much giving and lending of arrows. The society seems to want to extinguish in every way possible the concept of the meat belonging to the hunter.

A hunter chooses which arrows he will use. The owner of the arrow —who ipso facto owns the animal—may therefore be the hunter himself, who has chosen to use an arrow he made or one that was given him, or he may be a person, man or woman, who lent the arrow to the hunter.

There may be several hunters in the hunting party and several arrows in the animal, but this seems to cause no confusion or conflict. Every arrow is known, of course. The hunters can see which first penetrates effectively so that its poison could account for the kill. But I think that often it is arranged beforehand who will own the animal. A man asking another to accompany him might say, "Come and help me get a buck." Or "Old Gaú lent me an arrow and asked me to hunt for him. You come too." Incidentally, it was Old Gaú's arrow that was first shot into the giraffe that is depicted in John Marshall's film "The Hunters."

I think there is little or no dissension as to who owns the animal because it is not a cause for great stress; each hunter gets a share of the meat anyway. I think also that a man wants sometimes to be the owner of the meat in order to start the distribution off in the direction of his own relatives, but that one is also content sometimes not to have the onus of the main distribution.

If the animal is large, the hunters cut it up at the kill. If the whole animal is to be cut up in the encampment, any of the men may participate in the butchering. They cut the animal in a customary way each time, all know how to do it, all are skilled. If the owner of the animal is a man, he would probably work at butchering himself, and the hunters would probably help, but not necessarily so. Others might do this work. Women do not participate in butchering an animal, and we did not see any assist in carrying the meat around in the distribution, but we saw women carry meat at other times.

The first distribution the owner makes is to the hunters and to the giver of the arrow, if the arrow was not one the owner made himself.

Gao cutting up meat of a wildebeest

The meat, always uncooked in the first distribution, is given on the bone unless the animal is so large that the meat has been cut into strips at the kill.

In a second distribution, the several persons who got meat in the first distribution cut up their shares and distribute them further. This meat also is given uncooked. The amounts depend on the number of persons involved, but should be as much as the giver can manage. In the second distribution, close kinship is the factor that sets the pattern of the giving. Certain obligations are compulsory. A man's first obligation at this point, we were told, is to give to his wife's parents. He must give to them the best he has in as generous portions as he can, while still fulfilling other primary obligations, which are to his own parents, his spouse, and his offspring. He keeps a portion for himself at this time and from it gives to his siblings, to his wife's siblings if they are present, and to other relatives and friends who are there; possibly he gives only in small quantities by then.

Everyone who receives meat gives again, in another wave of sharing, to his or her parents, parents-in-law, spouse, offspring, siblings, and others. The meat may be cooked and the quantities small.

Visitors, even though they are not close relatives, are given meat by the people whom they are visiting. This social rule is strongly felt. Visitors may receive small quantities of cooked meat, which is like being asked to dinner.

Name-relatives often receive generous portions of meat because they have the same name as the giver or because their names associate them with his close kin, but this seems to be more a favor than an absolute rule. ≠Toma said there were far too many men named ≠Toma for him to give them special consideration.

The result of the distribution is that everybody gets some meat.

In the later waves of sharing, when the primary distribution and primary kinship obligations have been fulfilled, the giving of meat from one's own portion has the quality of gift-giving. !Kung society requires at this point only that a person should give with reasonable generosity in proportion to what he has received and not keep more than an equitable amount for himself. Then the person who has received a gift of meat must give a reciprocal gift some time in the future.

Band affiliation imposes no pattern on this giving. Except that the hunters are customarily given a forequarter or a hindquarter, no rule prescribes that any particular part of the animal must be given to any particular person or to any category of kin or affine. People give different parts of the meat and different amounts, this time to some, next time to others, more generously or less generously according to their own reasons. We are certain that the motives are the same as in gift-giving in general: to measure up to what is expected of them, to make friendly gestures, to win favor, to repay past favors and obligations, and to enmesh others in future obligation. I am sure that when feelings of genuine generosity and real friendliness exist, they would also be expressed by giving.

The distribution of an eland which was killed by Gao Beard of Band 2 will serve as an example of the way meat was shared on one occasion. On every occasion, the amounts given and the parts given would differ and the first recipients would vary. More than a hundred !Kung were present at Gautscha at the time of the hunt. Both Gautscha bands (Band

Lame !Kham and his family with a generous portion of meat cut in strips and hung on a branch to dry

1 and 2) were present. Bands 3, 4, and 7, and a sprinkling of people from other bands were visiting.

The hunting party was composed of four men: Gao Beard; his first wife's brother, //Ao, and his own brother, /Qui, both of whom lived with him in Band 2; and his brother-in-law, N!aishi [12.21], who was visiting at the time.

The party had hunted for eight days without success in heat so exhausting they had to lie covered with sand through the middle part of the day.

/Qui was the first to see the eland. It was a huge one. As /Qui had been asked to come on the hunt by his brother to help him, he told Gao Beard where the eland was and did not shoot at it himself.

Two boys joined the men to track the eland after it was shot. The party tracked it for three days and then found it dead from the poison. They cut up the meat and brought it to the encampment at Gautscha, which was two days' travel away. The hunt had lasted thirteen days in all.

Gao Beard was himself the owner of the arrow. The arrow had been given by one person to another five times. /Gao Music of Band 1, who had made it, gave it to his sister, /Goishay, who gave it to her husband, ≠Gao, of Band 3. He gave it to his brother, Gao [7.12], who gave it to his wife, Di!ai [7.13]. (Gao and Di!ai had returned to live in Band 3.) Di!ai gave it to Gao Beard, her brother, who shot the eland with it and who was responsible for the distribution of the meat.

Gao Beard first gave meat to the hunters who helped him, as was the custom. To N!aishi he gave a forequarter and to //Ao a forequarter and the head. (The hunters usually received a forequarter or hindquarter or an equivalent amount. The head was an extra gift.) The two boys who helped track got nothing, because their fathers would give them some, we were told. To our astonishment, /Qui was given nothing. Gao Beard explained that his brother would eat from his pot. (Actually he might eat more in this way as he would not have to share the cooked meat with anyone but his wife and child.)

Gao Beard's sister, Di!ai, who had given him the arrow, received the meat of the back and throat and the intestines.

Gao Beard kept the meat of the neck for himself. Continuing the distribution, he gave the rest of the meat as follows:

To his first wife, //Kushay, he gave both hindquarters, the meat of the chest, the lungs, part of the liver, and one hind foot. To his mother he gave the meat of the belly and one hind foot. To his half sister, //Kushay [12.20], and to /Gasa, the wife of his brother, /Qui, he gave one front foot each.

The amount given to his first wife was enormous. In addition to giving to her co-wife, also named //Kushay, and to her children and her co-wife's children, she gave a large portion of meat to her parents who lived with them in Band 2. (On other occasions the man had given directly to his wife's parents—not through his wife.) When the meat was cut up, //Kushay gave to her father, Old ≠Toma, four bundles of strips of boneless raw meat (it was somewhat dried by then). There were about ten or twelve strips to a bundle, about 2½ to 3 feet long. We guessed the weight of this gift to be about sixty to seventy pounds. She gave meat also to her two younger brothers, /Gao and /Gunda. (Her other brother,

//Ao, who had been one of the hunters, had got his share from Gao Beard.) She gave to her co-wife's father, ≠Gao of Band 4, and to Old /Gaishay of Band 4, her co-wife's MoFa. She then gave to six other persons, all in Band 1. They were: her cousin, Old Gaú (her FaSiSo); his two daughters, !Ungka and //Kushay; two other cousins (FaSiDas), Di!ai and !U, and !U's husband, ≠Toma.

The giving of raw meat went on. Old ≠Toma gave to eighteen people: his wife, six affines, three consanguineous kin, two name-relatives (i.e. a visitor whose father's name was ≠Toma and Old /Gasa, whose deceased husband's name was ≠Toma), and six other persons. Telling us the reasons for giving to the last six, whose consanguineous or affinal connections (if any) with Old ≠Toma were so remote we did not bother to trace them, he said of one, "He is an old man whom I like in my heart," and of another, "He was hungry for meat." In the end Old ≠Toma gave some of the meat back to his daughter, //Kushay.

Di!ai of Band 3, the giver of the arrow, gave raw meat to six persons: her husband's mother, his brother and his two sisters (all in Band 2), a visitor who was her HuSiHuBr, and her mother's brother in the visiting Band 7.

Persons who had by this time received substantial amounts of raw meat began giving to others. We recorded sixty-three gifts of raw meat. Doubtless there were more. After the raw meat was given, individuals shared their portions, cooked or raw, with parents, offspring, spouses, and others.

Meat is not habitually cooked and eaten as a family meal among the !Kung. When an individual receives a portion of meat, he owns it outright for himself. He may give and share it further as he wishes, but it never becomes family or group property. The men, women, and children may cook their pieces when and as they wish, often roasting bits in the coals and hot ashes and eating them alone at odd times. Or someone may start a big pot boiling and several people will bring their pieces to put into it at the same time, each taking his own piece out when it is cooked.

The sense of possessing one's own piece personally is, I believe, very important to the !Kung. It gives one the responsibility of choosing when to eat one's meat and struggling with hunger as best one can when it is finished, without occasion or excuse for blaming others for eating more than their share.

The !Kung are quite conscious of the value of meat-sharing and they talk about it, especially about the benefit of the mutual obligation it entails. The idea of sharing is deeply implanted and very successfully imposes its restraints. To keep meat without sharing is one of the things that just is not done.

GIFT-GIVING

The custom of gift-giving, in my opinion, comes second only to meat-sharing in helping the !Kung to avoid jealousy and ill will and to develop friendly relations. !Kung society puts considerable emphasis on gift-giving. Almost everything a person has may have been given to him and may be passed on to others in time. The !Kung make their artifacts, on the whole, of durable material and take good care of them; the objects may last for generations, moving in a slow current among the people. The dealings in gift-giving are only between individuals, but they are numerous and provide occasion, perhaps more than any one other activity does, for visits which bring groups of people together.

We gave cowrie shells as parting gifts in 1951 to the women in Band 1, the band which first sponsored us and with whom we stayed on each expedition wherever they were. When providing ourselves with gifts for the !Kung on our first expedition, we had had to guess as best we could what would appeal to them. The idea of cowrie shells came from seeing in museums so many West African objects encrusted with the shells. We thought the !Kung might like them as a novelty and bought a supply from a New York shell dealer. They came from the Pacific, and we amused ourselves imagining future archaeologists finding them in !Kung sites in the Kalahari, to their bewilderment. We carefully observed that there were no cowrie shells among the !Kung ornaments before we gave them. We gave to each woman enough for a short necklace, one large brown shell and twenty smaller gray ones. In 1952, there was hardly a cowrie shell to be found in Band 1. They had been given to relatives and friends, and they appeared not as whole necklaces but in ones and twos in people's ornaments to the edges of the area.

The !Kung have not developed special objects to use as gifts. Nor have they invested ordinary objects with special gift significance. What they give each other are the common artifacts and materials of everyday life. However, among those, some are more highly valued than others, as one would expect. I gathered that relative scarcity of material was a factor and that objects were appreciated for their beauty, workmanship, and appropriate size (a wide headband is better than a narrow one). People took an interest in remembering to whom an object had been given in the recent past, but the !Kung, who are present-oriented, do not place special value upon antiquity as such or systematically hold the distant past in mind.

The !Kung decorate their artifacts very little. (They have developed music and dancing but not the plastic or pictorial arts.) However, they delight in ornaments with which to adorn themselves. The most highly valued are the traditional ornaments of ostrich-eggshell beads, especially the wide headbands and the necklaces of five or six strings of beads that reach to the navel—the measurement of a good necklace. The creamy white of the shells is particularly becoming to the yellow-brown skin of the !Kung and is a relief from the monotonous gray-brown of the karosses that the women wear. The !Kung also like ornaments made with European beads of all colors, though white is preferred. They like

An ostrich-eggshell bead headband of traditional design, here worn as a necklace

To make the ostrich-eggshell beads, a woman first drills a hole in a fragment of eggshell. She then strings the fragments tightly on a cord and rubs off the jagged edges of the fragments with a stone till the edges of the disks are smooth and even. The woman in this photograph is Old /Gam, wife of Old ≠Toma. Whereas most of the older women wore few ornaments, Old /Gam bedecked herself as lavishly as the young women. Note three or four cowrie shells, gifts from us the year before, hanging on a string of beads from her head, and note her headband of European beads. Her pleasant smile was characteristic of her. (She is the woman who cooked the python.)

all beads, any beads, we were told; Gao Beard said that the only thing they do not like about beads is scarcity of them.[1]

They value artifacts that take time and care to make: the musical instrument (pluriarc) called *//gwashi;* a well-shaped wooden bowl; a long string of dance rattles. They also value metal implements and pots; these they obtain by trade.

The !Kung do not trade among themselves. They consider the procedure undignified and avoid it because it is too likely to stir up bad feelings. They trade with the Bantu, however, in the border-country settlements of western Botswana. The !Kung offer well-tanned antelope hides and ostrich-eggshell beads. For these they obtain tobacco, beads, knives, axes, malleable metal for making arrowpoints and assagai blades, and occasional files and chisels, fire-strikers, and pots.

The odds are with the Bantu in the trading. Big, aggressive, and determined to have what they want, they easily intimidate the !Kung. Several !Kung informants said that they tried not to trade with Herero if it was possible to avoid it because, although the Tawana were hard bargainers, the Herero were worse. /Qui of Band 1, a mild man, said he had been forced by a Herero, one whom he was afraid to anger, to trade the shirt and pants we had given him as a parting gift in 1952 for a small enamel pan and a little cup. /Ti!kay had more gumption. A Herero at the beginning of a negotiation with him brought out a good-sized pile of tobacco but took from it only a pinch when it was time to pay. /Ti!kay picked up the object he was trading and ran off. ≠Toma said with amused exaggeration that "a very good Herero, a respectable one, will give a handful of tobacco for five cured steenbok skins. A bad Herero will give a pipeful [he showed the size of his fingernail] for three skins." The Tawana values are a little better. A well-tanned gemsbok hide brings a pile of tobacco about 14 inches in diameter and about 4 inches high. The values vary. Some that were reported to us were three duiker or steenbok skins for a good-sized knife, five strings of ostrich-eggshell beads for an assagai.

The !Kung have become dependent on metal, especially knives, axes, and arrowpoints. They have been able to trade enough for every

1. The women always wove the headbands of ostrich-eggshell beads into the traditional design shown in the photograph. They wove European beads into a variety of designs. We had no idea how great a variety of original, subtle designs and color patterns !Kung women were capable of creating till Marjorie Shostak Konner had the idea in 1974 of providing some of the women with European beads she purchased, and asking them to make aprons. Her collection is fascinating.

man to have these implements. They could exist, however, without them and do still use a few bone and wood arrowpoints. Poison, not penetrating power, makes their arrows deadly.

The pots are Ovambo or Okavango pottery (the !Kung make no pottery themselves) or European ironware. The !Kung like to have a pot around to borrow sometimes; not everyone wants to carry one. They cook mostly in hot ashes. More for their novelty, I thought, than for their worth, the !Kung trade also for old oddments of cloth garments (they weave neither cloth nor mats), pieces of blankets, basins, and so on—things they do not really need but like to have.

Tobacco they need "to make the heart feel better." Oddly enough for these passionate smokers, tobacco was not given as much emphasis in gift-giving as one might expect. They do make gifts of tobacco, but when anyone lights a pipe he passes it around anyway; all present drag smoke into their lungs until they almost faint, and it does not seem to have mattered much who owned the tobacco.

Eland fat is a very highly valued gift. An eland provides so much fat that people can afford to be a little luxurious. They rub it on themselves and on their implements and they eat it. ≠Toma said that when he had eland fat to give, he took shrewd note of certain objects he might like to have and gave their owners especially generous gifts of fat.

Real property and the resources of plant foods and waterholes are not owned by individuals and cannot be given away. However, meat, once it is distributed after the hunt, and plant foods, once they are gathered, become private property and may be given. Artifacts are privately owned by the individual man, woman, or child, as outrightly owned if received as a gift as if made by the individual. The !Kung borrow and lend a great deal (thus supporting each other and aiding themselves in maintaining social solidarity), but this does not blur the clarity of ownership. Each object acquires some markings of its own from the maker and from use. It is easy for the !Kung, with their highly developed powers of observation and visual memory, to keep track of the commonest objects, know the ownership, and remember the history of the gifts.

As far as we know, no rules of avoidance govern the objects given to any category of person. For instance, although women, especially when menstruating, should not touch hunting weapons, lest the hunter's powers be weakened, they may own arrows that are given to them.

The gifts varied in quantity. One which /Ti!kay gave to ≠Toma was considered generous. It was a fine ostrich-eggshell headband, three ostrich eggshells, and a well-tanned duiker skin as soft as suede. Another generous gift consisted of a knife, an assagai, and a triple string of traded white European beads. Often gifts were less. The feelings persons have for each other, the degree of their past indebtedness, what they happen to possess and can give determine the generosity of the gift.

The acquisition per se of the objects is seldom, I believe, of primary importance to most individuals in gift-giving—that is, if the objects are their own artifacts. As the !Kung come into more contact with Europeans —and this is already happening—they will feel sharply the lack of our things and will need and want more. It makes them feel inferior to be without clothes when they stand among strangers who are clothed. But in their own life and with their own artifacts, they are comparatively free from both material want and pressures to acquire. Except for food and water (important exceptions!), with which the Nýae Nyae !Kung are in balance, but I believe barely so, they all had what they needed or they could make what they needed. Every man can and does make the things that men make and every woman the things that women make. No one was dependent upon acquiring objects by gift-giving.

The !Kung live in a kind of material plenty because they have adapted the tools of their living to materials which lie in abundance around them and are free for anyone to take (wood, reeds, bone for weapons and implements, fibers for cordage, grass for shelters), or to materials which were at least sufficient in quantity to satisfy the needs of the population. The Nyae Nyae !Kung have hides enough for garments and bags; they keep extra hides when they need them for new garments or when they want them for trade; otherwise they eat them. The !Kung can always use more ostrich eggshells for beads to wear or trade, but enough are found, at least, for every woman to have eight or ten shells for water-containers—all she can carry—and a goodly number of bead ornaments.

In their nomadic hunting-gathering life, traveling from one source of food to another through the seasons, always going back and forth between food and water, they carry their young children and all their belongings. With plenty of most materials at hand to replace artifacts as required, the !Kung have not needed or wanted to encumber themselves with duplicates or surpluses. They do not even want to carry one of everything. They borrow what they do not own. I believe that for these reasons they have not developed permanent storage, have not hoarded, and the accumulation of objects has not become associated with admirable status. Instead of keeping things, they use them as gifts to express generosity and friendly intent, and to put people under obligation to make return tokens of friendship. Even more specifically, in my opinion, they mitigate jealousy and envy, to which the !Kung are prone, by passing on to others objects that might be coveted.

Except, as ≠Toma said, that it would be surprising to see a man give a present to a woman who was not related to him (and vice versa I imagine), anyone may give to anyone. Degree or kind of consanguinity or affinity, having the joking relationship or lacking it, impose no requirements or restrictions. We did hear people say, however, that the k''xau n!a of a band may feel that he should lean well to the generous side in his giving, for this position focuses a little extra attention on him and he wants whatever attention he attracts not to be envious. Someone remarked that this could keep such a man poor.

The times of giving are determined almost entirely by the individual's convenience. The !Kung do not know their birthdays or anniversaries and have no special days of the year which they mark by giving gifts. Gifts are required by convention on only three ritual occasions. The type or quantity of the gift is not patterned, but the gift should be generous. The occasions are (1) betrothals and (2) weddings, when the parents exchange gifts and give to the young couple, and (3) the ritual of a baby's first haircut, when the !gun!a, the person for whom the baby is named, should give him a fine present.

Relatives give to young people with the idea of setting them up in life. Gao Beard gave an assagai and a kaross to /Gishay [1.22], saying it was his duty to see that the boy got some things because among the boy's relatives he was the most able to do so. The boy's father, Old Gaú, was very old, he explained, and did not have many possessions. People expect to wait a long time for young people to make return gifts.

The two rigid requirements in gift-giving are that one must not refuse a proffered gift and that one must give in return. Demi said that even if he might prefer not to be obligated to someone, he would accept and prepare to make his return gift. If a gift were to be refused, he continued, the giver would be terribly angry. He would say, "Something is very wrong here." This could involve whole groups in tensions, bad words, taking sides—even a talk might occur—just what the !Kung do not want. Demi said it does not happen: a !Kung never refuses a gift. (I thought of our Christmas giving and how one would feel if one's Christmas gift were refused.) And a !Kung does not fail to give in return. ≠Toma said that would be "neglecting friendship." A person would know that others thought him "far-hearted" and "this would worry him."

In reciprocating, one does not give the same object back again but something of comparable value. The interval of time between receiving and reciprocating varies from a few weeks to a few years. Propriety requires that there be no unseemly haste. The giving must not look like trading.

Incidentally, we were not included by the !Kung in their gift-giving patterns. They gave us a few things spontaneously which they thought we would enjoy—python meat for instance—but did not feel obligated to reciprocate for every gift we gave them.

Asking for a first-time gift or asking that a return gift be made after due time has elapsed is within the rules of propriety. People prefer that others give in return without being asked, but ≠Toma says he does not hesitate to ask if a gift is long overdue. If a person wants a particular object he may ask for it. Asking is also a means by which people play upon each other's feelings. One can test a friendship in this way. One can give vent to jealousy or satisfy it by acquiring some object. And one can make someone else uncomfortable. I thought that /Ti!kay (an intelligent man, but very touchy, self-centered, and—with us—uncooperative) used to ask for gifts in order to play with anger, arousing it for the sake of feeling it, as children do with fear, playing witches in the dark. His remarks one day indicated a mingling of feelings and purposes. He told us that one may ask for anything. He did, he said. He would go to a person's fire and sit and ask. (I could imagine him sitting and asking, his black eyes glancing around.) He would ask usually for only one or two things, but if a person had a lot, he might ask for more. He said he was almost never refused. However, if a man had only one pot and /Ti!kay asked for it, the man might say, "I am not refusing but it is the only pot I have. If I get another, you may come for this one. I am very sorry but this is the only pot I have." /Ti!kay said this would not make him angry unless he were refused too many times. To be refused too many times makes a person very angry. But, said /Ti!kay, he himself did not tire of people asking him for gifts. Asking, he claimed, "formed a love" between people. It meant "he still loves me, that is why he is asking." At least it formed a communication of some sort between people, I thought.

I have stressed the mitigation of envy and jealousy as the important value of gift-giving. !Kung informants stressed more the value of making a friendly gesture even if it is only a token gesture. It puts people under the obligation of making a friendly gesture in return. People are quite conscious of this and speak about it. Demi said, "The worst thing is not giving gifts. If people do not like each other but one gives a gift and the other must accept, this brings a peace between them. We give to one another always. We give what we have. This is the way we live together."

ABSENCE OF STEALING

One day, when I wanted to talk with a group of informants about what the !Kung considered to be a wrongdoing, I began with /Tikay. He said promptly, "making crooked arrows and fighting," but could not think of anything else that was a wrongdoing. Informants had previously said that not sharing food would be the worst thing they could think of. Others had mentioned that the breaking of the incest and menstruation prohibitions would be very wrong and that girls should not sit in immodest postures. No one seemed to think lying was very serious wrongdoing, and no one mentioned stealing. I finally asked directly, and Gao replied meditatively they had not thought to mention stealing because they did not steal.

We had heard of a man who took honey from a tree, honey which had been found and marked and was therefore owned by someone else. He was killed by the furious owner. That was the only episode of stealing that we discovered.

The !Kung stole nothing from us. Even when we went away on trips leaving several bands of !Kung settled around our camp site, we left our supplies and equipment unlocked, in the open or in our tents, with confidence that nothing would be stolen. Things that we lost or forgot in the !Kung encampment were returned to us, even two cigarettes in a crumpled package.

Stealing without being discovered is practically impossible in !Kung life because the !Kung know everybody's footprints and every object. Respect for ownership is strong. But, apart from that, /Tikay said, "Stealing would cause nothing but trouble. It might cause fighting."

During seventeen and a half months of field work with the Nyae Nyae !Kung (with Bands 1 and 2 and many visitors, up to about seventy-five persons), I personally saw only four flare-ups of discord and heard about three others which occurred in neighboring bands during that period. All were resolved before they became serious quarrels. Of the seven, four were flare-ups of sexual jealousy. Another one was the talk about Khuan//a's gift. Two were minor disagreements about going somewhere. On one occasion, Gao Beard coerced his young second wife into going with him when she wanted to stay visiting her parents. He coerced her swiftly and decisively by snatching her baby from her arms and walking off with him. In a flash, the wife ran a few steps and hit him on the head with her digging-stick, then she went around in a circle, stamping her feet in great, high stamps like an enraged samurai in a Japanese print, then she followed her husband. On another occasion, /Ti!kay gave his brother a shove for refusing to accompany him. None of the conflicts concerned food.

On a later expedition, in another year, John Marshall witnessed three serious quarrels. Anger flared more hotly than in the episodes I saw. One of those quarrels was about food. It was a dispute about the possession of an animal that had been killed. Another was about a marital matter; another about the failure of a curer to come to cure a sick child when he was asked. All three quarrels were resolved by talks. Vehement talking it was, but it stopped short of physical fighting.

I consider that the incidence of quarrels is low among the !Kung, that they manage very well to avoid physical violence when tensions are high and anger flares, and that they also manage well to keep tension from reaching the point of breaking into open hostility. They avoid arousing envy, jealousy, and ill will and, to a notable extent, they cohere and achieve the comfort and security which they so desire in human relations.

10 *Play and Games*

The arduous days in !Kung life are the days of hunting and gathering and the long days of walking when the people travel from one place to another. Days spent in the encampment when there is food on hand are anything but arduous. People stroll half a mile to the waterhole to fill their containers, perhaps to dance and sing together for a little while or just to sit and talk in the morning or evening coolness. The women carry away some of the ashes of the night fires and pile them at a little distance away from their shelters to tidy the place where they sit around their fires. That is the extent of their "housekeeping." People use the time during the days at home to make or repair their belongings. The women sharpen their digging sticks and perhaps do some bead work for a while. From time to time they clean and soften their karosses. They pound fresh bones between stones till they have about a quart of bone meal. This they rub, handful by handful, over the kaross, working its moisture into the leather. The men work on their hunting equipment, making arrows and poisoning them. They renew or repair any of their artifacts that need attention, sitting in groups in the shade the while, talking and singing. However, the !Kung artifacts are durable and do not often need renewing, so more time is spent in leisure than in tasks. People sit talking, smoking, playing with their babies, delousing each other's heads, napping, or just lying resting. Much of the time during the leisure days someone is making music. The children play all their waking hours, free play and structured games. The adults also play games.

The presence of our expedition at Gautscha in 1952–53 created an unusual situation which gave us an exceptional opportunity to see !Kung games. As I mentioned previously, we found as many as seventy-five to a hundred people encamped around us. Such numbers stimulated the playing of games. Although there was a tendency for boys of about seven to twelve to play together a good deal of the time and girls of the same age to do so also, there were no exclusive age groups. Adults played with the children and teenagers when they wished. Teenagers played with younger children. The little ones played with older children as best they could.

The games and play can be grouped into categories. Both boys and girls engage much of the time in physical activities such as climbing trees, swinging on swings they made themselves, or jumping rope. They also engage in play that imitates adult activity and at the same time serves as a learning process. In another type of play, groups of children play several dramatic games in which the actions are patterned rather than being free imitation of adult actions. The play that older girls and women most frequently engage in emphasizes rhythmic motion and singing. They dance little patterned dances and play rhythmic games, some that imitate animals but in a patterned way rather than freely. The game most often played is a ball game which is a dance itself. These rhythmic games include little feats of agility like hopping on one foot. Boys spend less time playing patterned games and engage more in physical activities, such as climbing trees. They play almost incessantly a game of stick-throwing in which they show their prowess, but no one wins.

Among !Kung games there is nothing like our hockey or football in which teams compete against each other. The !Kung do not play in teams, except at tug of war. Conflict is expressed between individuals, however, in the porcupine game; and in four little dramatic games conflict is expressed between parents and children, between humans and animals, between people who have and people who do not have cattle.

Mimicking animals is a pastime of men and boys. They mimic the walk and the way the animal carries and throws its head, catching the rhythm exactly. /Ti!kay could make himself uncannily like an ostrich; his sitting down on a nest and laying eggs was delightfully funny. Skill in mimicry has practical value as well as being very amusing. A hunter can let his fellow hunters know what animal he has seen without making a sound. The hunters also have conventional signs that they make with their hands. They indicate the relative position of the horns on the head of the animal, the wide-apart wildebeest horns or the upright harte-beest horns, for example, and they move their hands and forearms the way the animal's head moves.

Boys play little dramas of encounter and attack. One may imitate a lion, growling and springing at other boys who run toward him and leap away yelling before he seizes them. The boys played hyena by acting out an episode in which a hyena slips into the encampment at night when people are asleep and tries to bite them. The !Kung have tales of hyenas biting off a person's buttocks or a person's nose while he slept, and they tell of at least one actual episode of a hyena biting through a child's leg and trying to drag the child away to eat it. (The child, a little girl, was rescued, and she recovered from the bite.) In the boys' play, the people leap up, wave their arms at the hyenas, and yell and bang on a hard piece of hide to frighten the beast away with noise. (This is what they actually do if a real hyena or a lion appears.) On another occasion, one boy played he was a gemsbok, with sticks in his hair to represent horns. The other boys imitated hunters. They attacked and killed the gemsbok.

!Kung boys amuse themselves by mimicking people as well as animals. Probably girls do also, but apparently not as much. In any case, I noticed only the boys. They mimic peculiarities of posture and movement so cleverly that they leave no doubt as to who the model is. I saw the lame !Kham and Lame ≠Gao mimicked more than once. The ridicule did not seem bitter; I should call it mild ridicule. When the real ≠Gao or !Kham falls down, people laugh, and they laugh at the mimicry. In contrast, it seemed to me that the mimicking of animals showed a different spirit. There seemed to be no ridicule in it; rather it seemed to have overtones of intimacy and affection.

I find it interesting to note one lack in !Kung games. Whereas multitudes of children over the world play tag in one or another of its many forms, the !Kung children do not.

THE PLAY OF YOUNG CHILDREN

!Kung babies are carried most of the time by their mothers, tied in soft leather slings against their mother's side, where they can easily reach their mother's breast. They nurse at will. !Kung women have excellent lactation. All the babies are plump. The babies wear no clothes and are in skin-to-skin contact with their mothers. They sleep in their mother's arms at night. When they are not in their mother's arms or tied to their sides, they are in someone else's arms, or if they are set down to play they clamber over their elders as they lie chatting and resting, or play within arm's reach. The babies are constantly in the presence of

!U with her daughter, !Ungka Norna; !Ungka, ≠Toma's sister, for whom !Ungka Norna is named (her !gun!a) is on the left. Notice the baby's light skin. Notice the tortoise shells !U is wearing. They contain a sweet-smelling cosmetic powder. !Ungka Norna's beads are a gift from her !gun!a.

people who are gentle and affectionate with them and who are watchful. The babies have no special toys, but are allowed to play with any of the adults' possessions that come to their hands and mouths, except knives and hunting equipment. These items are hung carefully in the bushes, out of reach of children.

The !Kung never seem to tire of their babies. They dandle them, kiss them, dance with them, and sing to them. The older children make playthings of the babies. The girls carry them around, not as a task set

Girls made playthings of the babies.

them by their parents (though they might carry babies around for that reason also), but because they play "mother." The boys also carry the babies around, give them rides, and drag them on karosses (a favorite game). If the babies utter a whimper they are carried back to their mothers to nurse. Altogether, the babies appear to be as serene and contented as well-fed young puppies.

When people are sitting at leisure, they spend time teaching the babies. They help them to stand or to take their first steps between outstretched arms of the adults and they play little games with them. Three of their games are the following:

Young Duiker. The adult and the child sit close together—the child on the adult's knee, or the two beside or opposite each other. The adult pinches up a bit of skin on the back of the child's hand and then releases it; the child does the same with the adult's hand. Then each moves his two hands straight up and down with his palms facing each other, about twelve inches apart. The sequence is repeated. All the while the two are singing:

> The young duiker says "za za"
> The young duiker came running down.

Dung Beetle. This game is similar to Young Diuker. The adult and the child sit together in the same way; this time they pinch each other's eyebrows. Next they slowly bend their heads backward and forward, while making the up-and-down motion with their hands of Young Duiker and singing the syllable *zein* in a long drone. The sound represents the buzzing wings of the dung beetle in flight. The players then let their hands plop down, representing the dung beetle's plop into the dung.

Naming the Birds. A mother playing with a child bows her head rhythmically and points to the palm of her hand with the index finger of the other hand, saying each time the name of a bird: "The partridge egg is there, the dove egg is there, the guinea fowl egg is there," and so forth. Mothers said this was how they taught the children the names of the birds.

Boys and girls from about three to six play together near their family fires much of the time, but they also venture as far as the dance circle, where they chase each other around and play on the swing.

Much of the play of young children is imitation of the elders' daily activity. It is not surprising that one favorite theme they enact is hunting, gathering, preparing food, and eating it. The children take up the roles of men and women. The boys go out to hunt (they do not go far— twenty or thirty feet perhaps). They carry back leaves and twigs on carrying-sticks held over the shoulders, as the hunters carry meat. The little girls dig for roots with their mothers' digging sticks. They pound the "food" in their mothers' mortars and pretend to cook and eat it. Another favorite theme to enact is the ritual curing dance. The little girls clap and sing; the boys imitate n/um k''xausi and pretend to go into trance.

The little boys begin to try to keep up with the older boys as soon as they are able, and the little girls with the older girls. The girls have an easier time: the girls' play is somewhat more subdued than that of the boys. I was always impressed with the tolerance and patience of the older boys and girls with the little ones who kept getting in the way as they struggled to take part in whatever play was in progress.

THE PLAY OF BOYS

The most active players were the boys from about seven to eleven or twelve. They played together in a group most of the time. When many families were visiting Gautscha there would be present as many as ten or a dozen boys of that age. The older teen-aged boys and young adults who were present joined the young boys in some of their games.

Their play spaces were the cleared areas of the dance circles in both encampments of 1952–53, the space around the waterhole and the edge of the pan, and the space around the baobab trees. In the encampment of April–July 1953, the boys often played on a worn-down anthill near Band 1, and at another anthill, one with a tall pinnacle, east of the dance circle. They never went far afield. !Kung children of any age do not go far from the encampment into the featureless veld of grass and bush; they know not to.[1]

The boys played all their waking hours, turning from one kind of play to another through the day. They swarmed up the trees, hung from the branches, jumped down from them, played on the swing they had rigged to the tree near the dance circle, played their stick game, their *djani* game, their porcupine game (all to be described presently), dragged

---

1. The perils are real. The children have been taught from infancy to recognize them. For someone to encounter a leopard or a lion or to step on a snake is not a common occurrence, but is quite possible and actual occurrences are known to all. For children to get lost would be an ever-present danger if they were not taught to stay near their encampment. Only once in our experience some children strayed— a group of eight- and nine-year-olds. When they were missed, the encampment exploded into action. In minutes the men set out in tracking parties. The children had turned into the bush from the edge of the pan. They thought to come out again to the pan but had gone past it by that time. They wandered without landmarks till they happened to come to a little clearing which they recognized. They took their direction from it and were headed for the encampment when the men found them.

the babies on karosses. They made a variety of playthings for themselves
—little toy autos, for example, in imitation of our trucks. And they
played with bows and arrows. Every day they practiced shooting at the
pinnacle anthill, at birds and beetles and any little things that moved.

There was another side to the boys' play; they could be quiet. They
enjoyed being with Elizabeth and took to visiting our big tent (where
Elizabeth and I both had our work tables) to be with her and, sometimes,
to model with plasticene or to draw or paint with materials we had
brought.[2]

In my diary, I say their voices were so gentle, their play so gay but
so delicate that they did not disrupt anything and did not disturb
me even when I was making kinship charts. If the everlasting wind blew
our papers off the tables, Tsamgao picked them up for us. And he was
quick to open the zipper of the tent netting for us if either of us went
in or out.

The older teen-aged boys and the young men do not climb the trees
or play on the swing, but they sometimes play the stick game and often
the djani game with the younger boys. All boys and men play the porcupine game. Often they work on some new artifact or repair their bows
and arrows, or they lie in the shade doing nothing. But part of every
leisure day someone makes music—sometimes for hours at a time. Often
one of the men would tap quiet tunes on his bow with a stick. What the
young men liked best was to sing together the songs of the //gwashi,
while /Gao Music plucked soft rippling accompaniments on the strings.
If I could leave what I was doing, I would sit for a while in a bit of shade
nearby and let the music lift me out of the awareness of my discomforts
in the heat and the trials and frustrations of my work.

In the late afternoons, however, when the day begins to cool, the
middle-sized boys leave their stick-throwing or their arrow-shooting or
whatever they have been playing at; and the older teen-aged boys and
young men leave whatever they have been engaged in and congregate
wherever the girls congregate, most often by the edge of the pan.

There is always some singing and dancing, with someone playing a
//gwashi. Both boys and girls (and men and women also), in the informal
dancing as well as in the dancing of the curing ritual, dance with simple
restrained small steps, with very little movement of arms and torso, and
no erotic gestures. The boys and girls do not touch each other in dancing,

---

2. Elizabeth took material for modeling, drawing, and painting. She offered opportunity to children and adults to use the materials without suggesting to them what
they should do with them.

but they dance in each other's presence and are in unison in their response to the rhythm.

Presently, instead of dancing, they begin to play games. The boys and girls play separate games for the most part. The girls do not play the porcupine, djani, or stick-throwing games; those are exclusively for males. Boys and men do not play the ball game of the women and girls. There is some playing together, however. Little boys join the girls in playing the dramatic games, and the boys jump rope with the girls. The boys and girls play separate games, but they often play so near together in the same play space that they might almost be playing together. The boys barge in among the girls, playfully disrupting their games; the little boys get in the way.

The principal activity for the boys during these times of play in the late afternoon and evening is to perform feats of agility and of combat, and to make a show of strength before the girls. Most of all the boys, older and younger, tussle and struggle together. One lifts the other off the ground, carries him around, throws him down, and drags him about; the other in turn gets the better of his companion, lifts him and carries him around. Sometimes their tussling takes the form of wrestling; they grapple and strain to push one another down. Occasionally they fisticuff with much gesturing of arms and clenched fists. The wrestling and fisticuffing do not end in fighting—the boys have smiles on their faces; they break off, shouting and laughing, and run to tussle with someone else.

Sometimes the boys turn cartwheels and backward somersaults. They stand on their heads or roll over and over on the ground. One feat of agility is for one boy to run around holding the upraised foot of another; the latter hops after him on one foot as fast as he can. Another favorite game when this kind of play is in progress is for the boys to give each other "horseback" rides. Two boys form the horse, one behind the other. One bends over double and winds his two arms tightly around the waist of the second boy. A third boy rides on the back of the first. The "horse" gallops around.

The older boys may be joining in all this or they may be sitting nearby watching the girls. Meanwhile, as the boys are showing off their strength and agility, the girls are playing their gay singing games together.

THE PLAY OF GIRLS

Girls begin to take their place in the lifework of providing food earlier than boys do. The boys are not taken hunting by their fathers until they are about twelve. Younger boys, the !Kung believe, could not endure the lack of food and water that the hunters have to endure, nor keep up the walking pace that the men set. If there are adults remaining in the encampment during the day, the boys stay and play. Otherwise, they go with their mothers while they gather. Girls, on the other hand, begin to gather seriously by about nine or ten years of age. At that age N!ai gathered for herself and her young husband, /Gunda, accompanying her mother, Di!ai, and her aunt, !U, and //Kushay and !Ungka, all of whom usually went gathering together. At any given time, therefore, one usually sees more boys than girls playing in an encampment.

When girls are at home and engaged in play during the day, their play is quieter than that of the boys. We did not see girls construct playthings such as the toy autos of the boys. They play the //gwashi a great deal. They play with the babies, they play "house," building little shelters and imitating the actions of daily life in them. Although most of their games were active games and they did enjoy the swing, they engaged in less lively physical activities throughout the day than did the middle-sized boys who ran around so much.

The great forte of the girls is to play their ball game and other singing games in the late afternoon, with the boys watching them. They make a charming sight, bedecked with their ornaments and moving gracefully and rhythmically together. When the aloes first bloomed in the spring they wore wreaths of the pink blossoms on their heads.

None of the girls' games is a contest in which an individual or group of individuals, a side, is the winner. The girls play several types of games: games of agility, such as hopping on one foot and jump rope; dramatic games in which they enact a little story; and singing games in which they move together in close physical contact, sing and clap in rhythmic coordination. Whereas most of the boys' games develop their muscles, the rhythmic singing games of the girls, besides giving pleasure, develop the girls' ability to sing and clap with exquisite precision the complex music of the great curing rite, the curing dance.

GIRLS' GAMES

The Ball Game

The ball game, which involves singing, dancing, and clapping, as well as catching a ball, is a great favorite among the girls and women. Teenaged girls, older women with their babies on their backs, younger girls—

all group together to play this game. The number of players ranges anywhere from three or four to larger groups of fifteen, sixteen, or more. At
Gautscha, where many visiting girls were present, the game was played
every day. Boys do not play this game by themselves, and they do not
join formally in playing with the girls, but they sometimes leap in and
seize the ball to tease and annoy the girls.

The girls usually use a tsama melon for a ball, choosing one about
three and a half or four inches in diameter. If no tsama is available, they
use some other piece of plant food that is round and of suitable size.

To begin the game the girls stand in a loose line, all singing and
clapping. The girl at the front of the line, Girl A, who is holding the ball,
runs forward five or six steps in rhythm with the singing. She pauses,
waiting for a specific point in the musical period. While she waits she
dances: she turns swiftly to one side, then to the other, takes a long step
backward with one foot, does a little hop, and takes a long step forward
with the same foot—or else she makes some less precise shuffling step.

The women's ball game

When the proper moment in the music arrives, Girl A tosses the ball to the next girl in the line, Girl B, who has run forward to be in a position to catch it. (The girls toss the ball in different ways. The most usual way is for the girl to remain facing forward and with her right hand toss the ball back in a low underhand pitch, past the right side. Another common way is for her to turn to the left and, looking back, toss the ball with her right hand past her left side.) Girl A then runs on with free running steps and takes her place at the end of the line of singing, clapping girls waiting their turns. B makes her forward and backward steps; at the right moment she tosses the ball to the next girl, C, and runs to the end of the line. Thus they all take their turns over and over again tirelessly for long periods of play.

The girls are lively; they play at a fast tempo with great vigor and much laughter. They leap and bend, they run, throw, and catch, all with large, open, graceful gestures. Their excellent sense of timing holds them strictly in the rhythmic pattern, and they seldom miss the ball. The babies on their mothers' backs jounce and blink in apparent contentment.

Nicholas England discusses the ball game songs in his study of Bushman music. The songs are called T'ama Kwisi, tsama (melon) play. England writes:

> There are approximately one dozen ball game songs in central Nyae Nyae—"approximately" because the recordings taken over the past decade by the PHKE [Peabody Harvard Kalahari Expeditions] include several fragments that might or might not be part of this repertory. Apparently little change has occurred in the number since the first PHKE recordings were made in 1953; at that time there were ten (?) songs. During the 1957–58 expedition, the women sang the same ten songs of four years earlier along with two additional songs that had been added to the repertory. Like the Medicine Songs, then, the Ball Game Songs form a stable repertory that is slow to change. . . .
>
> Some of the songs have no designation other than simply "Ball Game Songs." On the other hand, some have specific titles and often concomitant program notes that everyone knows as the story behind the song.[3]

On the whole, the songs are sung without words, although sometimes a singer may choose to utter a few words pertinent to the subject.

3. Nicholas England, "Music among the ʒũ'/wã-sí of South West Africa and Botswana" (Ph.D. diss., Harvard·University, 1968), p. 645. The whole ball game section is pp. 641–653.

The songs are accompanied with clapping, but not with the //gwashi. The women and girls have another repertory of songs that they sing with //gwashi accompaniment, to be mentioned later. The following are some examples of ball game songs and their subject-matter:[4]

1. Scaly Anteater[5] (n≠hōi) Song—about the anteater's slow walk, which the girls imitate, and the way ants stick to his long tongue.
2. Grey Loerie[6] (kwāētshi) Song—about the bird's song, "kuri mama."
3. Puff Adder (!gai) Song—composed by Khuan//a. The women say it is a sad song about a bad thing—a lament. Old N!aishi, Khuan//a's father, was bitten by a puff adder. He had been trying to prod a springhare out of its warren and had pulled out a puff adder instead. He thought he had killed it, but when he picked it up, it turned and bit his hand. Friends cut and sucked the bite. He survived, but he was very ill for a long time. His hand was permanently damaged, and he has been unable ever since to twirl a fire stick. During that time Khuan//a was bitten by "something with many legs" (undoubtedly a scorpion). Her hand was terribly swollen and sore. It was then she composed the song commemorating the events.
4. Wasp (!gun /kedi) Song—a very lively song about a particular species of wasp that often stings the women when they are gathering plant foods. The wasps are bad things, the women say.
5. Beetle (//goni) Song—about a beetle with a short neck. The beetle pinches the women's fingers between its head and its neck, when they are gathering.
6. Caterpillar (//kugo) Song—composed by Khuan//a. The girls sing it when they are gathering certain caterpillars that the !Kung enjoy eating. The song praises the caterpillars.
7. Dance Rattle (joro) Song—about the larvae[7] that are found in the cocoons from which dance rattles are commonly made. The cocoons, I was told, have short, stiff hairs on them, which prick one's fingers; the !Kung rub them off with a piece of wood, and then they open the cocoons and cook the larvae in ashes. The words of the song describe people who, although their hands itch from the hairs, are happy to have the larvae to eat.
8. !Xwa[8] Song—about women gathering !Xwa roots. The women feel lively and happy and make a song about their happiness.

4. This list is a combination of information in my notes and information contained in England's study.
5. Smutsia temminckii.
6. Corythaixoides concolor.
7. Lasciocampid Trabala (England, ibid., p. 362).
8. Fockea sp.

9. Old Kaross Song—about a girl who has a ragged, worn-out kaross. Other girls have new karosses that are beautiful. The girl of the song laments that she has no one to give her a new kaross.

10. /Gao Song—this song, England writes, concerns "a very young boy who drank his mother's urine and got a good, round scolding because of it."[9]

England continues:

Women and girls compose these songs when they are moved to do so by some person, place, thing, or incident. For example, there is Hwan//'a[Khuan//a Music] and her puff adder experience; she also composed the Caterpillar song. Beautiful !Ungka, [Da of /Gaishay and Khuan//a from Kai Kai] composed the /Gao song. The other songs are composed by women whose names are known, but who are either dead or living somewhere other than central Nyae Nyae. In their visiting, the women learn songs from each other; but from the stability of the repertory, mentioned earlier, it appears that additions to the ball game repertory of an encampment or vicinage are not often made.

Musically, the ball game songs are similar to the medicine and eland songs. They are choral polyphonies with clapping, and often there are motives and phrases that are transferred from the medicine repertory, for example, into that of the ball games. However, certain differences are immediately apparent between the ball game songs and the other vocal music repertories.

First of all, the musical periods are shorter. Second, the rhythm patterns and periods of the ball game songs are distinctive; they are most often composed of asymmetrical combinations of pulses so that their flow seems uneven and somewhat bumpy by comparison to the more steady beating of the dance songs. The overall impression of the ball game songs is one of rhythmic catchiness and high variety.[10]

Variants of the Ball Game

I saw two variant versions of the ball game, both of which were less strenuous than the regular version. In one, the players danced around and around in a circle, singing and clapping; the girl who had the ball passed it underhand to the person behind her.

The other version, I was told, was invented years ago by Old /Gam's great-grandmother. In contrast to the regular ball game, this version in-

9. England, ibid., p. 647.
10. England, ibid.

volves little or no dancing. The ball is the seed of a palm fruit, !hani.[11]

I saw it played by four girls and three women one day in November 1952, when the hunters returned without meat but with a young palm tree they had found during their search for game. The girls and women stood in line, one behind the other, singing and clapping. The first girl, A, ran out in front of the others, turned to face the line, tossed the palm seed to the next girl, B, and ran to take her place at the end of the line. B ran out and tossed the ball to C, ran to take her place behind A, and so forth.

N≠a n≠a hau

This game is usually played by girls alone, but occasionally we saw young boys join in. The game is named for a tree, the n≠a, that has big thorns.[12] Hau is uttered as a high-pitched little howl, and I believe it is a howl, not a word. The words of the song the girls sang when they played this game mean "Come let us hook"—that is, come let us hook our feet together.

Four or five girls, or perhaps as many as six or eight, form a close circle. They all face forward. Each girl, lifting her right leg, bending it at the knee, and extending it slightly inward toward the center of the circle, hooks her right foot into the bend of the knee of the girl behind her. Thus hooked together, the girls hop on their left feet, clapping each time their feet touch the ground. They hop around and around in the circle, going quite fast. They may make two or three turns around the circle before someone loses her balance and breaks her hold, perhaps tumbling down. Amid squeals and laughter the circle falls apart. Then the girls hook again and hop around again, perhaps this time reversing the direction, hopping on their right feet with their left feet hooked.[13]

11. *Hyphaene ventricosa* Kirk. The palm fruits, Story says, are a little smaller than a tennis ball, and the seeds are about a half-inch smaller in diameter than the fruits.

12. The n≠a tree is *Ziziphus mucronata* Willd. (Story, p. 32). Story writes: "As a rule it is very thorny, with the thorns in pairs, of which one is hooked and the other straight." The edible berries also called n≠a come from this tree. The Afrikaans people call this tree *wag-n-bietjie*, "wait-a-bit." I was one time caught by a wait-a-bit. If a wait-a-bit catches you by a garment you can free yourself by taking the garment off, but I was caught by my hair. I had to call out for help and wait till someone came with a knife to free me.

13. Charles Béart, in *Jeux et jouets d l'ouest africain* (Mémoires de l'Institut Francais d'Afrique Noire, no. 42; Dakar, Institut Francais Afrique Noire, 1955) I, 256–258, mentions several West African games that resemble N≠a n≠a hau. He includes a Dogon game (reported by Griaule) in which three players hook their right feet together: A's foot over B's calf, B's foot over C's calf, and C's foot over A's calf. The players then hop around in a circle, singing and clapping. The game can be played either by boys or girls. The boys call it "Bird's-Nest," and the girls call it "My Turtle-Dove Nest."

N≠a n≠a hau

A Form of "London Bridge"

Two girls stand facing each other, holding hands, their arms straight out from their shoulders. The other girls who are playing take turns running between the two, ducking under their arms. As each girl runs under, the two lower their arms (still holding hands) and trap the girl, who wriggles and twists to free herself.

Four Riding Games

Girl A makes a stirrup with her two hands held behind her, fingers interlaced. Girl B places her foot in A's hands, pulls herself up, and holds onto A's shoulders while A trots around and gives her a ride.

Girl A bends forward, and Girl B, facing upward, lies on A's back. Girl C holds B's feet up off the ground. A and C prance around giving B a ride. (Boys also play this game.)

Two girls run around carrying a third between them, one holding her by her shoulders, the other by her legs.

Girl A holds Girl B head down against her back, B's stomach against A's back. B's legs are bent at the hips so that they stick out straight over A's shoulders and are held by A. A walks around carrying B in this way.

Jump Rope

Jump rope is primarily a girls' activity, but several times we saw boys (both young boys and teen-agers) join in.

The girls play with ropes about eight feet long. They use the ropes that women make (from the leaf fibers of the plentiful sansevieria plant) to bind grass thatch to the frames of their shelters. Women only bother to do this binding during the season of heavy rains, when fearsome thunderstorms strike the shelters, and gusts of wind tear at the thatch. The girls know how to make these ropes, and could make one for themselves if none were available.

Singing a song called //Haru, two girls swing the rope; the others jump in turn. //Haru is a plant food that people especially enjoy (*Lapeynousia cyanescens*, #18). We saw several versions of the game, and there are no doubt others as well. One girl, or two girls together, may run in and stay for several swings, jumping the rope each time it hits the ground; or girls may take turns running in, jumping once, and running out. The girls may run through under the rope while it is above their heads. Another version involves swinging the rope in a large revolution, so that it hits the ground on the downward sweep, and then in a small revolution in which the rope does not hit the ground at all. A girl runs in and jumps the rope on the larger revolution, steps back and waits on the smaller revolution.

The girls are lithe and agile, and, with their excellent sense of timing, they seldom miss.

Dolls

Megan Biesele has told me that she saw !Kung girls making dolls of wound strips of cloth in Botswana in 1972. Some of them were quite elaborate and fanciful. One, she says, had protuberant buttocks, abbreviated limbs, and a stylized grace reminiscent of the rock paintings supposed to have been made by Bushmen. As the group who had these dolls were in close contact with Tswana and Herero people and also had access to cloth, doll-making of this sort may well be very recent among !Kung children. I myself saw no such dolls in South West Africa; I observed no dolls made from any material.

Hopping on One Foot

Hopping on one foot is a regular activity of the girls in their afternoon play. They sing the ball game songs to accompany the hopping; if a girl has both hands free, she claps.

The girls hop in pairs or in groups of three or four. In one version of the game, Girl A and Girl B face forward, A in front of B. B lifts one foot; A reaches back and grasps it by the heel or the big toe; A prances forward and B hops after her, clapping vigorously. In another version, A and B face each other. A grasps one of B's feet and they move a few steps forward and a few steps back, B clapping and hopping back and forth as best she can. Sometimes a third girl, C, joins A and B in the first version of the game. A holds up B's foot, and B holds up C's; B and C clap and hop after A. One time four girls made two pairs prancing and hopping together as A and B do in the first version; on that occasion they sang a song named for an evergreen tree, ≠gwa.[14] In still another version, A and B face each other. A holds up one of B's feet, say it is the left foot, with her right hand; B holds up A's left foot with her right hand. They sing and hop back and forth, but neither can clap.

Hopping on Two Feet

The girls form a circle and hold hands. Keeping their feet as close together as possible, they hop, two feet together, around in a circle. The song they sing as they play this game is called !Kau !Kau. I do not know the meaning of the name.

Girls' Dances

The girls have a number of little dances, most of which are usually performed with singing; some are also performed with clapping. Several of the dances are line dances, one is a jumping dance, and one a twisting dance. Generally five or six girls take part.

14. *Combretum coriaceum* Schinz.

The one that I saw performed most often is called the "Dance of the Old Kaross."[15] Singing, the girls move slowly forward a short distance, all stamping their right feet at certain points in the song. Then they move backward in the same manner. The song they sing concerns a girl who has an old, worn kaross and wishes for a beautiful new one like those the other women wear.

Another line dance is called "Caterpillar." In this dance the girls perform a movement of the shoulders, neck, and head that thrusts out the chin without tilting the head. They make this movement twice and then make a tiny hop forward. After they have done this a number of times they begin to move backward in the same manner.

In a third line dance, the girls stand as close together as possible and lean forward, each leaning on the back of the girl in front of her. They move forward slowly; then they all fall over and, still holding on to each other, lie on the ground a moment, laughing.

A fourth line dance involves the girls running very fast around and around the dance circle, singing and clapping.

The jumping dance is performed by two girls who face each other, holding hands and singing. Both girls stand with their legs in a straddle —both right feet forward and left feet back, or vice versa. Then they jump and take the other position—left feet forward. The dance continues in this way, the feet going back and forth in rapid alternation.

For the twisting dance two girls face each other and hold hands by hooking their index fingers. They dance a little step together and then, still holding hands, one girl twists around clockwise while the other twists around counterclockwise, until they are back-to-back; another twist and they face each other again. They repeat this movement several times, sometimes reversing the direction of the twist. Several pairs of girls may perform this dance at the same time.

After there have been a few heavy squalls of rain, the pan at Gautscha fills and becomes a lake a few inches deep. The girls then bathe and dance in the water. I have an image in my memory of an afternoon when I heard singing away out in the pan and, looking up, saw fourteen slender dark figures dancing, seven upright and seven mirrored in the water. The girls, in a line, danced with prancing steps, kicking the water

15. Nicholas England reports ("Music among the ʒū'/wã-si," p. 647) that this song is also sung for the ball game. In view of this, it seems possible that the song that accompanies the "Caterpillar" dance is the same as the ball game song called "Caterpillar."

into a spray on certain beats of their song. After a time, still singing, they bathed and ran gleaming wet to put on their karosses and run back along the path to the encampment.

BOYS' GAMES

The Porcupine Game, or Axe and Assagai Game, or War Game

The three names above were used for a game that was frequently played by men and boys. The game is played in essentially the same way, whichever name is used; the variations are only variations in style of play and in what the players say is represented.

The game is one of conflict. The formalized gestures simulate combat between two men, not group combat. The men say that the game is a "fight," n!i, and when one player is vanquished by another, they say he is "killed," ⁻!khi. Their word for playing this game is ≠nam, which means, according to Bleek's *Dictionary*, p. 670, "to beat, strike, or play (music—as upon a bow)." Bleek has the !Kung phrase //a !ni, which she translates "to play the war game" (*Dictionary*, p. 513). Lee says that in the Dobe area, the !Kung call the game n!haie ("war").

The "axe and assagai" name for the game refers to the weapons the men pretend to hold in their hands. We did not succeed in tracing the history or the significance of the name "porcupine," !xum. We were told that the old people had said that was the name of the game, but had not said why.

Part of the action of the game resembles the game of "Rock, Paper, and Scissors" or the game that some American boys call "Beat Up."

The porcupine or axe and assagai game is exclusively a game for males; it is never played by women and girls, although they may stay nearby watching and joining in the laughter. Men and boys from the age of eight or nine (or thereabouts) to early old age play together. Little boys do not have the sense to play; the very old do not have the energy. The others play in any combination of ages.

The game is played in any open space large enough to accommodate the players. It is played whenever a group takes a notion to play—usually that would be late afternoon or early evening. The men enjoy this game and play it very often.

Any number of players may participate. We have seen groups as small as two and as large as seventeen or eighteen. There may be an odd or an even number. (Ten is the number that I will use in describing the game here.) The players do not win and lose by teams or sides, but as individuals.

The players usually seat themselves, facing each other, in two lines about three feet apart (occasionally they play for a time standing):

A   B   C   D   E
F   G   H   I   J

They pretend that each holds an assagai in his right hand and an axe in his left.

There is evidently no formal rule determining who starts the game. We were told that the man with the biggest assagai starts. When we asked who had the biggest assagai, the men replied that it was the one who said he had it. What would happen, we asked, if some other player did not agree and claimed that his assagai was bigger? That never happens, they said.

Assume that A starts. He challenges any player in the opposite line —say it is F. They play; if A "kills" F, A challenges another player in the opposite line, and so forth until A himself is killed. The man who kills him (say it is H) challenges a player in A's line, but not A. A, who is killed, remains seated in the line and takes part in the general action, but he is not challenged again until a new game starts. H continues to challenge men in A's line until he is killed by one of them. That man then becomes the challenger and so the game goes on. When all the players but one are killed, they start a new game.

The play between the challenger and the challenged consists in both men throwing out one arm or the other in haphazard order, right or left, but on a certain pulse in a definite steady rhythmic pattern.

The members of the expeditions attempted to gain an understanding of the rules governing "winning" in this rapid and complex game. We came up with several different sets of rules and so are not able to say with finality whether some of them are wrong interpretations or whether there are alternative rules by which the game may be played. One of the sets of rules, however, is corroborated by the observations of Richard Lee (personal communication). Since it is the only set of which we have independent confirmation, I set it down here:

A challenges B. If, at a crucial moment (apparently governed by the musical phrase) when the two throw out their arms, A throws out his right arm and B his left, or A throws out his left arm, and B his right, then A loses (is "killed"). If A throws out his right arm and B throws out his right, or if both throw out their left arms, then B is killed (see Fig. 13).

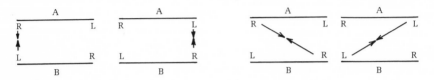

Fig. 13. "Kills" in the porcupine game

There appears to be no formality as to who starts the new game. It may be the man who was not killed in the previous game, but anyone who was enjoying the game and was vigorous, enthusiastic, and quick might be the first to resume the challenging.

All the while the challengers, the challenged, and all the other players, whether they have been killed or not, are accompanying the play with sound. They sit with their legs bent back under them, their buttocks resting either on their heels or on the ground between their heels. They sift the sand under their knees for thorns or sharp bits of stick, or they may place a kaross under their knees. As they play they thump the ground vigorously and loudly with their knees; soon they have beaten a hollow in the sand, two or three inches deep, with each knee. Their knees produce a loud, steady, regular percussion sound. The men add two more lines of percussion sound to the knee sound. Each man slaps his chest with his right hand, his thigh with his left hand, making a complex rhythmic pattern in rapid tempo. The arms of the challenger and the challenged are thrown out on a certain pulse in the rhythm pattern. The challenger often rises up on his knee and hurls his arm out with a yell as though throwing a weapon.

And all the while vocal sounds accompany the play. Intermittently the players may sing. When they do, the song is that of the Men's Dance or one of the songs of the Tshoma, the boys' initiation rite. But whether they slip into song or not, the players are constantly emitting grunts and gasps in a rhythmic pattern that fits into the percussion pattern of the thumping knees and slapping hands. And above the regular pulse of the thumping knees, slapping hands, grunts, and gasps are interspersed sharp hand claps, yelps, yells, shouts, cries of *oo-ha oo-ha*. In an exciting game, the latter sounds rise to a hubbub, but the regular pulse of the percussion sounds is always heard.

The play between the challenger and the challenged lasts for a varying number of seconds, until chance gives one or the other the victory—on the average perhaps ten or twelve seconds, but a player might be killed on the first throw. If there are enthusiastic players present and their mood is gay and the late afternoon air refreshing, the group might continue to play for an hour or two at a time. Two hours would be a long game, an hour and a half more usual. They often play for shorter periods. They always play for fun and with evident enjoyment.

Some men are considered to be better players than others. Gao and /Ti!kay were very good. ≠Toma was good too, although he was not as enthusiastic a player as the former men and often sat watching the play instead of participating. Of the younger men who were all good, several were thought to be especially so: //Ao, brother-in-law of Gao, /Gunda, the husband of N!ai, and //Ao Wildebeest.

A man can be a good player in two ways. Chance accounts for most victories, but if a man is alert and attentive and if he watches his adversary sharply, he notices if the adversary tends to fall into a habitual pattern of throwing out one arm or the other and can quickly vanquish him. The arms are all in constant rapid motion, slapping chests and thighs, making short feinting gestures of throwing, but a good player appears to be able to catch some clues and in a split second see which arm is coming. Some players in any case are victorious more often than others. An indifferent, lethargic player would fall easy prey to a skilled enthusiast.

The other way to be a good player in !Kung estimation is to be good at pantomime. Many !Kung are highly talented in imitating human and animal movements, and all are highly amused at clever imitation. People enjoy the players who act out their combats, throwing their arms with violence, as though hurling weapons, with yelps and yells. After a man has killed his opponent with his right arm (with his "assagai"), he may follow with a mimed blow with his axe—his left arm. Some of their gestures are stylized. Fluttering the fingers of the right hand means that the assagai is trembling. By flickering his hand past his ear, a player pretends that a missile has just whizzed by him. A sidewise slash of the left hand with the palm up means the wielding of the axe. A man who has just killed another makes a gesture of throwing something over his shoulder. This is the gesture people commonly make when they say that a person is dead.

On two or three occasions when the men called the game Porcupine, they wore porcupine quills in their hair and imitated porcupines to some extent. They made claw marks in the sand with their fingers, snarling ferociously; and when one was killed one time, he rolled into a ball and imitated a porcupine's twitching death throes till everyone guffawed with laughter, and the game paused till the porcupine was dead.

Apparently the players make no great ado about winning or losing. A man likes to vanquish his opponent in a given play, but no score is kept to see who wins most often. The fun is in the playing. I have seen boys' faces fall in sharp disappointment for a few seconds when they were "killed," but they wait their turn again and no one gets angry or sulky. The mood is gay, and there is much laughter. Most of the laughter pours upon the vanquished who laugh with the others at themselves. Approval is expressed in nods and smiles for the cleverness of the victor.

Tug-of-War

We saw only young boys play tug-of-war. They would form two groups of three or four boys each. The groups would sit facing each other, close together, the players in each group bunched together, their knees up and their feet more or less braced. For the rope they used a short length of hose, which someone on our staff had given them. Ordinarily they would have used a piece of sansevieria-fiber rope, or a piece of leather cut like a strap. The boys would grab hold of the hose and begin to tug, holding on tenaciously, straining and grunting, till those on one side pulled the other side over on top of them in a heap. Then they would untangle themselves and go at their tugging again. Sometimes the boys on one side would let go of the rope, and the others would all fall back.

One of the ancient tales of the !Kung tells how the fate of the Bushmen was decided by a tug-of-war. Long, long ago the Bushmen and the black people were one nation. One day the Creator commanded them to have a tug-of-war. The black people were on one side, the Bushmen on the other, in equal numbers. The rope the Creator made for them to pull had two parts to it, which were knotted together in the middle. One part of the rope, the part given to the black people to pull on, was made of the hides of animals, which had been cut into long, pliable strips and twisted together. (Such a rope is called a *riem* in Afrikaans.) The half of the rope that was given to the Bushmen was made of !hwi (sansevieria fibers). The tug-of-war began, and the rope broke. The black people had the *riem* end, the Bushmen had the !hwi end. This meant, we were told, that the black people got the best things: they got cattle, sheep, goats, and milk to drink; they also got the knowledge of hoeing and planting. The Bushmen got the less-good things: they make their living as best they can with !hwi. They make bowstring and snares with it, and thus they live. /Qui, telling this story to us one day, said that the Bushmen had been foolish to take the fiber end of the rope. Laughing, he said that he wished the pulling could be repeated now. He would see that the Bushmen took the *riem* end.

Stick Throwing

Stick throwing is a favorite activity of boys and young men.[16] I have the impression that the boys from about eight years old through the middle teens threw sticks for hours on end every day. Often the young men joined in. Smaller boys threw sticks too, imitating the older ones. The !Kung boys played very strenuously, setting a fast pace and pouring their vast energy into the game.

At Gautscha the boys played on the enormous ancient anthill that lay beside the shelters of Band 1. It was an ideal place for stick throwing. The material of anthills is very hard, quite unlike the loose, sandy soil that prevails in the Kalahari. This hill had long been abandoned by the ants and had been worn down by wind and rain till it was about five or six feet high at the peak. Its sides had come to the gentle slope of the "angle of repose" (the angle at which earth rests without sliding).

The boys prepare the sticks themselves by peeling off the bark and smoothing and tapering the stick. The finished stick is straight, two to three feet long, tapered at one end, and slender, but large enough in diameter (usually just under half an inch) to be fairly rigid.

Each boy takes a turn in the stick throwing. Holding the thicker end of the stick in his right hand,[17] he runs up to a certain spot and throws the stick with all his might. To make the throw, a boy swings his

16. Bleek reports that among the Nharo (Naron), stick throwing is "a man's amusement, even middle-aged men join in" (Bleek, *The Naron*, University of Cape Town Publications of the School of African Life and Language, Cambridge, At the University Press, 1928, p. 21).

17. All the boys I observed were right-handed. I assume there must be left-handed Bushmen, but in my casual observations I did not see any.

right arm back, up, and over in an arc. He slams his stick downward as hard as he can as his arm starts its downward swing. The momentum of his running goes into the throw. He puts the whole weight of his torso and the whole strength of his muscles into it also. By the time the throw has been completed the boy is leaning far forward, his right foot high in the air, his right arm sweeping past his left knee. The thick end of the stick, which the boy was holding, strikes the ground not far (ten feet or so) from the thrower. The stick bounces off and sails forward for varying distances—another twenty feet, perhaps. A thirty-foot sail would be a good long one. When they played on the anthill they aimed their sticks to hit just below the peak; the sticks sailed over the peak into the air beyond.

As fast as he can, the next boy runs to approximately the same spot (there is no marker or line drawn on the ground) and throws his stick. The boys take turns till all have thrown their sticks. Then they rush to pick them up, each his own, and repeat the performance, either throwing the sticks back in the opposite direction, or running to the original position and throwing again from that spot.

The boys do not appear to be in ardent competition with each other. No score is kept; no one emerges a winner from the session. Each boy tries simply to make the stick sail as far as he can. They take notice of a good throw and acclaim it, and the thrower smiles in pleasure. The fun seems to be in the action, in throwing well, and in seeing the sticks fly. Stick throwing develops arm muscles and helps to strengthen a boy's arms for throwing an assagai.

Rides on an Old Kaross

One of the boys' favorite games is pulling the younger children around on an old kaross. A young child or two is put down on the kaross, and two or three of the older boys take hold of the front part of the kaross and run as fast as they can, dragging the kaross behind them. The younger children delight in this game and always want a turn; the babies often seem not to want rides, but they get them anyway. Occasionally one of the older boys will get on the kaross himself, and the others will pull him around. The anthill at Gautscha was a fine place for the kaross rides.

Once I saw the boys play this game using, instead of an old kaross, a pair of gemsbok horns (still joined together by the top of the animal's skull) that had been discarded when the gemsbok head was cooked and eaten.

Airplane

The boys sometimes varied the kaross rides by carrying the kaross instead of dragging it. Four boys, one at each corner, would pick up the kaross and run around, carrying a small child in the kaross.

After November 1952 the boys called this game "Airplane." In that month we had an epidemic of flu. A man from Kubi had come on a visit to Gautscha.[18] He became very ill the night after his arrival. In four days he recovered and returned to Kubi, but people had been exposed to the infection, and soon they too fell ill. A number were visiting at Gautscha from several bands; in all there were seventy-two people encamped around us. The infection raced from one to another; people went down in waves like wheat before the scythe. As some improved others fell ill. We nursed them ardently, taking turns to keep a night watch, giving them water and food and giving them their medicines on time.[19] Supported by Merck's *Manual* we had decided to give antibiotics. All accepted our care gratefully and obeyed our instructions to stay and rest. They were too sick (with temperatures of 103° and 104°) to do much else. We were frantically worried nonetheless, and when our medicine began to run out we sent Charles Handley out to Grootfontein for help. He asked Dr. Malherbe to come back with him. They chartered a small plane and were flown in by Pilot Schink, who was famous in South West Africa for finding ways to land in the bundu. Pilot Schink had never been to Gautscha and did not know the way; he had to fly low and, with Charles Handley's help, follow the faint track our expedition trucks had made between Samangaigai and Gautscha. When the plane landed on the pan our little community of Bushmen and expedition staff was wild with excitement.[20] Dr. Malherbe examined all our patients, found only one with pneumonia, gave us our instructions and the medicine we needed, and flew away again, leaving us considerably comforted. In another few days everyone had recovered. It was after this that the boys called the kaross ride "Airplane" and ran about imitating the sound of the engine.

18. This man was Gumtsa, the father of N!ai. He had come to protest N!ai's betrothal to /Gunda.

19. We had not made gifts of food or water previously, wanting to observe the !Kung in their own ways of gathering and hunting, but during this illness we gave food and water to all.

20. This was the first airplane the Bushmen had seen close up, but it was not the first they knew of airplanes. Occasionally, a transcontinental plane crossed that part of the Kalahari high overhead. The Bushmen knew the planes were manmade but called them "vultures."

The boys played airplane in other ways as well. Tsamgao one day caught a large moth. He held it cupped in his hands and listened to its whirring wings, moving his hands back and forth in the air, saying "airplane, airplane." Then he threaded the live moth onto the end of a slender stick and ran with it while it whirred out its last moments of life.

On another occasion he caught a bird, tied a cord securely to its leg, and played airplane with it till it was too exhausted even to flutter any more. He then without concern abandoned it to die. This attitude toward living creatures was general among the !Kung, not peculiar to Tsamgao. They showed no concern for wounded creatures and no compunction for the pain they might be causing them. The boys shot thorns into beetles with little bows and left the beetles to die. Children (both boys and girls) pulled legs off live grasshoppers; they one day played with a baby rabbit till they killed it; and a boy once whacked to death a young mongoose, an animal the !Kung avoid eating. Our sentimental attitudes toward animals were not shared by the !Kung. To kill animals is the way of life among hunters.

Hobbyhorse

One day the boys tied a heavy cord between two trees and hung a piece of an old kaross over it for a saddle. One at a time they sat astride the saddle and pretended they were riding a horse.

Tree Climbing

Tree climbing is an activity of boys and men. For the men it is part of their work as hunters: they climb high in the baobab trees to look out over the country and see if game is stirring. Sometimes they hammer pegs into the tree to climb by; they had done this for one of the enormous baobabs near Gautscha.

The boys climb trees for pleasure. They climbed the baobab with pegs in it, but they liked another baobab better, one that had no pegs. They climbed this one frequently in spite of the fact that a big snake was thought to live in it. But there was an ever better climbing tree, not a baobab, that stood at the edge of the dance circle at Gautscha. Its branches offered more challenges to their acrobatic skills than the baobab's did: the boys walked upright along them, swung from them, jumped down from them, clung to them with hands and feet like sloths.

Swings

Swings were a delight for both boys and girls. The boys rigged them, knotting two or three straplike pieces of leather into a loop and slinging one end over a branch. The swing at Gautscha, more tame than some the boys made, hung from a low branch of the tree near the dance circle. A child sitting in it when it was at rest was not much more than two feet off the ground.

The children took turns pushing each other in the swing. Older children gave the younger ones a fair share of turns. Sometimes those who were waiting stood in a line in front of the child in the swing, at the farthest point of the swing's arc. One after another they took turns standing at the front of the line and letting the child swing into them with his legs stuck straight out. Some stood back so that his toes barely touched them; others let themselves be toppled over.

Bows and Arrows

When boys are about two years old their parents make little bows and blunt arrows for them to play with. From then on boys play at shooting. The boys at Gautscha aged from about seven into their teens did this a great deal. They made bows of various sizes for themselves. Tsamgao had made two bows, a tiny one about eight inches across when strung, and a larger one. From the tiny bow he shot thorns into dung beetles and any other little living thing that moved. From the larger bow he—like all the other boys—shot at birds, especially those that lived near the water hole. I never saw a boy hit a bird, but they never gave up trying. They also practiced shooting at a stationary target, an anthill not far from the encampment (not the old weathered one the boys threw sticks against and on which the girls made sand-patterns, but a pinnacle, about seven feet high). Sometimes their arrows penetrated it, but usually they just bounced off; in either case the boys could see where their arrows struck and could practice to correct their aim.

Autos

Not long after our arrival in 1952, with four trucks and a jeep, the boys at Gautscha took to making models of vehicles out of tubers or bulbs. They called these models "autos," pronouncing the first syllable "ow."

Tsamgao was the inventor. We guessed that he was about ten at the time. All the boys from about seven into early teens followed his lead and made autos for themselves, and playing auto became a favorite game, played for hours at a time. The boys pushed their autos with long, thin sticks or pulled them with sansevieria cords. They ran around and around in any of the nearby open spaces, imitating the sounds of motors starting and running in different gears. (They rather specialized in the roar of low gear pulling out of heavy sand.) Some of the boys made models of men and placed them in the autos as drivers; when they did so they named the drivers for themselves. Several of the autos were equipped with spare tires (actually the whole wheel with the spare). When Tsamgao changed tires he went through all the gestures of unscrewing the bolts, taking the tire off, placing the new tire on the axle, tightening the bolt again, pumping it up (with an imaginary pump), and testing the pressure (with an imaginary tire gauge). He would find the pressure too high and would let out some of the air, making a hiss; then he would imitate the sound of the starter and set forth again.

Tsamgao's original model was made out of a carrotlike root. The four wheels were slices from the small end, and the rest of the root was the body, with the wide end at the front. The body was partially hollowed out to represent the interior; a portion left unhollowed at the front was the hood. The axles were straight twigs running through the body and protruding on each side more than an inch. The wheels, properly rounded and with a hole gouged in the center, were set on the axles, and bits of soft bark were wound around the axles to hold the wheels on. Grooves were made in the wheels to represent tire treads. Headlights, the last detail of construction, were little onionlike bulbs fastened to the auto with tiny sticks.

The other boys' autos generally followed Tsamgao's design but were made from various roots and plant materials and had many variations in detail and proportion. Some of the boys later began to ask members of our expeditions for pieces of cardboard, discarded cartons, or file card boxes with which to make auto bodies; they also asked for empty film-spools to use as wheels for these larger autos.

Some of the younger boys (up to about seven or eight years old) played with a simpler kind of auto—an empty tortoise shell turned upside down, which they pushed around with a stick. The tire-changing and sound effects drama that accompanied play with the tuber autos was not evoked by the tortoise shells; mostly the younger boys just said "Brrrr."

Tsamgao's Gun

In 1955 we saw the boys playing with toy guns made out of reeds. We had not seen this on the previous expeditions. When I asked about them, I was told that the guns were copies the boys had made of one that Tsamgao had invented sometime after we left in 1953. All the boys and adults of whom I inquired stated that the gun was entirely Tsamgao's invention; no one, they said, had shown him how to make it or helped him construct it.[21] Once Tsamgao had made the gun, other boys copied it; there were several in use in 1955, of slightly varying size but of the same construction.

Tsamgao's gun was made of a 12- or 13-inch length of sturdy segmented reed that was hollow between the nodules. The reed, called n//ahru, was about ½ inch in diameter. About 4½ inches in from one end—the front or muzzle end—a slot was cut all the way through the reed. The slot ended at a nodule about 7 inches from the front. As there were no other nodules from this point forward to the muzzle, the barrel of the gun was hollow. Into the slot one end of a thin strip (about 12 inches long) of supple, resilient wood or heavy, peeled bark was inserted, protruding an inch or so below the reed. The strip arched back from the slot, above the reed, and the other end of the strip was inserted into a small cut in the reed, about an inch behind the nodule at the back of the slot. Another small cut had been made on the underside of the reed, and the end of the strip protruded below the reed from this cut as from the slot.[22] This strip was the gun's trigger.

Tsamgao's ammunition consisted of small darts 1½ inches long. They were made from pieces of strong grass or tiny reeds, with little

21. Tsamgao had seen our guns, and he had seen the fabulously old firearms of the Herero at Kai Kai on several occasions when he visited there with his family. I was told that it was one of the Herero guns that had inspired him. As I had never seen a toy gun like Tsamgao's among any of the Bushman or Bantu peoples I had encountered in 1951 and 1952–53, I did not inquire further to find out whether Tsamgao might have seen a Herero (or Tswana) child playing with a similar toy. This possibility did not occur to me until I saw in Béart (Jeux et jouets, I, 173) the drawing of a virtually identical toy made by Malinke children in Guinea. Béart remarks, moreover, that guns of this general design are found all over the world. Therefore, it must be considered a possibility that Tsamgao got the idea for his gun from a Bantu child's model.

22. This is the way I remember the gun, and it would seem to be the most efficient way of constructing it so as to hold the strip firmly in the reed. However, in Béart's drawing of the Malinke toy (and also in his drawings of other West African toy guns of the same type), the strip does not protrude below the reed—it is held in the reed only by the cut on the reed's upper surface. The photographs of Tsamgao's gun that were taken on our expedition fail to show this detail clearly.

Tsamgao's gun

thorns stuck into one end. To load the gun Tsamgao used his finger to press the end of the strip protruding from the slot firmly back against the nodule; holding the strip back he placed a dart in the slot, pushing the thorn-tipped point only a little way into the barrel, so that the other end of the dart still extended into the slot. To shoot he held the gun with both hands and took aim. His left hand steadied the butt, his right hand cradled the gun under the trigger, his right index finger held the trigger back firmly. When ready, he released the trigger, which snapped smartly forward and projected the dart through the barrel into the target—a piece of root lying about 6 inches from the muzzle. Tsamgao never missed.

Tsamgao's Camera

The inventive Tsamgao also carved a little camera out of a tuber, modeling it after our Leica. He carried it about, snapping pictures as we did, holding the camera to his eye and pretending to focus.

As these examples show, in each case it was Tsamgao who first made most of the inventions. He made the first auto, the toy gun, the camera, and the airplane. Other boys were quick to follow his lead, but he was definitely the innovator.

Djani

A *djani* is an exquisite winged toy. Tossed high in the air, it floats down vertically, spinning. Boys and young men play with the djani; girls never do. The game is a favorite one played almost every day for long periods at a time.

To make a djani, a boy uses a length of hollow segmented reed. The reed, though light, is strong. The length of the piece used varies: those I measured were between 10 and 13 inches long. A tuft of guinea fowl down is thrust into the top of the reed where it stays without glue or binding. About an inch above the middle of the reed, a guinea fowl feather about 5 inches long is bound to the reed in such a way that it slants out from the reed a little. The binding is sinew.

A thong is bound with sinew to the bottom of the reed, and a weight is attached to the djani by this thong. If a mangetti nut is used as the weight, a hole is bored through it with an awl, and the nut is strung on the thong which is then knotted at the end. A lump of gum from a tree may be used instead: while still moist, it is pressed around the thong and allowed to dry.

When I observed /Gaishay [1.18] making the djani in the figure, I noticed that he took care to trim the thong with a knife until it was the right width and perfectly straight. To trim the feather, he took from the fire a stick that was glowing at the end and burned the ragged edges off making the feather symmetrical.

The number of boys we saw playing with a djani was rarely less than three or more than six or eight, but there is no set number. Each boy holds a smooth straight stick about two feet long tapered at one end.[23] To begin playing, one boy throws the djani by hand up into the air as high as he can. Because of the weight on the end, the djani travels bottom end up. When the djani begins to fall, the weight straightens it into a vertical position, the feather and the tuft of down are caught by the breeze, and the djani floats down spinning. The breeze wafts it here and there, and the boys—leaping through grass and thorny brush as freely as little steenboks—run to be under it when it comes down. The

23. /Gaishay, in preparing the stick shown in the figure, peeled the bark off the tapered end but left it on the other end (the end he held).

The djani

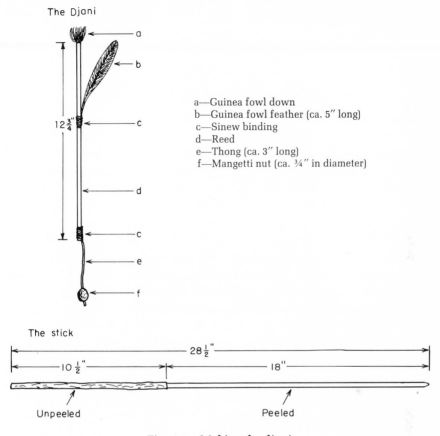

The Djani

a—Guinea fowl down
b—Guinea fowl feather (ca. 5″ long)
c—Sinew binding
d—Reed
e—Thong (ca. 3″ long)
f—Mangetti nut (ca. ¾″ in diameter)

Fig. 14.   Making the djani

object is to catch the djani on the stick and toss it up again before it touches the ground. The boys are skilled at this; they catch the djani at the thong and with a strong flip of the stick hurl it back up into the air high above the trees.

Not infrequently a djani gets caught in a tree. If the boys cannot reach it by climbing, they do so with a springhare hook.

Competition among the boys is not systematic, but each likes to toss the djani and tries to be the one to catch it, and I have seen a boy do a bit of pushing and shoving to get another boy out of the way.

In Bleek's *Dictionary* (p. 32), the name of the toy, spelled "dzanne," is listed (with the definition "plaything, shuttlecock") as having been reported by L. C. Lloyd, whose research into the !Kung language took place during the years 1879 to 1882. The djani may be a toy of great antiquity. It plays a crucial part in both the !Kung and the /Gwi tales about the giving of fire to mankind. The tales follow.

The !Kung Tale of How Fire Was Given to Mankind

Long, long ago there was a man named /Ka /Kani. This man had fire, and the name of the fire was *doro*.[24] With his fire /Ka /Kani cooked food for himself and his children. All other people ate raw food. /Ka /Kani had a food called //*haru,* a white root dug from the earth. There was a man named Huwe. One day Huwe went to visit /Ka /Kani.[25] /Ka /Kani was not at home; only his children were there. The children were eating. Huwe asked them to give him some food. They gave him some, and when Huwe ate it, he said, "Oh, you eat nice cooked food. We eat raw food. How do you cook your food?" The children answered, "Our father has a nice thing and he always gives us cooked food. We do not eat uncooked food. He does all good things for us." Huwe said, "I shall come back tomorrow and eat this kind of food again."

The next day, Huwe came back. Before he reached their dwelling place he saw /Ka /Kani and his children digging for roots in the ground. Huwe hid himself behind a tree and watched. When /Ka /Kani and his children had dug enough roots, they returned to their dwelling place. /Ka /Kani went to the place where he hid his fire sticks. He took them and started to make a fire. He twirled and twirled the upper fire stick, and as he twirled he said, "Fire will come, fire will come." Fire did come, and /Ka /Kani built up the fire and started to cook the roots that he and his children had dug. He then hid his fire sticks again.

---

24. The !Kung word for fire is -*da*. *Doro,* said to be the name of /Ka /Kani's fire, is given as a noun and a verb in Bleek's *Dictionary* (p. 28). As a verb, *doro* means "to twirl, pierce, bore, rub fire." This verb occurs in central and northern Bushman languages. *Doro* as a noun appears in southern, central, and northern languages and is translated in the *Dictionary* as "fire stick" or "tinderbox."

25. Our family collected different versions of this tale. The version presented here was told me by Old /Qui [Band 7]. His name for the protagonist of the tale, the fire giver, was Huwe. This is one of the names of the great God of the Nyae Nyae !Kung. In other versions of this tale, the name given was ≠Gao N!a, which is another of the names of the great God, and the name usually given to the protagonist in the !Kung tales. In other versions of this tale, I heard the name /Ka /Kani pronounced differently—/Kai /Kani in one version, /Kai /Kini in another. In Botswana, this character is known as /"xe tsunini, which is short for /"xashe (/Gaishay, a man's name) tsunini. Doke reports /ka/ka:ne as a !Kung word for "upper fire stick" (Bleek, *Dictionary*, p. 305). It seems likely that this word is the same as the name of the man who possessed fire. Fire Stick seems to me a most appropriate name for the possessor of fire.

All the time Huwe was watching. He watched very carefully when /Ka /Kani hid the fire sticks. When the roots were cooked and /Ka /Kani and the children were preparing to eat them, Huwe came out from his hiding place and went to them as a visitor, and they all ate together.

Huwe then said, "Now we must play." /Ka /Kani asked what game they must play. Huwe made two djani that had guinea fowl feathers, and he and /Ka /Kani began to play. But the djani did not fly well, and Huwe could not get /Ka /Kani away from his dwelling place. So he said, "The guinea fowl feathers are no good. We must get paouw feathers." When they put the paouw feathers on, the two djani flew high. /Ka /Kani tossed his djani to the eastern side. Huwe tossed his to the western side. And then Huwe opened the wind, and the wind came from the eastern side and blew /Ka /Kani's djani over to the western side. /Ka /Kani followed it and passed Huwe and went farther. Huwe followed. When /Ka /Kani was far away, Huwe ran back to the place where the fire sticks were hidden. He seized the sticks, broke them into little pieces, and threw them over the whole world crying, "All the world is going to get fire now! Fire! Fire! Through the whole world!" /Ka /Kani stopped his play and came and looked at Huwe. Huwe told him, "It is not right that you alone should have fire. From now on you will not be a person. You will be a little bird." And /Ka /Kani was changed into a bird called ≠ore.[26]

Since then there has been fire in every piece of wood, and all men can get it out and cook their food. These events were told by the old old people. They happened long ago.

The /Gwi Tale of How Fire Was Given to Mankind and How the Sun Was Created

Pisiboro[27] went looking for berries. When he returned to his home he saw Ostrich nearby eating some berries. Pisiboro walked up to Ostrich. Just as Ostrich lifted his hand to pick some more berries, Pisiboro smelled fire. Ostrich had fire under his arm; it was a coal. Pisiboro noticed this. He went back to his home; he slept, and in the morning he

---

26. The bird ≠ore, we were told, comes in the season of the rains. It has a red collar, a green chest, a black spot on its head, and white stripes on its cheeks.

27. The protagonist of the /Gwi tales had three names. Pisiboro was the name used in most of the tales. We were told that another of his names was //Gama, but we did not hear this name used. The third name was N!iriba. The portion of the present tale that concerns the creation of the sun was told to us by Ukwane on two different occasions. The first time he told it, Ukwane used the name Pisiboro for the protagonist; the second time he told it he used the name N!iriba.

went again to the place where Ostrich was picking berries. Both he and Ostrich picked and ate berries for a time. Pisiboro presently told Ostrich to try to pick the berries that were highest up. When Ostrich reached up, Pisiboro grabbed the fire from under his arm and ran away with it. Pisiboro ran and ran with it, till he came to an anthill. He threw the fire onto the anthill and the fire broke into bits. After that Pisiboro told the fire to run and hide in a ≠uri bush and also to go into all the fruit bushes and into all the stones it could find. Pisiboro disappeared in a bush called n≠i n≠i.[28]

After that Pisiboro made a *zani* [the /Gwi word for djani]. He took the wing of a korhaan. Then he took fire and burned the edges of the wing all around. Then he bound the wing to a reed with a cord. The wing was near the top of the reed. On the other end of the reed he tied the coal also with a cord.[29] (Thus he made a zani.) He tossed the zani up into the air with a stick. It fell and he caught it with his stick and tossed it again, hoping to toss it so high it would not fall again, but it fell. A third time he tossed it. This time it stayed up. It is the sun. It cut the night that was there and made the day and the night. Thus Pisiboro had light. Before that time, people had been living in darkness. The sun gave them light.

GAMES PLAYED BOTH BY GIRLS ALONE AND BOYS ALONE
Patterns in the Sand

Boys playing "Tortoise," as they said, made a pattern in the sand with their feet, singing a song the while. Moving backward and taking very small steps, their toes turned out, they printed each step carefully and symmetrically, and each time dug their toes in more deeply than their heels, to represent the tortoise's footprint.

Girls also made patterns in the sand with their feet. Those I saw moved very slowly forward, their toes slightly turned out, overlapping one tiny imprint with the next. The pattern resembled overlapping leaves. The girls said it did not mean anything, it was just play.

---

28. Ukwane told us that the ≠uri bush has yellow fruit, and that the n≠i n≠i bush is the one from which the /Gwi cut sticks to use as the upper fire stick. He went on to say that Pisiboro told the fire to go into all the fruit bushes so that its heat would ripen the fruit and people would have ripe fruit to eat. Ukwane also said, in response to a question about the fire's going into all the stones, that if one has a piece of metal he can strike a spark of fire out of the stone with it.

29. Ukwane told us that /Gwi boys weight the *zani* (and he did so when he was young) by attaching a piece of the nest of the Penduline Tit (*Anthoscopus minutus* [Roberts, *Birds*, No. 530]), rolled into a ball.

Sound Patterns Made with Feet

The !Kung—men, women, or children—if the fancy takes them, and a suitable object presents itself, enjoy dancing and tapping their feet in such a way as to make rhythmic patterns or to imitate familiar sounds, like a tap dancer on a vaudeville stage. The suitable object would be a stone or log or root with a smooth, flat, slanted surface. They stand in front of such an object and with incredible speed hop and stamp on the ground and tap their feet on the stone or log.

Some were extremely skilled in this play. One woman could imitate the sound of a galloping horse to perfection. Two men had worked out a rhythmic pattern together. Their four feet moved so fast, stamping and tapping, that one could not follow them with the eye, but one could follow with the ear a flawless intricate rapid rhythmic pattern. Little N!ai knew a certain stone and always danced upon it when she passed it, making a gay rippling pattern of sound.

Sound Patterns Made with Hands

Girls make a sound pattern by patting their foreheads and lips in rapid tempo.

String Figures

On a few occasions we saw young women, girls, and young boys make string figures. I do not think that string figures are a highly developed art among the !Kung, and they did not seem to be a frequent pastime; but I cannot speak with certainty about this.

I am able to identify one string figure that was made by several people on different occasions. I do not know if the !Kung make other string figures in addition to this one. A few of the unsystematic photographs taken by members of our expeditions seem to show stages in the construction of a second (or possibly a second and a third) string figure, but the finished figures are not shown, and I am unable to identify them.

The figure I can identify is shown in the photograph. It is recorded in Jayne's *String Figures*, where it is called "Osage Diamonds."[30] Mrs.

---

30. Caroline Furness Jayne, *String Figures: A Study of Cat's Cradle in Many Lands* (New York, Charles Scribner's Sons, 1906), pp. 24–27.

N≠isa, the young wife of /Gao Music, making a string figure

Jayne saw it made in 1904 by an Osage Indian from Oklahoma. She writes that the figure has also been collected in the Hawaiian Islands and in Ireland.

Wedgwood and Schapera record the same figure among several

made by the Kxatla in Mochudi, Botswana.[31] The Kxatla call the figure *Setswaldô,* "A Gate."[32] The authors cite reports of the figure for the Temne, Sherbro, Kru, Mende, BaToka, BaRotse, Asena, Yoruba, and BaThonga.

The !Kung use the method common to the Osage and Kxatla in making the figure.[33]

During the 1957–58 expedition, of which I was not a member, N!ai was seen making a string figure on her toes. In the film that was made of her, I see that she used both hands to manipulate the strings.

In making the string figures, the !Kung use either a cord made from sansevieria fiber or a lighter-weight cord made of fibers from a long, carrot-shaped, carrot-colored root.

MIXED GROUP GAMES

Tsi tsi gwara

A possible translation of this name is "Behind behind move." Whereas I saw some games played almost every day, I saw *tsi tsi gwara* played only twice. The !Kung tended to play the less-structured games more commonly than the structured ones. Tsi tsi gwara is structured in form but has no drama associated with it—at least no one seemed to know of any. Any number of players may participate; they may be male and female. One occasion on which we saw the game played was a July morning in 1953. A group of young women and girls and younger boys played it with evident enjoyment on that occasion. Old /Gasa, Old //Khuga, and //Kushay (wife of /Qui) had much to say in teaching the young boys what to do.

31. Camilla H. Wedgwood and I. Schapera, "String Figures from Bechuanaland Protectorate," *Bantu Studies* 4 (Dec. 1930), 251–268. The figure in question is shown in Figure II of Plate I, and on p. 257 (Figure II): its construction is described on pp. 255–256. Of the Kxatla the authors write: "The BaKxatla of Bechuanaland Protectorate arrived there some sixty years ago, having left the Western Transvaal, their former home, as the result of conflict with the local European authorities" (p. 252).

32. Other names reported for the figure by Mrs. Jayne and by Wedgwood and Schapera are: *Ma-ka-lii-lii* and *Pu-kau-la* (Hawaiian Islands); "The Ladder" and "The Fence" (Ireland); "Four Eyes" (Mende); *Amadande* (BaToka); and "Calabash Net" (Yoruba). The name "Osage Diamonds" is Mrs. Jayne's own—her Osage informant had no name for the figure. Mrs. Jayne also writes that the figure "is known among Indians, sometimes as 'Jacob's Ladder.' " I unfortunately did not know enough about string figures at that time to ask the !Kung if they had a name for the figure.

33. A person uses his right hand to pick up the left rear index string, places it over his left thumb, and then uses his left hand similarly for the right near index string. Mrs. Jayne says this is the usual Indian way. This way of beginning is called Opening A.

The players form a circle facing inward (see Fig. 15). A's left hand holds B's right hand, B's left hand holds C's right hand, and so forth; this is Position 1. They begin to dance around in a counterclockwise direction, with big sideward steps, moving faster and faster till some of the players begin to fall down. As they stumble, the players beside them pull them up without letting go their hands. To keep their handholds is a point of the game.

After dancing in the circle a moment or two, H and A let go their handhold and the circle swings open to become a line. H is its leader. He begins the second phase of the game by running under the raised arms and held hands of A and B. Gripping each other's hands, all the players in the line follow after H. They run under from front to back, and as they do so they turn to their right. C is the last player to run under. He is holding B's left hand, and his motion of running under makes B spin completely around in place, turning in a clockwise direction. Coming to a stop, B is standing close to A facing in the same direction as when he started. His right arm has been pulled up across his chest, his right hand is on his left shoulder clinging to A's left hand; A's left arm is pulled up across B's back. B is in Position 2.

C stands beside B as before, still holding his left hand. H now repeats the maneuver. Running up in front of the line of players he swings the line after him and they run under the arms and held hands of B and C. C spins around as B did and stands close beside B in Position 2. The maneuver is repeated till H, the last, spins himself around and all the players are standing in Position 2.

The players then unwind. H turns himself completely around, counterclockwise. He then unwinds G by moving behind him and ducking through the line (from back to front) under the arms of G and F. (The players are standing close together, and those who pass through the line do not run as freely as in the winding process.) This move turns G to his original position. H, followed by G, moves behind F and ducks under the arms of F and E. H, followed by G and F, passes under the arms of E and D. Thus the whole line is unwound, the handholds (ideally) still unbroken. When the ten young boys were playing, however, they did lose their handholds a few times. In one instance, a young woman with her baby on her back had difficulty passing under the arms because her baby's head got caught. So that none of the players would break their handholds that time, Old /Gasa sprang up from where she was sitting watching and pushed the baby's head through.

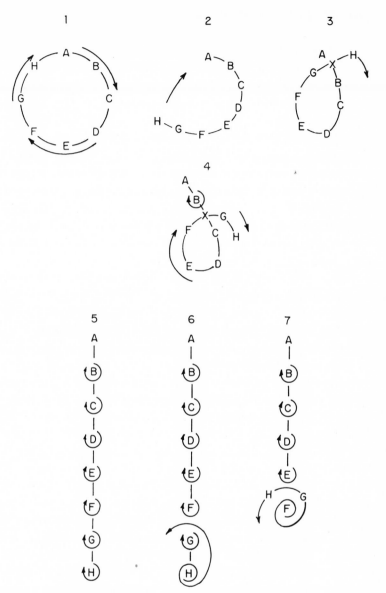

All players
in position 2

— indicates that the players are side by side holding hands
x indicates the place in which the line files under the upraised arms of two
  players
Encircled letters indicate that the players have turned in the direction
  of the arrow.

Fig. 15.   The tsi tsi gwara game

When the players had unwound, they began again and played the whole game through once more, more smoothly the second time with less twisting the wrong way and breaking of handholds. One time they formed a circle while in Position 2 and joggled around in it a couple of times before unwinding.

This game is played in the United States. Three young women—two from Chicago and one from Massachusetts—have told me they played it when they were children. They call it "Rattlesnake." The song they sing with it spells out the word "rattlesnake" letter by letter. I did not play it as a child in California. I never saw or heard of the game till I saw it played by the !Kung.

Four Dramatic Games

Four games are little dramas acted out by the players. The names of these games are: Frogs, Ostrich, Cattle, and Python. All four are dramas of conflict. In Frogs and Ostrich, the conflict is between parents and children; in Cattle, it is between a person who owns cattle and one who does not; and in Python, it is between humans and pythons. It is interesting that these three pairs—parents-children, herders-hunters, and humans-animals—are three of the basic polarities of !Kung life in general. The three kinds of conflict represented are also prominent in the folklore.

Although they did not play these games often, the !Kung find them very enjoyable. Women, girls, and boys between the ages of about eight and twelve all play them together. (An exception here is Python, which I saw played once by an all-boy group and once by an all-girl group but not by a mixed group.) The games are definitely not part of the repertories of men or older boys. Nor do little children (younger than about eight) play—they do not have enough sense, we were told. The men, older boys, and children stand around watching or play their own games nearby. Occasionally one of the men barges in and disrupts the game momentarily, imitating the players or simply clowning around.

As in so many other instances, informants could not tell us anything about the origins of the games, nor did they have any stories or lore to explain the symbolism. Not even gray-haired Old Demi could throw any light on these matters; he could only reiterate, "That is the way to play the game; the children know that is the way."

All four of these games—and two others (Tsi tsi gwara and N≠a n≠a hau) as well—were played at Gautscha the July morning I spoke of previously. I will base my description of the games on the way they were played on this occasion, noting variations that I observed at other times. The people of Bands 1 and 2 were all at Gautscha that morning, and a number of people were visiting from Bands 4, 5, 7, and 9. It was a day of leisure: there was still meat from the last hunt; the women had gathered plant food the day before. A pleasant breeze stirred. The mood of play welled up and a group of ten young women and girls gathered to play in the space between the encampments, where the dance circle was. Eleven young boys joined them. Several old women and young children came to watch, and occasionally the old women joined in the play or waved their arms at the players, calling out their approval or disapproval of the way the games were being played.

We had seen the games played before, but not all in the same session of play and never with more vivacity. The players were in the mood. I attributed their mood to the leisure of the day and the pleasant weather, but more especially to the fact that a goodly number of people were present, including several gay, lively girls who greatly enjoyed playing together.

Frogs. Of the dramatic games, Frogs is the only one that has no song. When I asked the children the name of the game, they imitated the sound of frogs so skillfully I knew at once what the name was. It also differs from the others in its chaotic ending, in which the players dash about shrieking, chasing each other all over the encampment. Both Ostrich (which has other similarities to Frogs) and Python end in a certain amount of tussling and shouting, but nothing compared to Frogs.

I saw two different versions of Frogs, a "short" and a "long." The one played that July morning was the short version, which omitted many of the details of the long one.

In both versions the players sat down in a close circle, facing inward. One was chosen to play the part of "mother of all"; the rest of the players were her children. (I was told that a boy could be chosen for the parent's part; he would be called "father of all." However, I only saw young women play the part on this July morning. The mother was Zuma [2.2], sister of Gao Beard.)

Once the mother was chosen, the game began. The mother, seated with the other players, tapped each of her children on the ankle with a stick. As she tapped them, each lay back full-length on the ground, as though asleep. (At this point in the short version, the mother got up and walked away, omitting all of the long-version action described in the next paragraph.)

The mother then pulled some hairs from her head and placed them on an imaginary fire in the center of the circle. The hairs, I was told, represented frogs the mother had gathered and was cooking for her children to eat. Presently (the frogs presumably having cooked long enough) the mother called to the children, and they all stood in the circle. The mother then went to each one, tapped him on the chest with a little leafy twig, and asked him to go and fetch her mortar and pestle so that she could pound up the crisp, roasted frogs and make them ready to eat. Each child turned away, refusing. The mother, with an expression of annoyance with the children, went to fetch the mortar and pestle herself.

While she was away, the children got up and ran off in all directions to hide. They hid behind shelters or clumps of bushes, inside the shelters, wherever they could. (In the long version, when the children got up to hide they stole the frogs from the fire and ran off with them.) The mother came back and acted out her anger at the children, scowling and making threatening gestures. Then she began to run here and there, looking for the children. Whenever she found one she held him and struck him on the head with her forefinger, breaking his head (we were told) so that his brains (n/ani) ran out. (In the long version the mother would then lean over the child and, sucking at his head, drink his brains.)

On that July morning, this final part of Frogs was pandemonium. When Zuma caught them, the children squealed and struggled and pretended to cry. They broke away and dashed about, Zuma chasing after them. Zuma's baby howled, jerking and bouncing on his mother's back. Two young women, Khuan//a Music and N≠isa (wife of //Ao Wildebeest], who had not been among the players at the beginning of the game, joined in with Zuma and chased the children, striking them with their forefingers like Zuma. Two children still hiding were found by other children and dragged to Zuma to have their heads cracked. In the end everyone was chasing everyone else, shrieking and laughing in wild excitement. Some children had picked up sticks and were whacking others' heads with them. The sticks were light, but the blows were real. When the tumult subsided, all went off to sit in the shade and rest.

Ostrich. To begin this game the players all held hands and sat down in a loose circle, facing inward. The young woman, Khuan//a Music, who had been chosen to play the part of Ostrich (a boy could have been chosen, I was told), remained outside the circle, holding a bunch of leafy twigs. The players began to sing (without clapping): "My old father, O, give us some meat." (Another time when I saw the game played, a young woman again taking the part of Ostrich, the players sang, "My old mother, O.")

With a rush Ostrich ran and leaped over the arms of the players into the circle. The players all jumped up, still holding hands, and began to bounce up and down in place; after a moment the bouncing subsided, and the song as well. Ostrich then began to move around the circle, offering each player one of the twigs she was holding. The twigs represented meat. Each player refused the meat, making some complaint. "The meat is too little," one said. Another said, "We do not like this meat." Another said, "You gave us good things before; what you give us now is nonsense." (When the game was played a second time, later that morning, this section was done differently: each player bit off a piece of the leaf and spat it out with noises of disgust instead of complaints.) After every refusal Ostrich, frowning, threw the twig at the player's chest. When all the players had refused the meat, Ostrich went around the circle again, stopping in front of each player and kicking sand at his feet. The sand represented fire—Ostrich was burning the players' feet. The players tried to jump out of the way of the sand.

Then Ostrich went around the circle a third time, thrusting out her buttocks at each player and pretending to fart at him (a most insulting gesture, the !Kung feel). Again each player tried to jump out of the way. But this last indignity was apparently too much for the players to bear, for, resuming their song, they all began to jump up and down, shouting the words of the song and creating a great hubbub of anger at Ostrich. Ostrich also jumped up and down; as she jumped she pointed upward with the forefinger of her right hand.[34] Then she sought to break out of the circle and escape the anger of the players: bouncing across the circle in rhythm with the song, she threw herself against the barrier of arms and tightly held hands, trying to squeeze under. Several times the players prevented her, tossing her back to a standing position. At last she broke through between two of the boys, but one of them caught her and,

---

34. This gesture seems to be a traditional part of the game: once I saw a player tap Ostrich's shoulder and demonstrate the gesture, which Ostrich (a little girl, not Khuan//a Music) had omitted. Ostrich promptly began jumping again, this time making the gesture.

making a great show of striking her with his arm, pretended to kill her. She fell down, and all the players swarmed over her, pretending to pluck off her feathers.

I saw this game played at other times with several variations. Once Ostrich brought a single branch with many twigs on it, instead of a bunch of twigs; once she brought a handful of long, coarse grass; once she made a fourth round of the circle with long, sideward steps, placating the angry players by bowing low to each after she had thrust out her buttocks at them.

Cattle. In this game two players, /Gasa [2.5], wife of /Qui, brother of Gao Beard, and //Kushay [1.23], represented people, and the rest cattle. /Gasa was the owner of the cattle; //Kushay had none. The plot was simple; //Kushay stole /Gasa's cattle, one by one; when //Kushay had them all, /Gasa stole them back, one by one; then //Kushay took them again —and so forth, until the players were tired of playing. In contrast to the naturalistic whacking and struggling movements of Frogs, the conflict in Cattle was represented entirely by stylized movements.

The game began with /Gasa and //Kushay facing each other, all the cattle lined up behind /Gasa. /Gasa and //Kushay and some of the other players began a charming song about "cattle of mine" that was sung (unaccompanied by clapping) throughout the game; the rest of the cattle lowed and mooed (except for one of the younger boys, who persisted in barking like a gemsbok the whole time). The words of the song were:

> We nama, we nama gumi sa
> Gumi sa o mi i si.

(*We nama*, I was told, is rigmarole; *gumi* is "cattle.") At certain points in the song /Gasa and //Kushay gesticulated at each other, waving their arms emphatically and looking stern. Then //Kushay began her attack and /Gasa her defense. The combat took the form of a dance. Both players danced with smooth-flowing little running steps, their bodies bent over, arms held low in front of them; they tended to look at the ground rather than at each other. /Gasa danced in an arc in front of the cattle, moving first to the right of the line and then, dancing backward, to the left. //Kushay, meanwhile, danced in a sinuous line (sometimes figures of eight), advancing nearer and nearer to /Gasa and the line of cattle. She faced always in the direction of her steps until she came close to /Gasa, but then she threw up her hands (so that they were just above shoulder height, and in more or less the same plane with her head and shoulders) and began to dance in arcs like /Gasa's, moving backward as well as forward. /Gasa also threw up her hands and began to mirror //Kushay's steps. The whole dance lasted through several statements of the song; then, at a given point in the song, //Kushay darted past /Gasa, seized one of the cattle by the arm, and led the player across to her side to stand behind her. The cycle began again: //Kushay and /Gasa gesticulated at each other and danced their combat, and //Kushay captured another of the cattle. When she had them all, /Gasa began to take them back.

At one point in the game, when /Gasa had only a few cattle left, three cycles went by without //Kushay's capturing any. During these turns, /Gasa's dance was somewhat different: she stayed closer to the line of cattle and danced in shorter arcs, with both arms extended behind her. The line of cattle also swayed this way and that, staying behind /Gasa as she danced. When the moment in the song for one of the cattle to be captured had passed, //Kushay returned to her side, and she and /Gasa went through the gesticulating and dancing again.

It was my impression that the point of the game was the plot itself, rather than any competitive test of the players' skill in capturing or defending the cattle. //Kushay and /Gasa, smiling broadly, performed as gentle and graceful a combat as one can imagine.

Since the !Kung are hunters and gatherers with no history of possessing cattle, one wonders if they adopted the game from their cattle-owning neighbors, the Tswana. Ledimo, our interpreter, said that the children of his tribe (Batawana) play the game, but that with them the characters are mothers and children. On the other hand, Bleek reports an almost identical game, which she calls the "Ox Game," played among the Nharo Bushmen:

> [The oxen] stand with their arms curved over their heads to represent horns, make big eyes and low. One player is the owner, another the claimant. These two dance about in front of the oxen, chanting: "My oxen they are, I refuse to give them; Thy oxen they are not, I refuse them; I say my oxen they are." Meanwhile the claimant gradually catches one ox after another and pulls it over to his side. When all are caught, the game is finished.[35]

The language of the song !Kung children sing in their version of the game is neither Nharo nor Tswana, but !Kung.

35. Bleek, *The Naron*, p. 19.

Python. On that July morning eleven young boys played Python; on another occasion as many girls played it; on a third occasion only seven girls played the game. The girls' version was the same as the boys', except that the girls omitted the lying down at the beginning.

The boys formed a chain by sitting down one in front of the other as close to each other as possible. Each stretched out his legs on either side of the boy in front and hooked his feet over the thighs of that boy. For a moment they all lay back, one on top of the other. Presently they sat up, and two boys jumped up from the chain and ran ahead to a clump of grass, where they crouched down. The boys in the chain began to sing (without clapping), and the whole chain began to move slowly forward, the boys hunching themselves along on their buttocks. With each hunch the line undulated, the first three boys swaying to one side, the next three boys swaying at the same time to the other side, and so forth.

The words of the song were:

> We wanted to go gathering;
> People went gathering.
> We wanted to leave; people left.

When the line drew near to the crouching boys, they sprang forward on hands and feet and attacked and routed the line. They seized one boy and pretended to strike him; the rest of the boys in the line all jumped to their feet and scattered, shouting and laughing. In a moment the boys in the line returned and made gestures at the attackers as though they were hurling something at them.

The undulating, slowly moving line looked so snakelike that I expected it to represent the python, but I was told that the line represented people going to get water and also going for plant foods. The two boys in the clump of grass were a mother python and her baby in a pool. They attacked the people, my informant said, and drove them away.

Bleek describes the game (the "Great Water Snake Game") as played by Nharo children.[36] The players in the line (all girls) were people going for water. The chain stopped occasionally, and the girls pretended to dig and eat a water root. A boy played the water snake. He flicked sand at the people, pretending that he was squirting water on them. At last he jumped up and seized a victim and pretended to swallow it; at this point, the game ended.

36. Bleek, *The Naron*, p. 19.

11 Music for Pleasure

Continuing in the vein of leisure days and recreation, I want to describe briefly the songs and instrumental music that are so much a part of !Kung daily life.

The !Kung are a music-loving people. Most of the time someone in a !Kung encampment is making music. People sing to their babies to soothe or entertain them. They sing to enliven their tasks and their games. They sing at the waterhole and in leisure hours by their fires. Everyone sings, almost everyone plays an instrument. Although some are more talented as musicians than others, and some take more interest than others in playing and singing well, none are specialists in any of the several repertories of music, and no one performs before others as musicians in European culture perform at concerts before an audience. People sing and play for their own delectation, and all participate to some degree in all aspects of the musical life.

I divide !Kung music into two categories, ritual music and music that is not ritual. Here I only mention the ritual music in passing; I shall have more to say about it when I describe the rituals in a forthcoming volume. Three !Kung rituals have special music as an integral part of the ritual. They are:

The Menarcheal Rite. The music of this rite is the Eland Music, some of it the most ancient of all !Kung music, Nicholas England tells us.[1] It is sung only by women and only during the performance of the rite. In some instances of the performance the women's singing is accompanied by the faint clink of two pieces of metal struck one against the other.

---

1. Nicholas M. England, "Music among the ʒũ'/'wã-si of South West Africa and Botswana" (Ph.D. diss., Harvard University, 1968), p. 578. All subsequent references are to this work.

Tshoma and Men's Dance. Tshoma is the boy's initiation; the men's dance is a preliminary to tshoma. The music of these rituals is sung only by men. No instruments are used to accompany the songs.

The Ritual Curing Dance. During the dances, the many ritual songs are sung by men and women in full chorus. The women accompany the songs with clapping, in intricate rhythm patterns. The only instrumental accompaniment is the swish of the cocoon rattles that the men wear wound around their legs. !Kung music reaches its highest development in the interplay of the several singing lines of the men's and women's voices and the women's clapping lines. The ritual curing music is not restricted to the curing dance. The music is sung anywhere, anytime, by anybody.

Music that is not ritual includes several repertories, as follows:

Men's Bow Songs. These are played only by men on their hunting bows or on bows made to be used as musical instruments.

Music of a One-Stringed Violin. This music is played only by men.

Women's Ball Game Songs. These and a few other singing game songs were mentioned in the previous chapter.

Songs of the //Gwashi. These include two repertories, one sung by men, one by women.

I have the impression that the music most often heard in an encampment is the music of the curing ritual. Individuals who are singing to their babies or just bursting into snatches of song for their own pleasure usually sing snatches of the curing music. But the bow music and the songs of the //gwashi are also often heard.

The !Kung we knew in the years 1951–53 and 1955 had no drums, though in the surrounding Bantu cultures drumming was highly developed, especially among the Bantu peoples of the Okavango River. There all night long one hears the sound of the drums played at extremely rapid tempo, the patterns of this delicate, magical music endlessly repeating themselves. The soft air carries the sound for miles along the river, filling the night with it. It seemed that it penetrated one's being without having to be taken in through the mind. I had never heard drumming like it; I had heard nothing like it in the world. In 1961, !Kung boys had acquired a couple of drums and were beating them happily and well, but they were not producing any magic.

It is interesting to note also that the Nyae Nyae !Kung had no thumb-pianos in the 1950's, although in the surrounding Bantu cultures, thumb-pianos were common. England reports that he saw two thumb-pianos introduced in 1961 (p. 221). Megan Biesele found numerous thumb-pianos among the !Kung in Botswana by 1970. England surmises that in the earlier years the !Kung did not have enough suitable metal to make thumb-pianos. They needed what metal they could acquire for arrows (p. 224). Why had the !Kung not made drums, one wonders. They had plenty of hide and wood. One can only guess that they were not interested in making drums. Their ancient ritual music is entirely vocal, the rattles and metal pieces being of such minor importance in the music that they can be disregarded as instruments. As to their instruments, the !Kung were imbued with the sound of strings, primarily the bow, and with the quality and the patterns of sound that strings generate.

I have had numerous occasions to refer to England's splendid dissertation on !Kung music, and I hereby refer the reader to it again for a full description of all aspects of the music and a full musical analysis. I presume only to point out a few of the interesting aspects of the music and to indicate, by describing the songs of the //gwashi, some of the concerns of the !Kung that are given expression in song.

THE HUNTING BOW

The !Kung have had their hunting bows and have played music upon them for unknown ages. England says that probably the bow was the precursor of all other stringed instruments and has had a basic influence on the tone systems of Bushmen and other African peoples (p. 77).

Every man has a hunting bow which he keeps with him constantly. To play music on this ubiquitous instrument is a very common practice. Hunters while away the time with bow music when they are walking mile after mile, perhaps following game they have shot. In the encampment, bows are always at hand for any boy or man to play.

There are several variations in the technique of bow playing. A man, first of all, adjusts the tension on the bowstring. For hunting, the string is very taut; for playing, the string is loosened so that its fundamental, open-string tone is, England tells us, in the range of D to B flat (p. 80). Using the simplest and most common technique, the man places the head end of the bow in his mouth, which serves as a resonator. (The head end, called "head" because it is held up in shooting, is the end

The hunting bow played as mouth bow

around which the string is simply looped.) England calls the music produced by this mouth technique mouth-bow tunes; the !Kung call them bow songs, *n!ao ⁻ts'i-si* (p. 85).

To make his music, the player either strikes the open string with a piece of reed or small stick that he picks up anywhere, or he plucks the string with his forefinger. He may hold his hand against the bow moving only his finger, or he may pluck with a free wrist. Using this technique, the player has one fundamental tone, the tone produced by the open string as he plucks or strikes it. The air in his mouth cavity is set into vibration and, by altering the size of the cavity, to use England's words, ". . . the player isolates (by sympathetic vibrations of the air) different partials of the tone. The resulting sound is a succession of harmonic intervals that consist of the fundamental string pitch and one of its partials, the fundamental sounding as a drone to the delicate little melody of the overtones" (p. 82).

The men casually twiddle and improvise a great deal in their bow playing, and they also play little tunes, which, although they are not given names, are musical entities, established in the bow music repertory. They repeat the tune over and over for many minutes with a a number of variations—a method used in all Bushman music. England says of the mouth-bow music, "Casual as it is, then, and unconsequential as its little tunes may seem, the mouth-bow n!ao playing cannot be underestimated as a more or less constant influence on the tonal concepts of the Bushmen" (p. 88). To my ears, the gentle little tunes of the mouth-bow music were very pleasant; I never tired of them.

!GOMA

When a hollow object other than the mouth is used for a resonator, the playing of the hunting bow and the music produced by the playing are called *!goma*. !Goma music is more complex than mouth-bow music. Insofar as I know, there are two techniques in playing !goma. In one, the player holds a gourd against his stomach with his left hand and with the same hand presses the bow against the gourd. He manipulates the size of the air chamber in the gourd and controls the overtones by contracting and distending his stomach. In this kind of !goma playing, the player stops the bowstring about five inches from the top with his thumb and forefinger. He thus produces a second tone and has two fundamentals to use, the tone of the stopped string in addition to that of the open string, both with their overtones. The two fundamental tones are of basic importance to !Kung music. England says of them, "For the jū [that is, the !Kung], at least, and for most other Bushmen as well, the two fundamentals used in bow playing and their lowest, strongest overtones (partials 2–4) seem to appear constantly in the music as a formative and regulative set of tones for the scale system" (p. 97).

The player using a gourd resonator instead of his mouth is free to sing, and thus adds another line to the music to increase its complexity and make what England calls three-part counterpoint (p. 93).

This system of !goma playing has its importance—especially as it has influenced the !Kung scale system—but playing in this way appeared not to be a popular pastime, at least where we were. I suppose the technique of controlling the overtones is rather difficult. This !goma bow playing was not to be compared in popularity with the mouth-bow playing, the singing of the curing dance songs, or the songs of the //gwashi.

In the second manner of !goma playing, two players play the bow simultaneously. At any time I saw the bow played in this way, the two players were boys (that is, not men—women and girls never play the bow), and the spirit of the performance was more the spirit of a game than that of a musical rendition. These musical games were great fun.

For a resonator, the boys place a hollow object over a shallow hole scooped out in the sand. They liked our enamel wash basins for resonators. One boy holds the bow, one end of it pressed against the resonator, the other against his shoulder. It is the function of this boy to stop the string. He does so by pressing his chin firmly on the string, usually at a place that produces a tone a minor third above the tone of the open string. In this kind of playing, using this kind of resonator, the overtones are not brought out. The player alternates his two tones in various rhythmic patterns.

The second boy sits at the lower end of the bow and twangs the string with a light stick or reed, with very rapid wrist motion. The stick is used as a plectrum and strikes the string with a downward and an upward stroke. The second boy produces lively and highly varied rhythm patterns on the background of the two tones of the open and closed string. The two players frequently change places. I suppose the twanger's wrist gets tired, and the chinner's chin gets tired.

Most of the musical games played in this way are in imitation of animals. Each animal is represented in the music by its own rhythmic pattern. Often the rhythms seem actually to catch the motion of the animals—a kudu leaping, for instance. The boy who twangs makes imitative motions of the animal with his free arm and his head. A hyena game seemed to catch the rhythm of the sounds hyenas make. I remember most vividly the lively /Gwi boys in central Botswana playing their bows in this way and playing hyenas copulating. Invariably, a group of children gather to watch the players and to take turns playing, and they all contribute to the imitations, crawling, pouncing, or leaping around and making the animal sounds.

THE MUSICAL BOW

The !Kung make a musical bow on which they use a wire instead of a sinew string. They divide the wire into two lengths by tying it against the bow stave at about the middle. These bows, called braced bows, or wire bows, were adopted from the Bantu, but long ago. Even the old men could not remember a time when the !Kung did not make them and play them. It happened that the !Kung we knew in 1952–53 and 1955 did not have a braced bow; at least I do not remember having seen one played. England, however, observed such bows in 1957, and has described them and the repertory of music played upon them [p. 126 ff].

THE ONE-STRINGED VIOLIN

The origin of this instrument is obscure, England tells us (p. 184). It was brought to Nyae Nyae within the memory of the old men (p. 188). The !Kung call the instrument the tin can bow, *do n!ao,* though it is not what we would call a bow. It is a stick about three feet long with a hollowed-out trough extending most of its length. It is strung with wire which is fastened at the top and wound around a tuning peg that is inserted near the bottom end of the stick. Its resonator in our day was a five-gallon oil tin placed over the top of the stick; in the past it was something else. To play the instrument, the man sits down. He rests the upper end of the instrument against his left shoulder. He hooks the little finger of his left hand around the tuning peg, his other fingers around the stick, his thumb moves up and down to stop the string. The instrument is played with a tiny bow about three inches long, strung with hair from an animal's tail. The player moistens the bowstring with saliva. He holds it in his right hand and gently rubs the string with it in a circular motion. He rubs at certain points, where the nodes are that produce the overtones he wants for the tune he is playing. England tells us that all the tones brought out by the little bow are overtones, a unique feature of the instrument (p. 184).

The player and others sing along with the instrument if they wish. They hum the main tune or a counterpoint to it. There was not a large repertory of do n!ao songs. England records six; one has the intriguing title of "Lion Fear" (that is, fear of a lion). The others were (p. 206ff.): Water Song, Springhare Song, Gemsbok Song, Duiker Song, Kuru N!omer (an insect). Only men play this instrument, and not many are interested in learning it. Its technique is rather difficult. Among the people of Gautscha when we were there, only //Ao Wildebeest played. To me the tones were squeaky, and the music eerie.

THE //GWASHI

The //gwashi is a pluriarc. This is the general appellation for stringed instruments of this type. The !Kung make two versions of the instrument. The two are the same in form and range of sizes, but one has four strings and is properly called //gwashi, while the other has five strings and is properly called ≠gauka. The !Kung have fallen into the way of using the appellation //gwashi for both, and we have followed them in that practice.

England's long chapter on the //gwashi includes information about the distribution of pluriarcs in Africa and the advent of the //gwashi in !Kung culture (pp. 251–355). He tells us that pluriarcs exist in the west of Africa, roughly speaking, from the Niger River to the Kunene River, in three clusters, north, central, and south. The instruments of the different clusters vary in their shapes, sizes, the materials of their construction, the number of strings, and the methods in which they are played. The form adopted by the !Kung derives from the southern cluster and came to the !Kung through the Ambo people of Ovamboland (p. 285).

One of the stories which England heard about the //gwashi was a legend-like story about a man named K"ao N//ai, who is said to have made the first //gwashi. His wife had left him and had gone with her own people to the north. He followed her to try to persuade her to return to him. She and her people shot a gun at him and drove him away. On his sorrowful return journey, he passed through a mangetti forest. There he stopped and made the first //gwashi. He made it of mangetti wood. England points out that the gun in the story is a foreign element, and that it suggests contact with non-Bushmen in the north, probably Ambo. Ambo pluriarcs have five or seven strings. England believes that it just might be that K''ao N//ai did make the first four-stringed pluriarc, the //gwashi. Bushmen, England adds, are the only people in the southern cluster to play a pluriarc of four strings (pp. 282–284).

Old Demi first saw a //gwashi when he was a young man visiting near Karakuwisa. England, relating the dates to events in the German Herero War, believes the year was 1905 (p. 287). People still remember the names of men who were clever at learning to play the //gwashi when it was new to the !Kung. They learned at Samangaigai, and they taught others. From there the skill spread southward into the Nyae Nyae area.

//Gwashisi are made from mangetti wood, which is soft and easily carved. Mangetti logs are cut into pieces ranging from about fourteen to sixteen inches in length, about seven to nine inches in width. A hollow six or seven inches wide, four or five inches deep, is chopped with an adze or scraped out with a knife in the mangetti log. A thin plate of mangetti wood is placed over the hollow. The plate is fastened to the body of the //gwashi with little leather thongs inserted into matching pairs of little holes, one in the plate, one in the body, burned into the wood with a red hot awl. At the front end of the log, holes are burned to receive the sticks to which the strings are tied. The red hot tang of an assagai blade is the right size for these holes. These holes may be burned right through the solid front part of the log as far as the hollow, or not so far. The holes may be four or five in number. Into them are thrust slender sticks which have been scraped and smoothed. The sticks are about one-fourth inch in diameter, a foot more or less in length.

Strings made of sinew cord are attached in slots at the back end of the plate, brought forward, and wound around the sticks. The instrument is tuned by tightening or loosening the strings and by bending the sticks slightly one way or another. The two outside strings of the five-stringed instrument are called female strings, the middle string is called the male string.

Two repertories of //gwashi songs exist, those that men sing and play, composed for five strings, and those that women sing and play, composed for four strings. Men and women are not constrained by rules of avoidance from touching each other's instruments. Women frequently play the five-stringed instrument, but, when they play songs of the women's repertory, they tune the //gwashi with the women's tuning and play on only four of its strings. I did not observe a man playing a four-stringed instrument, though they may do so.

The five and four strings are tuned differently. The player holds the //gwashi in both hands with the sticks at the top. He tunes from right to left, string one being the farthest to the right as he faces the instrument. England describes the tuning of the instruments. On the five-stringed ≠gauka, string one is G (this is the G an octave and a half above middle C); string two is tuned to E, a third below string one; still going down the scale, string three is D; string four is C (the octave above middle C); string five is B (one note below string four). England gives two tunings for the four strings of the //gwashi. In the first, string one is G, the same G as in the ≠gauka tuning; string two is C (the octave above middle C); string three descends one note to B; string four rises to E. In the second //gwashi tuning, string one is G, string two is D, string three is B-sharp, string four is F (pp. 317, 351). Needless to say, the notes do not have the absolute precision of a professionally tuned European instrument. But though the notes may be off a bit from the precise G or C of a European instrument, the player carefully tunes his intervals so that they sound right to him in relation to each other.

The strings are plucked with the thumb and forefinger. On the five-stringed instrument, strings one, two, and three are plucked with the right hand, four and five with the left. On the four-stringed instrument, two strings are plucked by each hand.

The system of tones used in the composition of //gwashi music derives from the musical bows, England tells us. The tones are, he says, "1) the two fundamentals a m3 [minor third] apart, played in all bow songs except the simplest hunting-mouth-bow technique; 2) the third partials [overtones] of these fundamentals which figure prominently in the bow melodies of the mouth-bow type, as well as in the vocal melodies that are sung to bow accompaniments . . . ; and 3) the infixed tone a M2 [major second] above the lower of the two fundamentals" (p. 333).

The music of the //gwashi consists of the music of the instrument and singing; both are called "songs of the //gwashi, //gwashi ⁻ts'i." The songs may be sung without the instrument, or the instrument played without singing. However, the instrument and the voice are usually combined. A person may sing and play alone or one may play and a group join in the singing. The !Kung do not make an orchestra of their instruments. Only one is played at a time.

Almost everyone plays the //gwashi—at any time, in any place. Children make a plaything of the instrument, girls and boys play for fun, and men and women play whenever the mood is upon them. Many lack talent and skill, and their playing is mere strumming. There are, however, a few excellent musicians among the !Kung. At Gautscha, Khuan//a Music and /Gao Music were outstanding.

The melody ripples rapidly and softly from the strings. The instrument states the melody of the song. The singers pick up the phrases of the melody and weave them skillfully together in varying contrapuntal arrangements. England described the singing as follows (p. 341):

> Several singers would draw upon the same musical materials, choosing the melody line that they desired at the moment and adding their individual variations in the process. As they severally alter the materials . . . , they would bring into being a contrapuntal complex constantly changing throughout the performance as the musical period was repeated again and again. Just as in the two versions of Tshi Baba by /Gao, there would be no predicting the exact tonal and rhythmic content of any one iteration of the period until it actually happened; for there is no constraint on anyone to perform a specific melody or its variation at a given time. Yet it is possible to know roughly what melodies will be sung merely by listening to a solo version of the song, for a solo singer presents successively the materials that would be heard simultaneously in an ensemble rendition.

A minority of //gwashi songs have no titles. The composer of them was evidently concerned only with the musical idea. They can be called "absolute" music. The majority of //gwashi songs, however, have been inspired by something other than a musical idea. They are "program music." They have titles that proclaim what the songs are about. An experience is behind each. They commemorate an event or they reflect a mood. Each has a little story connected with it.

I consider the music of the latter category of //gwashi songs to be as pure as the "absolute music" in the sense that it does not imitate sounds that are not actually musical sounds. The song may be about the sound of branches rubbing together in the wind, but its utterance is a purely musical utterance; it does not imitate the rap or whine of the branches.

Although they have titles and stories behind them, the songs are not literary verses set to music. They are often sung without any words

Khuan //a [5.7], the musician, and her //gwashi

at all. The singers vocalize syllables or humming sounds, a, o, oo, or perhaps ha, hoo, or mm or hnn. Sometimes, however, the singer will utter a few words that pertain to the subject of the song, not in any set way, but as his whim dictates. The singer might sing a song about a bird without words for a while, and then, to add to its poignancy, spontaneously insert the words "Daybreak, I cannot sleep," implying that the chatter of the birds wakes him. Very often, the words "my mother" are uttered, "mi tai." They might be uttered, for example, in the song that laments a hunter's failure. When I questioned them, the men said they did not know what lay behind the tradition of singing the words "my mother, my mother." They just sing them.

The melodies are not lengthy musical statements, but the singers may repeat the song over and over, continuing for any length of time they desire.

The songs of the //gwashi that we heard and have notes on are listed below, twenty-seven men's songs, fifteen women's songs. (The latter do not include the women's ball game songs or other singing game songs mentioned in the previous chapter.) England, who was in the Nyae Nyae area in the year 1957–58, found that seventeen of the nineteen men's songs he recorded were among the songs we had recorded five years before and were still in the repertory of the !Kung.

THE MEN'S REPERTORY

Songs Addressed to the Instrument

1. //Gwasi ⁻Ts'i /Ne, //Gwashi Song One
   The song was also called _//Ka'a ⁻Ts'i /Ne, Mangetti Song One. The men explained that they referred to the tree, not the nut, and that they call the song mangetti song because the instruments, the //gwashi and the ≠gauka, are made of mangetti wood. They sang the words, "The skin (n/o) of the mangetti is speaking to me." They also sang, "My mother, my mother, mi tai, mi tai." The "mangetti skin" and "mother" were uttered from time to time in the other songs addressed to the instruments.

2. //Gwashi Song

3. //Gwashi Song

4. //Gwashi Song
   The singer sang, "The //gwashi respects me."

5. //Gwashi Song
   The men sang, "The //gwashi has a song. The mangetti has a song."

6. //Gwashi Song

7. //Gwashi Song

Songs of the Mangetti Forest

8. _//K'a ⁻Ts'i, Mangetti Song
    The singer sang, "Let us sing a //gwashi song," and later he sang, "Where shall I be?" The implication is that the person will be in a mangetti forest gathering nuts.
9. !Gum ⁻Ts'i, Winter Song
    The words interspersed in the song from time to time were: "Winter has come," "Let us sing winter," "My mother, my mother."
10. _//K'a !Gu !Ka, Mangetti Water Heart
    The men sang: "The mangetti has one song," "The mangetti is in a sandy place," "Water (collects in its) heart." A man named Dam, who lived at the time at Samangaigai, composed this song. People from Gautscha who visited learned it from him.

Songs of Birds and Wind in the Trees

11. _!Ka, Redwing Partridge[2]
    I asked if the sound the bird made was imitated in the song and was told it was not. The song, I was told, was composed by a man named Short Demi who lived near Samangaigai. He addressed the song to the bird because the bird is good to eat.
12. Op Op Op
    The !Kung call two birds _!ka, the redwing partridge and the red-crested korhaan.[3] This song is about the red-crested korhaan. The title refers to the birds' chatter, but the chatter is not imitated in the music.
13. Ko Ko Ko
    The song is about a bird that pecks a tree. The title, but not the music, imitates the chopping sound.
14. !Kañ N≠uru Ts'a !A Mi (tree rubbing I hear above me)
    Short Demi of Samangaigai made this song, which is about his hearing tree branches above him rubbing together in the wind.

Songs about Hunting, Failure and Success

15. K"ao N//ai ⁻Gunni ⁻Tã Na
    This is a very old song composed by K"ao N//ai who made the first !Kung //gwashi. The title of the song means that he failed in

---

2. *Scleroptila levaillanti levaillanti.*
3. *Lophotis ruficrista.*

hunting (⁻*gunni*, to hunt,⁻*tã*, to be unable, *na* indicates unfinished action [Bleek, *Dictionary*, p. 142]). The men like the song and sing it to lament when they fail in hunting.

16. To Play a Bad Trick

The title here is a paraphrase of a !Kung verb which I cannot spell and cannot find in the dictionary. I was told the verb was used when someone surprised another person and played a bad trick on him. The verb occurs in the ancient tales in which ≠Gao N!a, the protagonist, is always playing bad tricks on people. He raped his daughter-in-law and ate his brother-in-law, for example. His wives played a bad trick on him when they pushed him into a pit that was full of excrement. In the song, fate in the form of hunting plays a bad trick on the hunters, and they get no game.

17. Another Song about Failure in the Hunt (Title lacking)

The men who were singing said they sang the song when they have been hunting and get nothing. The song represents their weeping. "My mother, my mother" was repeated over and over in lament.

18. Eee yaw yaw

These are sounds the men make in singing this lively song, not words. The men sing the song when they have eaten a lot of meat and are in a happy mood.

Songs about Marriage

19. !Goa ⁻Ts'i, Marriage Song

A man had two wives. He could not please them both. He loved one more than another. This is an old song that came to Nyae Nyae from a distant place.

20. N!ono Khwe

N!ono is a man's name, *khwe* is "person." N!ono is a man who lived at Samangaigai. He had two wives who were jealous of one another. They behaved badly, and N!ono made the song to chastise them. Words in this song say that N!ono wants to divorce both the wives and return to his own parents. He did not do so, we were told; he only wished to do so.

21. Gama Gama

A young man asked to marry a girl, but her parents refused to give their consent. The young man made the song. The singer sings the words, "They refuse, they refuse," and "Gama gama

/kwa tsau a (gama gama not woman yours)." I failed to learn the meaning of *gama gama* and whether it is one word or two. One meaning of *gamagama* as one word is the noun "bracelet," which is not appropriate here. The men who tried to explain to me the meaning indicated that in the context of the song the word is a verb. They said that if a man loved his young second wife and divorced his old first wife against her wish, one would say he *gama gamaed* the second wife, and the first wife would weep and say "gama gama."

22. A Lament for a Lost Love (Title lacking)
   A deserted wife weeps for her husband. (Although the song is about the grief of a woman, it is a song in the men's repertory, composed for five strings.)

23. A Lament for a Lost Love (Title lacking)
   This is the plaintive lament the young man, /Ti!kay, sang at /Gam when his jealous wife, //Aha, drove away his beautiful young third wife, /Khoa.

24. A Lament for a Lost Love (Title lacking)
   The same young man made a second song about his loss, an equally beautiful song.

Songs of Chagrin

25. ≠Gara, To Beg
   A man who lived at Samangaigai long ago made this song. Hunters killed an eland. The man went to the people whose eland it was and asked for meat. He heard the people talking against him, saying that he had come to beg, and that he had a short face. They gave him some meat, but it was cooked meat, not raw meat. Chagrined at having been given cooked meat instead of a more prestigious gift of raw meat, he went home and made the song.

26. Tshi Baba
   If a man has no leather bag in which to carry the food he has gathered, he makes a bundle of small branches or of bunches of long grass, places the food inside the bundle, and ties the bundle with cord. Such a bundle is called a *tshi baba. Tshi* means "things"; England translates *baba* as "makeshift" (p. 661). The song was inspired when a man with such a bundle was ridiculed. People laughed and said he was so poor he did not even have a bag. He

left those people and later took up his //gwashi and made this song. The Nyae Nyae people learned the song somewhere. They do not know where nor do they know the man's name.

27. !Kãn (or !Gãn) ≠Em ≠Em

The words of the title are "tree broken broken." I paraphrased them and called the song, "The Song of the Old Stump." The story of this song has been mentioned before. A hunter separated from his companions found himself alone when evening came. In the dusk he saw a man in the distance and ran to him, glad that there would be two together by the fire that night. But when he came near, he found only an old stump. After singing the song on one occasion, the men laughed and remarked that the stump made a fool of the hunter.

THE WOMEN'S REPERTORY

28. Song of a Forest, !Kãn !Gu

The song is about a mangetti forest when rain is falling, and the countryside is turning green. The women are pleased with the greenness of the mangetti trees. They know that the food plants are growing. There is water in the hollows of the mangetti trees.

28. Mangetti, _//K'a

A happy song that women sing when they are in a mangetti forest gathering nuts.

30. /Gui Song

A song about little birds with red beaks that flock to the waterhole. They waken the people in the morning with their chatter as they fly overhead.

31. Dove Song

32. Tsi Song

A song the women sing when they have gathered tsi. The song is a lament for the way they would feel if they found the footprints of another people in the tsi place and all the tsi gone. The women sing a few words in this song. They say, "(They) follow the footprints in the tsi place."

33. Eland Song

A song about a cow eland. There were many elands together. The hunters killed one, a cow, and the people were pleased to have meat. This song is very old.

34. Song of the White Ants, Guriko !Gum[4]

When the people gather the white ants as the ants fall from nuptial flight, they sing this song in expression of their pleasure at having this delicious food.

35. !Xe Song

A song about a man of this name. People were displeased with him because he ill-treated his mother. They made the song to chastise him. (Did he improve his ways after the song was made, I asked. I was told that he did.)

36. I Am Alone, Mi Kwara Ju (I [have] no people)

The song is sung by girls if they are in a sad mood and fear that there will be no one with them to give them food.

37. The Two Baús, Baú Tsa

I have mentioned this song before. It is the song about the two jealous, quarrelsome co-wives who disturbed the whole encampment with their wrangling, and who mended their ways when they heard the song sung from the shadows.

38. Short !U, !U!Goma

Short !U and Sa≠gai were co-wives of N!ani. Short !U was not a good co-wife. She was jealous of Sa≠gai. She wanted to keep their husband to herself. Sa≠gai's children made a //gwashi for themselves, and when they had made it, they composed the song about Short !U's objectionable behavior. Did Short !U reform, I asked. No, she did not, the women replied. She was not ashamed, she flaunted herself. The women said they like to sing this song because it is a very beautiful song, musically speaking.

39. Khwova

Khwova, a young girl, did not like the man to whom she was betrothed. She rejected him and married another man. Her betrothed still loved her and made the song to mourn his loss of her. This happened long, long ago away in the west. The song is also very beautiful, the women say.

40. Two Women

A song about two women who used the kin terms tūn and !guma for each other. The Gautscha people do not know who the women

4. Termites, popularly called "white ants," of the order *Isoptera*. After nuptial flight, the male termites fall to the ground and lose their wings. On the rare occasions on which the !Kung are present when a nuptial flight occurs, the !Kung in great excitement gather the termites and eagerly eat them alive. We were present on one such occasion.

were. The song came from the north. The women were friends. They loved each other and paid so much attention to each other that they neglected the other people with whom they lived. What is more, they were both given to backbiting. People were tired of their constant criticism, and someone made a song. Like the two Baús, the women mended their ways.

41. A Man Was Waiting for the Moon

He was "visiting." In this instance, I took the word "visit" to be a euphuism for sleeping with a woman. He was waiting for the moon to rise so that he could travel back to his own encampment in moonlight rather than in darkness.

42, 43. Dama !Kumsi, and Dikira

Two of the women's songs are about Herero. One is called Dama !Kumsi, Herero Legs. The implication of the song is that the Herero had or wanted to have sexual intercourse with a !Kung girl. The other song is Dikira. This is the name of a Herero who does not give enough food to the people who work for him. The people long for food. This is a sad song.

The //gwashi songs, always lovely, are most enchanting when sung by groups of good singers, accompanied by an accomplished //gwashi player. When a group of good singers, who know many songs, are enjoying a singing session, they may sing for an hour or two at a time. They do not perform for others. They sing for their own pleasure, but the songs fill the air and all can listen and enjoy them. !Kung life mingles arduousness with ease, anxieties with supportive human relations. In all its aspects, it is lightened by music.

Appendix 1
Band Charts

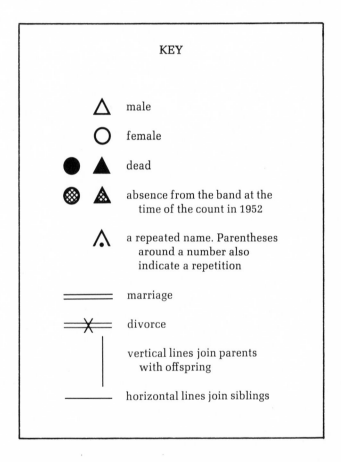

KEY

△	male
○	female
● ▲	dead
⊗ ▲	absence from the band at the time of the count in 1952
△̣	a repeated name. Parentheses around a number also indicate a repetition
═══	marriage
═╳═	divorce
│	vertical lines join parents with offspring
───	horizontal lines join siblings

Numbers have been assigned to the individuals in the band charts for the purpose of identification. The numbers are composed of the band number and a number for the individual within the band—1.1, 1.2, 2.1, 2.2, etc. An X in the number—e.g. 1.X3—means that the person is dead. A Q in the number—e.g. 1.Q2—means that the person is counted as a member of the band but was temporarily living elsewhere at the time of the count in 1952. The numbers do not express any hierarchical order of persons.

Segments, groupings of families within the large bands (Bands 1, 2, 10, and 12), are separated by heavy vertical lines. The numbering of the segments is not sequential on the page. The segments and the order in which they are numbered are explained below.

Age is indicated approximately as follows:

YC	0– 7	years old
C	8–15	years old
YA	16–24	years old
A	25–50	years old
O	50	years or older

In Figs. 16, 17, and 18, following the charts, forebears who do not appear on the band charts have not been assigned numbers, e.g. //Ao and !U in Fig. 16. For spouses and offspring (omitted in the figures) of persons listed in boxes see band charts. Siblings of the generations listed in boxes are given in order of age. Relative age of siblings in ascending generations is not indicated. Dead siblings are not recorded.

Charts are provided of ten bands in the Nyae Nyae area to show examples of large and small bands and to show the relationships through which people come together to form bands. The charts record the living people who were the members of the bands at the time the first count was made in 1952. If charts were to be made of these same bands at another time, they would show some of the same people in the band together, but there would be movement and change to record also. Only a few dead forebears are included to show key relationships. Space does not permit the inclusion of abundant genealogical material but, in Figs. 16, 17, and 18, a sampling of genealogies shows how relationships extend throughout the area. Bands that neighbor each other are especially rich in linking relationships. The two Gautscha bands provide an example. The Deboragu and Nam Tshoha bands and the Tsumkwe and Khumsa bands do also. Genealogies of the members of Bands 12 are not given, but this band has similar interwoven relationships with the other southern bands, Bands 13–16.

Bands 3, 4, 5, 6, and 9 are not complex. The charts show quite simply all the relationships involved—who are the "owners" of the territory, who are the incoming members of the bands.

The larger bands, Bands 1, 2, 10, and 12, and Band 7, though it is not large, are complex. They are composed of groups that I call "segments." Each segment has its own internal bonds of relationships that make it a unit. The segments are joined in the band by consanguineous or affinal bonds; in the instances before us, each is held by a single bond to one other segment.

In Band 1, Segments 1 and 2 are both composed of the "owners" of the territory, the kxai k"xausi, and their incoming spouses. See Fig. 16 for the relationship between Old N/aoka [1.13] and Old Gaú [1.20] as "owners," as well as the relationship with Debe [1.X1] and /Khoa [1.X2], who were incoming members in their generation. Old N/aoka and Old Gaú pass the "ownership" to their descendents. Although the members of Segments 1 and 2 are related, and although they live together closely most of the time, I count them as two segments because they do cleave at the segment line when they separate to go to different places to visit or gather. They do not live as one "household," but as two separate but adjacent family groups. Segment 3 in Band 1 is composed of people who belong to Band 4. Gao [1.8] is the son of Old /Gaishay [4.1]. He comes into Band 1, and brings his first wife, N/aoka [1.7], and his whole extended family, through his marriage with his second wife, Di!ai [1.9], daughter of Old N/aoka, sister of !U [1.15] and Lame ≠Gao [1.14].

Note that in Band 1, in Segments 1 and 2, the living incoming spouses happen to be men married to women Gautscha "owners." They are ≠Toma [1.16] from /Gam (the band he belonged to is disbanded, its affiliations were with Band 14), and /Qui [1.24]. Gao [1.8] in Segment 3 is another male incoming spouse to Band 1. (See Figs. 17 and 18 for the genealogical background of Gao and Fig. 17 for that of /Qui.)

In Band 2, Segments 1 and 2, like those of Band 1, are composed of "owners" of Gautscha and their incoming spouses. Fig. 16 shows the relationship between the two segments. They live as two separate but adjacent family groups, as do Segments 1 and 2 in Band 1. Note that whereas in Band 1 the incoming spouses happen to be men, in Band 2 it happens that of seven incoming spouses married to Gautscha "owners" five are women. Old Xama [2.7] came from Band 7. /Gasa [2.5] came from Band 5. /Gam [2.17] and ≠Nisa [2.21] came from /Gam. //Kushay II came from Band 4. //Kushay I is an "owner" of Gautscha, as is her husband, Gao Beard [2.9]. Of the two men, Gao [2.1], a son of Debe of Band 24, came from Tsho/ana, /Tuka [2.15] came from the vicinity of Epata.

Segment 3 in Band 2, like Segment 3 in Band 1, is not an integral part of the band. Segment 3 comes into Band 2 through the marriage of Gaú [2.25] to Khuan//a [2.24], sister of Old /Gam [2.17]. Gaú was in bride service. Gaú, Old /Gasa [2.35], his mother, and his two sisters, ≠Gisa [2.31] and N/aoka [2.36] belong to Band 3 where ≠Gao [3.4], also a son of Old /Gasa, is the present k"xau n!a. Short /Qui [2.37], husband of N/aoka, and Dam [2.32], husband of ≠Gisa, belong to Band 12. Short /Qui and Dam and their families were living in Band 12 when we first saw them. They came to live with Gaú in Band 2 shortly after. The people of Segment 3 have three choices of residence, Band 3, Band 12, or Band 2, that is, as long as Gaú chooses to stay in Band 2.

In Band 7, Segment 1 was composed of the old k"xau n!a, Old /Qui [7.2], his wives, offspring, and his son's wife's mother, //Kushay [7.6]. Segment 2 was only briefly present in Band 7. It was composed of Gao [7.12], another son of Old /Gasa, and his wife, Di!ai [7.13], daughter of Old Xama [2.7], sister of Gao Beard [2.9]. Gao [7.12] belongs to Band 3 .where his brother ≠Gao [3.4] is k"xau n!a. He had recently married Doïn [7.11], granddaughter of Old /Qui, as his second wife and was in bride service for her. In 1953, that marriage dissolved in divorce, and Gao and Di!ai went back to live in Band 3.

In Band 10, Segment 1 is composed of the "owners" of Tsumkwe and their spouses (see Fig. 18). Segment 2 is composed of the family of //Ao [10.21] from Tsho/ana. They are in Band 10 temporarily through the marriage of /Qui [10.7], the son of //Ao and N≠isa, to two daughters of Baú [10.12] and Gao [10.13].

Band 12 at /Gam was more complex than any of the others. When we were with the band it had six segments. Unfortunately, the genealogical superstructure that would show the relationship between some of the segments was lost to memory. Band 12 people appeared to be singularly uninformed about their forebears. One of our interpreters, with whom we had only recently begun to work and whom we had not yet trained to avoid interjecting his own questions or remarks into an interrogation, became exasperated with the replies of, "I do not know," and said to Khwova [12.7], "You seem to be an old woman. How is it you are so ignorant about your relatives?" She replied, apparently without taking offense, "I am not old. It is hunger makes me seem so." She left his accusations of ignorance without comment.

Gao [12.29] in Segment 1 was the k″xau n!a of the band. He was a young man; his first child was only about two years old. Gao's father, !Kham [12.X11], had been k″xau n!a before him. Gao could tell us little about his father except that he had been, as Gao said, the "biggest" k″xau n!a at /Gam. That would mean probably that his family had been established at the /Gam water longer than the family of the k″xau n!a of Band 13, a position claimed by /Ti!kay [13.14]. /Ti!kay's position was not substantiated by the rather confused genealogical data we managed to gather from that band, but that !Kham had been the "big" k″xau n!a and the person who gave people from other places permission to take the /Gam water was substantiated by the explicit statements of several persons in addition to those of his son, Short Gao [12.6], Short /Qui [2.37], Dam [2.32], Old Debe, leader of Band 13, and Old /Ti!kay, k″xau n!a of Band 14, all concurred.

Segment 2 of Band 12 was composed of Kuara [12.22] and his family. Kuara is a brother of Gao's deceased mother, Baú [12.X12], and of her old sister, Old Khwova [12.28], who lives with Gao, and of another of Baú's sisters, /Khoa [12.17], who lives with her family in Segment 3. Kuara and his family were present in Band 12 because of the drought. Ordinarily, they live with Band 15 of Domn!a. That is the band from which Kuara, Gao's mother, and the two other sisters stem. When the waterhole at Domn!a dried, Kuara took advantage of his Band 12 connections and settled down between his two old sisters. He expected to return to Band 15 when the water permitted. Old Khwova and /Khoa live permanently with Gao, insofar as any residential pattern is permanent. I count /Khoa and her family as living in a separate segment from Gao's, however, because they lived separately in the encampment, next to their daughter's husband's people, i.e., the people of Segment 4. The daughter is N≠isa [12.15]; her husband is /Qui [12.14]. They provide an example, incidentally, of a marriage between two people in the same band. Although not prohibited by the marriage regulations, provided the couple's consanguineous or affinal bonds permit it, a marriage within a band is nevertheless unusual.

Segment 4 was composed of Short Gao [12.6] and his family. Short Gao felt that he was as firmly and clearly an integral part of Band 12, as much a kxai k″xau, as Gao. /Ti!kay [12.X6], Short Gao's father, and !Kham [12.X11], Gao's father, had been related and had belonged together in Band 12. When !Kham died and Gao, his son, was still a young boy, /Ti!kay had become the leader of the band. The two young men, Short Gao and Gao, were equally ignorant of the relationship that united their fathers. They could tell me the names of their grandparents (apparently none of the grandparents were siblings), but nothing at all about their great grandparents. In all probability, a sibling relationship in the great grandparents' generation existed, and the two young men are second cousins.

The one person who came into a band on the basis of a name relationship, rather than through a consanguineous or affinal bond, is Old //Kushay [12.12]. Her deceased daughter was named Baú and that gave her a name bond with Old Baú [12.13] with whom she lives. Old Baú lives with her daughter, Khwova [12.7], and her son, /Qui [12.14]. Old //Kushay left Band 13 because she hated //Aha [13.13], the first wife of her deceased daughter's husband, /Ti!kay [13.14]. /Khoa [12.10] was /Ti!kay's third wife before //Aha drove her away with her shrill, vociferous jealousy.

Tshi!ko [12.1] and her family, Segment 5 of Band 12, came from the band to which Dam [2.32] had belonged, a band that broke up because their waterhole dried completely, not in the present drought but some years before. Dam and Tshi!ko had connections with Band 12 through an ascending generation that are now forgotten, like the relationship between !Kham [12.X11] and /Ti!kay [12.X6]. Tshi!ko has additional affinal connections. Her two sons married daughters of Khwova [12.X5], who was a sister of /Ti!kay [12.X6].

Old Gao [12.37] and his family, Segment 6, came into Band 12 from Band 13 through the marriage of Sebe [12.30] to Gao [12.29], the young k″xau n!a. The connection between Old Gao and Sebe is one of the stretched-out connections. Sebe is Old Gao's son's second wife's daughter by a former marriage of the son's second wife. Old Gao's son and his wife came to live with Sebe, and Old Gao and his wives came to live with his son, all simply because they prefer living in Band 12 than in Band 13. They might return to Band 13 any time they wished to do so.

I enjoyed Old Gao immensely. He was cheerful, agreeable, and willing to talk with me about anything under the sun. His second wife, Old //Khuga [12.41], did not find him so agreeable. She apparently was thoroughly annoyed with him and declared herself divorced from him. However, she liked to live with her sister, Old Gao's third wife, //Kushay [12.38], so they made a little ménage à trois in spite of the declared divorce. I may add that Old Gao and //Kushay lived at one fire, and Old //Khuga at another, but the fires were only about eight feet apart, and I think we should take the declaration of the divorce with a grain of salt.

Continued on
page 389

BAND 1—GAUTSCHA
SEGMENT 3

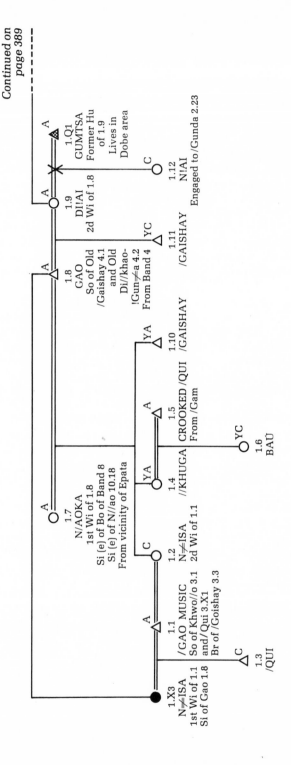

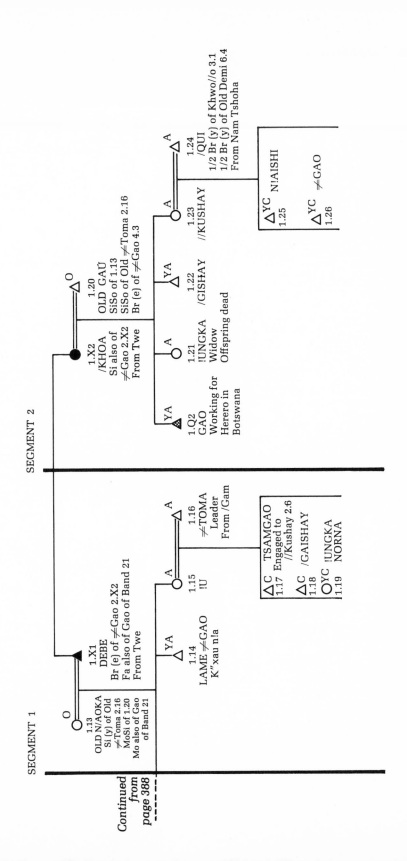

SEGMENT 1

SEGMENT 2

Continued
from
page 388

1.13
OLD N/AOKA
Si (y) of Old
≠Toma 2.16
MoSi of 1.20
Mo also of Gao
of Band 21

1.X1
DEBE
Br (e) of ≠Gao 2.X2
Fa also of Gao of Band 21
From Twe

1.14
LAME ≠GAO
K"xau n!a

1.15
!U

1.16
≠TOMA
Leader
From /Gam

1.17
TSAMGAO
Engaged to
//Kushay 2.6

1.18
/GAISHAY

1.19
!UNGKA
NORNA

1.X2
/KHOA
Si also of
≠Gao 2.X2
From Twe

1.20
OLD GAU̶
SiSo of 1.13
SiSo of Old ≠Toma 2.16
Br (e) of ≠Gao 4.3

1.Q2
GAO
Working for
Herero in
Botswana

1.21
!UNGKA
Widow
Offspring dead

1.22
/GISH̶AY
Offspring dead

1.23
//KUSHAY

1.24
/QUI
1/2 Br (y) of Khwo//o 3.1
1/2 Br (y) of Old Demi 6.4
From Nam Tshoha

1.25
N!AISHI

1.26
≠GAO

BAND 2—GAUTSCHA

SEGMENT 1

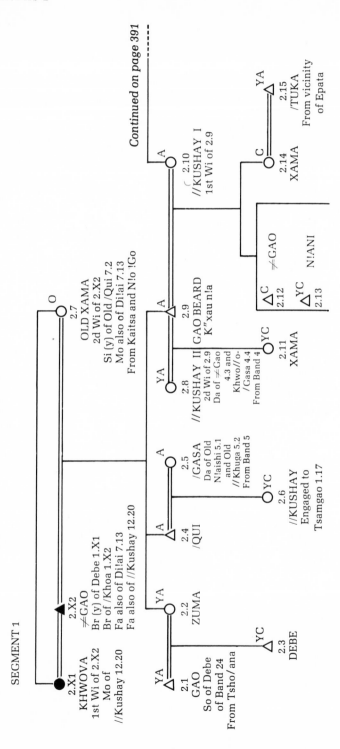

Continued on page 391

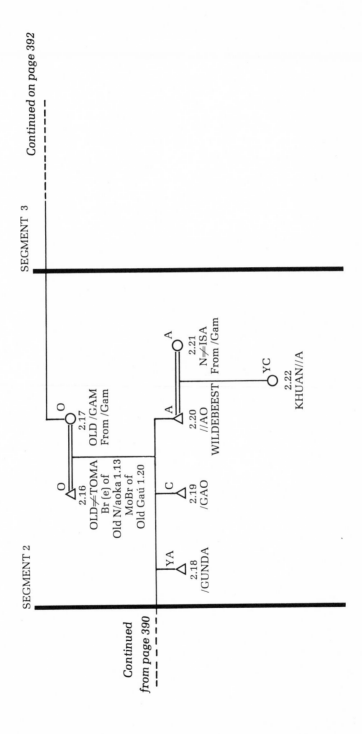

Continued on page 392

SEGMENT 3

SEGMENT 2

Continued
from page 390

O
2.17
OLD /GAM
From /Gam

O
2.16
OLD≠TOMA
Br (e) of
Old N/aoka 1.13
MoBr of
Old Gaú 1.20

A
2.21
N≠ISA
From /Gam

A
2.20
//AO
WILDEBEEST

YC
2.22
KHUAN//A

C
2.19
/GAO

YA
2.18
/GUNDA

SEGMENT 3

Continued from page 391

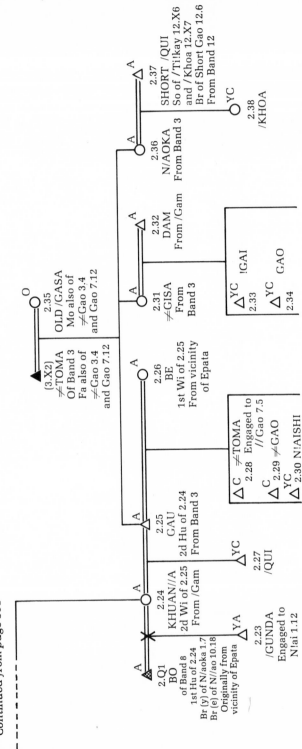

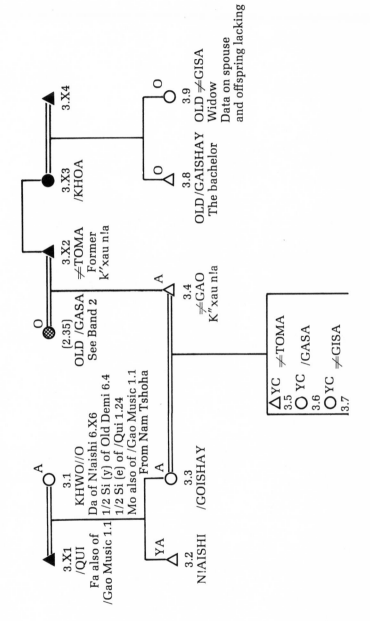

BAND 3—KAUTSA

BAND 4—DEBORAGU

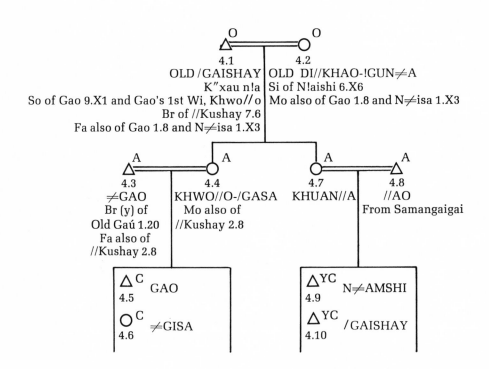

BAND 5—DEBORAGU

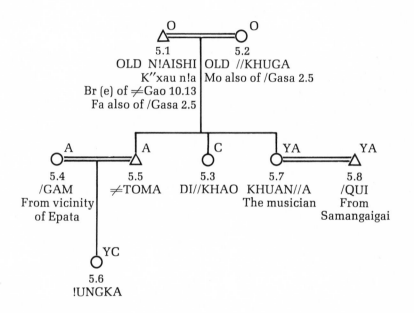

BAND 6—NAM TSHOHA

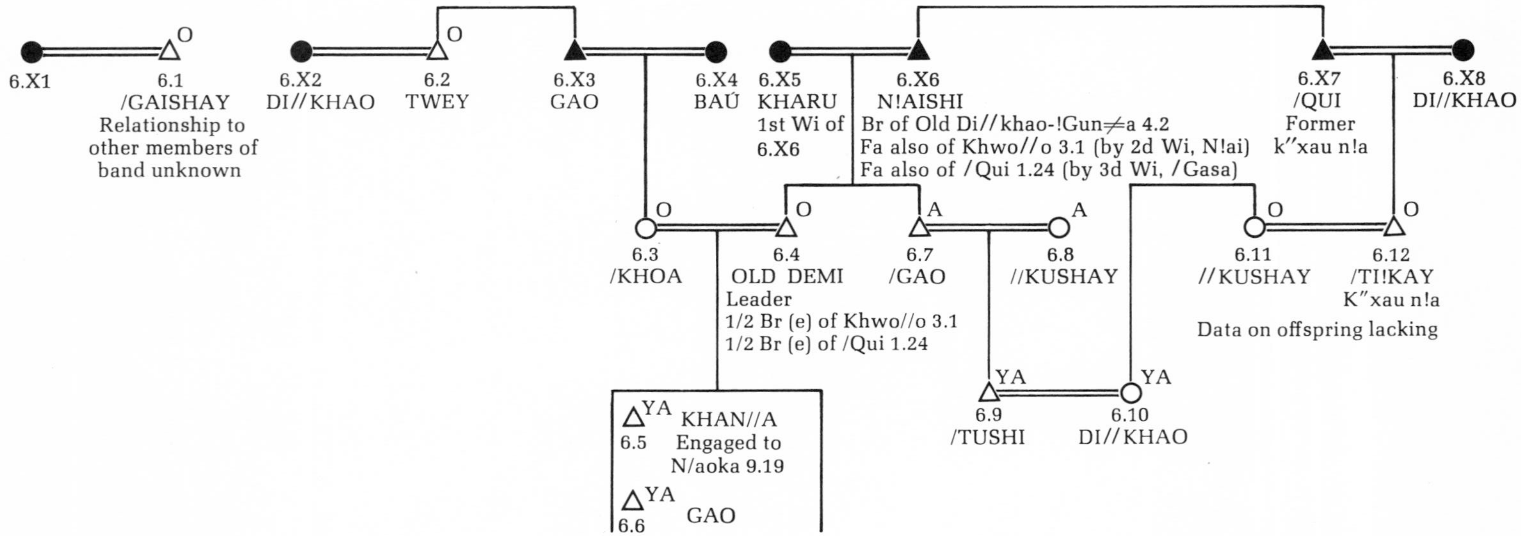

6.X1

6.X2
DI//KHAO

6.1
/GAISHAY
Relationship to
other members of
band unknown

6.2
TWEY

6.X3
GAO

6.X4
BAÜ

6.X5
KHARU
1st Wi of
6.X6

6.3
/KHOA

6.X6
N!AISHI
Br of Old Di//khao-!Gun≠a 4.2
Fa also of Khwo//o 3.1 (by 2d Wi, N!ai)
Fa also of /Qui 1.24 (by 3d Wi, /Gasa)

6.X7
/QUI
Former
k"xau n!a

6.X8
DI//KHAO

6.4
OLD DEMI
Leader
1/2 Br (e) of Khwo//o 3.1
1/2 Br (e) of /Qui 1.24

6.7
/GAO

6.8
//KUSHAY

6.11
//KUSHAY

6.12
/TI!KAY
K"xau n!a
Data on offspring lacking

6.5
YA KHAN//A
Engaged to
N/aoka 9.19

6.6
YA GAO

6.9
/TUSHI

6.10
DI//KHAO

BAND 7—N!O !GO (Winter), KEITSA (Summer)

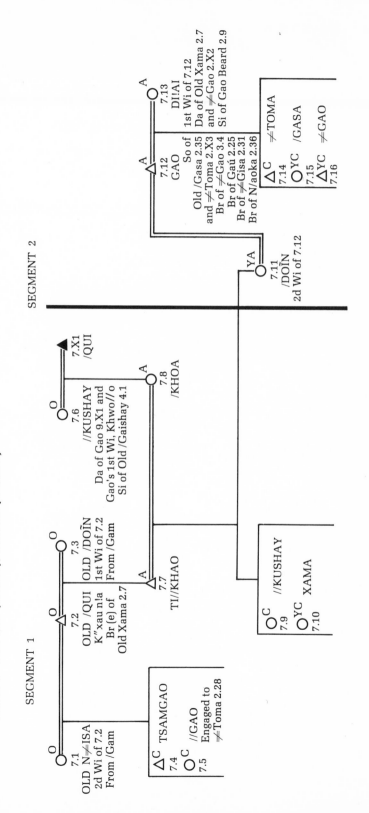

BAND 9—KHUMSA

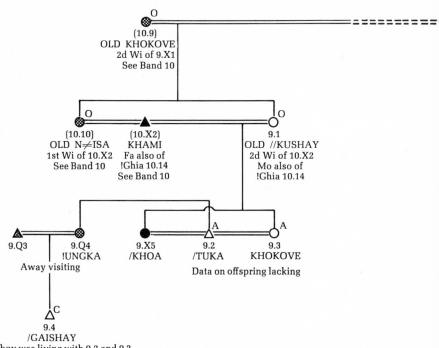

9.4
/GAISHAY
This boy was living with 9.2 and 9.3

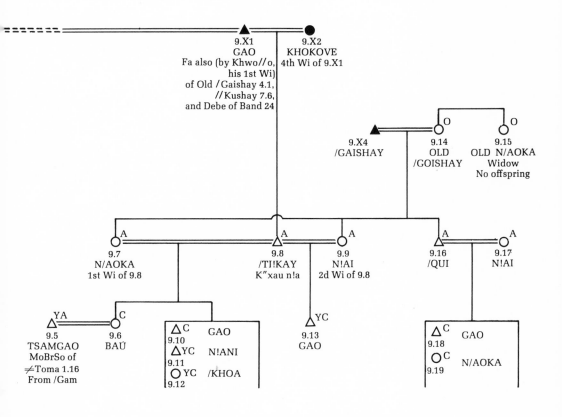

BAND 10—TSUMKWE

SEGMENT 1

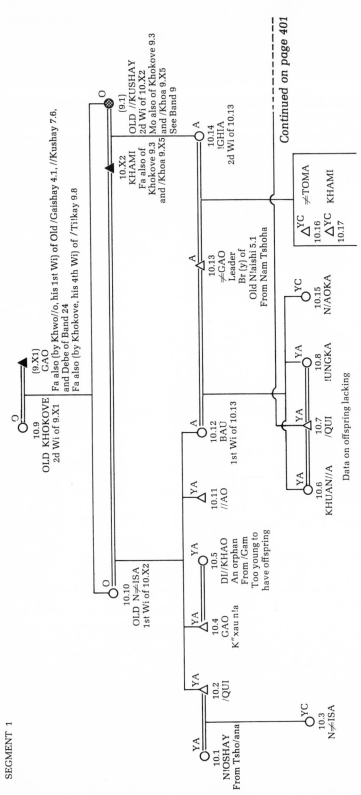

Continued on page 401

SEGMENT 2

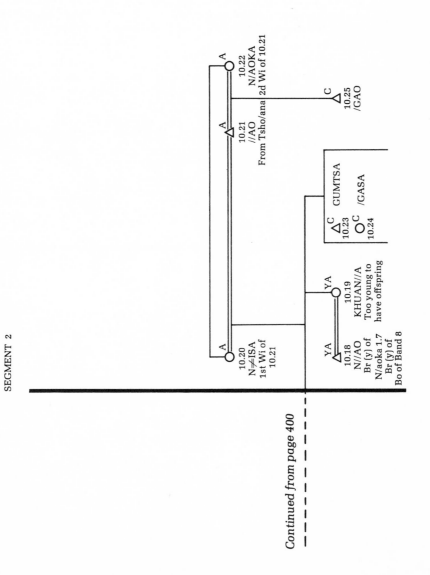

Continued from page 400

BAND 12—/GAM

SEGMENT 5

SEGMENT 4

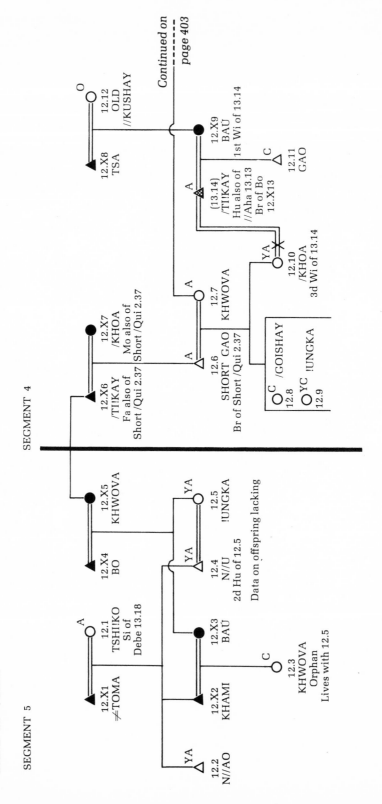

Continued on
page 403

12.12
OLD
//KUSHAY

12.X8
TSA

12.X9
BAÚ
1st Wi of 13.14

12.11
GAO

(13.14)
/TI!KAY
Hu also of
//Aha 13.13
Br of Bo
12.X13

12.10
/KHOA
3d Wi of 13.14

12.X7
/KHOA
Mo also of
Short/Qui 2.37

12.7
KHWOVA

12.X6
/TI!KAY
Fa also of
Short/Qui 2.37

12.6
SHORT GAO
Br of Short/Qui 2.37

12.8
/GOISHAY

12.9
!UNGKA

12.X5
KHWOVA

12.X4
BO

12.5
!UNGKA

12.4
N/U
2d Hu of 12.5

Data on offspring lacking

12.1
TSHI!KO
Si of
Debe 13.18

12.X1
≠TOMA

12.X3
BAÚ

12.X2
KHAMI

12.3
KHWOVA
Orphan
Lives with 12.5

12.2
N//AO

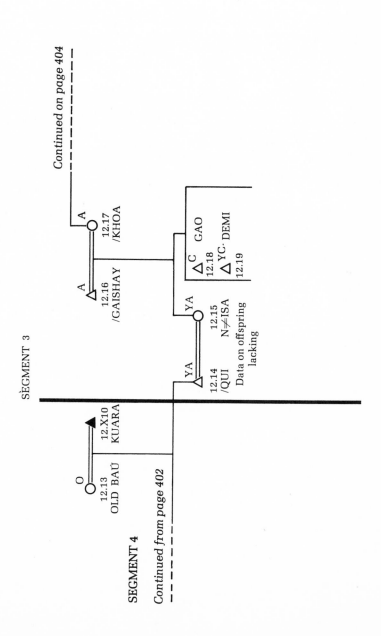

SÈGMENT 3

SEGMENT 4

Continued on page 404

Continued from page 402

A
12.17
/KHOA

A
12.16
/GAISHAY

C GAO
12.18
YC· DEMI
12.19

YA
12.15
N≠ISA

YA
12.14
/QUI
Data on offspring
lacking

12.X10
KUARA

12.13
OLD BAÛ

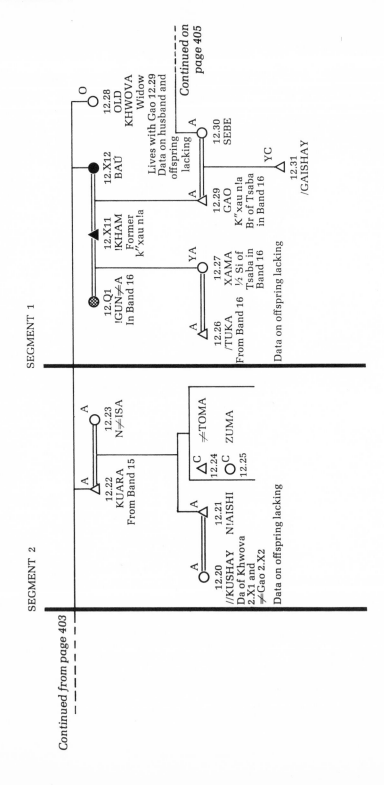

SEGMENT 1

SEGMENT 2

Continued from page 403

Continued on
page 405

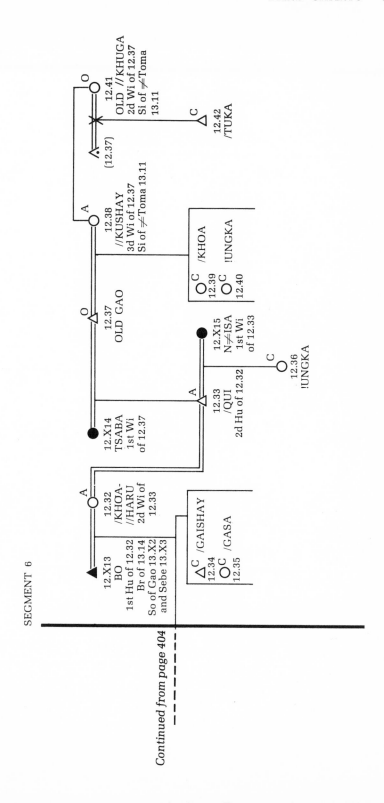

SEGMENT 6

Continued from page 404

Fig. 16. Relationships of members of Bands 1 and 2 in Segments 1 and 2 of each band

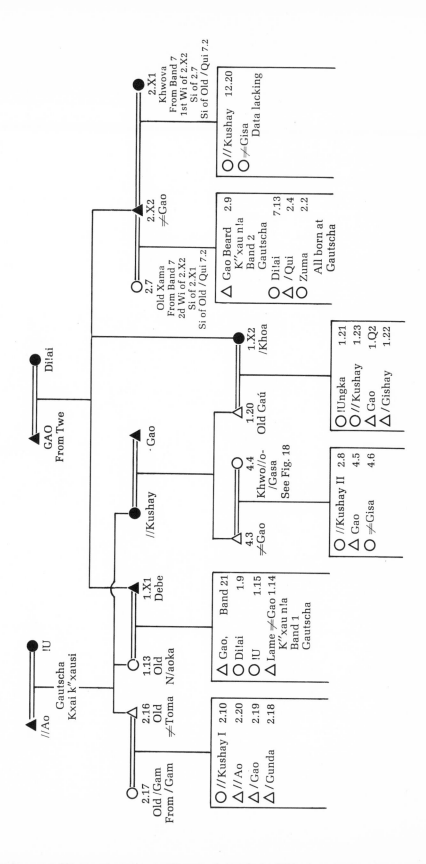

Fig. 17.   Relationships of members of Bands 4, 5, 6, 10, and Segment 3 of Band 1

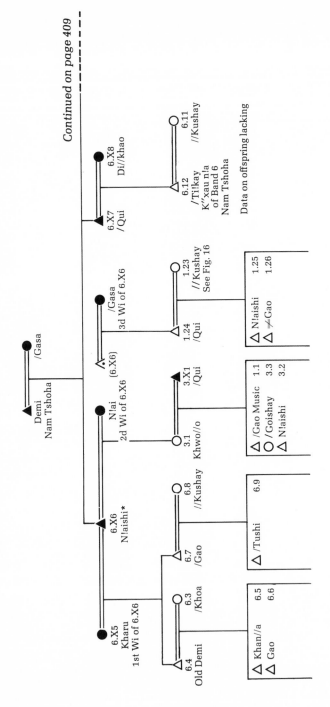

Continued on page 409

*N!aishi 6.X6 provides an example of a broken social rule. He married a woman who had the same name as his mother.

Continued from
page 408

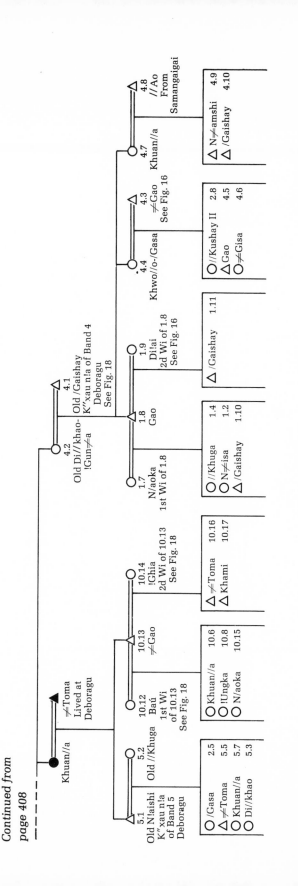

Fig. 18. Relationships in Bands 9 and 10: Descendants of Gao 9.X1 and three of
his four wives

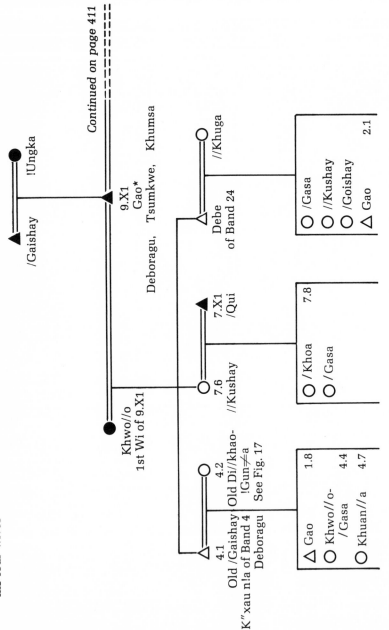

Continued on page 411

* //Gao was the third wife of Gao 9.X1. At Gao's death she went to Botswana,
and the people of Nyae Nyae lost track of her.

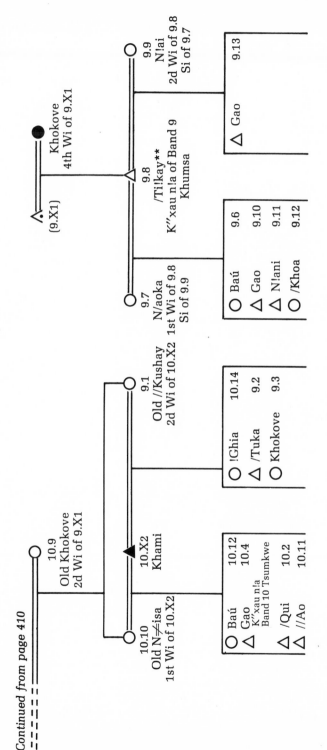

Continued from page 410

**/Ti!kay 9.8 belongs to the generation of his older half-brother, Old /Gaishay 4.1, but being the youngest of Gao's offspring, he corresponds in age to a younger generation, that of Gao 1.8, ≠ Toma 1.16, and !U 1.15, and /Ti!kay's children correspond to theirs in age.

Appendix 2
!Kung Artifacts

ANIMAL MATERIALS

Hide

Made and used by men
  breech clouts
  specially shaped belts worn by
    hunters to hold arrows fanned
    out at their waistline within easy
    reach when they are shooting
  back aprons sometimes worn at the
    ritual curing dances (not a ritual
    practice)
  headdresses of hide with fur or hair
    left on, worn at the dances (not
    a ritual practice)
  small karosses used not as cloaks
    but as windshields
  caps (a few)
  oracle disks
  covers made of scrota for quivers
    and for horns used as containers
    in which poison beetle larvae are
    carried
Made by men, used by women
  front aprons
  small karosses worn around but-
    tocks or for carrying babies
Made by men, used by all
  large karosses, the whole hide of an
    antelope, preferably gemsbok
  sandals
  bags (sewn)
  bags of whole skins
  tobacco pouches of scrota

bracelets, armbands, knee and ankle
  bands
necklaces
thongs

Sinew

Made and used by men
  bowstrings
  wrappings for arrow shafts (the
    poison adheres well to sinew)
  binding for hafts
  snares
Made by men, used by all
  strings for //gwashi (musical
    instrument)
Made by men or women
  fine rolled cord

Horn

Made and used by men
  horns fitted with leather covers for
    carrying arrow points and poison
  horns for cupping
Used by all
  horns for pipes
  horns for spoons

Bone

Made and used by men
  connecting parts for arrow
  arrow points (few)
  dishes for mixing poison

Made and used by women
  fresh bone, pounded to powder,
    used to clean and soften karosses

Porcupine Quills

Used by men
  arrow points
  ornaments worn in hair

Cocoons

Made by men
  dance rattles

Birds' Nests

Used by men and women
  tobacco pouches (nests of the
    penduline tit, *Anthoscopus
    minutus*)

Shell

Made by men, used by all
  ostrich-eggshell water containers
  tortoise-shell dippers
  tortoise-shells for dishes
Made by men, used by n/um k″xausi
  tortoise-shell containers in which
    medicine is kept
Made by men, used by women
  tortoise-shell cosmetic containers
Made by women, worn by all
  ostrich-eggshell beads

Feathers

Used by boys on djani toys
Worn by all occasionally in hair

VEGETABLE MATERIALS

Wood

Made and used by men
  bows
  spear handles
  axe, adze, or assagai handles
  knife handles
  knife sheaths
  springhare hook handles
  fire sticks
  hatchet bow (musical instrument)
Made by men, used by all
  digging sticks
  carrying sticks
  stirring sticks
  mortars and pestles
  bowls
  spoons
  fire paddles
  //gwashi (musical instrument)
  one-stringed violin
  djani toys
  beads

Made by women
  frames for shelters

Reeds

Made and used by men
  arrowshafts
Used by all
  sip sticks

Bark

Made and used by men
  quivers from the bark of the root of
    Acacia uncinata Engl.
Used by women
  strips of bark to bind grass thatch
    on shelters
Used by all
  pieces of bark for dishes and spoons

*Fiber from sansevieria leaves, aloe
leaves, n!oa tree roots, other roots*

Rolled by men and women
  cord

Made and used by men
  cord for carrying nets
  cord for snares
Made and used by all
  cord for ornaments

Grass

Made by men and women
  stoppers for ostrich-eggshell water
    containers
  ornaments
Made by women
  shelters
Made by children
  toys of grass folded and woven to
    suggest animals
Used by all for beds
Used by women
  strips for tying frames of shelters
    and for tying grass on in times of
    high wind
Worn by all as head and chest bands

Tsi Nuts

Used by all as beads
Used by boys as weights for djani toys

Gum

Used by men
  an adhesive black gum from the
    bulb of a plant used to glue sinew
    bindings to arrows and bows and
    to mend utensils
  an adhesive yellow gum used to
    glue together components of
    arrows and tanged assagai blades
    into the holes in the wooden
    handles into which they are
    inserted
  a sticky substance exuded from a
    rarely found parasite plant called
    chi chi. It is smeared on branches
    of trees for catching birds

STONE

Made by men
  arrow straighteners
  pipes
Used by men for
  sharpening blades
  hammers

  anvils
  weights to stretch nets
  marking graves
Used by women
  powdered red earth for ritual marks
    on face

OBTAINED BY TRADE WITH BANTU

Malleable Metal and Wire

Made and used by men
  arrow points
  assagai blades
  springhare hooks
Made by men, used by all
  pipes
  awls—the !Kung sew by punching a
    hole in material with an awl and
pushing a thong or sinew or fiber
cord through the hole. Men are
the sewers, they do fine neat
work. Women drill holes in
ostrich-eggshell beads with awls
  knives

Used by men
  axe or adze blades
  chisels (few)

files (few)
fire strikers (few)

Miscellaneous Objects

Used by all
beads—copper, glass, shell
pots—Bantu clay, European iron

pipes (few), European briar, old
cartridge shells
enamel basins and cups (few)
old scraps of garments and blankets
oddments such as buttons for
ornaments

Appendix 3
John Marshall's Films
of !Kung Bushmen

An Argument about a Marriage	color	18 minutes	16 mm.
Bitter Melons	color	30 ″	″
A Curing Ceremony	black/white	8 ″	″
Debe's Tantrum	color	8½ ″	″
A Group of Women	black/white	5 ″	″
The Hunters	color	72 ″	″
A Joking Relationship	black/white	12½ ″	″
Lion Game	color	3½ ″	″
Men Bathing	color	14 ″	″
N/um Tchai: The Ceremonial Dance of the !Kung Bushmen	black/white	19½ ″	″
Playing with Scorpions	color	4 ″	″
A Rite of Passage	color	14 ″	″
The Wasp Nest	color	20 ″	″
N!owa T'ama: The Melon Tossing	color	14½ ″	″
!Kung Bushman Hunting Equipment	color	37 ″	″

These films, with the exception of "The Hunters," are available through Documentary Educational Resources, 24 Dane Street, Somerville, Massachusetts. "The Hunters" is distributed through Films Incorporated, 1144 Wilmette Avenue, Wilmette, Illinois 60091, with offices in New York, Los Angeles, and Atlanta.

Tables

Figures

Index

Aardvark, 14, 128, 129, 134

Aardwolf, 124, 127

Acacia, gum from, 121–122

Adansonia digitata L. (≠m) (baobab), 117–118

Address: kin terminology for, 240–241; respectful, 243, 246–249

Adultery, 279, 280–282

Affines: defined, 203; joking relationships with, 206–207; terms applied to, 214–223, 229–230; primary, 214–219, 220, 229; secondary, 219–222; and spouses of relatives, 223; and incest taboos, 254–256, 258

Age: not reckoned in years, 53–54, 163; of gathering, 96, 97, 322; of hunting, 97, 130, 321–322; of band members, 162; and kin terms, 227–228; and name-relationship, 238; of marriage, 268; of playing games, 314

Aged, the, 53, 97–98

//Aha [13.13], 183, 264

!Ai Ha !O Pan, 78

Airplane game, 339–340

Altruism, 288

Ambo, 23

Ancestors, of Bushmen, 29, 31, 32, 41–45

Andara, 24

Angola, 16, 23

Animals: as food, 124–130; !Kung identifications of, 124–126; avoidance of eating, 127; weights of, 129; hunting of, 130–155; mimicking, 314, 368–369; lack of sentiment toward, 340

Annona Stenophylla Engl., 118

Antelope, 136–137, 306

Ants (*!kxon*), 128

//Ao [2.20] (//Ao Wildebeest), 59, 141, 175, 226, 300, 335

Arrow poison, 92; and small stature, 33; effect of, 137–138, 150, 152; from beetle larvae, 147–149; process of applying, 149–151; no antidote for, 150; from *!gaowa,* 151; from *n/i !go,* 151; knowledge of, 152

Arrow straightener, 145

Arrows, poisoned, 137–138, 152; in hunter's quiver, 144; design of, 145, 148 (photo); size of, 145–146; shaft of, 146; points of, 146–147, 307; release of, 148 (photo); not touched by women, 177; always at hand, 288; and ownership of prey, 296–297; owned by women, 307

Artifacts, 188, 303, 304, App. 2; stone age 49–52; sufficiency of, 9, 308

Assagai, 138, 145

Auen (NI), 16

Australopithecines, 30

Autos, game of, 341–342

Avoidances: of foods, 127; connected with hunting, 177; of names, 245–246, 248–249; sitting, 249–250; of entering shelters, 250; of asking for food, 250; speaking, 250–251; and incest taboo, 253–259

Bags, hunting, 144

Bahti, 159

Ball game, 322–327

Band 1, 19, 157; at Gautscha Pan, 6, 197; presents for, 10; territory of, 71; productive areas of, 103; food of, 104–107; hunters in, 133; family phases in, 174–175; relationships in, 182; *kxai k"xausi*